BOB UECKER feels more fortunate than most former big leaguers, because he has no feelings of frustration, of promise unfulfilled. He knows he got the most out of his talent—and it wasn't much. This is from the man whose greatest thrill in baseball was watching a guy fall out of the upper deck in Philadelphia—who loved being in the minor leagues, and who once shagged fly balls with a tuba. What he lacked in talent, Uecker made up in high jinks. His stories are hilarious, his insights keen, and his heart is as big as a diamond . . .

"An engagingly droll journeyman's view of the national pastime."

—KIRKUS REVIEWS

MICKEY HERSKOWITZ is a broadcaster for Houston's KPRC-TV and a nationally syndicated sports columnist.

CATCHER IN THE WRY

Bob Uecker
and Mickey Herskowitz

A JOVE BOOK

Baseball cards from the collection of Larry Fritsch, 735 Old Wausau Road, Stevens Point, WI 54481. All interior photographs not otherwise credited are from Bob Uecker's personal collection.

Cover photo courtesy of Lite Beer from the Miller Brewing Company of Milwaukee, WI.

This Jove book contains the complete
text of the original hardcover edition.
It has been completely reset in a typeface
designed for easy reading, and was printed
from new film.

CATCHER IN THE WRY

A Jove Book / published by arrangement with
the authors

PRINTING HISTORY
G. P. Putnam's Sons edition / August 1982
Jove edition / May 1983

ISBN: 0-515-07255-9

Jove books are published by Jove Publications, Inc., 200 Madison Avenue, New York, N.Y. 10016. The words "A JOVE BOOK" and the "J" with sunburst are trademarks belonging to Jove Publications, Inc.
PRINTED IN THE UNITED STATES OF AMERICA

Acknowledgments

When people ask who made me a broadcaster, or a baseball humorist, I give them the names of a dozen pitchers in the National League.

But I also want to express my thanks to Merle Harmon, who talked me into doing an audition with ABC; to Alan (Bud) Selig, who gave me my first opportunity in broadcasting with the Brewers; and Al Hirt, for letting me try out my brand of comedy on the stage of his nightclub. I just recited the highlights of my career and the audience thought it was hilarious.

The efforts of many people went into the making of this book, but a special debt is owed to Mark Stillwell, the president (retired) of the Bob Uecker Fan Club (also retired).

To Gus, my father,
who was never surprised
when I struck out.
He would have seen the humor
in all the good it did me.

Contents

Introduction

MOST OF WHAT I have written here is true, especially those descriptions and examples of how I struggled to become a lifetime .200 hitter in the major leagues.

Some of what I have written might have happened, but didn't, and some could only have happened in the dark corners of my own imagination. I have not used any arrows, cartoon balloons or parenthetical asides to tell you which is which.

Those who love baseball as a game, the way I love it, will know the difference, and they are the ones for whom this book was written.

Preface

THIS IS BILL LEE, the rather unconventional pitcher for the Montreal Expos, on the subject of catchers:

"Catchers anticipate. They try to receive vibrations, waves. Catchers have to be very sensitive. Their attention wanders a lot. So you have to stop, shake them, get all the screws back in the right place. If my catcher wants to come out to the mound and tell me how bad I am, I'll say, 'You're right, so what shall we do about it?' I give everybody their own space."

When Bob Uecker was asked if he would like to select a friend, perhaps a former teammate, to say a few words about him and possibly provide an insight for his book, he said he would take his chances with Tim McCarver. It was an interesting choice, the obvious conclusion being that one catcher understands another. Certainly, these two do.

Uecker was McCarver's backup at St. Louis in 1964, the year the Cardinals won the pennant in a four-team pileup. Tim retired at the end of the 1980 season after a remarkable career that spanned twenty-one years. He was the first modern catcher to play for four decades, in most years a splendid performer, always a hard-nosed one.

He recalls catching a rookie lefthander named Steve Carlton in the spring of 1965, then having the young man approach him in the clubhouse and say, earnestly, "Hey, hey, you've got to call more breaking pitches when we're behind the hitter."

By then McCarver was moving into his sixth season, having established himself in the World Series as a coming star. He backed up the startled pitcher against a wall and screamed at him, "You sonofabitch! You got a lot of guts telling me that. What credentials do *you* have?"

That, as Tim describes it, was the beginning of a long and beautiful friendship, tight enough that the Phillies would bring him out of one retirement just to catch Carlton.

Between Uecker and McCarver—one catcher to another—there was never any pugnacity. When Tim became a broadcaster in Philadelphia, Bob was among his well-wishers. He knew McCarver would have to make it the hard way. There is not much comic material in a baseball career as solid as that one.

Perceptive and direct, McCarver may blow a few of the covers Uecker has created for himself, but here he is:

When I roomed with Uke in 1964, people were always saying to me, "I'll bet that's a zany room." It wasn't zany at all. You'd go down to the lobby or out to the parking lot and there'd be a string of guys telling one Uecker story after another. But he isn't one of those people who has to be *on* all the time. When he wanted to relax, he got away from people. I guess that's one of the ironies of his life. Maybe it's true of any humorist.

The thing is, you never knew what was going to come out of that imagination. Once he invented something called the Ugly Card Game. He had a friend who was a police detective in Philadelphia, who kept sending him pictures of prisoners, until he had collected fifty-two of them. We would deal them out and play a version of War. You put three cards down and one face-up. The ugliest won the hand. I was the judge in case of a tie and each guy would challenge.

There was one woman's picture in the deck. I'll never forget her. She wore a wide-brimmed hat with a feather in the back that did a kind of corkscrew. She had Coke-bottle glasses, and a half-moon scar that curled right under her nose up to one eye. She was ugly. It isn't often that you can look at someone straight on and see into their nostrils.

Uke saved that card, had it whittled down to wallet size, and would just wait for someone to come up and ask about his family. He'd say, "Doin' great. My wife just sent me a recent picture," and he'd whip out his wallet. All small talk around Uke went right down the tube.

I used to wonder at what went on in his mind. All those army sergeant routines. None of it was written down. You'd think the guy had rehearsed for years. He'd be a platoon leader, demanding to know who filled the motor pool with water. When they were thinking of making him a coach, in Atlanta, he walked around like he had a pocket watch, timing everybody. He picked up all the bullshit clichés.

He and Ray Sadecki used to broadcast the news in the clubhouse. They bought a metal frog with a key in its back, and they'd wind up the frog and have it clacking in the background. That was their tape. They'd set it up on a bench and read stories out of the paper . . . Dateline: Tel Aviv . . . and there was no way to ignore them.

I know he played for some managers who didn't understand him. I think Johnny Keane did. John was a serious man, but I think he appreciated Bob, his sense of humor.

Uke really did have some talent. The first thing you looked at was his defensive ability. His throwing arm and glove. I haven't an envious bone in my body, but I envied his arm. His relaxed, quick hands.

It's strange about catchers. They really root for each other. There isn't the kind of envy you find among pitchers. You see a guy on the mound and there is always someone in the bullpen thinking, "If he fails, I may get a shot." Catchers don't have that. I guess we got banged up too much to be jealous.

One thing about Uke, he would fight anybody. He was a docile guy, but he'd come to the front very quickly. He didn't like to call knockdown pitches, and Gene Mauch called them all the time with the Phillies. But if there was a guy you wanted next to you in a fight, it was Uecker.

Bob used to make up nicknames. He called me T-bone. He was one of those people who had a knack for immediately becoming your friend just by the way he spoke your name. T-bone. Timmy. A very affectionate thing. Not too many people are caring enough to cultivate a trait like that.

I remember listening to him talk about his dad, after his dad had his operation. It was touching, and funny. He's so comfortable that you don't feel bad laughing. Uke is so outlandish that if you missed a little, you missed a lot.

—Mickey Herskowitz

CATCHER IN THE WRY

PART I

The Bob Uecker Story

*In which a poor but honest smartass from a
small beer town in the Midwest goes off to
win fame and fortune in baseball, and is
never heard from again. . . .*

"I was the first hometown boy to sign with, and play
for, the Milwaukee Braves. Technically, I wasn't born
in Milwaukee. My folks were on an oleo run to
Chicago, and my mother was due any day. On
Highway 41, just out of town, she got the pains. My
old man swung the car off the exit ramp and she
dropped me in a mangerlike area. There were three
wise men standing under an exit light . . . one had
oleo, one carried butter, the third was a baseball
scout."

Weeks later, my mother took me off milk and fed
me beef jerky to toughen me for the Cinderella story
that was to follow.

1. A Funny Thing Happened on My Way to Cooperstown

IN JUNE AND JULY of every year I go through the same ritual—an ordeal, really—of waiting for the telephone to ring. I am waiting to be told that the dream of my lifetime has come true.

I am waiting to be told that I, Robert George Uecker, known as "Mr. Baseball" to a generation that never saw me play, have been elected to baseball's Hall of Fame.

But the call doesn't come. And I realize there is no point in getting nervous or uptight. My record speaks for itself, and the fans, at least, haven't forgotten me. I go to the Old-Timers' games now and I know I haven't lost a thing. I sit in the bullpen and let people throw garbage at me, just like in the old days.

Actually, given the way things work now in our National Pastime, and were I just a few years younger, I too could be the object of a bidding war. I would play out my option, declare myself a free agent and twenty-six teams would be drooling. I would probably have to take

3

my phone off the hook. Can you imagine what the market would be today for a defensive catcher who had a career lifetime average of .200?

And I mean on the nose. Not .201 or .199. A cool .200, lifetime. A lot of retired players joke about being a career .200 hitter, but I was the real article. Modestly, I'd say I could command a salary today of one hundred fifty thousand dollars per annum as a backup playing sixty games. Of course, if the team I signed with was deep in catching and only needed me for thirty games, I'd be worth two hundred thousand. The fewer games they needed me for, the higher the minimum bidding would go.

Of course I'm not a few years younger, and bidding wars or not, I can't but feel a warm glow of nostalgia when I think back over my years in the big leagues. I played with three teams, in four cities, under six managers. My teammates included four Hall of Famers: Henry Aaron, Eddie Mathews, Warren Spahn, Bob Gibson.

In my heart of hearts, I believe my accomplishments were as great as theirs. What did it mean for Aaron or Mathews to hit their .350 or their forty homers? Anybody with ability can play in the big leagues. To last as long as I did with the skills I had, with the numbers I produced, was a triumph of the human spirit. I played thirteen years of pro ball, and remember all but the last six clearly. Up to the very end of my career, I was still being judged on my "potential."

Many times I have been asked how a player knows when he is washed up, through, at the end of the line. Willie Pep, the former boxing champion, once said that you could look for three signs: "First your legs go. Then your reflexes go. Then your friends go." My friends went first.

In baseball the clues were more subtle. In my case, I began to get the hint when my bubble gum card came out and there was a blank space where the picture was supposed to be. Sporting goods companies offered to pay me *not* to endorse their products. I got to the park for what the manager had announced would be a night game, and found out they'd started at 1:00 P.M. I came to bat in the bottom of the ninth, two out, the bases loaded, my team trailing by a run, and looked over at the other dugout and saw them already in their street clothes.

When a player is sold or traded, he may feel a certain rejection. But when he gets cut, well, the news is traumatic. He is face to face with that moment of final truth, that he will never put on a big league uniform again. Nor is it easy on the manager who has to break the news. How do you tell a man that his career is over, that the only life he had ever known is behind him?

I'll never forget how it happened to me. I went to spring training with Atlanta in 1968. The manager was Luman Harris. I opened the door to the clubhouse and Luman looked up and said calmly, "No visitors allowed."

I suppose it is safe to say that my sense of humor caused me to reach the big leagues at least a year late, and my sense of mischief drove me out a few years too soon. But I hung around long enough to prove that my first manager was wrong, the one who sent me back to the minors with the warning, "There is no room in this game for a clown."

There was, and is, a place for Bob Uecker, it pleases me to report. Actually, I still have the view I always had—from behind home plate. Today I'm just a few tiers

higher than field level, as a broadcaster for the Milwaukee Brewers and ABC television. I enjoy my job. It's
a lot safer up there, and I don't get booed as much as I
did when I was catching. As a matter of fact, my career
might have been prolonged if Clete Boyer had hit one
less home run in 1967.

That year a Honda dealer in Atlanta had a promotion
going at the ball park. Any player who hit a homer or
pitched a shutout in the month of September received a
free Honda. Boyer hit one the last day of the season. The
next morning I dropped by his apartment to road-test it. I
was shoeless and shirtless when I roared off down the
street in front of Clete's place.

A pack of dogs, excited by the noise, began chasing
me. Feeling for the brake, my feet got tangled, I hit the
gas instead, jumped a curb and tipped over. I was lucky
to get away with a broken right arm and a pair of badly
slashed feet.

The cast was removed three weeks before I was to
report to camp the following spring. When a trainer tried
to "work out" the adhesions by yanking and twisting my
arm, he rebroke it. My arm was back in a cast when I got
to Florida, and the Braves put me on the roster as a
player-coach.

My luck continued pretty much in that vein. One day
the club went to Orlando to play the Minnesota Twins,
and I stayed behind because of my arm. Billy Martin was
the manager of the Twins then. Billy had been with the
Braves at the end of his career, and was still friendly with
Clete Boyer and Deron Johnson. He gave them a jug of
martinis to take back on the bus. I was to meet them that
night at the Cock 'n Bull restaurant in West Palm Beach.
I had been waiting maybe a half hour when they
appeared. They were loaded when they got off the bus.

The three of us were sitting at the bar, when the next thing I knew some drunk had jerked Boyer off his stool. I spun around, got to my feet and slugged him. He skidded through the dance floor area. The bartender jumped across the bar and yelled, "Bob, dammit, no more, that's all!"

I didn't want any more problems, but as I got up a friend of the first guy hit me across the head with a full beer bottle. Busted my head wide open. When I reached up and felt the blood I thought, "Oh, jeezus." I knew it wasn't beer. Not even light beer. Beer isn't red and sticky. The wound later took forty-eight stitches to close.

A terrific fight was breaking out all around me, like a scene from a "B" western. But at that point I had one goal in life: to get the hell away from that bar. I staggered out the nearest door and found myself looking at a dead-end alley, so I had to go back in and walk the length of the place to the front door. The cops were just pulling up to the curb as I fell into my car. Jim Britton, one of our pitchers, drove me to the hospital. I had my head sewn and paid the bill, $175. I went back to my hotel room, expecting to find Boyer. He wasn't there. I called the Cock 'n Bull and whoever answered said, "Yeah, he's still here. They're both here."

The doctor had wrapped my head in one of those white bandages piled up like a turban. I put on an old fishing hat and went back to the bar. Deron and Clete were sitting right where I had left them. They were so drunk they had never moved. Deron looked up and said, "Hot damn, look who's back. Uke's here. Give us another round."

I wasn't worried about Deron. His wife was in town and she could do the worrying. But Clete was rooming with me and it was past curfew and I had to get them out

of there. I finally did. I dropped off Deron at his
bungalow and half-carried Clete back to the room.

The next morning my head was killing me. I felt like I
had the hangover they were saving for Judas, and no
matter how hard I tried, I couldn't get Boyer out of bed.
At ten I went to the ball park and told Luman Harris what
had happened. He said, "Okay, go back to your room
and if any of the writers call tell 'em you were in a car
wreck."

I finally got Clete awake and he left for the park. At
one o'clock he was back. Luman had found him asleep
under the stands. After the game that day, I drove to the
hospital to have my bandage changed. Now the news
comes over the radio: *Three Atlanta players involved in a
brawl.*

A week later the Braves released me. I guess they
thought I had been a bad influence, but since I was so
good at getting into trouble, they offered me a job in
public relations, which is how I wound up making
speeches and doing the game color on television.

I am able to look back on my career now with few
illusions. The highest salary I ever drew, twenty-three
thousand dollars, came after my best season . . . that's
right, the one in which I played the fewest games. But I
had my share of thrills. Probably the biggest was when I
started my first game for the Braves, in my hometown of
Milwaukee, in April 1962. My folks, my friends, my old
schoolmates were there. And they were all cheering.

We were playing the Giants that day and Juan
Marichal was pitching. I had his bubble gum card and
that told me all I wanted to know about Marichal.

Before the game. Birdie Tebbetts, our manager, said
he knew a lot of my relatives were in the park, but he
didn't want me to be nervous or uptight. I assured him I

was fine. I had been in the minors six years waiting to get here and I was ready to play.

As I walked toward the batting cage, he hollered after me: "Kid, you're doing good, except that up here in the big leagues most of us wear our athletic supporters on the inside of our uniforms."

I hit my only home run that year—the first of fourteen in my career—off Diomedes Olivo, a forty-two-year-old rookie relief pitcher for the Pittsburgh Pirates. When the ball landed in the seats, the fan who caught it threw it back. Years later, someone turned up a tape of that home run and put together a strip for a roast-and-toast, with a staff announcer giving it the H.V. Kaltenborn treatment:

"The great power hitters of days gone by recall their first home runs in the major leagues, their eyes filled with tears and their voices shaking with excitement, every detail of their first round-tripper as clear as if it had happened yesterday. It's the same for all the great ones . . . Steve Bilko, Harry Hannebrink, Clint Courtney, big Albie Pearson, Curt Blefary and Ed Bouchee.

"And so it is for Robert Uecker. He remembers that first looping line drive and so do all his fans. Recall with us now that thrilling day when Bob stepped to the plate still looking for Number One. Here's the play-by-play, as it happened, with Earl Gillespie at the microphone:

"'. . . oh and one, the pitch swung on and a drive [voice rising] INTO DEEP LEFT FIELD . . . GOING BACK TOWARD THE WALL . . . IT MAY BE . . . IT'S BACK AT THE WALL . . . HOME RUN FOR BOB UECKER!!! Well, Bob Uecker . . . quite a thrill . . .'"

Gillespie's description was followed by five minutes of the kind of laugh track you hear at a carnival fun house, interrupted by a wailing siren and Earl's voice repeating, over and over, "Well, Bob Uecker . . ."

Actually, a home run I remember even better than my first was a grand slam I delivered a few seasons later off Ron Herbel of the San Francisco Giants. After I connected, the manager, Herman Franks, came out of their dugout to remove the pitcher, and he was carrying Herbel's suitcase. For some reason, other teams took me lightly.

If you are really going to appreciate my career—and I am not sure it can be done—I guess we should start at the beginning. I was your average hot-shot athlete in high school, an all boys school in Milwaukee. My father wanted me to learn a trade. I did. By the end of my first semester I could hot-wire a car. Baseball and basketball were my games. As a freshman I was six feet one and weighed 130, and the other guys would wear my jockstrap as a wristband.

In class, my commitment to education was less than total. I had some growing up to do, and one day it occurred to me I might get there faster in the service. What helped me reach this decision was the fact that my father spent more time at school than I did. I was a total failure. I even flunked shop. I couldn't make a bread-board. In 1954, at nineteen, I enlisted in the army.

My baseball career began there, at Fort Leonard Wood, Missouri, where they had a sign inside the post that said: IF YOU SCREW UP IN KOREA THIS IS WHERE THEY SEND YOU. During orientation, an officer asked if any of us had played college or pro baseball. I raised my hand. He asked where I had played, and what position. I told him I had been a catcher at Marquette, which never had a baseball team. But I figured, correctly, what could they know about Marquette?

I had pitched in sandlot ball and the Braves had scouted me two years earlier, at seventeen. I had done some catching too, and I knew the base team was going to lose its starter, Bob Schmidt, in the spring. Before being drafted, Schmidt belonged to the San Francisco Giants. Later, at Fort Belvoir, I joined a team whose shortstop was Dick Groat, who would be my teammate at St. Louis.

A friend of my father's, Louie Zimmerman, talked the Braves into scouting me as a catcher. He was the editor of a German newspaper in Milwaukee, which shows you how casual the scouting system was back then. When I got out of the army I signed with Milwaukee for a three-thousand dollar bonus. The amount bothered my father at first. We were a poor family and, frankly, he didn't have that kind of cash. Finally, he scraped it up and got me to leave home again.

For the signing ceremony, the Braves' officials took us to one of the city's swankiest restaurants. My dad was so nervous he rolled down the window and the hamburgers fell off the tray.

My dad's name was Gus. He was a tool- and diemaker from Basel, Switzerland. He was also the best man I ever knew: stubborn, funny, impatient, generous and proud.

I remember reading a story about Ernie Banks, and how his father worked and sacrificed to give Ernie the chance to play ball. His father never saw the sunlight, leaving the house before dawn and getting home after dark. When Ernie signed his first contract with the Cubs he sent a three-word telegram to his father: "WE DID IT."

I relate to that story. My father got on my ass all the

time. He never said, in front of me, that he thought I could play, and at home, listening to the games on the radio, whenever I came to bat he would turn to my mother and say, "Ach, he'll probably strike out."

But without him I would never have gotten a shot. In the minors, when I was making $250 a month and the money ran out, he was right there. He was a great mechanic and a hard worker, who never let his family—his wife, a son, and two daughters—go without the basics, even in the meanest days of the Depression. He could always make three or four dollars a day working on cars.

When I got to the Braves to stay, in 1962, he was all fired up about it. Birdie Tebbetts was the manager then and they became drinking buddies. Birdie would tell me later how he would needle my old man, saying how horseshit I was, and Gus would argue with him. By the end of the season he was second-guessing Birdie.

Gus had a fearful circulation problem in his legs, a condition that caused him endless grief. He was a big man, in his sixties, when his legs were amputated.

He had kept his troubles to himself, as he usually did. The first indication I had came from my mother, who told me he had to sleep at night in a chair with his feet on a heating pad. They were always cold. My first day back, at the end of that season, I walked into his house and made him lift his trousers and show me his legs. They were black and blue from the toes to the knee.

Had he consulted a doctor, which he had never done in his life, his legs might have been saved. But he was proud and stubborn and he suffered on his own terms.

I practically dragged him to a doctor. The examination revealed that gangrene had already set in. He was in surgery the next day. Nylon tubes were inserted in both legs to replace the veins and increase the circulation of blood.

The operation seemed a success—for one full day. I spent the night at his bedside. The next morning he started clotting. Now the doctors had no choice but to amputate. They could not even wait for my mother to return to the hospital. I was the one who had to sign the papers. Later, I was the one who had to tell him.

I don't think my father's death, a few years later, saddened me any more than the sight of him being wheeled out of the operating room, his legs gone.

He was in the hospital for twenty weeks, and my old Milwaukee teammates helped him get through the bad times. I would walk into the room and Warren Spahn or Eddie Mathews or Johnny Logan or Lew Burdette would be visiting him. My father wasn't allowed to have liquor in the room, but they would sneak in a couple of bottles and after two or three hours we would all be blasted, including my old man. The nurses could never figure out why he was so cheerful.

I came home from St. Louis the next year and he had thrown away the artificial legs the doctors had fitted to him. He was more comfortable with smaller ones, and he had rockers attached so he could shuffle along and not fall. When he had them on he looked like Toulouse-Lautrec.

The first time I walked into the house and saw him on those short legs, I just cracked up. He didn't mind, so long as I didn't cry. I couldn't stop laughing. You could push him back and forth, like a rocking toy. He loved it. We were both whacko. We had exactly the same sense of humor.

For months he stayed close to home. He was embarrassed to go into his favorite gin mill on those little legs, and he couldn't use the restroom in his wheel chair. He had to carry a jar with him. I went by the house one day, threw a jacket on him, lifted him out of the wheel chair and drove him to the tavern, the Meadow Inn. His drinking and card-playing buddies were waiting for him. He had the time of his life.

I was in Atlanta in 1968, the season after my playing career had ended, when his heart gave out. Twice I flew to Milwaukee to be with him after major attacks. I was with him in intensive care when he had what the hospitals call a Code Four. I watched the doctors restart his heart with an electric shock and by pounding his chest. In the process, they cracked a couple of his ribs.

They literally brought him back to life. A few days later, he told me he was really hacked off. He said he felt himself going, everything was soft and mellow, and suddenly everyone was beating on him.

I made my mother promise that she would take him out of the hospital as soon as he could be moved. If he was going to die, I knew he would rather it happen at home. And so he did.

He went home with strict orders not to listen to any football or baseball games on the radio or TV. Of course, he paid no attention. Gus died two months after he left the hospital, during the 1968 World Series between the Tigers and one of my old teams, the Cardinals. I knew then, if I hadn't before, how important it was to me, and to both of us, that he had been able to see me play in the big leagues.

Sure, I had my critics, people who swore I would never make it. They never bothered me. I always thought I was bigger than baseball and I think my record proves it.

2. Down on the Farm

IN OUR SOCIETY, big league has become a synonym for "first class." A friend once told me of the time Judge Roy Hofheinz was trying to get a bill passed that would allow construction of his domed stadium in Houston. As part of a public relations blitz, he flew some sixty politicians and news people out west.

They stopped off in Los Angeles to stare at an enormous hole in the ground that would become Dodger Stadium, then flew on to San Francisco, where Candlestick Park was nearing completion. Everywhere they went the propaganda machine kept rolling: this was big league; that was *not* big league; this was what you had to do if you wanted to go big league.

The junket ended in Las Vegas, with dinner and a show that featured one hundred topless, statuesque showgirls. Red-eyed and hung over, the party landed in Houston just after dawn, the early morning sun all but blinding the passengers. Amid the groans and stirrings, a man named Morris Frank, known for his twangy East

Texas wit, looked out the window of the plane and saw his wife among a small crowd gathered at the ramp.

"Wal," said Morris, stretching his arms, "it sure was great seein' all them big-league boobies, but it's back to the minors today."

One way or another, I spent some of the best years of my life in the minors. I feel sorry for any ballplayer who never had to work his way up through a farm system, who never lived on sliced meat sandwiches or dressed in clubhouses where your locker consisted of a nail driven into a board. It is like going through life without ever riding on a train.

I am going to ramble a bit now, which is the way I remember the minor leagues, as a slow, rambling, breezy time in my life. I loved it, the way people dressed and talked and thought, the way they cared and didn't mind showing it.

My dad drove me to the bus station and I reported to my first spring training camp at Waycross, Georgia, to an old air force base where the Braves' lower farm clubs trained. I had just received my discharge from the service, and here I was back in the barracks.

A player who has never gone through *that* kind of camp, where the prospects numbered in the hundreds, can never really appreciate spring training. They would pin a number on your back—you might be Number 317—and each morning a crowd would collect around the bulletin board in the camp office to see who had made the Greyhound squad that day. Meaning, adios.

The signs over the toilets warned, DON'T FLUSH WHILE SHOWER IS RUNNING. This was an invitation to every guy who walked in to flush the commode and scald whoever was in the shower. You would walk out of there with a red stripe down your back.

After curfew we'd string a wire across the barracks about knee high and wait for the drunken night watchman to make his rounds. The high point was hearing his body hit the floor. Days later, when the night watchman thought he had the knee wire figured out, we would string it neck high and almost garrote him.

Ah, memories. There were no fences in the outfield, and many a player chased a deep fly ball into the high grass, spotted a snake, and came out faster than he ever went in.

If you were lucky, you might wind up with the hand-me-down uniform of your favorite big-league player. A little tape here and there and the pants would look fairly decent.

Thus prepared, I joined my first professional team, Eau Claire, in the Northern League, in the late spring of 1956. I was twenty-one, just out of the service, making $250 a month and six dollars a day on the road for meal money—just enough to keep you from gnawing on the table leg in your favorite café.

I got off to a miserable start, even for me, and at midseason was batting just .171 with seventeen runs driven in. So the Braves had me reassigned to Boise, Idaho, in the Pioneer League, and I went on to have the kind of summer people used to have in their dreams, when summers didn't cost much.

Boise was about thirty games out of first place when I got there in July, and the Braves had sent down a whole new team in an effort to pull the club out of last place. Boise was the quintessential minor-league town.

They had an old fart who, when all the new players came in, vowed not to shave until we were in first place. By the end of the season his beard was down to his knees. The fans had what they called a Hustle Fund. If you hit a homer you got five dollars, and they passed the hat in the stands. The winning pitcher got five. A triple was worth three bucks, a double was worth two and a single got you a dollar. If you hit a homer you could stop by Pierson's Café the next morning for a free breakfast.

With all those incentives going for us, we caught fire, came from thirty games out and won the pennant on the last day of the season.

At Eau Claire, I had gone something like oh for fifty before I picked up my first hit as a pro, a grand slam homer at Warsaw. But at Boise I was hot from the start. I batted .312 and drove in forty-one runs, with thirteen homers. Lots of free bacon and eggs.

A local VIP named A. J. Archibald owned a bus line that ran junkets—by bus—to Las Vegas. They were motor homes with a toilet and card tables. When one was available he loaded it with fresh fruit and let the ball club use it on road trips, some of which covered seven hundred miles. Hell, I didn't see how they could travel in a style any fancier in the big leagues.

Our manager was a low-keyed, soft-spoken Southerner named George McQuinn, who played first base on the only St. Louis Browns team ever to reach the World Series (in 1944). In 1947, he helped bat the Yankees to the pennant, playing on the same team with Joe DiMaggio, Phil Rizzuto, Tommy Henrich, King Kong Keller and a rookie named Yogi Berra.

McQuinn never talked about his big-league career, which was just as well. When you are that low in the minors, you can't relate to the New York Yankees. We didn't know about anything outside the Pioneer League, and that was how we liked it. What we related to were the signs McQuinn posted in the clubhouse, such as the one that read:

THROUGH THESE DOORS PASS THE HUSTLING BOISE BRAVES.

He arrived when we did, at midseason, and had just the right touch for a bunch of eager, know-nothing kids. He was the same, win or lose. "Now you boys," he would drawl before every game, "you got to get out theah and do youah job."

Every night was an anecdote. Rufus (Big Train) Johnson was one of the three blacks on the team. He was on first base one night during a power failure—we had them regularly—and when the lights came back on Rufus was standing at third, as if nothing had happened.

Boise was the kind of place where the groundskeeper lived at the ball park, in a cabin under the stands, with his wife and kids. He was in charge of the fireworks display. One night he was half in the bag when he started lighting them. After the first few, about four hundred of them went off at the same time, knocked down the left field fence and burned up his quarters. It was beautiful.

The ball park held three to four thousand people and was jammed every night. It was a neat, pretty park surrounded by mountains. Years later, when I was with the Braves, we came back to Boise to play an exhibition game, and the other fellows asked me about the lights, the infield, the power alleys. I told them the place was great, wait until you see it, a miniature Dodger Stadium.

When I got off the bus and walked into the park, I couldn't believe my eyes. There were only about ten light poles, and it was so dark a cat burglar would have felt right at home. The guys really got on me.

But what I remember best about my first year in the Pioneer League was the ball park at Missoula, Montana. I had heard stories about a trap door behind home plate and I thought people were bullshitting me.

Missoula was a farm club of the Washington Senators, and the fans had a theme song, "Hurry Back, Timber Jacks." We walked into the park and the players were taking batting practice, future big-leaguers like Jim Kaat, Jay Ward, Chuck Witherspoon. I saw the trap door and I still couldn't believe it.

When the starting lineups were announced, the trap door flew open and out popped the players, led by their manager, Jack McKeown, while the organist played "Hurry Back, Timber Jacks." The fans loved it, just loved it. The trap door was flush with the ground, ten feet or so behind the catcher, and once inside, you walked down a stairway that led to the home team's clubhouse.

During the game, if you had to answer nature's call, you just grinned sheepishly and made a very public exit. In most parks you walk to the end of the dugout and through a tunnel, or around a corner. Here you had to walk behind the catcher and open the trap door. Everybody knew where you were going. It was like dropping your pants.

My minor-league career took me from Boise to Wichita, Evansville, back to Eau Claire, to Atlanta, back to Boise, Atlanta again, Jacksonville, Indianapolis and Louisville. I was in more hotel rooms than the Gideon Bible.

One of our stops in the Northern League was the Grand Hotel in Fargo, North Dakota, a transient hotel right next to the railroad tracks. The steam engines hissed and whistled and tooted all through the night. The lobby was a famous gathering place for drunk Indians.

On the kind of money we made entertainment was scarce, and we killed a lot of our idle time with water fights. We would start small, filling rubbers and dropping them out the window on people walking by. Then we would graduate to buckets; balancing them on top of a door, poised to spill on the first luckless soul who entered. By the end of the night, we were taking the fire hoses off the wall and facing each other in the hallway like gunfighters. With one spray you could knock a guy clear across a room.

It was a small world and at times a silly one. But twenty-five years ago, you didn't go into pro baseball thinking you had an automatic ticket to the big time. At least, you didn't say so out loud, not if you were a hustling Boise Brave, or even a Timber Jack.

We were like guys trying to break out of a prisoner-of-war camp, knowing that every so often a lucky bastard got through. Our goal was to move up to a higher league the next season. Each move was a step closer to the Taj Mahal.

But in those days a lot of fine players with great records never got out of the minors. The times had changed. The country had changed. The people had changed. But in 1956 baseball had just begun to change. The Braves were in Milwaukee, the A's were in Kansas City, the Dodgers and Giants were heading west. There were still just sixteen cities on the big-league map, and too many players for too few teams. An infielder in the Braves' system could bat .300 for ten years in Triple-A and never stick in the majors, with Mathews, Logan or Schoendienst ahead of him.

So the minors would become his career. He would marry a local girl, get a job in the off season, and enjoy the fact that he was recognized in the community, a small-bore celebrity.

I was fortunate in the minors to have managers who guided and encouraged me and moved me along to the next rung. They were always trying to convince someone in the Braves' office that I could play, even if I was not always convinced myself.

One was Bob Coleman, a legendary manager in the minors, who had won something like twenty pennants by the time I played for him at Evansville in the Three-I League. Bob was in his sixties then, a brawny, gruff, hard-bitten guy who had the look of an old sea captain. He owned a German shepherd named Silver, and he continued the line as each dog died, so now he was up to Silver Five.

Coleman had a habit of sitting naked after a game in a beach chair, with his balls dangling between the canvas webbing, and Silver Five curled up under the chair, snapping at flies. I don't mean to be crude, but players new to the team were endlessly fascinated by that sight.

That damned dog attacked me once. We were in spring training in Waycross, Georgia, and I was warming up a pitcher when the ball got away from me and rolled past the chair where Bob was sitting, in uniform, with Silver Five at his feet. I ran toward the ball and the dog leaped on me, got his teeth into my hand and wouldn't let go. He thought I was after the old man.

With the uniforms we wore then, he could have grabbed me anywhere but the hand and not broken skin. The uniforms were all hand-me-downs from other clubs, blousy things that made most of us look like we were suffering from elephantiasis.

That down-home atmosphere was what I missed when I finally got to the big leagues. You never saw a manager with his pet German shepherd dozing under his chair, and they didn't take you out to eat on Sunday after a road game, either. Bob Coleman did.

A manager in the minors was likely to be a father

figure. And, the way it worked out, you were likely to need one.

In the 1960s the minor leagues began to shrink, some said because of television, soaring costs and competition from other sports. Today the character of the farm system has changed. You used to get a mixture of young prospects, veterans playing out the string, and ex-big-leaguers hoping for the one good streak they needed to make it back.

Now the old-timers are virtually gone. The market is for kids only. And those who don't make the majors in two, three, or four years usually return to college, or move on to something else. No more will you find a fellow spending a dozen years in the minors, beating his way from town to town.

I am not sure there would be room for a Bob Uecker in the minor leagues today, much less the majors. My brand of horseplay probably would not be tolerated, unless more talent than mine went with it.

In my last year in Triple-A ball, I almost joked myself out of the league. At midseason the Braves sent down Stan Lopata, and he took over as the regular catcher. I went out to the bullpen and began to look around for new ways to amuse myself, and my friends.

Fireworks have always been one of my weaknesses. On the Fourth of July, I talked the fellow in charge of the fireworks display into giving me one of his launching tubes and thirty boomers, those heavy-duty jobs that go off like artillery shells.

I carried them out to the bullpen and stored them, with the idea of lighting one each time we hit a homer, as a celebration. They had a fuse a foot and a half long and I wasn't sure I had the courage to light one. But that same night Neil Chrisley homered, and I put a match to the fuse and everyone in the bullpen scattered. We were hiding under benches, behind bunkers, hands over ears.

The boomer rose out of the tube with a soft poof, like a bazooka's, and just as Chrisley reached second base the thing exploded—like a sonic boom. The crowd came unglued. In the bullpen, the boys cheered.

To my surprise, the general manager liked the reaction and told me to keep it up. I continued to set off a boomer after every home run for the next few weeks.

Then John McHale, the president of the Braves, flew into town to look over the club. When he left, I was told to forget about the fireworks. The people in the homes across from the ball park had been sending telegrams to Milwaukee, complaining that the boomers were going off as late as ten o'clock at night, damned near knocking them out of bed.

For a while I thought the Braves might hold it against me. But I guess they were impressed with my team spirit. The next year I was in Milwaukee, a big-leaguer, at last.

3. Planet of the Apes

BY THE TIME I went to my first spring training camp with the Braves, in 1961, there was one thing I knew. I could make people laugh. Most rookies approach their first training camp as though they were raising the flag on Iwo Jima. Not me.

Chuck Dressen was the manager that year. At the end of camp, he sent me back to the minors with the deathless words: "There is no room in baseball for a clown."

Even though I believe he was wrong, and I believed it then, I can see how Dressen might have felt that way.

Billy Martin opened the season with the Braves, and was traded after six games. Billy was at the very end of his stormy career, and still years away from his even stormier service as a manager, during which he would be fired by the Twins, the Tigers, the Rangers and the Yankees, twice. Billy would gain immortality as the last manager ever hired by Charles O. Finley, who sold the Oakland A's some weeks later, in 1980.

Johnny Logan was another kindred spirit in that camp. He would be traded the next year and out of the big leagues in two.

The three of us were on the scrubs. In the fifth inning of those spring training games, if the Braves were losing, Dressen would send in the reserves. We would shout and jump around and pound our gloves and, in general, act as though we were being sent in to save the game. We really pissed off Dressen.

He never forgave some of us for making fun of his cooking. He considered himself a gourmet cook, and frequently prepared a large vat of chili, his specialty, for the coaches, the writers, and his guests. He never offered any to the players.

For this and reasons less worthy, we would slyly drop cigarette butts, matches, and sand from the butt box into the chili when Dressen wasn't watching. Later, we would sit there and watch the VIPs eat that mess and laugh ourselves right out of the room.

I heard that the quality of Dressen's chili remained high the rest of the season, but the team didn't perform so well. He was fired with twenty-five games left and Birdie Tebbetts replaced him.

That year, 1961, would be the last full season I would spend in the minors. I batted .309 with fourteen homers at Louisville, and when I reported to the Braves the next spring I felt almost as though I belonged.

I would be hailed as the first Milwaukee native to play for the Braves. Later, I would be hailed as the first Milwaukee native to be traded by the Braves. Hometown boy makes good.

When I joined them the Braves were a fifth-place team going nowhere. Del Crandall was the starting catcher and a great one. I appeared in just thirty-three games and batted .250—just right, not high enough to raise their hopes or low enough to cut my pay. I woke up to a new world every day, thrilled to be in the big leagues, grateful to be around people I had heard and read about for years. But it was tough to be a young catcher working with a veteran pitching staff.

One day I went out to the mound to talk to Lew Burdette, after a couple of runners had reached base. When I got there, he said, "What the hell do you want?"

I said, "Nothing. I just came out to give you a break."

Lew said, "Don't be coming out here. I don't want you out here. They"—and he waved his gloved hand at the crowd—"think you're giving me advice. And the only thing you know about pitching is that you can't hit it."

My reaction was to go back behind the plate and tell the hitter what pitches were coming. I understood Lew's position.

Still, my stay with the Braves was not without a splash of reflected glory. I was on the receiving end of the game that made Warren Spahn the winningest left-handed pitcher of all time. Spahn was a joy to watch, a master craftsman. Some nights I would catch him without using signs. He didn't have the big breaking ball. Spahnie had a popping fast ball, screwball, and slider. If he wanted to pitch inside to a right-handed batter the pitch was always going to be a fast ball or slider. If he wanted to pitch away, it was going to be a fast ball or screwball.

The only sign I gave him was *in* or *out*. I'd just put up the mitt as a target. He would mouth the words: "Where do you want it?" And I'd mouth back: "In the web."

You can do that when you win and, in those days, Spahn nearly always won.

But overall the Braves had declined from their World

Series years, '57 and '58, and had become the one thing baseball fans can't accept. A mediocre team. Not good enough to compete, not bad enough to be lovable.

I would go on to sit on the bench for a lot of losing teams. Fans often asked me how the players were able to stay up, stay ready, when it was August and the sun was blazing and your team was out of the race?

I can only answer for myself. I would just go out and get likkered up. Same way under pressure. Just go to the bottle. The game is easy when you go out there and play it straight. But when you take half a jug of V.O. and toss it down, you make the game a challenge. I used to get a big kick out of someone coming up to me after a game and asking about a certain play, and I couldn't remember it.

In my day, which was before the age of the mega-bucks, these were the little things that held the players together. I do concede that the players are better behaved today. Chewing tobacco was more popular in my time. You would get dressed and walk onto the field in your clean, white, sanitary socks, with your shoes shined, and somebody would come up and drop a bad wad right on your ankle. Seemed like it was always just before the gum card people were going to take your picture. (Some habits are hard to outgrow. I admit it: I still chew. Even on airplanes.)

The funny thing is, people never believed me when I told them it didn't bother me if I didn't get to play. In the darkest, most insecure corner of my soul, it didn't. I always figured the more I played, the closer I was to going back to the minors.

For years, whatever reputation I had as a player was based entirely on my label as a "good defensive catcher who only needs a chance to play," and on my ability to hit . . . Sandy Koufax.

Koufax? *That* Sandy Koufax? Right. I hit him. I hit him hard. Neither one of us ever figured out why. But whenever Sandy is interviewed about the hitters who were tough on him, he always mentions my name. And he usually gets a laugh, even though he means it.

One night, with Koufax on the mound, the Dodgers gave me an intentional walk to load the bases and bring up the pitcher. Tom Gorman was the umpire and John Roseboro was catching. As I tossed the bat toward the dugout, I turned to the two of them and said, "Boy, if this ever gets out you guys are going to get a letter from the commissioner."

It was obvious I was not going to catch much in Milwaukee. Behind Crandall they had a fine young rookie coming up in Joe Torre. I would be gone from Milwaukee in 1964. (The Braves would be gone in 1966, bound for Atlanta.)

They did me what turned out to be a great kindness. The Braves traded me to a St. Louis team that was going to put on a terrific stretch kick and win the pennant in the National League. The season would be two-thirds gone before anyone knew the Cardinals were in the race—including the Cardinals.

My immediate role seemed to be to provide another character for the clubhouse act developed by Tim McCarver and Ray Sadecki. They had worked up a number of zany routines, inspired by the popular Jackie Gleason show, with Tim as Crazy Guggenheim and Sadecki as Joe the Bartender.

The movie *Planet of the Apes* would not be released until four years later, but in 1964 the two of them were ahead of their time. They went out and purchased gorilla

masks. They wore them everywhere. On the plane, on
the bus, in the clubhouse, sitting around naked in their
hotel room. Believe me, many a maid went tearing out of
their room, towels and bedsheets flying.

Some nights they would take a suit coat and trousers
and concoct a dummy, stuffing it with sheets and pillows.
Then they would arrange the clothing just so, put the
mask on top and stick a cigar in his mouth and prop him
up in one of those big, overstuffed chairs. Now, their
room might be ten floors above mine, but they would
carry that creation down the stairwell at four o'clock in
the morning and knock on my door. I would get out of
bed, stumble to the door, and there would be this ape,
with a cigar in his mouth, sitting in a chair in the hall.

As a near legend among the fringe players of my time,
I was a natural choice to be commissioner of the Batting
Practice League, formed among the pitchers and reserves
in St. Louis. We actually played a game every day. We
chose up teams and had lineup cards. Even as the team
was clawing the Phillies and Reds in the real pennant
race, we were holding our own.

We used to get to the park early for the BPL. There
was a lot of money involved. Ron Taylor was the captain
of one team and Sadecki captained the other. As
commissioner, I also had to pitch batting practice. One
day, Ron Taylor's team hit out of turn. Sadecki let them
bat and then, as the rules require, called it to my
attention.

I walked off the mound to get Taylor's lineup card, and
when he saw me coming he ate it. I mean, as I got within
a few feet he yanked the card out of his pocket, stuffed it
into his mouth, chewed gamely and then swallowed the
pieces. It was better than a spy movie.

Afterward, Sadecki insisted we follow Taylor around

until he went to the toilet and passed the lineup card, so I could rule on whether his team had batted out of turn.

I drew the line at this indignity, but on the scrubs the craziness went on day in and day out. At the end of the year we awarded the trophies.

All in all, the '64 Cardinals were the perfect team for a player whose personality demanded expression. There was talent on the field, intrigue in the front office and madness in the clubhouse. We were curiously untouched by the pressures of a pennant race. We did not even know we were in one until September. This was the loosest, goosiest team ever to come from ten games behind to reach the World Series, a drive in which Robert George Uecker played his own, as shall be seen, crucial part.

PART II

Inside Baseball

In which he reveals that if an athlete works hard, stays in shape, never gives up, and hits .200, he can attract one of the funniest fan clubs anyone ever had.

"There were a great many people who thought that the Cards had made a mistake, trading two ballplayers for one Uecker. As the season wore on, Uecker proved that they were indeed correct . . ."

4. The Fan Club

THE STORY YOU are about to read is true. The names have not been changed to protect anybody, innocent or not, on the theory that if I'm willing to use mine so should they.

Some years ago the zaniest and most unlikely fan club in the annals of baseball was formed. The story behind it is the stuff of legend. How it came to be, the spirit and purpose of the club, the tenacity with which its hero was supported, would melt the heart of a Greek statue.

In 1964, a student at Drury College in Missouri, Mark Stillwell, and his brother, Paul, noticed that the St. Louis Cardinals had not won a game in which I had played from the start of the season until the second of July. This record struck them as worth celebrating, and they did so in what I thought was a commendable and logical way.

They organized The Bob Uecker Fan Club.

In four years the club attracted over five hundred members (names and addresses are on file with the club president, as well as the FBI and the CIA). Sweatshirts bearing my name and likeness were manufactured. An official matchbook was printed, a slogan adopted ("Bob Uecker is a Great American"). Attempts to plan an appreciation day had to be postponed, either because I kept getting traded or because the school cafeteria was not available.

It is hard to say what forces came together to start such a movement. I suppose it was a natural reaction to the pressures of the Vietnam War. Those were turbulent years.

Mark Stillwell was a clean-cut, otherwise normal college type, the sports editor of the Drury *Mirror*. We kept in touch during his undergraduate days, and later when he served in the navy. Eventually he returned to Drury as the school's director of sports information.

I don't think I ever met more than three or four club members at a time. Every so often one of them would show up at whatever ball park my team happened to be in, and if I played that day the news would soon be all over the campus. They would report back with all the excitement of a bird watcher sighting a gray-speckled spanarkel. "He went oh for three," they would say, breathlessly, or, "he chased a ball all the way to the backstop."

When Mickey Mantle retired, he began receiving scrapbooks kept by his fans throughout the country, more than fifty of them. Sometimes late at night he would take one out and thumb through it. "It gave me goose bumps," he said, "to know I had that kind of effect on people."

My first reaction to hearing that I had a fan club was to say nothing, and to lie low for about two weeks, until I could see if Ray Sadecki or Tim McCarver was behind it. There came a day when I received in the mail from Mark the scrapbook the club had maintained, in three or four volumes. Turning the pages, my entire career flashed before my eyes. It was a little like drowning.

The tone was set with the introduction, a little defensive, I thought, like a lawyer appealing to have a guilty verdict overturned. To quote Mark Stillwell, "This book is an attempt to present the case of Bob Uecker. Sometimes it is straightforward, sometimes it is biased against Bob Uecker and, mainly, it is biased in favor of Bob Uecker."

Now I like that approach. I am reminded of the vacuum cleaner salesman who knocks on a customer's door and says, "Let me give you the pros and cons of this product."

Mark goes on: "It was the kind of sudden impulse thing I couldn't explain, and this hurt my presentation. But my heart was soon fully in it and my enthusiasm won me a lot of support.

"This (scrapbook) tells it all. The pictures and words vividly record the course of the Bob Uecker Fan Club and the successes and failures of Bob Uecker. (It) is all collected here, and this is probably the greatest conglomeration of Bob Uecker data ever assembled anywhere."

The casual fan may feel that the kid was taking a lot for granted, not knowing what they might have had on file at, say, the British Museum. But when I first read that paragraph, I could envision the scrapbook being made into a television docu-drama, the highlights of my career in baseball: Bob Uecker getting on a plane to start a road trip; Bob Uecker sleeping on a plane; Bob Uecker getting off a plane.

The club caught on. Where all the members came from I never knew. I am not sure I wanted to know. I was told that several were under ten years of age. The oldest was ninety-two.

By the time the club was organized, I had spent nine years in organized ball—two of them in the majors—and had made fifteen moves to ten different cities.

As a big-leaguer, I had appeared in eighty-six games, with forty-one hits in 186 times at bats for an average of .220. I had scored sixteen runs and driven in fourteen, with five doubles and two homers—all in less than three seasons.

Jeez, no wonder I had my own fan club.

Mark Stillwell took special note of one part of my game: "There is a lot said about Bob Uecker's speed. Most everybody generally agrees that he is one of the slowest runners in the game. He had a race with Dick Groat in spring training to see who was the slowest on the team and Groat outran him. The fact also stands out that Uecker has stolen six bases in his career. All, however, before 1960, and all in the minor leagues. He swiped one base at Eau Claire in 1956 and two at Boise the same year. He got two more at Boise in 1958 and one at Jacksonville in 1959. And that's it."

This, I think, came under the heading of what the boys called "some of the good stuff" they had learned about my career.

Another item from early in the scrapbook: "Paul saw Uecker play in a minor league game at San Diego in July of 1963 against San Diego. Uecker played for Denver. He batted sixth and grounded out twice and walked as Denver lost, 3-0. His name had been left off the scoreboard and the box score in the San Diego paper the next day spelled his name 'Uekcer.'"

When the Braves traded me to the Cardinals only a few days before the start of the 1964 season, getting catcher Jim Coker and outfielder Gary Kolb in return, I was just another journeyman ballplayer. Although manager Johnny Keane announced that I had been obtained to back up Tim McCarver, and "make our catching solid," I did not instantly capture the hearts of the people of St. Louis. As the president of my own fan club would later observe: "There were a great many people who thought that the Cards made a great mistake, trading two ballplayers for one Uecker. As the season wore on, Uecker proved that they were indeed correct. He fielded like a slow, wounded turtle behind the plate. He ran like a batting cage with a flat tire, and he hit like he didn't know what the word meant. He cost the Cards some ballgames with poor throwing and hit into double plays or made outs at key spots. His batting average dwindled to the .200 mark. He became the butt of some jokes and his very presence in the lineup gave the Cards a defeatist attitude. He seemed to be a loser like the Cards hadn't had since the days of Dal Maxvill. He became the scapegoat. People began to blame things on Uecker. And Uecker deserved every bit of it."

At this point, you might conclude that the fans were not yet solidly behind me. No matter how poorly things were going for me, no one made excuses. They told it like it was with a bluntness that would have made Howard Cosell weep.

The diary of the 1964 season went on: "Johnny Keane constantly used pinch hitters for him and never played him unless McCarver was about to drop and it was the second game of a doubleheader and the team was on the road and the Cards were facing a lefthander.

"Uecker went from bad to worse to terrible. It seemed that the Cards just couldn't win with him in the lineup. Through the first three months of the season, the Cards lost every single game in which Uecker's name appeared

in the box score. No matter what he did, it never
failed . . . when he played, the Cards lost."

Some athletes can't handle compliments and are
embarrassed by praise. Thank the Lord I'm not one of
them. My patience paid off.

"On July 2, 1964, baseball history was made in
County Stadium in Milwaukee. The St. Louis Cardinals
won a game in which Bob Uecker played. Of course, he
didn't play the whole game. That would be expecting a
little too much. Uecker, whose true talent was probably
revealed when he won a cow-milking contest in Houston, has given Harry Caray what is probably another
good omen, and the Cardinal announcer values such
things.

"He caught three innings and the Cards maintained a
4-3 lead and finally won a game with him in the lineup.
He was rushed to a hospital for immediate observation.
Cardinal fans across the country postponed plans for the
biggest event of the year in St. Louis, Bob Uecker Night,
at which they intended to assassinate him.

"Uecker entered the game in the seventh. The Cards,
thanks to Julian Javier's second homer in two games and
tenth of the year, and a couple of pinch hits, had tied the
Braves, 3-3. The Braves brought in Hank Fischer to
pitch. Since Johnny Keane had unwisely batted for
McCarver, he had no other catcher. It is not unwise in
itself to bat for McCarver, but the thing is that when you
do you have to use Bob Uecker behind the plate. So,
when Fischer came in to pitch to Flood, who should
come riding in on the golf cart with him but Uecker, to
catch the seventh, eighth, and ninth. (The fans) shuddered. Another game lost, they figured. Flood walked
and Brock hit a sacrifice fly to center to give St. Louis a
4-3 lead.

"In the bottom of the seventh, Bob Humphreys walked the frst man he faced and sent him to second on a wild pitch. Same old Humphreys, we all thought. Then, Humphreys proceeded to retire the next nine men in a row to save Ray Sadecki's ninth victory of the season. He even struck out two men. When Uecker batted, of course, he was called out on strikes. Typical. The only reason the Cards won is that nobody, with the possible exception of Humphreys, knew that it was Uecker behind the plate."

The Uecker jinx had been broken. And a strange coincidence took place. The Cardinals caught fire. Cautiously, Keane tried me again. In a game at Pittsburgh I went hitless in five trips, but the Cards collected twenty hits and breezed, 12-5. The same week I caught again, and we rallied for eleven runs in the eighth innng to win, 15-7.

There was magic in the air. I refer to the scrapbook: "Four nights later, Uecker actually got a base hit. His batting average had dwindled to .173 and he boosted it to .179. On the twenty-fifth of July, he caught a full game. He came to the plate five times. He had three walks and two singles, scoring twice. He caught an excellent game and even got several closeup shots on national television when he *got hit in the neck by a foul tip*.

"He now had twelve hits in twenty games and his average was back around the .200 mark. He has four runs for the season and two runs batted in. Clearly, he intends to play a better brand of baseball for the rest of the season than he started with. . . . As Harry Caray said this afternoon, 'This is the catcher we traded for.'"

Blissfully unaware of the activity stirring on my behalf, I found myself blending into what had become, surprisingly, a pennant-contending team. At midsummer, the rumors were buzzing around the league that Johnny Keane was finished in St. Louis, to be replaced at the end of the season by Leo Durocher.

But, suddenly, the Cardinals had begun to make a charge at the leaders. On the last day of August, we beat the Braves, 5-4, to pull within a couple of games of the second-place Reds. The Phillies seemed uncatchable, but as Yogi Berra once said, "It's never over until it's over." My single in the last of the ninth drove in the winning run to beat the Braves. We had rallied from four runs down, and earlier I had hit my first homer of the season off Denny Lemaster. The crowd went berserk. I had the spirit. So did my fan club, which I still did not know existed.

In Springfield, the kids at Drury College were taking credit for turning around the pennant race. On the day the Bob Uecker Fan Club was started, the Cardinals were a game under .500 with forty-seven wns and forty-eight losses. Since then we had won thirty and lost thirteen, a .697 pace. No doubt about it. The formation of the club had coincided with the revival of the Cardinals as a factor in the pennant race. It was almost metaphysical.

Their "strange impulse" had undergone a change in character. The club was still a put-on—hey, my kind of game—but no longer a put-*down*.

I was soon to meet my two truest believers. On September tenth, with the Reds in town, the Stillwell brothers drove to St. Louis and arrived at Busch Stadium, wearing their designer sweatshirts and armed with their membership list and a carton of matchbooks. Mark recorded the scene: "I watched Uecker for a while as he sat in the dugout comparing hands with Ken Boyer, and then he came out to play catch with his faithful friend, Bob Skinner. There were several kids in the front row of the box seats looking for autographs as Paul and I boldly walked down into an area which is no-man's-land for autograph hunters because of the nasty attitude of the ushers."

They had not been at the railing long when the printing on their sweatshirts caught my eye. I left Skinner and walked over to investigate, a little wary, my grin getting wider as I drew closer. Mark made the introductions and said, proudly, "I'll bet you didn't know you had a fan club with one hundred seventy-six members down in Springfield, did you?"

I laughed out loud. "No," I said, "I sure as hell didn't. You aren't the ones who have been booing me, are you?"

They assured me they were not. I signed a team picture and two scorecards, and Mark gave me a personalized Bob Uecker matchbook. I stuck it in my back pocket and went off to catch infield practice.

Mark continued his observations: "Happily, I went back to my seat to watch the Cards do battle with the Reds. Uecker caught the first game (of two) and reached base on an error in the second inning. Ken Boyer hit a towering two-run homer in the third to give the Cards the lead, and the first hit off Gibson was a line drive by Deron Johnson in the fourth into the left-field seats. Uecker grounded solidly into a double play in the fourth and bounced out in the seventh. He was on deck in the ninth when McCarver got the game-winning hit. The Cards won, 3-2.

"As I walked into the park I had been confronted by a teenager in civilian clothes talking to a scorecard vendor. I recognized him as Bob Baker, the Cardinal batboy. He said, pointing to my shirt, 'How many of youse are there?' I told him, one hundred seventy-six. 'Where are

you from?' he asked. I told him Springfield. He asked if
we were all boys. No, I replied, we do have some girls.

"All day people would look at my sweatshirt and
either snicker, or come right out and laugh or make some
smart comment or wisecrack. It was almost as if nobody
ever heard of Bob Uecker and none of them ever
appreciated him.

"However, it was late in the second game when I saw
a sign above the Cardinals' bullpen in left field that read
BOB UECKER ALL STAR. (There was another sign in front
of the hot-dog stand in the left-field bleachers that said
ED SPEZIO FAN CLUB.)

"Lou Brock homered in the first, McCarver homered
in the seventh and Flood singled in Javier in the ninth
with what was the winning run in a 3-2 victory that tied
the Cards and Reds for second place.

"Later, we were walking up Sullivan Avenue and a
young lady in a car saw my sweatshirt, leaned out the
window and said, 'I agree.' I turned around, astonished,
and yelled, 'Hey, a real Bob Uecker fan.'

"We decided to go to Stan Musial's restaurant to eat,
but they told us we couldn't come in with that kind of
attire. They were rather nasty about the whole thing, I
thought. Maybe I should have had a McCarver sweatshirt on. We finally wound up eating at the old standby
way out on Chippewa, at Chuck-a-Burger."

End of a perfect day.

The boys went back to the campus to push their
membership drive with new vigor. I didn't *really* take it
seriously, but, what the heck, in the weeks since the club
was founded the Cardinals had swept from seventh place
to second. Lay that secret handshake on me.

I am not the kind of player who lived by batting
average alone. And I do feel that I made a contribution to

the team's pennant charge, if only by helping to maintain the morale of the club. Actually, I won two or three games with clutch base hits, but there is no point in going into all the details. It gets to be too much like walking through a garden, admiring the roses, and saying over and over, "Here's another beauty."

Actually, I was getting my share of playing time. On September thirteenth, I was behind the plate when we became the first team since 1923 to score in every inning. We pounded the Cubs, 15-2, racking up eighteen hits—off six Chicago pitchers—and taking advantage of seven errors. Curt Simmons got the win, his fifteenth of the season. At Drury College, the club members said the game was a tribute to my greatness.

A moving team has a grace all its own. The Cardinals could do nothing wrong in September, winning twenty-one of twenty-nine games, and squeezing past the Reds and the Phillies in one of the wildest of all pennant races.

The Cardinals had approached the season with a huge question mark. Stan Musial, one of the game's legendary hitters, their spiritual leader—and left fielder—had retired. A spot in the lineup that had not required a second thought in twenty years was suddenly wide open.

Four players were tried there as the club limped through the season's early weeks. Just before the All-Star break, a trade with Chicago brought in Lou Brock, in return for pitcher Ernie Broglio. The deal was not a popular one in the locker room. Ernie had been a proven winner, and was one of the few players who never failed to laugh at our skits. Not much was known of Brock, a young outfielder with speed, a slight build and a newsboy's innocent face.

After a slow start, Lou began to run and hit. Left field ceased to be a problem. In another trade, Roger Craig arrived to help Barney Schultz in the bullpen, and Bob Gibson found his control and got hot.

Of course, there was another, less obvious factor. I suppose some people will feel that my quoting from the scrapbook, at this point, is merely a device I can hide behind to appear modest, to avoid saying things that sound self-serving. The best way to answer that charge is to quote from the scrapbook: "On July 26, 1964, the Bob Uecker Fan Club came into existence and was an immediate and lasting success. We of the club don't pretend to take complete credit for the events which occurred in the city of St. Louis and which culminated on the afternoon of October fourth when the St. Louis Cardinals became the National League champions. However, we do point to the record and will continue to point to it as long as skepticism to our cause appears.

"One quiet fact stands out. Prior to the time the Bob Uecker Fan Club was formed, the Cardinals were in seventh place. After that, they won forty-six and lost only twenty-one and rolled past team after team until they had moved into the National League throne room. They then defeated the New York Yankees to win the World Series.

"We don don't claim that *we* won the pennant. We don't claim that Bob Uecker won the pennant. And we don't claim that the Bob Uecker Fan Club won the pennant. We simply point to the record before and after the formation of the Bob Uecker Fan Club!"

Credit aside, I enjoyed the race as both a player and a spectator. In what has become one of the more celebrated collapses in all of baseball lore, the Phillies blew a lead of six and a half games with twelve games to play. "It was like watching someone drown," said Gene Mauch, the manager.

Gus Triandos, the big Greek catcher, called it "the year of the blue snow."

Meanwhile, the Reds were gallantly trying to win the pennant for their manager, Fred Hutchinson, who was dying of cancer, and who gave up the team to Dick Sisler in August. Sisler was called the "acting manager," a phrase with a reassuring temporary ring to it. But the Reds would never again jump to the orders of Fred Hutchinson. He knew it and they knew it. He died in November.

For the Cardinals, the finish was not without its bittersweet moments. The club at one point won eight in a row, five over the Pirates, to leap past the Phillies and Reds into first place.

The race went down to its final weekend, whereupon the Mets almost ruined it for us. The Mets. The lowly, comic-book Mets. They beat us in the first two games. They were like cockroaches. It wasn't what they ate or carried off, it was what they fell into and ruined. We still needed a win to clinch the pennant, and Gibson delivered on the final day.

So the Cardinals surprised not only the Phillies, the Reds, and the experts. They surprised the Cardinal ownership. Bing Devine, the team's general manager, and Johnny Keane's closest friend, had been fired in August, with the club trailing in third place. The papers were saying that the manager's job had been offered to Leo Durocher. Keane kept his silence.

Now here were the Cardinals, meeting the New York Yankees in the World Series. Mantle, Ford, Skowron and Howard. Naturally, the Series went the distance, and Bob Gibson beat the Yankees in the seventh game, on two days' rest, starting because, in the words of Johnny Keane, "I had a commitment to his heart."

As Jack Benny might have said, "W-e-l-l-l-l." Do you think the Cardinals's owners were red-faced when Keane's team turned around and won both the pennant and the World Series? Hastily, they broke off talks with Durocher. Keane was offered a new contract, with a respectable raise.

John was in the sweetly ironic position of being able to tell them to take their offer and stick it in a beer can. Which he did. In a startling postscript to the Series, the losing team fired its manager, Yogi Berra, and replaced him with the manager of the winning team, Johnny Keane. Sadly, he joined the Yankees in time to catch them on a downward slide, and was fired in 1966, proving again that in baseball, as in politics, there are no final victories.

According to my calculations, in my six years in the majors I did not play in 675 games, not counting All-Star games. A lot of the games I did not play in were big games, historic games—involving names like Stan Musial, Willie Mays, Roberto Clemente, Henry Aaron, Frank Robinson; two or three no-hitters, marathons that lasted eighteen or twenty innings, things like that.

Looking back over my entire career, I am proudest of the World Series I did not play in for the Cardinals in '64. Tim McCarver caught every inning of every game.

For the Series, McCarver batted .478, scored four runs, drove in five and even stole a base. In all sincerity, I doubt that I could have improved on his performance.

But in all modesty, I can say that I probably received as much publicity as any fellow could for not playing in a World Series. Before the first-game ceremonies in St. Louis, I was on the field shagging flies with the rest of the scrubs. All the players were using gloves except me.

I was wearing a tuba. That probably requires an explanation.

There were four Dixieland bands on the field that day to entertain the crowd before the game. When the band in the left-field corner took a break, I noticed a tuba sitting there, looking neglected.

So I whipped it on and started catching fly balls with it. I didn't catch them all. A few, possibly several, hit the rim. The Cardinals later received a bill from the tuba player, wanting to be reimbursed for the damages. I had to kick in for it.

The Series turned out well, and that was as close as I came to getting into it, so you would have to say the money was well spent.

5. The Best Defensive Catcher
in the League

MY LAURELS MAY be the only thing I never rested on in my career, and I know my fans felt the same way. By way of a preamble to the 1965 season, the fan club recorded this touching thought: "Last year our goal was to get one member for each point in Bob Uecker's batting average. A late spurt gave him a .198 average, leaving us slightly short . . ."

That spring of 1965, coming off the championship season, I found myself with the kind of opportunity second-stringers dream about and seldom get. Tim McCarver broke a finger toward the end of camp and was out of action opening day and longer. I figured to get a chance to catch every day.

Now being a second-stringer is just about the most awkward role in sports. You have to accept the fact that the only way you will see any substantial action is for the fellow ahead of you to get hurt. If it happens, you have to be ready, but you can't appear too eager or too pleased. I mean, you can't go up to Tim McCarver every day and ask, "How's the finger?"

Red Schoendienst had succeeded Johnny Keane as manager of the Cardinals, and every day I read in the papers how he wasn't worried by the thought of having to go with Uecker. "He'll get better with more work," said Red.

Of course, this went contrary to my own theory, which was that the less I played the more likely I was to stay in the big leagues. But I prepared myself to take the risk. At least once in your life, you have to gamble. I had a heckuva spring, hitting over .300 and even banging a couple of homers.

I was the starting catcher on opening day of 1965, with Bob Gibson on the mound, when the defending champion Cardinals met the Chicago Cubs at Wrigley Field. It was just another typical day in the life of Mr. Baseball, meaning that:

—The game was called on account of darkness at the end of eleven innings with the score tied, 10-10;

—The Cards scored five runs in the top of the first and Gibson, one of the great pitchers of his day, couldn't hold the lead;

—I tried to steal home in the fifth inning and was out at the plate . . . I thought the sign had been flashed for the suicide squeeze bunt, but apparently it hadn't. I was sorry about that;

—I drew a walk with the bases loaded in the first inning to drive in a run;

—In the sixth I crashed into the field boxes chasing a pop foul and badly bruised my left kneecap. There went my career as a temporary regular catcher. The Cards had to press into service Dave Ricketts, a utility man who had been signed two days before as an insurance move.

The omens were not good. My personal historian, Mark Stillwell, took note of the crisis: "The St. Louis Cardinals won the 1964 pennant with a furious stretch drive. Then they won the World Series. With the same team looking much improved, they were picked by many to win again in 1965. But they started badly, losing five of their first six games and eight of their first twelve. Clearly, action was called for as something had to be done to pick the team up. Something *big* was needed. The Bob Uecker Fan Club moved in and stemmed the tide."

Mark and three other members of the club, Joe Fisher, Mike McCloskey, and Mike Wright, arranged to be in St. Louis on Friday night, April 30, to watch a four-game, weekend series against the Pirates. I was not in the lineup as we won the first two games, both by scores of 3-2.

On Sunday, the boys got to the ball park early: "Uecker was standing out in front of the left field wall. Eventually he wandered in and went into the dugout. When the team came back out, he started playing catch with Boyer and Carl Warwick. McCloskey had a poster that had Uecker's picture on it and I yelled at Uecker and held it up for him to see. A broad grin crossed his face. Shortly he came over and I took some pictures of him. I asked him if he was going to catch one of the games and he said he was. After the dugout interview, I got the attention of Cardinal announcer Harry Caray. I handed him a clipping from the Drury *Mirror* (the student paper) and he started reading it eagerly with a smile on his face. He asked me if he could keep it. I was only too glad to oblige.

"Then the game started. Donn Clendenon and Willie Stargell homered off Gibson in the first to put the Pirates ahead, 2-0. Then, in the bottom of the first, it happened. At roughly 1:25 P.M., Harry Caray uttered those immortal words: 'Members of the Bob Uecker Fan Club are here today, hee hee, from Drury College.' Short, simple, and to the point.''

I didn't play in the first game as the Cards came back to win, 9-5. Mark continues: "Then came the big second game. Uecker's moment of glory . . . The Pirates had used sloppy Cardinal fielding and a general clobbering of Bob Purkey to get three runs and there were still men on first and second with two out in the third and Del Crandall at bat. He drilled a single to left and Jerry Lynch came charging around from second.

"Lou Brock fielded the ball in left and threw toward home. It wasn't a particularly strong or impressive throw at all. Uecker had to go several feet into foul territory away from the baseline to get the ball as Lynch barreled down the line toward home. At the last instant, Uecker grabbed the throw on one hop and lunged at Lynch. He stretched himself out horizontally and just managed to tag Lynch on the shins. Lynch bowled him over and Uecker quickly bounced up with the ball clenched tightly in his fist. The umpire raised his right arm high. The crowd roared. I was the loudest.

"In the lower third he got to bat. A wild cheer came up from our section after the play he had made to end the top of the third. Then he hit a long fly into right that had us all on our feet. Bill Virdon ran a long way and finally caught up with the ball on the warning track in front of the wall.

"Bob Veale was tough for the Pirates. As the bottom of the eighth rolled along, Veale was breezing, 4-1. He had given up just one hit (a homer by Ken Boyer) and fanned nine. Then came his downfall. Bob Uecker stepped to the plate.

"With grace and poise, Uecker took a ball in the dirt. Crandall said something to the umpire as he picked up the ball and through my field glasses I could see Uecker grinning out of the side of his mouth. He carefully watched the second pitch go high. We were pulling for him now, vocally, and I think the people around us sensed it as they kept turning around. The next pitch came in and was again low. Ball three! One more and we had a base runner. Veale wound up. He fired. It was inside! Uecker trotted down to first base as the four of us gave him a standing ovation. Veale had faltered. Just to make things exciting, he threw over to first to try and get Uecker. (Imagine Uecker trying to steal.)

"That brought up Phil Gagliano to bat for Barney Schultz. The crowd was up and hungry for a rally. We were up, too, yelling to Gagliano for a hit and warning Uecker not to get picked off. Uecker is one of the slowest men in the league. The danger of his scoring on a triple by Gagliano was only slight.

"Gagliano amazed everybody as he lined a shot off the right-field wall. Uecker took off for second base. The ball bounded away from the right fielder as McCloskey took a picture of Uecker lumbering along and we all cheered wildly in an effort to give him more speed. The ball bounced into the bullpen and the pitchers there scattered. It rolled under the bench and the right fielder chased it there and picked up the bench and looked for the ball and then kicked it away and had to run after it again.

"By this time Uecker had reached second base and was getting a little tired and had to slow down from the brisk pace he had been setting. The right fielder located the ball, but tripped over the pitching rubber in the bullpen and fell headlong out on the grass. The ball kept rolling away. Uecker was digging for third, but was obviously laboring. The right fielder picked up the ball and fumbled it a couple of times and let loose a weak throw that rolled into the second baseman, who also fumbled it. Uecker started his slide. The second baseman dropped the ball and picked it up and threw toward third and it was another weak throw. The ball bounced in the dust and caromed off the third baseman's forearm and into the waiting arms of the pitcher who also bobbled it before he picked it up and flipped it back to the third baseman, who tried to put the tag on the sliding Uecker. The play was close. He was safe!

"It was at this point that Joe Fisher remarked, 'He looked like he was goin' up a forty-five-percent grade.' By now we were all ecstatic that Uecker had started a rally that might conceivably change the course of the ballgame. Curt Flood came up and promptly singled to left and in a blaze of speed, coming from a second wind, Uecker roared home with his second run of the season to make it 4-2. There was loud shouting in our box and shaking of hands as our boy finally got off the base paths and into the dugout. McCloskey grabbed my arm and pointed to the scoreboard. 'That run up there belongs to Uecker,' he shouted at me.

"Then Lou Brock singled and Gagliano came in to make it 4-3. Groat bounced into a double play, but Flood scored to tie it up. Boyer lined out to the shortstop to end the eighth. We went wild, as the game was tied. And Veale had been taken out.

"In the bottom of the ninth, Bill White led off against Al McBean. All he had to do now was homer and the Cards would win. He hit the second pitch into the right-field pavilion for a 5-4 win. The Cards had won four straight from the Pirates and had reached the .500 mark for the season, and had climbed in three days from tenth in the National League to a tie for fourth.

"The boys had come through in the clutch. And Uecker was in the center of it all. As Joe remarked to me in the three-run rally in the eighth, 'He broke it open.' There was a woman in front of us who was enjoying our antics as much as she was the game. She turned around and looked at me and said, 'You're right! Uecker did it.' And then she turned to her husband and I heard her say, 'I never heard of Bob Uecker in my life until today.'"

I see that game, that rally, and that remark as a microcosm of my life. I guess it would be easy for some people to say that anyone's career could sound exciting if you described every pitch of it. On the other hand, perhaps not.

I am not trying to make a big deal of the fact that I drew a walk and scored the run that got us back into a rather meaningless game in May. Someone had to get us started. Nor do I care to say where that play ranks among all the most unforgettable plays of my career. That would be like trying to single out your favorite noodle at a spaghetti dinner. But out of that narrative, the line that appeals to me most is, *"Uecker started his slide."* The line has a kind of melancholy ring to it.

The season rocked along. McCarver and I were still nagged by injuries, but we struggled to stay in the lineup. A few days later, I hit my first home run of the season, but it went to waste. The Giants scored five runs in the top of the tenth inning to break a tie and beat us, 10-5. It was a weird inning, and I figured in it in a prominent way.

We had Ray Washburn on the mound. There were runners at first and third with one out when Ed Bailey, a backup catcher who was even slower then me, batted for the San Francisco pitcher. He swung at an 0-2 pitch and rapped a grounder toward Phil Gagliano at second base. The perfect double play mix: crisp ground ball, slow runner.

Phil charged the ball and juggled it. Then he picked it up, decided he had no chance to get two, and fired a strike to home.

The only problem was, I wasn't there. The ball almost hit the plate umpire in the gut. I had headed down the first-base line. If Gagliano fielded the ball cleanly, I needed to back up the relay to first. Meanwhile, the winning run scored and the Giants went on to get four more.

After the game, Bob Broeg, the veteran St. Louis baseball writer, bumped into Tom Sheehan, the round, red-faced Giants' scout who always reminded me of a house detective. Broeg told Sheehan that, man and boy, he had been watching the Cardinals for forty years and had never seen that play.

"No," boomed Sheehan, in his big, bass voice, "and man and boy, I'll bet you've never seen many catchers, either, whose last name begins with the letter *U*."

As the 1965 season unfolded, it developed that beneath the clown's mask, inside my bench-warmer's shell, beat the heart of a semi-regular and might-have-been .300 hitter. I darned near blew my image.

In May, Red Schoendienst decided to platoon me with Tim McCarver. I started twelve games. We won eight of them. That month the Cardinals made their best and last bid to move into first place, pulling to within a game and a half of the Dodgers.

My fan club began to suspect that they had created a monster. On May fifth I cracked my first homer of the season, against the Giants. Three nights later, I started rallies with a walk and a single, and kept the Phillies from scoring the winning run in the ninth by tagging out Alex Johnson on a close play at the plate. Over the radio network, Harry Caray exulted: "How Uecker ever held that ball I'll never know."

Like monks recording their daily prayers, my scribes committed every word to the club scrapbook.

May 16—"Uecker had a hit to raise his average forty points to .190. Jack Buck spoke for all of us when he said, 'Uecker has been really stinging the ball, but it just isn't falling in.'"

May 17—". . . threw out two runners attempting to steal, was the middle man on a double play and blocked the plate to keep the Phillies from scoring. Harry Caray called his arm 'phenomenal.'"

May 20—". . . had a hit and scored run as Bob Gibson won his eighth, 12-2."

May 21—". . . laced a single to center in the fourth, with a 2-2 count and the tying run on second, to drive in his third run of the year and raise his average to .214 (the highest it has been in some time). Two innings later he walked. It seems as if every time Uecker catches, he walks once. Never twice, but always once, except Thursday when he was hit by a pitch. He obviously has a good eye at the plate."

It is dangerous for an athlete to believe his own publicity, good or bad. I never believed mine, partly because I never read any until after I had retired. But for a fleeting moment there, in 1965, I was getting very good ink indeed.

In late May, we beat the Dodgers twice to cut their lead to one and a half games. I collected two hits off Claude Osteen and two—of course!—off Sandy Koufax, one a double that just missed being a homer.

I was only in the lineup against left-handers, which meant that I could look forward to a parade of people named Koufax, Bob Veale, Chris Short, Bo Belinsky, Dick Ellsworth, Al Jackson, Jim O'Toole and Claude Osteen. I had to adopt a new philosophy. I learned to dread one day at a time.

The win over Koufax turned out to be the high point of our season. I scored the winning run and lifted my average to .286, at the time the third highest on the club, behind Curt Flood and Lou Brock. We should have known right then that the Cardinals were in trouble.

Out last hurrah came in Los Angeles, on July 25, when we beat the Dodgers in ten innings, 3-2, before a crowd of fifty thousand. As luck would have it—I am trying to be humble about this—I had two hits off Koufax, one a homer. Poor Sandy. He was the greatest pitcher of his time, and whenever I stepped in to face him he didn't know whether to laugh or to cry.

After that we went right down the tubes. The Giants swept a three-game series from us at home, and by the first week in August we were just over .500 and out of the race. Typical of the way the season had gone, McCarver and I went on the injury list at the same time, just as we had in April. Once more Mike Shannon was yanked from the outfield to fill in as the emergency catcher. Tim had a spiked left thumb. I had a split right thumb. Between us we had a complete set.

Sometimes there is no way to explain why a championship team takes a pratfall. Some call it the Fat Cat syndrome. But the Cardinals had to fight too hard in 1964, won too late and by too little, to be complacent. True, we had changed managers, but Red was a clone of Johnny Keane: a good man, quiet, serious, diligent, with the same way of handling a team.

We had virtually the same lineup that had won the World Series. Yet at the point where we had begun our pennant drive the year before, our tank was empty. Injuries nagged us. Simmons and Sadecki won fifteen fewer games. Boyer, White, Flood, and Brock saw their averages drop between twenty and forty points. When the locusts come, they devour everything.

During this period I made an interesting discovery. These were all players with high standards, which they had set for themselves. When they failed to meet them, the fans and the management came down hard. I had no such problem.

I found myself a more frequent guest on Harry Caray's postgame radio show, reserved for The Star of the Game. I appeared in September after a win over the Mets, during which I picked a runner off second and singled off the shortstop's glove. The hit at first had been called an error.

Harry asked me if some players didn't worry a lot about whether balls were called hits or errors.

"Some players," I admitted, "will get on first base and reach down and pick up a handful of dirt and when nobody is looking, they'll glance up at the scoreboard."

Harry said, "What do you do when it's a close call?"

I said, "I reach down and pick up a handful of dirt and when nobody is looking, I glance up at the scoreboard."

"I guess you like to see them call it a hit."

"Well, I always like to count 'em as a hit myself," I

replied. "I count everything—hits, walks, fielder's choices, everything. If I hit the ball good, I count it."

Harry asked, "Well, by your own system, what are you hitting right now?"

"Six-forty-three," I said.

There was not a lot to laugh or cheer about by the time the Cardinals ended the season at home. We stood in front of the dugout while Lou Brock received a plaque at home plate for breaking the club record with sixty stolen bases. Without turning my head, I whispered to McCarver, "If I had been in the lineup every day that could be me out there."

I did, in fact, have my best season in the majors. I played in fifty-three games, batted 145 times, with thirty-three hits, seventeen runs, seven doubles, two homers and ten runs batted in—all career highs. I hit a hard .228.

I was the catcher when Roy McMillan, of the Mets, stepped in the batter's box to start his two thousandth game. When Sandy Koufax set the National League record for strikeouts in a season, 349, I was the hitter he fanned to tie the record.

Over the years we had a great personal rivalry, Koufax and I. Thank the Lord I didn't destroy the boy's confidence.

Although the Cardinals had tumbled to seventh place, I had performed reasonably well as a spot starter. No one would blame me for the decline. No one had said, "As Uecker goes, so go the Cards." I felt secure. I even thought I might get a small raise.

What I got was a trade to the Philadelphia Phillies, along with Dick Groat and Bill White. In return, the

Cardinals received pitcher Art Mahaffey, outfielder Alex Johnson and catcher Pat Corrales.

The news broke on October 27, 1965, on the heels of a trade that sent Ken Boyer to the Mets. The fan club felt betrayed and outraged. The kids stopped just short of asking the president to double the guard at Pearl Harbor.

Mark Stillwell took the news harder than I did: "To trade Bill White after the job he has done is in itself a crime against humanity. To trade Dick Groat might be partly understandable, much as the Boyer trade was. But to trade Uecker was the unkindest cut of all. This is an unpardonable sin. And, when you don't get anything for him in return, it's doubly bad.

"Myra Becker called me over in English and told me the Cards had traded Bob Uecker. I almost fainted. I called Dave Schulty down at the newspaper office and he confirmed the report. Never in my life had I been so sick about something. Joe Fisher almost keeled over when I told him. I can't in any way rationalize trading White, and I can't even stomach trading Uecker.

"The first thing I did was to write a story for the Drury *Mirror,* letting the world know that the Bob Uecker Fan Club will not desert its hero in his time of great need. Then I prepared to write a nasty letter to Bob Howsam, the general manager of the Cardinals, who perpetrated this great crime."

Howsam was not popular with the players, although I hasten to add that being popular with the players is not essential to being a general manager. At times, it isn't even desirable. But Howsam had replaced Bing Devine, who had spent his life with the St. Louis franchise and was widely admired for his fairness.

Howsam was no amateur. He had a long family history in sports, and had set minor-league attendance records in

Denver. He was a large, affable man, with a round face and a high, soft voice. He sounded a little like Liberace. He liked to dash off memos and post clippings on the bulletin board in the clubhouse, and the players are suspicious of anyone who makes them read things.

What Howsam had done was to follow an old and honored custom. It is called cutting the payroll. Baseball teams prefer to rebuild with younger players, especially those with low overheads. Boyer, Groat and White drew hefty salaries. I was thrown in, I think, just to confuse people.

A pained and angry letter from Mark Stillwell poured into the Cardinal offices the day after the trade:

Dear Mr. Howsam,

I've been a Cardinal fan for a long time and I don't know when anything has happened that has disappointed me and disgusted me so much as the trade just completed with the Philadelphia Phillies.

In Bill White, the Cardinals had the best defensive first baseman in the National League, and also one of the most dangerous power hitters around. In Dick Groat they had a smart, steady ballplayer who knew more about the game than most shortstops ever learn. In Bob Uecker, they had the best defensive catcher in the league and one of the strongest throwing arms in baseball. These are three men I would seriously doubt that the Cardinals could afford to (lose) unless they obtained some outstanding talent in return.

In Art Mahaffey, we've picked up a discontented pitcher who won just two games. Pat Corrales has good minor-league credentials, but not overly impressive. Alex Johnson may be the sleeper in the deal, but he'll have to hit more than eight home runs to help the Cards.

If Red Schoendienst doesn't get an ulcer trying to decide what he has left when he gets to St. Petersburg next spring, I'll be surprised. But, while you're at the trading game, see if you can clear up some of this sadness by unloading part of this horde of pitchers that has piled up and come up with a bona fide power hitter.

> Yours truly,
> Mark Stillwell
> President
> Bob Uecker Fan Club

Nowhere, this side of politics, do people get madder, or choose up sides faster, than in baseball. A single trade can disrupt the pace of an entire city. People honk their horns. They are rude to each other in elevators. Children wet their beds.

We lost some of this emotional outpouring when the free-agent traffic began. When a player sells himself on the auction block, and his team gets little or nothing in return, the fans can't argue about which side got the better of the deal, or wonder how the front office could be so stupid. As a former player, I have mixed feelings about free agency. It is like coed housing in college. We are shocked and confused, and we ask why didn't it happen twenty years ago?

Howsam's answer to Mark was stock front-office stuff, soft-answer-turneth-away-wrath:

Dear Mr. Stillwell,
Thank you for your letter of October 27 regarding the recent trade.

Naturally, it is never pleasant to trade ballplayers that have played such good baseball for the club and were so popular. But in order to try to keep our ball club strong and in contention, it is necessary to make changes.

When a trade is negotiated, it is the thinking of the entire Cardinal organization. Our manager is consulted, our scouts are consulted, because they are the ones who thoroughly check the records and actually watch the various players throughout the year; our minor-league department is consulted to find out what they know about the player or players involved. I could never be part of trading a player on the spur of the moment. A lot of research goes into the players we receive in a trade and also into a player before we trade him. We feel we have made trades which will be beneficial to the Cardinals.

I appreciate your interest, and thank you for taking the time to write to me. We hope you will have the opportunity to see many games in the new stadium next year.

> Kindest regards,
> Bob Howsam
> General Manager

In other words, they were not going to call off the trade. Uecker was going to Philadelphia, a town where, on Easter, they boo the little kids who don't find eggs.

6. Uecker's Last Hurrah

THE PHILLIES, like the Cardinals, were a team trying to regroup. No manager had survived more adversity than Gene Mauch. His first team had established a major-league record by losing twenty-three straight games in 1961. Near the end of the streak, they came off a road trip to find a large crowd waiting for them at the airport in Philadelphia. They figured, obviously, it was a lynch mob. A pitcher named Frank Sullivan called out, "leave the plane in single file. That way they can't get us with one burst."

But the fans came to welcome them home again, to cheer, to give them support. There is no way to know what makes a Phillies fan tick. They rallied behind Gene Mauch, and in time he gave them a contender, only to see the Phillies blow a ten-game lead in the nightmare season of 1964. The next year they were never a factor, and now Mauch had decided to retool the club.

I felt at home with the Phillies, when I reported to camp at Clearwater in March. The roster included such cashews as Richie Allen, who liked everything about a ball park except getting there; Bo Belinsky, the flamboyant left-hander who thought he had been Rudolph Valentino in a prior life, and John Boozer, a pitcher whose idea of fun was to eat bugs and worms and watch people gag. He did a better job in the clubhouse than D-Con. He would be talking to a writer and one of the players would hand him a live worm or a beetle. Some of the reactions were terrific.

Belinsky reported to camp two days late, explaining that he had been trapped by a snowstorm in Texas on the drive from California. Those Texas snowstorms can be murder.

In addition to the ex-Cardinal trio, Mauch had traded for Phil Linz, an infielder the Yankees had fired for playing the harmonica on the team bus after a loss, and Jackie Brandt, who once watched part of an All-Star Game while sitting in the dugout in the nude.

The Phillies had a terrific roster. I don't mean in talent, but in names, the kind that headline writers loved, like Wine and Boozer, and the kind that just had a certain ring, like Ferguson Jenkins, Cookie Rojas and Clay Dalrymple.

I had been brought in to back up Dalrymple, a seven-year vet and an underrated fellow, whose .213 average in 1965 was well below his form. Clay hit from the left side, which meant that once again I would have a chance to start against the left-handers. It was hard to tell if I had made any progress. I had been traded to my third team in three years. The Phillies issued me uniform Number 10. I had worn 9 in St. Louis and 8 in Milwaukee. Was this progress?

When the players talked about the best and the brightest managers, the name of Gene Mauch often came up. He was quick-tempered, but he did not give up on people easily. His career as a player had been similar to mine. He was a shortstop who always seemed to line up behind someone better, such as Phil Rizzuto, with the Yankees, or Pee Wee Reese, with the Dodgers.

Frustrated, still a kid, Mauch once confronted his manager, Casey Stengel, in the dining room of a hotel where the Yankees stayed. "Dammit, Casey," he blurted, "I've got to play."

Stengel looked up from his soup and nodded. "Go talk to Mr. Rizzuto," the old man said. "If it's okay with him, it's okay with me."

Mauch was the most intense manager I ever knew. He would sit on the bench with his arms folded and his eyes never stopped moving. He didn't miss a thing. They used to tell a story about when Mauch was playing for the Red Sox, and on the way to the airport the team bus got stuck under an overpass. The driver and the team got out to study the problem. Finally, Mauch said, "Let the air out of the tires and fill them up on the other side." And so they did.

I was in the lineup on opening day, 1966, caught Chris Short and drove in a run with a single as we beat the Reds and Joe Nuxhall, 3-1. Then a really uncharacteristic thing happened. I hit home runs on consecutive days at the end of April. In my first six games, I had produced four hits, half of them homers, and driven in six runs. A curious start, it was worth three stars and a full, hand-lettered page in the scrapbook:

TWO HOMERS
IN TWO
DAYS!

BIG UKE
IS STARTING TO
FIND THE RANGE

ONLY 505 CAREER
HOMERS BEHIND
MAYS & OTT!!

Ah, yes, the future stretched ahead as smooth and inviting as the Pennsylvania Turnpike. When I connected for my third homer on Memorial Day, against the Mets, Mark wrote a story for the school paper at Drury, and mailed a copy to Bob Howsam. The Cardinals were in the process of sending Mahaffey and Johnson to the minors. The trade was looking rather one-sided for the Phillies.

The story went like this: "Bob Howsam has finally, publicly, admitted in May that he was completely wrong in October. The story we got then was that we were trading White, Groat, and Uecker for Johnson, Corrales, and Mahaffey because we (the Cardinals) were fully committed to our youth movement.

"Well, it doesn't look too good for smiling Bob. How can you say you're in a youth movement and trade a thirty-one-year-old slugger like White and then keep a broken-down, thirty-seven-year-old pitcher named Curt Simmons, who only pitches against the Phillies and can't beat them?

"With his homer, double, and three runs batted in on Memorial Day, and his two singles two days later, Uecker raised his average to a lusty .266. With three homers . . . he seems likely to get a new career high in every hitting department, and last year had been his best. He's hitting better than either Bill White or Dick Groat,

the men he was traded with, and that ought to make him
the big man in the deal. The key man in the deal!

"Howsam, you're an idiot."

With aplomb, Howsam wrote back:

Dear Mr. Stillwell,

   Thank you for sending along the article which
appeared at Drury.

   It's nice to know, too, that you have remained
Cardinal fans.

   We hope you and your Fan Club will have the
opportunity to visit the new Busch Memorial
Stadium and see the Cardinals play. I think you'll
enjoy it.

> Kindest regards,
> Bob Howsam
> General Manager

The first time the teams met in 1966, the Phillies
edged the Cards, 5-3. Bill White singled home our first
two runs. I singled to open the winning rally and scored
the tie-breaking run on a bases-loaded walk to Groat,
who had two hits. It's true, hitting well is the best
revenge.

On June 3, I slugged my fourth homer of the year,
equaling the total for my entire big-league career. The
blow was off an ex-teammate, Ray Sadecki, then
pitching for the Giants. By the All-Star break I had
raised my total to six, the same number as John Callison,
a guy who was usually good for twenty-five to thirty a
season.

I would have felt great, except that everybody around
the Phillies kept wondering what was wrong with
Callison. Four teams figured to stay in the pennant race

most of the way, the Dodgers, Giants, Pirates, and the Phillies. We needed a big year from Callison. In fact, we needed a big year from everybody.

The point should be made right here that it can be harmful for a fellow who doesn't hit homers to suddenly start banging a few. It is like a guy who discovers girls late in life and thinks he can catch up all at once. And the next thing you know, you are in a jar at the Harvard Medical School.

But sooner or later you have to try. You see a Richie Allen twitch a muscle and the ball flies off the bat and lands five hundred feet away. And you think, is there any reason I can't do that? The next thing you know, your hands are down at the end of the bat and all your weight is on your heels.

In a way, those homers, hitting in the .270's, and getting four (4) votes for the All-Star Game may have been my undoing. Up to then my theories had stood the test of time, like milk of magnesia: 1) The more I played, the closer I was to getting shipped out, and 2) the better I performed, the more they expected.

If I had been content to just hit .200 every year, all singles, and throw out a runner now and then, I might have played as long as Gaylord Perry. Your body doesn't wear out very fast when you catch a game every four or five days.

On July 17, I tagged my seventh homer in what turned out to be a fifteen-inning win over the first-place Giants. On the Phillies, only Allen and Bill White had more, even though a total of twelve players had started more games.

I had no personal goals in mind, which was just as well because I did not hit another homer during the rest of the season.

We stayed in the race until September, then became the first of the four contenders to fade. Chris Short won twenty games and Jim Bunning finished with nineteen. A late-season slump by Bill White was costly, but he drove in 103 runs and popped twenty-two homers.

Seasons that end badly tend to blur, a series of pitches half-forgotten at the moment they are half-missed, in games that are half-played. But it was a thrill, that year, to watch Richie Allen, young and untamed, blossom into a superstar. He hit forty home runs and fought Hank Aaron for the title down to the final days. He drove in 110 runs and batted .317. And he was going to get stronger and better. He would in time overpower this game and, unfortunately, himself.

Allen was one of baseball's new talents, a prodigious long-ball hitter. He preferred horses and cars to the company of people, but he was seldom loud or rude. He asked only to be treated like a man. In view of what Richie accomplished, the request did not seem unreasonable.

Part of his problem was that no matter how much he accomplished, it was never enough to satisfy all of his critics. Some just didn't like him, his color, his style, his habits. Others simply felt that he didn't get the most out of his huge gifts. Many a time, on his way to the plate, Richie would tell us he was going to take two strikes and see if he could hit one pitch. He would do this against some of the best pitchers in the league. He drove Gene Mauch wild, but more often than not he came through. He was just that good.

Richie did not take direction well, he was careless about the time, and he liked to sip the cooking sherry. We would get in the back of the plane, glowing slightly, and sing harmony, all the old barbershop songs. We were a happy pair.

I was a witness to the events that led to Richie's famous car-pushing accident, which left him with a mangled hand. Someone had given him an old stock car. He had it at the ball park one day, and he invited Dick Groat, Bob Skinner and myself to ride back to the Presidential Apartments with him. On the way, he tried to show us how to speed shift a stock car, and going from first to second he jammed the gears into reverse. The gears locked. We pushed the jalopy over to the side of the road and that was where it stayed, until Richie had it towed to his apartment.

I don't know how long the car stayed there, but at last he decided to move it. He tried to push the car from the front and his hand slipped and went through the headlight. From then on his hand was like a claw, after the surgeons did what they could to repair the tendons. After that I called him "Crash" Allen. A lesser man would have been finished. Richie regained the use of his hand and played ten more stormy seasons.

My own season was a deceptive one, as my seasons sometimes were. In the final weeks my average shrank to .208. But I had almost as many runs batted in (thirty) as I did base hits (forty-three). I saw the most action of my career, catching seventy-six games and playing one inning at third base, although I no longer remember why. It probably had to do with whatever strategy Gene Mauch was using that night.

I figured I had done well enough to go another year, and that was as far as I ever planned. Big-league baseball players, as a group, fool no one but themselves. We are like Oskar in *The Tin Drum*, the little boy who would not grow up.

My fan club was growing older. It had somehow acquired 476 members, and the hard cord were now seniors preparing to graduate. We were bonded, in a curious kind of way. They were like having your own private gag, my Pookah, my Harvey the Rabbit made real. They redeemed my view of life; that the world belongs to those who know when to laugh at it. I am not sure what they got in return, other than a hero without the trimmings, a hero who could never let them down.

Well, almost.

At midseason, Mark had made the following entry in the scrapbook: "Since 1966 will probably be the last really active year of the Bob Uecker Fan Club, it seems significant that we should set a definite goal for ourselves. It would be altogether fitting and proper for the Phillies to get into the World Series and for Uecker to be the hero, but we have a much simpler goal.

"We want Uecker to either hit a triple or steal a base. He has never done either in his five-year career in the big leagues and we think it's high time for one or the other . . . We realize he isn't fast, but a determined man ought to be able to accomplish these things.

"He may not know how we feel about this. I ought to write and tell him."

Which he did. To no avail. Another year without a triple or a stolen base.

I continued to hear from the club. They had subscribed to the Philadelphia *Inquirer*. They had mailed a check to the Phillies for a yearbook and team pictures that as yet were undelivered, and they were thinking about setting fire to Connie Mack Stadium.

That winter I received a funny-serious letter from Mark:

Dear Bob,

The second volume of the Bob Uecker Story is all but complete and it looks like it's going to be every bit as good as the first. We had a lot of material to work with this year, largely because you came through with your best season. I only got to see one game, a Monday night affair at Pittsburgh late in August, but you delivered a key, run-scoring single.

The Cardinal fans discovered something this year. When you were traded for Corrales, we went from two catchers to one and your friend McCarver had a fine year but he had to play 150 games and that's a few too many. I think that is one trade that will go down in the books as a disaster for St. Louis. Now that Charlie Smith is gone, I'll see if we can't figure a way to get you back and let you play third base. . . .

I'll be graduating from Drury next May along with my number-one sidekick, so we won't have as much time for active fan-clubbing. The Navy has plans to send us somewhere for three years, but I'll get to St. Louis before July and catch some Phillie-Cardinal games. We're all hoping you'll turn in another fine year in 1967!

Sincerely,
Mark Stillwell
President
Bob Uecker Fan Club

The reference to Charlie Smith is worth noting now. The Cardinals traded Smith that winter to the Yankees in return for Roger Maris, who had chased Babe Ruth's ghost across the summer of 1961. It was an even trade, one for one. Does anyone remember Charlie Smith today, except as the answer to a trivia question? Funny game.

The problem with being a fringe player is that just about the time you get comfortable with a team, you're gone again. Wherever I had played, the scrubs banded together and developed our own esprit de corps. I don't think any of the teams ever suffered for it, although I am not sure all of my managers would agree. On the Phillies, we called ourselves The Avengers, and the group included Bobby Wine, Phil Linz and Jackie Brandt. Richie Allen was an honorary member. He was a great player, but he had the heart of a truant.

The career of another fellow, who was to become a special friend of mine, ended that year. Harvey Kuenn batted .296 for the Phillies and decided to call it a career. He was thirty-six, had played fifteen seasons and finished with a lifetime average of .303.

He had been a principal in one of the most publicized trades ever made. Harvey won the batting title at Detroit in 1959, and then was swapped for the man who had won the home run title, Rocky Colavito of Cleveland.

I admired Harvey as a fine agitator and one of the smartest hitters I had ever been around or caught behind. He stood in the deepest part of the batter's box and defied the pitcher to throw the ball on the outside corner of the plate. That was a pitch he could kill. He was an all-fields, line drive hitter, but if his team needed a run in the late innings to tie or win, he could take you downtown.

After our playing days, both of us came home to Milwaukee. Harvey joined the Brewers as a coach. I'm on the radio crew. And our friendship continues.

In February, three years ago, his right leg was

amputated because of a circulatory problem. By the end of spring training, he was walking on an artificial limb. By winter, he was playing golf every day. Sometimes a fellow as big and active as Harvey Kuenn finds it hard to accept such a blow. But those who knew him as a great athlete found out he was much more. He wouldn't let life slip one over the outside corner, either.

We were not far into the 1967 season when I knew my days with the Phillies were numbered. I went to the plate one night as a pinch hitter, and when I looked to the third-base coach for a sign he turned his back on me.

The trade that sent me back to the Braves, my original club, for another catcher, Gene Oliver, was announced on June seventh. In truth, I felt a little guilty about leaving Philadelphia. Richie Allen was brooding and threatening not to play. I felt like a hostage who had been released early.

The next morning, Rich said he wasn't going to the ball park anymore. I called Donald Davidson, the Braves' road secretary and an old friend, and told him I couldn't report right away. He pleaded with me: "Uke, dammit, you got to get your ass down here. Joe Torre is hurt and you're the only catcher we have."

When I left, Allen was still boycotting the ball park. Soon I heard from Charlie Meister, in the Phillies' front office: "You have to talk to Richie. He hasn't suited up since we made the trade." I called, reminded him that the Braves would be flying into Philadelphia for a three-game series that weekend, and convinced him to go back to work.

Of course, it didn't take much to keep Richie away from the ball park. He didn't like to practice. Always felt it wasn't in his contract. He had signed up just for the games.

I was fortunate to room with great, normal players like Eddie Mathews, and an occasional pure flake like Roger Craig.

Craig, my roomie in St. Louis, had one of the most uneven careers any pitcher ever had. He helped pitch the Dodgers to a pennant in 1959, and in two seasons with the Mets lost a total of forty-six games.

Influenced, perhaps, by his term with the Mets, Roger loved horror movies and sometimes imagined that he was in one. He had a problem with his neck for a while and wore a brace. I would open the closet door to put away my coat, and find him hanging on the inside of the door, his brace looped over the hook.

Those are the pictures you take out of baseball, more than the runs, hits, and errors. You remember the players and the people and the rhythm of the towns.

I honestly liked Philadelphia. The fans there were smart and mean and you could count on them. One of my biggest thrills in baseball was watching a guy fall out of the upper deck in Connie Mack Stadium. The crowd booed when he tried to get up.

On the other hand, I wasn't sure what to expect in Atlanta. The catching job would belong to Torre when he was well. But Paul Richards, the general manager, wanted to turn Phil Niekro into a starter, if he could find someone to catch his knuckleball.

The Braves had undergone many a change since I had last worn their uniform in 1963. For one thing, they were no longer in Milwaukee. Spahn, Burdette, Mathews and Crandall were gone.

When I walked into the Braves' clubhouse to rejoin the team I was given the white-carpet treatment. Literally. Joe Torre had laid out a path of white towels from the door to my new locker, above which were two handwritten signs. One, from Joe, had a heartfelt simplicity to it: THANK YOU VERY MUCH. GOD BLESS YOU.

The other said, LOTS OF LUCK. YOUR BUDDY, PHIL NIEKRO.

There was a third Brave eager to see me and renew an old acquaintance, Henry Aaron. Henry thought he had an old score to settle. The talk was just beginning to stir about his chances of breaking Ruth's career home-run record, and he accused me of taking one away from him in 1965.

Curt Simmons was on the mound that day for the Cardinals in St. Louis, Aaron had been frustrated by Simmons' assortment of slow curves. This time he ran up on the ball before the curve could break, and the pitch exploded off his bat, bouncing off the roof of the park in right field.

As Henry remembered it, I called the plate umpire's attention to the fact that he had stepped out of the batter's box. The umpire disallowed the homer and called him out.

The night I rejoined the Braves, Henry grinned and said, "If I miss Ruth's record by one homer, I'm going to be looking for you, Uecker."

I had to tell Henry the truth. It wasn't me. Tim McCarver was the catcher who took the homer away from him. But it was the sort of thing I would have been proud to do.

I was still a backup catcher, still the twenty-fourth or twenty-fifth man on the roster, still in the twilight of a mediocre career. But something was different this time. In a small way I had become necessary. All because of a maddening pitch that had carried Phil Niekro to the majors and now threatened to carry him right out.

It was a toss-up whether the batters hated to hit against Phil's knuckler as much as the catchers hated to catch it. He had played on teams in the minors where the catchers had simply refused. And he had lost more than one game when a third strike rolled back to the screen while the winning run crossed the plate.

I had caught Barney Schultz, in St. Louis, and Bob Tiefenauer, in Milwaukee, then the only other pitchers to rely almost exclusively on the knuckleball. I had one other thing going for me: my reputation as a defensive catcher. It occurred to me that when you don't hit much, teams tend to exaggerate your defensive skills.

I caught every game Niekro started the rest of the season, and I caught every day while Joe Torre recovered from his injury. In late June I had the biggest day at bat of my career, hitting my first grand-slam homer, off Ron Herbel of the Giants, and knocking in five runs.

Soon Niekro was giving me credit for keeping him in the big leagues. He was still doing it in 1981, fourteen years later. I don't know if this was the case, or a polite overstatement, but it was nice of Phil to say so. I am glad to claim him as the legacy of my big-league career. He won 150 games in those years, mostly for losing teams, and he is a fine legacy to have.

Niekro had a good slider and fastball, still has, but the knuckler was his strikeout pitch and he knew I wasn't afraid to call it with a runner at third. Every time he started I went through the same ritual before the game. I took four aspirin for the headache I knew I would have afterwards.

Once, after Phil had beaten the Pirates, 2-1, our trainer, Harvey Stone, looked up from rubbing his arm and told a reporter that Phil could probably pitch the next night.

Paul Richards overheard him. "No, he couldn't," Richards said, immediately.

"Why not?" asked the writer. "He needs more rest?"

"No," said Paul, "but Uecker does. Every time Niekro pitches, Uecker is the one who needs four days' rest."

Another problem with not having much talent is that it's hard to tell when you have begun to slip. But if I was on my way out of the big leagues, I was going more or less in style, and my fan club was going with me.

Baseball lore is filled with tearful stories of great players like Ruth and Mantle visiting hospitals and then slugging homers for a little sick kid. I made the same promise once, struck out three times and then found out the kid was an out-patient.

When it really counted, when it was not just a matter of drama but of justice, I am proud to say that I came through. When the Braves met the Cards in St. Louis on Sunday, July 23, Mark Stillwell showed up at Busch Stadium. Later, he described what happened: "There are in sports certain moments that come along perhaps only once in a lifetime. If you can take part in those special occurrences, you can treasure their memory always. If you miss them, you've missed them. The Home Run was such an occurrence.

"I was due to leave the twenty-fourth for Southern California to begin three years of active duty with the Navy. A Navy publication had recommended that the departing sailor should endeavor to spend his last hours at home with his loved ones. I did just that. I drove to St. Louis to see the Cardinals play a doubleheader with the Braves . . ."

I sat out the opener as the Braves lost, 3-1. In the nightcap, I started and struck out my first time out. Mark continues: "When he came up in the fourth with one out and nobody on, I snapped a picture of him taking a cut at the plate. A couple of pitches later Uecker got around on what was probably a hanging curve and hit a long fly ball down the line toward left field. It looked like just a routine fly ball and it hadn't sounded particularly solid but it kept carrying, and carrying, and finally fell deep into the loge reserved seats in left field for Uecker's third homer of the year.

"As Uecker started the home-run trot around the base paths, I realized what I had just witnessed. I set up a clamor like few around me could believe or understand. It dawned on me that I was the only guy yelling for Uecker in the entire crowd . . . I may well have been the only member of the Uecker Fan Club ever to see The Great One crack a home run."

In retrospect we know how he must have felt. I am told that some people never forget the first time they heard Heifitz play the violin, or Caruso sing an aria, or watched the sun set on Bo Derek's body. The homer had no bearing on the outcome of the game, which the Cards won, 8-3, to sweep the doubleheader. Of the thousands who were there, only two of us had any reason to care or remember it, and I am not so sure about myself.

So much for history. The Braves finished sixth and fired manager Billy Hitchcock. I played in eighty games, the most of my career, and hit .150, my lowest ever. I did lead the league in one category, and I could not have done it without Phil Niekro. I was charged with twenty-seven passed balls. The next-highest total was sixteen.

I kept intact my career record of never having stolen a base or legged out a triple. It was a letdown to the kids at Drury College, but I hoped they would overcome it in time.

And so the stage was set for the series of events I have described earlier: the accident on Clete Boyer's motorcycle, the barroom fight in Fort Lauderdale, my release as a player and coach, then signing with the Braves as a speaker and occasional broadcaster.

In 1971, Alan (Bud) Selig offered me a chance to return to Milwaukee as a full-time member of the radio crew. I jumped at it, completing a cycle as the first Milwaukee boy signed by the Braves, traded by the Braves, fired by the Braves, and hired by the Brewers.

As I think back on the zaniness of my years, I am grateful for the career I had. I mean, one good season and I might have blown my entire future in broadcasting. Today I speak frequently at banquets around the country, and the audiences often include youngsters. I always try to leave them with one sincere thought. If you can't play a sport . . . the hell with it.

As for the fan club, I never really felt that I deserved it. Of course, I have arthritis in one knee and I don't feel I deserve that, either.

And I am still in touch with Mark Stillwell, who was born to be a public relations man, and whose enthusiasm now serves the football Cardinals. After I had begun to appear as a repeat guest on the *Tonight Show*, I received a long and nostalgic letter from Mark. He closed by saying: "My brother asked me last week what the greatest satisfaction from the fan club had been. I told him it was being able to say that we had followed your career from the time you were a tuba player for the 1964 World Champions."

PART III

Outside Baseball

In which he looks at the world of radio and television; and a strike that could have hurt everyone except Bob Uecker, who can always go back into the service.

"He (Dave Winfield) also wanted a voice in team trades, more beef in the ground patties, and the right to change his name to Ronald McWinfield."

7. All My Tonights

WHEN ANYONE ASKS ME how to break into radio and television, I never know where to begin. Or where to end. I might tell them this truth: You have to be lucky. It isn't enough just to be crazy.

The only training I ever had was as an occasional guest on a postgame show. Of course, I also called the play-by-play of hundreds of games for the boys in the bullpen, broadcasting into a beer cup.

My career is a confirmation of one of the basic laws of success: Anything is obtainable if you don't need it.

There are advantages to not being a star athlete. When you retire no one feels cheated, and the adjustment to the Real World is more gentle, emotionally as well as financially. Some athletes need a decompression chamber when the time comes to take off the uniform. They suffer withdrawal pains when the cheering stops.

While it lasted, while the player was hot, the wine flowed and the dollies came waltzing through the green pastures and big offers and big deals became a part of his daily routine. Later the offers turned small and the deals disappeared.

The fringe player doesn't miss the cheers and his standard of living doesn't undergo a dramatic change. My highest salary in baseball was twenty-three thousand dollars. In a few years I would be earning more than that, from telling people what a failure I was.

I was perfectly content with my life in Atlanta in 1969, working in the speaker's bureau for the Braves and doing the color on their telecasts. Now and then I did a turn at the Playboy Club, managed by a friend of mine, John Barnes, who had once run the business end of Al Hirt's club in New Orleans.

That year Barnes talked Al into opening a saloon next to the Playboy Club, featuring the Dixieland sound and look, with jazz and red wall fabric.

Hirt flew in for the opening of the club and John asked me to ride out to the airport with him to meet the great trumpet player. Al got off the plane wearing a Cossack hat and a full-length fur coat and a dark beard. You got this overpowering impression of *fur.* If he had landed in the Himalayas, the natives would have set traps for him.

It was because of Al Hirt that I became a frequent guest on the *Tonight Show,* a debt I will describe later.

Even before we shook hands I knew we would hit it off. I began to rip him immediately about his size. Al is the best kind of friend to have, the kind you can't embarrass, and vice versa. And we have both tried.

Every November I try to spend three weeks in New Orleans, working with Al in his club on Bourbon Street. It has become a tradition. We drink, we jam, we fish. I have never found a more fulfilling way to spend my time. The part I enjoy most is not drowning.

Once, after an all-night jam session at the club, we

drove to Shell Beach, Louisiana, a forty-minute drive from New Orleans, to the fishing camp where Al keeps a boat. He filled a cooler with sandwiches and beer and booze. The party included his clarinetist, Pee Wee, and his brother, Little Gerald, who is the same size as Al and looks just like him except that his beard is red.

Al and I climbed into one boat, a twenty-eight-foot whaler, and the others, Pee Wee, Gerald and a couple of fellows from the club, climbed into a larger one. We were still feeling frisky from the night before when we headed for the bayous, fifteen or twenty miles out. It was a damp, chilly morning and Al had on his Russian outfit, the hat and coat, with the collar turned up. The other boat took the lead and we followed, with Al at the controls.

We were going wide open through the canals, curving and hooking, kicking up a spray on either side of us. I was sitting forward in the whaler and saw the first boat make a wide turn. We didn't seem to be slowing and I suddenly realized Al was going to have to cut it pretty short if we were going to make the turn. So I looked over my shoulder to say something and I discovered that Al was fast asleep.

When I realized there was no hope of making the turn I began to scream at Al, my face reddening in the wind. The swamps were coming up fast. When I saw he wasn't going to wake up, much less throttle back, I stood up in the front of the boat. I am not sure why I did, unless it was to get a closer look at the disaster rushing to meet us. When we hit the bog I was like a missile going through the saw grass.

I landed face down, arms out, covered with muck and mud, and with only two thoughts on my mind:

ALLIGATORS AND SNAKES.

I struggled to my feet, rising out of the primeval goop, which was like quicksand, and turned to walk back to the boat. What I saw looked like a scene from *Boom Town*, with mud flying thirty feet in the air, as though we had brought in oil. The engines were still wide open. When I pulled myself back aboard, Al was no longer sitting in the same spot. He was on his hands and knees with his head stuck in the bait box. I yanked him up by the back of his coat. He was still asleep, live shrimp dangling from his beard like weird Christmas ornaments.

The group on the other boat had watched with horror as we went aground. They came alongside, their faces pale and anxious. That was their meal ticket sitting there, slumped over the bait box. Gerald said, "Christ, what happened?"

"Al was showing me a scene from 'Victory at Sea'," I said. "The son of a bitch fell asleep, going thirty miles an hour. We were wide open."

Finally, Al yawned and opened his eyes. When it became obvious he was unhurt, we all started laughing so hard nobody could speak. He looked at us suspiciously as he picked the shrimp out of his beard.

Another time I went out with Al and Pee Wee. On the way in, Al decided to sleep and he stretched out on the floor between a fishing chair and the side of the boat. We docked, took off the fishing gear and unloaded, then woke him up. He didn't move. "Hey, I'm stuck," he yelled. "I can't get out."

We thought he was joking. But he was wedged in. I don't know if the boat shrank or Al expanded, but it took us fifteen minutes of maneuvering to get him out of there. The longer it took the more nervous and ill-tempered he got. He had visions of becoming a permanent fixture, like the figurehead on a Viking sailing vessel. I had a great plan for getting him out of there quickly, but we couldn't find a harpoon.

Al Hirt has a heart bigger than a bass fiddle. When I married my wife, Judy, he made all the arrangements, picking the day, the church, the minister, and the music. He likes people, enjoys their successes, and is just as comfortable in the company of a Catholic priest as he is in that of a baseball player.

One of his closest friends in New Orleans was the fire and police chaplain, Father Pete Rogers. He would tell people, proudly: "Fodda Pete leads the world in talking guys down offa bridges. How many you talked down this year, Fodda? Seventeen?" Al would shake his head. "He's a great man. If I was the boss I'd make him pope."

Al was a child prodigy who could play the trumpet at six. At Jesuit High, in New Orleans, he was on the football team as a sophomore, changing uniforms at the half so he could march with the band. His father, a cop, made him quit football to concentrate on his music.

He owned a small piece of the New Orleans Saints in the early years. At the games he would walk through the stands and swing into "When the Saints Go Marching In." The noise of the crowd would explode, until opposing teams complained they could not hear the signals. Now Al only plays for the Super Bowl and other religious holidays.

And while it is true that in professional sports many owners can sing the blues, Al Hirt is the only one I know who ever made a living at it.

I knew the first time we met that he was my kind of degenerate. When Al opened the club in Atlanta, he invited me to take the stage during his breaks. I did a half hour of what I usually do. After the show, Al's agent,

Jerry Purcell, approached me. He asked me if I'd like to appear on the *Tonight Show*.

I thought to myself, "Yeah, sure, the *Tonight Show*. Me and ten million other characters."

Ten days later, I found myself walking through a curtain and taking a seat on a couch next to Johnny Carson. Purcell had called and told me to fly to New York. I went on that night, after meeting with Carson's talent coordinator, Craig Tennis.

That night, for one of the few times in my life, I was scared spitless. I was not a comic. Never thought of myself as one. I had performed in nightclubs and not been nervous, partly because I was always half boiled. I walked around backstage, trying to keep straight in my mind what I wanted to say. No one knew who the hell I was. I don't remember seeing any other faces. There were people there, but they didn't seem to have faces. That was how I knew I was nervous.

Whatever I said that night worked. The audience laughed. After the show I heard Carson turn to Ed McMahon and ask, "Is this guy really a baseball player?"

Three weeks after the first time, I was invited back. What happened next was not exactly the classic show biz story, with instant stardom and headlines in *Variety*. Nor did I rush out and hire an agent named Max.

But my career began to move. My speaking fees rose. ABC hired me to be a part of the original crew for *Monday Night Baseball*. I was signed to be a guest host on other national shows, such as *The Midnight Special*. For a guy who spent the better part of his life behind a mask, I suddenly had a face people knew.

Whatever the benefits of being on the *Tonight Show*, I accepted them without guilt or pressure. I have been a

THE MAN
WHO MADE
MEDIOCRITY
FAMOUS.

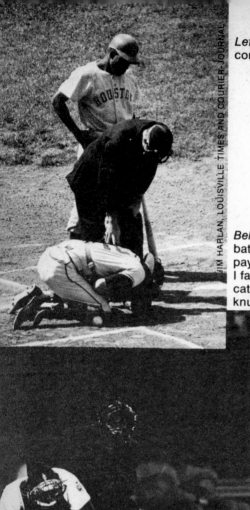

Left, looking for my contact lens.

Below, umpire and batter (Doug Rader) pay no attention as I faint after finally catching this knuckleball.

The young player is easy prey for seductive baseball groupies such as Phyllis Diller.

D. ELLIOTT

Big league athletes are subjected to the most malicious and unfounded rumors (Number 6 is Clete Boyer).

Left, Dick Bertell (Cubs) slides in. The worst part of being a catcher is always having your back to the camera.

Right, Tony Cloninger (Braves) slides in.

Above, Rico Carty (Braves) slides in.

Below, Harvey Kuenn (Giants) slides in.

Above, John Roseboro (Dodgers) slides in.
Below, Vada Pinson (Reds) slides in.

Above, Cardinals call time to review my performance.

Below, Being forcibly removed from the game
(by my own team).

Here I am trying to score from second on a three-base hit;
out on a close play.

Celebration in Cardinal clubhouse after team announced
I would not play in 1967 World Series; Carl Warwick pours.

One of my first bubble gum cards.

BOB
UECKER
MILWAUKEE BRAVES   C

I tricked the Topps people by posing lefthanded; no one noticed.

CARDS
CATCHER
BOB UECKER

With Del Crandall and Joe Torre in Milwaukee; too bad the other two never made it.

Once again the guys told me it was a night game; with Del Crandall, Henry Aaron, and Ed Mathews.

Joe Garagiola made the airwaves safe for ex-catchers.

Original Monday Night Baseball crew—Warner Wolf, Bob Prince and Bob Uecker became household words (the household was in Menomonee Falls, Wisconsin).

The cleanest shave I ever had; at World Lumberjack
Championships.

Yes, Johnny, I am...

Al Hirt and me filming a segment for the
Un-American Sportsman.

Al Hirt points me to the stage, I think.

A man for all seasons.

Diving for scuba in the Bahamas.

Portrait of a star.

guest always for the fun of it—mine, if not theirs. I don't consider what I do to be show business. Or journalism. Or an art form. Or even a business. I don't consider it to be a lot of things. I broadcast sports, mostly baseball. My work is to these other things what recess is to school.

But I saw quickly that the exposure on the *Tonight Show* was terrific, the best stage ever created for anyone with a movie, TV series, song, or toy to sell. Of course, what makes it all work is Johnny Carson, his wit, discipline, and generosity.

If I were to rate Carson in baseball terms, I would say he can do it all: hit, hit with power, field, and throw. I don't know if he can run. It is hard to tell about a man you usually see sitting behind a desk.

I am not sure that even his most devoted fans really understand what Carson has achieved. There is simply no one else in the field to compare with him, with the freshness and endurance of the show he has done night after night, year after year. Though himself a master comic, he is probably the finest straight man alive. I found him generous when it counts most, when no one is watching. During a station break, sitting there, chatting idly, he would coach me a little: "You ought to be saying more about this," or "drop in another line about that."

As many amateurs do, I had a habit of protecting myself by warning him: "You've probably heard this one . . ." Johnny assured me, "Hey, I don't hear every joke in the world."

There is a kind of art to the way he puts you at ease, once you slip into the chair next to his. You can sense the empathy he has for a struggling comic or singer. He is a contained and private man, even with his staff, but not in a selfish way. I admire him for trying to keep his personal life separate from the show and his career.

I have a theory about Carson. I believe one reason he has survived so long, and so well, is that he has less ego than his critics think. He isn't always drawn to the center of the stage. He doesn't have to be "on" all the time.

Some performers feel obligated to crack jokes to a bunch of strangers riding in an elevator. I understand that feeling. Part of my disposition demands that people find me funny or amusing. If I were on a show, or at a banquet, and the laughs didn't come, I would drop my pants. Anything. I would get that laugh.

Carson would merely shrug, do a Jack Benny pause, and go on to the next one.

I never had the same determination about baseball, and maybe that was my undoing. No matter how badly I wanted to get a base hit, I knew the other guy was trying to stop me. And I might be overmatched. In front of an audience, no one can stop me but myself. The audience is on your side (usually).

I feel fortunate to have been on the *Tonight Show* when there occurred one or more Unforgettable Moments. I was a guest the night Burt Reynolds sat in for Johnny, and another guest was his ex-wife, Judy Carne, the actress and comedienne, who had emerged as a star of the new hit show, *Laugh-In*.

Burt took me aside backstage and confided, a bit nervously, that they had not seen each other since their divorce, three years or so earlier. "I don't know what the hell is going to happen," he said, "so if it gets a little tense or shaky feel free to jump in."

I came out first, then Judy, then Helen Gurley Brown, the editor of *Cosmopolitan*. It was the night Helen suggested that Burt pose for the centerfold in *Cosmo*. We all played around with that thought for a while, and Burt asked if I would do such a thing. I said, "Sure. As long as they'd let me wear a pair of shin-guards, I'd be all right."

Judy teasingly suggested that he could cover himself with his hand, and Burt immediately shouted, "You mean MY ARM, MY ARM."

The show was bright and funny. My own impression was that there still existed a warm affection between Burt and Judy. And, of course, he did pose for *Cosmopolitan*.

I was on another night with a guest named Foster Brooks, listed on the schedule as a professor from Harvard, or some such. We chatted backstage. I did my bit, and then Foster was introduced, and the moment he walked through the curtain I thought, "Oh, jeezus, the guy is plastered. Fifteen minutes ago he was sober, now he's just destroyed." I was embarrassed for him, until I realized, about the time the audience did, that he was doing his drunk act. He was hilarious. And later I learned he doesn't drink at all.

Don Rickles used to tape his television series, *CPO Sharkey*, in the studio next to the *Tonight Show*, and I would drop by to watch him work. I discovered early that I could play on his insecurity. It's true; like most comics, Don is sensitive and his feelings are easily bruised.

We developed a kind of ritual. He always asked me how I liked his show.

"Okay," I would say, forcing the word. "It was okay."

"No, dammit, how did you like it?"

"It was okay," I repeated, "but it wasn't you."

Now Rickles would give me that ear-to-ear grin, the one that makes him look like he should be sitting on a lily pad. "No, really, what did you think?"

"Hey, Don, if you want me to say it was great, if that's what you need to hear, yeah, it was great."

Then I would walk away and, over my shoulder, I'd whisper, "But it's not you."

Rickles is a fanatic about baseball and most other sports. He wasn't big enough to play sports in school, he says, "But I was always the kid who helped the gym teacher take the names of those who weren't practicing."

He can create a caricature, even his own, with words. "Actually," he says, "I would like to be a general manager and have the guys come and get them girls and sit and drink with them and tell them what bad years they had."

Once I offered to leave tickets for him any time the Brewers were in town to play the California Angels. His eyes lighted up. He said, "My kid really loves baseball. Do you think you could take him down to the clubhouse and show him around?"

I promised I would. Rickles was in Las Vegas when the next trip rolled around, but I called his house and talked to his son, a pre-teenager.

"This is Bob Uecker," I said.

"So what?" he said.

"I promised your dad I'd leave you tickets to the ballgame."

"Who cares?" he said.

The kid didn't go to the game. To this day I think Rickles put him up to it. Or else he is a Dodger fan.

The real pleasure, for me, of being on the *Tonight Show* was the chance it provided to meet and work with Burt Reynolds and Rickles, and other guest hosts such as David Brenner, David Letterman, Bob Newhart, Robert Klein, David Hartman and Joey Bishop—all these in addition to Johnny.

Not even Avis has gotten more mileage out of being Number 2 than Ed McMahon. The friendship of Ed and John, their loyalty, the fun they have, is part of what makes the *Tonight Show* an appealing place to be. Another key is the quality of the staff, starting with Freddie de Cordova, the producer; Jack Grant, the stage manager; Craig Tennis, Ginny Fosdick, Shirley Woods, and the fellows in the booth, Bob Ostberg and Bobby Quinn.

Many a night I have sat backstage for hours after a show with Tommy Newsom or Doc Severinsen, and the guys in the band, having a few pops and talking baseball.

There is no need to pinpoint which night it was that almost didn't end, causing me to nearly miss a baseball broadcast for the only time in my career. Nor will I mention which member of the staff was with me when I so nearly disgraced myself.

I didn't think I had a problem when I missed my flight at 10:00 P.M. I could still catch a breakfast flight in time to join the Brewers in New York for the game the next evening against the Yankees. And I would not have had a problem, except for a slight miscalculation. My plane was not leaving from the airport where my friend dropped me that morning, in a condition less than clear-headed.

The clerks at the airline counter were bemused, and offered me a place to lie down, when I tried to explain that the Brewers were in New York, I was in the wrong airport, and my partner, Merle Harmon, was off some-where televising a World Football League game. There was no one else to do the radio broadcast.

While my ticket was being changed, I placed a frantic phone call to Bob Sullivan, the team's equipment man, at the hotel in New York. I tried to sound calm, but after about thirty seconds of his saying, "I can't understand you, what was that?" I realized it wasn't working.

Finally, I said, "Look, Sully, get hold of Tom Ferguson and go up to the booth when the game starts." (Ferguson, now a vice-president and traveling secretary with the Brewers, had started out as a clubhouse boy with the Braves.) "Just open the show for me. Talk about anything. Talk about the difference in laundry prices in New York and what it costs to clean the uniforms. I'll get there as early as I can."

It looked as though baseball was about to record another first. An equipment man was going to open the radio broadcast of a game between the Yankees and the Brewers. Alas, I got the next flight out, grabbed a cab to the ball park, and collapsed in the booth five minutes before air time.

I don't think Sully or Fergie will ever forgive me for depriving them of his big chance.

8. The Boys in the Booth

MY TRAVELS LED ME one summer to what I thought would
be a quiet night in Cincinnati, the kind of night you
expect in Cincinnati. I should have known better.

It was the Sunday before a Monday night baseball
game, to be televised over ABC. Sharing my table in the
hotel dining room were Howard Cosell and Chet Forte,
our director.

Cosell and Forte have known each other for years,
ever since Chet was the nation's leading scorer in
basketball his senior year at Columbia. Once, before a
game, Chet agreed to be a guest on Howard's radio show.
As they waited for a cue, the little guard asked, "What
are we going to talk about, Howard?"

"Relax, kid," said Cosell. "Leave it to me. You'll do
fine."

Whereupon Howard opened the interview, turned to
his guest and said, "Chet, is it true that some of your
teammates hate to pass to you because you shoot so
much?"

As Rick said to Louie on the airstrip at Casablanca, it was the start of a great relationship. Chet knows Cosell so well that he is able to finish most of his meals, no matter how much Howard agitates the people around him. And Howard is one of the most artful agitators of this or any other time.

In the middle of dinner, two young ladies approached our table to confirm that the voice they were hearing really belonged to Howard Cosell. On a good night, Howard's voice can be heard in every corner of a restaurant, into the kitchen, and out the service door.

An incurable flirt, although a harmless one, Howard soon had a dialogue going with the one named Cindy, a blonde in her early twenties. When he learned that their boyfriends were at a table a few feet away, he raised his voice and said, "If those fellows continue to bother you, my dear, I am going to send Bob Uecker over there to break their legs."

Every few minutes, Howard would toss off a line of that general substance, and I began to get some hard looks from their table. I made a mental note of the fact that both were young and burly and they were drinking, not eating. Cindy was enjoying Cosell's attention, and I guessed that it was only a matter of time until her friend came over and hauled her away. You get a premonition about those things and you can almost put a watch to it.

Soon enough, this brute of a guy sidled up to the table and stood there looking puzzled. He put a hand lightly on the girl's shoulder, but before he could speak Howard warned him, "If you touch Cindy again I'll have Uecker tear your head off."

At that point, I leaned across the table, my chin almost touching the butter dish, and whispered: "Howie, I just want you to know something. This guy may drop me, but if I have time to get off one punch, you're going down with me."

As luck would have it, he was as curious about Cosell as she was. There was no menace in him, although you would not have been reassured if all you had heard was his name and avocation. His name was Tyrone Malone and he drag-raced SEMIS. He invited us out to the hotel parking lot in the morning for a demonstration.

When we arrived at the parking lot after breakfast, we rubbed our eyes in disbelief. He had three huge trailers painted red, white, and blue, with enough chrome on them to make the Hell's Angels weep. Probably cost a half million each. A tractor was attached to the back of one. Behind another was a truck, on the back of which was a frozen whale, with a catwalk leading up to it so people could get a close look.

In the mouth of the whale was a photograph, an eight-by-ten glossy of Gregory Peck, taken from a scene in the movie *Moby Dick*.

I have no idea how long that whale had been on the back of that truck. I did not ask. All I know is, that odor was the foulest I have ever smelled in my life, and I am a guy who has been in a baseball locker room after a doubleheader when the second game went eighteen innings.

Naturally, Tyrone Malone wanted to know if one of us would like to join him for a run in the parking lot, to get a feeling for this kind of drag racing. Naturally, Howard and Chet insisted they could not deny me this honor.

I took a pack of cigarettes and tucked them in my shirt sleeve and rolled up the sleeve the way I had seen drag racers do in the movies. Then I climbed into the cab of that monster next to Tyrone Malone, who is a six-footer, about 230, with brown hair and arms larger than most people's legs. He was leaning out the window, watching Cindy kick out the tire blocks, and telling me out the side of his mouth how he travels to fairs all over the country, drag racing his semis. I noticed Cosell and Forte moving back, smiling and flashing me the victory sign.

Tyrone dropped it in gear—he put it on the floor, as they say in CB talk—and announced: "I'm going to put the hammer down now."

I said, "Do whatever you want. I'm just along for the ride."

Tires smoking, he proceeded to run that baby through the parking lot, one hundred fifty yards long, and had the truck up to sixty miles an hour when he hit the brake. I was amazed that a diesel that size could burn rubber. After that run, he backed up and made another. I rattled around in that cab like a dice in a cup, the truck was vibrating so hard.

When I stumbled out of the cab, Chet and Howard said they were trying to remember the last time they laughed so hard. They thought and thought, but didn't come up with anything.

The first six years of my career with ABC—I started in 1975—went pretty much in this vein, by accident or design I can't say. In a sense I am their off-the-wall editor, the Walter Mitty of the staff, the fellow who will try anything once, or even twice, if once is not enough.

The baseball strike of 1981 afforded me a rare chance to report on the world lumberjack championships at Hayward, Wisconsin, held every July, in what would normally be the heart of the hardball season.

Lumberjacking is a hugely popular sport in Australia and New Zealand, and in our upper central and north-western states, where the timber industry is strong. They have a circuit, a mystique, and a following all their own, like rodeo.

On the first day of competition one fellow fell seventy feet and broke both his legs. In the speed climb, their tools are a telephone lineman's spike and a safety rope. They pull themselves to the top of a one-hundred-foot pole cut from a California redwood—the amateurs stop at seventy feet—ring a bell and then descend. Some go down so quickly they scrape the skin off their arms. The man who fell lost his safety strap.

These are among the strongest, bravest, craziest characters in the world. I watched them and wondered how our best athletes would compete against them. That is, if they could get in the same kind of shape, able to saw through a thirty-inch log in twenty-four seconds, using a chain saw powered by a motorcycle engine.

In another event, they put a thirty-inch log between their legs, raise an axe sharpened like a straight razor, and at the gun split the log with three or four swings. One guy had the wrong angle on one swing and almost took off his right calf.

On the third day, there was a break from the log rolling and axe swinging and pole climbing, and the TV crew and the contestants relaxed on a moonlight sail along the Namagagon (an old Indian word meaning fielder's choice). I joined the jacks for drinks and good talk.

You would not mistake any of them for adagio dancers. They were huge men, most with beards, their humor robust and earthy. I found that they needled and insulted each other just as baseball players do, and I jumped right in.

As the boat glided along, and the drinks went down smooth, I asked a New Zealander named Jim Wass if what I had heard was true: that a lumberjack was so tough he could shave himself with an axe.

He said, yeah, it was true.

I told him Americans were tough, too, and I vaguely remember making a speech about Paul Bunyan and his blue ox Babe. At one point I asked Wass if he thought he could shave me, if I was having an appendectomy. I am not sure what the appendectomy had to do with anything, or where I had in mind his shaving me, but he said, yeah, he could.

The next day I had forgotten the whole conversation. We had set up our cameras in front of the grandstand, which encircled a small lake. There was a pier nearby where the lumberjacks did their chopping. We had a clear view of the pit on the other side, where two hundred-foot pole rose against the sky, and two men climbed at a time.

Our producer, Ellie Riger, came up to me and asked if I was ready to go. I thought she was talking about an interview, and I looked around me, sort of absently, and asked, "Anyone special you want me to talk to?"

She said, "No, I want you to do the shaving thing."

I said, "The shaving thing?"

She nodded.

Just then Jim Wass strolled up, cradling a five-pound, single-bladed axe. The conversation of the night before started to come back to me. I heard myself say, "Oh, God, I was only kidding about the appendicitis."

But I was game. And I knew instinctively that the film would be something nice to stick in the show, the tough-but-oh-so-gentle shtick. People were moving around and rearranging cameras. Wass took out a pumice stone and started sharpening his axe.

I watched closely for a moment, then asked, "Is this thing going to do the job?"

He spit on his arm, wet it down and shaved a patch of hair. Then he looked up at me and said, "Don't worry about it."

I still did not feel quite the level of confidence I felt the stunt demanded. Every few minutes Wass would test the blade. The third time he cut himself and a small ribbon of blood ran across his arm.

I thought to myself, maybe this guy isn't as good as he says he is, or else we should have gone home earlier last night. Out loud I said, "Look, try that on my arm." So I wet my arm and the hair wouldn't come off. The blade would not shave my arm. I wondered about my face. I don't consider myself vain, but whether you are handsome or ugly, it is nice to have a face.

It was too late to back out. I touched the blade with my finger and it really did feel sharp as a razor. So I sat on a log, and while the cameras rolled and a few people shot still pictures, Jim got out a can of cream and I lathered up. He proceeded to shave me just like a barber, lifting my nose, tightening the skin under my neck.

As soon as he started I could tell he knew what he was doing. I looked down at the ground where the wood chips were and I didn't see any blood, and I didn't hear anybody cry out, "Oh, shit!" So I knew it was okay.

If I have a weakness, or even a talent, for ideas that are slightly off center, it wasn't something I developed for network television. It is an extension of what I have been doing all my life.

A few years ago, as a promotion, the Brewers decided to inflate a hot-air balloon before a game at County Stadium. Merle Harmon suggested that we could make history by doing a part of the broadcast from inside the gondola of the balloon. Specifically, my part of the broadcast.

The balloon, they assured me, would be tethered to a light tower and would not be allowed to rise above a couple hundred feet. We would not ascent at all if the winds were over twelve hundred feet because the stadium was in the landing pattern for the airport in Milwaukee, Mitchell Field.

On Saturday morning, the day of the game, the first thing I did was check the weather. It was windy as hell outside. I felt a surge of relief as I left for the park.

People were clutching their hats and women's skirts were flapping as I walked through the press gate. Hot-dog wrappers and small objects whipped through the stands. The players were bending against the wind as I walked onto the field.

And in front of the fence in center field, the ground crew was trying to blow up the balloon. They had decided to at least do the pregame show from the gondola. The pilot, or captain, was directing the work, which had a certain mad urgency about it. The gondola was on its side, and things began to go badly as soon as they turned on the gas. The guy who was fluffing up the silk was burned by the flamethrower they use to heat the air, and needed first aid.

The captain told me, over the howl of the wind, that we would get her airborne, have the ground crewmen hold the lines, and let the balloon float around the park for a while. The crowd would love it, he assured me.

I climbed into the gondola with the unhappiest-looking radio engineer in captivity. We went on the air, and I tried to do the pregame show, and the wind kept tipping over the gondola. We were bouncing up and down like a golf ball on a driveway, and the guys on the ground crew were running around in all directions, eight or ten of them, trying to hang on to the ropes.

We would get up about fifteen feet, then bang down and tip over. I was hanging on to a safety bar with one hand, holding on to the microphone with the other, and my feet kept flying out from under me. The captain was yelling up at us, telling me to stop kicking the gas tanks, I was letting out the air.

We must have looked like those early slow-motion films of the rockets that kept falling off the launching pad. After twenty minutes of banging up and down, the gondola turned over and dumped us out, like kittens from a basket. The crowd never did figure out what we were supposed to be doing, but they loved every turbulent minute of it. When the engineer and I crawled off the field, they cheered.

As far as I know, that was the last time anyone attempted to broadcast a baseball game from a hot-air balloon.

Given the record of my own playing days, the bosses at ABC clearly decided that I was qualified to work on a show called *The Superstars*. I have done several, and my speciality has become the unusual, if not impossible, scene-set.

The first *Superstars* show I ever helped report, in 1976, I made my arrival by sea. Bob Goodrich and Roger Goodman, the director and producer of the show, had brought the crew to the Bahamas, where the water sparkles in the noonday sun and the sands are as fine as salt. They asked if I could suggest something funny for the opener. I said the first thing that popped into my head: "Why don't I put on a suit of clothes and swim in?"

Their eyes got big as saucers. Bob said, "Would you really do it?"

When I saw them next they were toting a box from a discount store in Freeport. It contained a double-breasted coat, slacks, shirt, and tie. Fully dressed, I waded about one hundred yards out into the water.

On the beach, Al Michaels, Don Drysdale and Reggie Jackson opened the show. Al mentioned the fact that Bob Uecker was supposed to be there but had not yet arrived. In the background, you could see me behind them, fighting my way through the surf.

I finally made it ashore and dragged myself onto the catamaran. The three·of them all shouted, "Uke's here," and Drysdale looked me over and asked what happened.

Panting, I replied, "I had some extra time, so instead of flying to Freeport I took a boat. We were having a party and it got kind of loud and the captain told us to quiet down. We ignored him and started throwing bottles over the rail with notes. He came back a second time and told us either to get quiet or he'd put me overboard. I told him he didn't have the guts, and that was the last thing I remember."

We were back in Freeport in 1976, after the Olympics in Montreal. This time we did a scene-set—in the middle of the summer—with me decked out in a full winter ski outfit, trying to ski down the sand to Frank Gifford, Don Meredith and Reggie Jackson. I had supposedly taken a wrong turn on the cross-country trail in Montreal, and ended up on the beach at Freeport.

The joke worked fine, except for the fact that I had never skied before, the boots were a size eight and a half and I wear a ten, and we had to do three or four takes while the sweat poured out of me as though from a garden hose. Of course, I didn't really ski. I just sort of shuffled along, with a pole in each hand, yodeling as I went.

Another time I was to do an opening with Gifford at the swimming pool, and Frank wasn't told what to expect. I put on every piece of equipment I could find that would be used in the *Superstars*: flippers, a snorkel mask, a pair of size nineteen tennis shoes over my neck, a bowling ball in one hand and a tennis racket under my arm. I came walking out and Frank looked up from his commentary just in time to see me talking through the snorkel. He got on a laughing jag and it took us six takes to get through the scene.

They are a good gang to work with, Keith Jackson, Michaels, Gifford, the entire SS army. I have a special respect for Chet Forte, a small, dark, snappy fellow who has won seven or eight Emmy awards. More important, his sense of humor is as warped as mine.

It was Forte who came up with the idea for the Gorilla Trick.

For years, on the football side of Monday night, Cosell had conducted a running gag with me as the target. Whenever a team appeared with a mascot, or a fan dressed in a chicken suit, or as an owl or a robot or a horse, anything weird, Howard would say, "Well . . . I . . . see . . . Bob Uecker . . . is . . . here . . . tonight."

Then Gifford and Meredith and Fran Tarkenton picked it up and began to act as Howard's spotter: "Hey, Howard, there's Uecker," pointing to someone dressed as a bumblebee or a duck.

In December of 1980, Chet called me from Miami, where he was to direct a game between the Dolphins and

New England. I was to fly down a few days later to film another *Superstars* show. He asked if I could fly in early, and be there in time for the game.

A car was waiting for me at the airport Monday afternoon. I was taken by the freight elevator to my room in the Sonesta Beach Hotel, and stayed there until the broadcasting crew—Cosell, Gifford and Tarkenton—left for the Orange Bowl.

At the stadium I went directly to the truck and waited there with Forte and Bob Goodrich. We watched the game on the monitor. At one point, Chet punched up a picture of a guy in a Santa Claus suit. Gifford said, "There's Bob Uecker."

Cosell added, "Yes, he's just back from the baseball winter meetings."

A canary feather all but fluttered from Chet Forte's smiling lips. "Now's the time," he said. I felt like an agent about to be dropped behind enemy lines. They had gone to a costume store and purchased a gorilla outfit. I slipped into the suit, walked into the end zone and put on the mask. A technician with a hand-held camera was ready to cue me as soon as the boys mentioned my name.

He gave me the cue.

I took off the gorilla mask.

A sort of gargling noise came from Cosell's throat. It was beautiful.

If Howard Cosell personally found the answer to poverty, high interest rates, and bad officiating, there would be those who criticized him. The truth is, Howard is the kind of guy who will pull you out of a ditch. He performs countless acts of kindness, large and small, without getting (or wanting) credit for them.

On the Sunday before the baseball strike, Cosell flew

into Kansas City for the telecast on Monday night of the game between the Royals and the Yankees. That afternoon the Brewers were in town.

Howard caught a cab from the airport to the park, sat in the booth the entire game and kept up a running repartee with my partners and me. I compared him to Richard Arlen, the old, stylish actor who always wore a scarf.

Howard repaid the compliment by saying, "Personally, Uke, I don't understand what Bud Selig sees in you or why he keeps you on the air."

At the end of the game, as he left the booth, I said, "Nice to have seen you, Howie."

He said, "I wish I could say the same."

When Cosell was unable to appear at a roast and toast in my honor in Milwaukee, he sent instead a tape-recorded message. Imagine you can hear Howard's voice—it should not be difficult—as you read these words.

"People who have studied baseball in Milwaukee from its very beginning usually associate the sport with such names as Aaron and Mathews, Spahn and Burdette and Logan and Adcock and Bruton, and all the rest from the halcyon days of the Braves.

"And now those who are contemporary think of Caldwell and Hisle and that brilliant band of youngsters who are on the field for a young and promising and exciting team. You can throw in Bando's name, if you will, though he is hardly worthy of mention [note: Sal Bando was at the banquet] . . . but the point is, those of us on the inside of the so-called national pastime *know* that only two names ever really mattered in Milwaukee baseball . . . Osinski and Uecker. Osinski, of the spitball, and Uecker, of the knuckle head. Matter of fact, Bob, the more I've watched your career in broadcasting, the more it has made me realize the truth of what I have so often said, that there are only two professions in America where you can begin at the top. Prostitution and sportscasting.

"I don't know what your plans are for the rest of your life, but one thing is certain. You have got to find the right business. What you are doing now is purely and simply not for you, Uke. People in the broadcasting industry know it. And in your heart you know it, too. You've got to get out. *Now*. Test yourself, even as you did in baseball; when you knew you stank and couldn't play you accepted the fact, hung around for years . . . unsung . . . a third-stringer, copying down Joe Garagiola's old jokes, trying to get a dry, understated delivery that would, from time to time, get you on the Carson show and would produce lower ratings than anyone else in the history of that show.

"Now is the time to face reality, because you're still young enough to get out. If it means unemployment for a year, two years, whatever, fine! You can surmount adversity. Remember, adversity is what produces character. Now you've got to take a whole new look at your life; who you are, where you're at, what you are all about. And when you deduce all of that you will find that you are NOTHING. You are all about NOTHING.

"I'm glad they are roasting you tonight, Uke. It's the right way to go out."

I can hear those words, or read them, and immediately tell you three things: He did it without notes. He did it in one take. He got as close to the bone as you can get—as Don Rickles and Jack Carter and the great insult artists have always done—without causing actual pain. He is brilliant.

We were doing a baseball telecast in Minneapolis once and at one point Howard used the word "truculent." He looked at me and said, "Obviously, you don't know what I am talking about." I said, "Sure I do. If you had a truck and I borrowed it, that would be a truck-you-lent." Howard waited a beat and said, "Need I say more?"

I will let you in on a secret. For all of his blather about the "tired litany of the ex-jocks," and his belief that the networks are too quick and eager to take them on, Cosell respects those who work at the craft. And, although the self-put-down is part of my style, I do work at mine. I prepare. On the air, I care about being right. I had everything to learn about voice and delivery and the technical side of broadcasting, and I spent ten years learning them. I didn't try to wisecrack my way through it.

And like Cosell, I am not afraid to be controversial. I was among the first to take a stand when the question arose of whether to admit women reporters into the locker rooms. The issue was clouded with passionate speeches about freedom of the press, the First Amendment, and equal rights.

Not many people wanted to tangle with the true, bedrock issue, which is: If you were a lady, and found yourself in a clubhouse with twenty-five naked guys, would you look?

As a personal matter, I favor admitting women sportswriters and sportcasters to the locker rooms. I can't think of any place that figures to be more instantly improved by a few whiffs of cologne. But I do suspect that the ladies get distracted, even though they insist that they need to be there to write their stories. Sometimes, when you read their articles the next day, in the middle of a word you will notice a capital letter.

Sure, I can understand why some of the players are embarrassed by having women around while they (the players) are undressed. I know when I'm working in the broadcasting booth, and I'm nude, I don't want strangers coming in there, either.

The transition from player to announcer was hard for me in only one respect. There is a great temptation, for a former player, to be overly critical of the athletes now on the field. I just have to watch myself. It would not be fair for me to expect these fellows to do things the way I did them. Not fair at all.

And that is why my role on the Monday night telecasts is so clearly defined. The other guys can get all excited about the home runs and no-hitters and triple plays. I'm the one who gets excited when the catcher holds on to a third strike—or the warmup tosses. If the catcher drops a pop foul, I'm the one who explains how he did it. I'm the only one who knows his frame of mind.

I am at my best on passed balls. I'm like the expert at a golf tournament, or a coach at halftime. I am able to diagram the play for the viewers.

Now back to you, Howard.

9. One Strike and We're All Out

IT WAS LIKE a variation of the question that George Patton once posed to his troops, and kids of a later generation asked their fathers: "What did you do in the war, Daddy?"

Only this time the question was: "What did you do during the strike?"

I heard it all over America in the midsummer of 1981. The stadiums were still idle when Johnny Carson, on the *Tonight Show,* asked me how I had been spending my time.

I told him I had planned to go back into the army. I figured I still owed them a few weeks, having gone AWOL in 1956 after a disagreement with my first sergeant during hand-grenade training. He wanted me to use a lob throw, the way they do in the movies. I preferred a baseball throw, which is more accurate and gets better distance. We argued and I went over the hill. And never went back.

Unfortunately, when I contacted my nearest army

recruiting office I learned that I had leave time coming, so I had to continue with my broadcasting.

Carson nodded and asked, "What are you going to do when you leave here?"

I said, "Tomorrow I'll be at Craters of the Moon, Idaho. I'm going around the country promoting unsportsmanlike conduct school for kids. This is for youngsters in peewee football, basically. If the referee throws a flag, we encourage the kid to blow his nose on it and hand it back. Or they can slip a little Crazy Glue on the tip of his whistle and watch him pull his lip off."

Johnny did a double-take. *"Craters of the Moon,* Idaho?" he repeated.

The funny thing is, he thought I had made it up. But there really is such a town, at the foot of a volcano, just outside of Boise. It was the scene of the last major eruption in the United States prior to Mount St. Helens. When I was in Class C ball, our bus trips used to take us right by there, and the players would try to remember whose face the terrain reminded us of.

If the loss of eight weeks out of the 1981 season proved anything, it proved that baseball is as strong and elastic as ever. A strike nobody wanted was followed by a split-season plan that nobody seemed to like, and it all worked fine.

That hole in the middle of the schedule meant that there would be no twenty-game winners, and no hitters who drove in one hundred runs. But the teams came back to four new pennant races, and isn't that why God created September?

Like many fans, I had a sinking feeling that the rest of the season was going to be wiped out. In which case, these things would have happened:

—The company in the East that packs Delaware River mud into cans, to be used to rub the gloss off new baseballs, would have gone out of business (for years we have begged them to diversify).

—The sportswriters would have fanned out across the country, interviewing the players at their new jobs in feed stores and filling stations. They would have found Pete Rose on a sandlot in Philadelphia, crouched behind first base, waiting for a game to break out.

—With the billions saved by fans not buying tickets, parking their cars, or eating hot dogs, popcorn, and peanuts, the nation's economy might have turned around. People would have invested in the stock market or remodeled their homes. The rest would have gone into certificates of deposit.

It is a good thing the strike ended, after all. The longer it went on, the more people argued about it on radio call-in shows, and the harder the media tried to explain the issue, and the madder and more confused everybody got.

Both sides claimed that money was not the issue. The owners said they needed to be compensated, off the twenty-five-man roster, for a player lost to free agency. They needed this, they said, to protect the "competitive balance." The players said they liked the system the way it was. They were fighting, they said, to protect a right they had "won in court."

The issue was money. Since 1976, player salaries had tripled, thanks to the seven-figure, multi-year contracts the owners were tossing at so many free agents.

The compromise that ended the strike after fifty playing dates were canceled boiled down to this: The most a team can lose for signing a free agent is the twenty-fifth man on its roster. The fans really didn't care who won or who lost. The reaction of the fans was: Shut up and deal.

When the walkout began, I asked myself what I would have done if there had been a reason for striking when I was still a player, making my twenty grand or less? And there were probably a lot more reasons than there are now.

The players have a point when they ask why they should make life easier for the owners, just because the owners lack the discipline to do it themselves. On the other hand, it is pointless when the players say, as they have said repeatedly, "The owners wouldn't be paying those big salaries if they couldn't afford them." What has affording it got to do with anything? That is why credit cards were invented.

Given a choice between winning and running up costs, the owners unfailingly will choose to win. The need to win tops anything else that life can offer. They already know how it feels to be rich.

It is hard at this point to work up any sympathy for the players or the owners. When a utility infielder, or a pitcher who wins fourteen games, can sell himself for five hundred thousand dollars a year, even the players giggle softly. They also take the logical position that it isn't their duty to stop it.

If someone reminds them that they could kill the fowl that lays the golden egg, they are likely to shrug and respond, "The fowl will find a way to survive."

So the players want to keep the *status quo,* which, in the words of an old country preacher, is Latin for "de mess we is in." They like their freedom, their salaries, their thirty-five dollars a day in meal money. You give the average housewife thirty-five dollars a day and she will feed five people and have her hair done with the change.

An ex-player, who played for modest wages and probably got what he deserved, risks coming off like a sourbelly if he doesn't stand with the troops. But some of what the players say is wearing thin.

I heard Dave Parker, of the Pirates, tell an interviewer: "This game is harder than people think. Some days, we're out at the ball park eight or nine hours." An image of a pipefitter smashing his beer can through his TV screen came to mind.

After Andy Messersmith signed with Atlanta for a multi-year contract valued at a million and three-quarter dollars, a TV reporter asked why the negotiations had dragged out for months. "Was it just a matter of money," he asked, "or was there a principle involved?"

"Well," said the pitcher, "it started out as a money thing, but then it became a principle thing."

There was a kind of wild poetry to Andy's words. For most athletes today, the principle is clear: Grab it while you can. A career in pro sports is short, unlike that of a brain surgeon, or even a judge, who gets to sit down a lot.

A popular parlor game today is to wonder what players of the stature of Babe Ruth, Ty Cobb, Joe DiMaggio, or Ted Williams would bring in the current market. Clearly, Ruth would not receive a contract. He would get a partnership. As his widow once noted, "In my husband's day .280 hitters were not regarded as stars. They sat on the bench." I could have sat on the bench in Ruth's day, as easily as I did in my own.

In 1981, Dave Winfield, a lifetime .280 hitter, signed a ten-year contract with the New York Yankees said to be worth fifteen million dollars, not including bonus

clauses. Winfield won his free agency after the San
Diego Padre refused to meet his price or his personal
demands. It was rumored that Dave wanted a veto in the
event Ray Kroc, the McDonald's hamburger tycoon,
decided to move the club. He also wanted a voice in
team trades, more beef in the ground patties, and the
right to change his name to Ronald McWinfield.

Do you remember when sports was the nation's escape
from the hustle and bustle of everyday commerce? Now
the athletes no longer merely sign contracts, they cut
deals. The owners grumble, but pay, and some of them,
such as George Steinbrenner and Ted Turner, don't even
grumble. The players, of course, are having orgasms.
Big money, rather than big performance, has created
today's breed of superstar. When a streak hitter like
Reggie Jackson can get a candy bar named after him,
you conclude that the word "superstar" has been
devalued. Or even the word "candy bar." Of course, I'm
not jealous. I had one named after me, too. The Zero bar.

As a close observer of trends, I have kept myself
prepared in the event of another strike. Radio stations
recreated old games and newspapers ran old box scores
during the last one. The owners missed an opportunity
by not keeping the parks open and showing old baseball
movies, such as *The Babe Ruth Story,* or *Pride of the
Yankees,* or *The Winning Team,* which starred Ronnie
Reagan.

I will continue to keep open as many options as I can.
I still have several business ventures, including the
various Bob Uecker academies. One is my famous
Passed Ball School for kids. We teach young catchers
how to miss the ball. I got the idea from people asking
me what was the best way to catch a knuckleball. I told

them that what worked for me was to wait for the ball to stop rolling, then just pick it up.

Of course, we also have adult education classes, such as our School for Tall-Building Climbers. I got this idea after two fellows climbed the World Trade Center in New York. The work is exciting, although I must admit that up to now our graduates have enjoyed very little success. Two of them failed to climb the C.N. Tower Building in Toronto, seventeen hundred feet high. We prefer that they start off with something smaller, such as a one-story building, or a Winnebago.

The most important warning we give our students, when they go through spring training, is: Don't touch the ledges! We consider this to be of life-and-death importance. There might be pigeon droppings on those ledges. The first time you grab the ledge, and you feel the pigeon droppings, your natural instinct is to say, "Aaagghh," and let go. And that is that.

During an earlier baseball strike—there have been three since 1972—I went into a sport fishing investment with my friend Al Hirt, the jazz trumpetist. We set up the company in a first-class way, printing a four-color brochure that showed Al floating in a swamp near New Orleans, with me sitting on top of his stomach with my feet in the water, and holding a rod.

I decided to back out of the deal after I found out how Al wanted to fish. One day we got into a boat and I looked around and didn't see any rods or reels, just a tackle box. He said not to worry about it. Fifteen miles out into the lake he cut off the motor, opened the tackle box and took out a stick of dynamite. I was appalled, having always considered myself a pretty good sportsman.

Jumbo, as his friends call him, lit the fuse and pitched the stick into the water. With his first cast we got about two hundred fish. After two or three more I said, "Look, I've had enough of this." With that he picked up another stick, lit the fuse, handed it to me and asked if I wanted to fish.

It was my only throw but I guess we got another one hundred fifty, and most of them were already cleaned. But that was the end of my sport fishing venture.

I hope there will never be another strike in baseball. But if there is, I won't be hurt. I can always go back into the service.

PART IV

Short Subjects

In which he examines the mystique of spring training, managers, umpires, and the underworld of Little League.

"Baseball owes me a lot. If I had to go into the tank to lose a game, I would do it. I was not one of those guys you had to go back two and three times to ask a favor. And this is what I tell kids. You have to make up your mind sooner or later, do you want to be good, or do you want to be a tanker?"

10. It Happens Every Spring

"WELCOME TO DIAMOND THREE, men. During your stay here you will be taught the art of fighting snakebite, how to survive for days without water, and how to extract water from the cactus plants behind second base. You will never see people out here. You will learn not to care when dirt gets in your bubble gum. And you will be given a chance to play baseball at its very worst. Welcome to Diamond Three, men."

Okay, so it won't make the world forget General George Patton's speech to the troops on the eve of D-Day. But this was my welcome each spring to the other scrubs, in my role as honorary captain of the irregulars, with the Braves, the Cardinals, and the Phillies.

Spring training was my favorite part of the baseball season. One year, with the Phillies, I took a call in the clubhouse. Hanging up the phone, I turned to the fellows around me and said, casually, "It was my wife. She wanted to know where I've been all winter."

They call it the Dreamer's Month. In March, on paper,

125

every team looks stronger than it did a year ago, and they are counting heavily on a player they got in a trade with a team that no longer wanted him.

It's the same every year. The rituals never vary. A pitcher may have nothing more on the ball than the autograph of the league president, but in March they all look like the reincarnation of Walter Johnson.

In short, spring training is a fantasy land, a place where rookies with rheumatism hit .400 and the ball *sounds* louder, whether it is off the bat or landing ka-pow in the catcher's glove. Reality doesn't sink in until mid-April is on the calendar.

Even the managers can sometimes suspend their critical judgment. In places like Bradenton and Orlando, West Palm Beach and Phoenix, they say to themselves, "Well, we all start even, and why shouldn't it be me this year?"

They also tell each other things like: "So help me, Max, this kid could be another DiMaggio. His name is Higgins or Hawkins, I'm not sure which, but he's sensational . . . gawd, if he could only hit."

Many people have the impression that players in the spring stay on a pretty tough schedule. The first two weeks are the worst. The pitchers and the catchers have it harder than anybody. They pitchers have to run, run, run. The catchers never get a break. You have to stick around until everyone is finished throwing. Or throwing up.

Anybody could do it.

Actually, the biggest setback the American players ever suffered was when the Japanese teams began making occasional visits to Florida. You get an idea of how well-conditioned the American baseball player is when you see a runner in June try for three bases. No sight is more pathetic, no effort sorrier, than the spectacle of a baseball player legging out a triple.

Sliding into the bag, he calls time for the ostensible purpose of dusting off his uniform. But he is so pooped, so exhausted, that you begin to think that his next move is to call in the paramedics.

By contrast, the Japanese go to something that resembles a Marine boot camp. They scale mountains, run obstacle courses and climb ropes.

At major-league training camps in the U.S., the players will touch their toes, run a little and then play golf, unless they prefer to go fishing. Fishing will give a man a hell of a workout, especially if he gets a bite every three hours.

A majority of the players manage to avoid the Spartan existence of camp life itself. They bring along their families, renting places on the sands of Vero Beach and St. Petersburg—or, if they are based on the desert, they occupy an oasis with pools at Scottsdale, Arizona.

The Japanese player, summoned for reville at six in the morning, will go for his bowl of rice under a thatched roof before he is asked to take a run up Mt. Fuji. This is an athlete lean and hard, and ready to leg out a triple.

For me, personally, the great thing about spring training was working on my tan. When the weather was bad I would just get liquored up and do a handstand and bring a flush to my face. Works almost as well.

It used to be, in the days before football and basketball were played twelve months a year, and golf and tennis players were not yet let in through the front door of the country club, that sports fans had little to do but wait for the start of spring training. There were always those first exciting clues that told us the season was just around the corner.

You would see a page-one photograph of a few early arrivals doing sit-ups or hopscotching their way through a broken field of old tires, or two guys throwing a medicine ball at each other's stomachs, a fairly decent target at that stage of training.

Of course, from my own experience I can tell you that those photographs were usually faked. In all probability, the ball wasn't even a medicine ball. More likely it was a rubber beach ball and a photographer borrowed it from a little kid at the going rate of twenty-five cents an hour.

No doubt the players tossed it around for a total of five minutes, at which point they noticed the sun was out and retired to the clubhouse for a beer.

All of which goes to the very heart of what spring training is all about. Traditionally, baseball players have never deliberately built a muscle in their lives. They have believed that either you had muscles or you didn't. March was a month to get the old timing and coordination down pat, and to prepare your *head*. Once you were in the right frame of mind to open the season, why, your body had no choice but to go along.

If nothing else, spring training is a rich and bottomless source of stories that reflect the romance and character of the sport. In a less frantic age, the teams traveled by train, and the players had time to talk about the sport and to agitate each other and concoct all kinds of wild schemes. They would do this traveling north out of Florida, with the countryside flashing by the window. The scenery, it should be noted, is not particularly absorbing, unless you happen to be attracted to cabbage palms and slash pines.

So the boys would sit around thinking up subjects to argue about, and this led naturally enough to a lot of enduring tales. One of them concerns the grizzled old catcher, Clint Courtney, known in the pits as Scrap Iron.

In his salad days, Courtney caught for the old Washington Senators, and one spring he promoted a footrace between Pedro Ramos, his battery mate, and Don Hoak of the Cincinnati Reds.

The teams were barnstorming through the South together, and the players entered into one of those club-car arguments about who was faster, Ramos or Hoak.

Ramos was then a skinny young pitcher who could fly, but nobody realized it because he did not know how to get off to a proper start. And, besides, he seldom got a base hit. Courtney baited the Cincinnati players by claiming that, "Anybody beats my man, he's got to put his feet down real regular."

So they decided to hold the race before a game in Chattanooga at one hundred yards. The guys on both clubs started making bets, and on the way north Courtney would stroll through the Reds' part of the train hustling bets that would be covered by the Washington players. Altogether, the pot was rumored to have reached seven thousand dollars.

The day before the race, Courtney received permission to go on ahead of the clubs to set up the racing course at the Chattanooga ball park. The players arrived in a state of great excitement, and everyone lined up along the way, most of them near the finish line.

At the starting point, Hoak crouched in the accepted American track stance, while Ramos was standing up with his arms dangling at his sides. As everyone expected, Hoak got off on top. He quickly opened a lead of about five yards, and then—as Courtney told it—here came Pedro Ramos.

He cut the margin down gradually, caught Hoak, then

won it pulling away. Ramos beat him by about ten yards, to the utter amazement of the Cincinnati players.

They paid off, and some of them probably do not know to this day that Clint Courtney's course measured *one hundred and twenty yards*.

The phrase "It happens every spring" wasn't invented to describe the craziness and mass optimism that grips baseball at that special time of the year, but it fits as snugly as a catcher's mask.

In the spring, even the writers are easily spoiled and tend to be temperamental. Chicago scribes are the treasurers of a classic story that dates back to when big-league teams moved like wrestlers from town to town, picking up expense money as they headed north to open the season.

The hero of this story is T-Bone Otto, a legendary Chicago scribe who was covering the White Sox on a tour across West Texas. The White Sox had played the Giants in a town called Alpine, and after finishing his account of the game, T-Bone Otto turned upstream in search of refreshments.

He looked all over town, a task that didn't consume a great deal of time, and found every eatery shut as tight as the lid on a jar of bees. When he returned to his hotel, grouchy and thirsty and hungry, he was informed that the White Sox had just purchased the contract of Willie Kamm, an infielder of some promise. He sat down at his typewriter and pounded out a story that began:

"ALPINE—In this lousy little Texas town, where a man can't get anything to eat after 9:00 P.M., the White Sox today acquired Willie Kamm."

Of course, a fellow doesn't have to be clairvoyant to

guarantee that certain things will happen every spring, such as:

—A manager who has no one else to play the position will announce, dramatically, that a certain rookie has the job until he loses it.

—The players who grumble the most about how hard they are working will sneak away after a game to play eighteen holes of golf.

—At least one player will be laid up with a serious sunburn.

—A guy who never hit over .220 in his life will say that this year he is going to wait for his pitch.

—No matter how homely the waitress in the motel coffee shop is, she will get a big play from the single players if she owns a car.

—Every manager will say at least once in every interview that, "You can always use another pitcher."

—An actor will put on a uniform and work out with the Dodgers.

—A player who was traded from a contender to a last-place team will be quoted as saying that he is glad to be with a team that wants him.

—The manager of a second-division club will predict that his team will be improved. (He will be fired in August by the general manager who put the team together.)

—George Steinbrenner will make headlines by criticizing his manager, another owner, one or more of his players, or all of these.

—Billy Martin will make headlines by getting into a fight, or by not getting into a fight.

—Yogi Berra will be credited with a funny remark that was originally uttered by a nightclub comedian.

—A sports columnist will warn that salaries have

gotten so out of line, the fans are being turned off, and the sport is in danger of dying. (A new attendance record will be set.)

—A star player will not report to camp, threatening to retire unless his contract is renegotiated. Both sides will wind up happy. The club will announce that it did not renegotiate the contract, which would have set a poor precedent, but merely extended the contract at a slightly higher figure. The player will have missed the first week or two of camp, the most boring part.

It was a matter of pride with some players never to report to camp on time. Mike Marshall, the great relief pitcher who had his finest years with the Dodgers and the Expos, was always working toward another degree in college, and usually showed up around St. Patrick's Day to chase the snakes out of Florida.

My old friend Richie Allen sometimes arrived on schedule, then quickly disappeared for several days to have his eyes checked, or to go visit a sick horse.

One of the masters of this art was the colorful Orestes (Minnie) Minoso, who held out not for financial gain, but because he loved his native Cuba and preferred to stay there as late as possible in the spring. Once, reporting five days late to the Cleveland camp, he was met by an irritated Hank Greenberg, then the general manager of the Indians.

"Suppose," Hank asked Minoso, "you were in my position?"

"You mean if I Greenberg and you Minnie?" asked Minoso.

"Exactly," said Greenberg.

Minoso smiled. "I pat you on back and I say, 'Minnie, you good boy, you fine fellow, you hustle all the time. All right if you take off four-five days.'"

• • •

As a player, I always went to spring training in Florida, where the early weather was often so cool and so wet that the newspapers had to use pictures of last year's bathing beauties dipping their toes into the Atlantic.

There is always a basic conflict in the spring between management and the players. The management prefers an environment that is almost hermetically sealed, and goes to great lengths to keep the players away from the nearest beach, fearing that such a place offers too much in the way of temptations. The players complain that there are never enough temptations.

I can assure you that both complaints are justified.

One of the things I hated most about spring training was the long bus rides starting at 5:00 A.M. to play another team across the state. As they say, everything gets easier with practice except getting up in the morning. I would never recommend to anyone getting up before dawn to drive to a spring training game between say, the Braves and the Red Sox. Still, it might be worth doing once. You would remember it a long time, and that would save having to do it again.

But it really boils down to keeping things in perspective.

Once, we headed out of our camp at West Palm Beach to play a B game against the Twins at Orlando. We followed the coastal highway to the Astronaut trail, until our bus took us past the launching pad at what was then Cape Kennedy.

Poised like a great white bullet on the gantry was the rocket that would carry the crew of one of the Apollo flights toward the moon. The bus grew quiet. All of those aboard swung their eyes to the window and stared out through the early-morning mist, across the Banana River, at the huge ship visible through the wispy clouds like the first glimpse of the mountain Bali H'ai, in the movie *South Pacific*.

Finally, the silence was broken. From the back of the bus came the voice of one of the players. "Gee," he said, "it makes our B team game with the Twins seem almost insignificant."

11. The Fearless Leaders

DO YOU HAVE trouble keeping track of which manager is with which team, and who was there before him? Of course you do. It is like trying to understand the price index on pork futures. It is even more confusing than keeping up with the ex-husbands of the wife of New York's Governor Carey. It makes your eyeballs burn.

In 1961, Phil Wrigley, the reclusive owner of the Chicago Cubs, decided to try a perfectly bold experiment. He decided not to have any manager at all. Instead, he appointed what he called a board of rotating coaches, six of them, each to take his turn at the helm of the team for a period of weeks.

The experiment ended in 1963, after it had become apparent that the Cubs played just as miserably without a manager as they did with one, and thus were deprived of someone to take most of the blame.

Charley Metro happened to be the coach-of-the-month during a game in 1962, when he was ejected for arguing with an umpire. At that moment, Joey Amalfitano, an infielder with Houston, jumped out of the visitors' dugout, pointed to the Chicago coaches sitting in a row, and shouted across the field: "Okay, each of you guys move up one seat!"

I played under six different managers in my six years in the big leagues: Birdie Tebbetts, Johnny Keane, Red Schoendienst, Gene Mauch, Bobby Bragan and Luman Harris. They were an interesting cross-section. Tebbetts was warm, outgoing, fatherly, quick with a funny line. Mauch was smart, hot-tempered, always trying to stay three innings ahead of the other guy. He surprised me one night, when I saw him quietly holding hands with his wife in a hotel lobby during spring training.

Keane was a gentle, proud man, who had spent his life in the minors, whose playing career was ended by a beanball, who managed farm clubs for twenty years and had one year of glory, when the Cardinals won the pennant for him in 1964.

Red Schoendienst had been a championship player in Milwaukee and St. Louis. He was no back-slapper, but he was businesslike and fair. Bragan had the look of a bartender in a Gay Nineties saloon; he smoked cigars, played the piano, liked a good laugh. Luman Harris had pitched for Connie Mack, was tough but not threatening.

All of them had one thing in common. All of them, sooner or later, would get fired.

You conclude that it takes a special kind of rainbow chaser to want to be a baseball manager. When Dave Bristol was hired in Atlanta, a reporter asked if he considered himself a fiery type of manager. "I guess so," he replied, "I've been fired three times." Later, he moved on to the Giants, and was fired a fourth time.

Do you know what the average tenure is among big-league managers? Two and a half years. Migrant fruit picking is more secure than that.

You begin to get the idea that the best way to get a manager's job is to be delivering bottled water to the team's office at the moment the last one is getting fired.

When Gil Hodges was named the manager of the Washington Senators, his old Dodger boss, Walter Alston, was asked for his reaction. "I'm happy for him," said Alston, "that is, if you think becoming a big-league manager is a good thing to have happen to you."

Hodges inherited a last-place team in Washington. One night, after another loss, Frank Slocum, a former newsman who had worked in the commissioner's office, stood in his doorway. "The Dodgers just released Gino Cimoli," said Slocum, mentioning a former Hodges teammate, and an outfielder of average talents.

Wearily, Hodges looked up from his desk. "Why are you telling me this?" he asked.

"I thought he might be able to help you," replied Slocum.

"Frank," said Hodges, "did it ever occur to you that if I thought Gino Cimoli could help this club, I'd quit right now?"

No one in America is second-guessed more often, or hears more unwanted advice, than the manager of a big-league baseball team. And that includes the President, plumbers, and producers of X-rated movies.

The fact is, one manager in twenty can influence a team emotionally. Technically, in terms of the moves that are open to him, a manager can win or lose—actually decide the outcome—of possibly eight to ten games a year, tops.

When a team finishes poorly, and elects to bring in a new field leader without making any serious roster changes, it is doing just one thing. It is grandstanding for the fans, saying to them: "Your good ownership is doing something, trying to bring you, our deserving fans, a winner."

Richie Allen used to say that the public is mistaken when it believes that managers are fired. "They aren't fired," said Richie, "they are only moved, like players. If you want to say that managers are fired, then I've been fired four times." That is a new but not unreasonable way to look at the practice of teams' hiring managers who have been fired elsewhere, usually more than once.

Considering the nature of the job, and the insecurity of it, you tend to ask yourself why any sane person would pursue this line of work. The answer is twofold. First, the job satisfies the power needs that exist in most of us. A manager controls twenty-five men, plus a staff. His words are recorded by press, radio, and television. His friendship and company are sought by important people, at least while he remains on the job.

What else could the average manager do that would pay as well and be as exciting? They will tell you that it beats operating a crane, driving a bread truck or selling jock-straps.

Yet the pressure of the job changes them as people. Even playful, fun-loving types like Bobby Bragan and Luman Harris became more serious and touchy and less approachable.

With a few exceptions, they turn into people you have trouble recognizing. Of course, Walter Alston stayed the same: quiet, aloof, steady as a rock. Casey Stengel was nutty and lovable when he won, more so when he lost. And nothing will ever change Billy Martin. He was a tough s.o.b. when he played and when he managed and he will still be on the day he dies. And I love him for it.

I was fond of Bobby Bragan and I still am. He had a great sense of humor. But he was more fun to be around when he was a coach than when the Braves hired him as their manager.

The first thing Bobby did when we returned to Milwaukee after spring training was go out to the bullpen and tear down a kind of recreation room the boys had created out there. We had taken wire clippers and cut out part of a snow fence and made an area for ourselves. We built a table, suspended it from under the stands, and arranged several boxes and crates so you could play cards and eat. The little guy who drove the scooter to the pitcher's mound was named George, and we would bribe him with a dozen baseballs and have a steady supply of hot dogs or bratwurst or whatever we wanted.

Bragan knew about the arrangement from his days as a bullpen coach with Houston. So he had everything ripped out and fired poor George. Bobby, Bobby. Where did we go wrong?

The year before, when Bragan was a coach, the hot-foot was just epidemic in baseball. Players would be sitting on the bench, watching the game, and you would crawl from one end of the dugout to the other, sticking matches in their shoes and lighting them, and then see those feet go up like someone running the keyboard on a piano.

Inevitably, the action got more complicated. Guys would smoke a cigarette down to about a half inch and stick it in your belt loop—even while you were on the field. I looked up one time and our second baseman was out in the field, beating out flames on his uniform.

The planning was elaborate, like spies preparing to blow up a factory. One trick was to chew a stick of gum, then press it against the side of the victim's shoe. You could just touch the cigarette but to the gum and it would hold. When the cigarette burned down far enough, it would go right through the leather, and the poor fellow couldn't get his shoe off fast enough.

Or someone would light your shoelaces. All of a sudden your shoes split right down the middle and the laces were gone. It was just one piece of nonsense after another.

One day the Houston team came into County Stadium, and Turk Farrell found me before the game. He said, "Uke, bring some lighter fluid out to the bullpen." I said, "Whaddya gonna do?" He said, "Just bring it. We're gonna torch Bragan."

I gave Farrell a can of fluid and he stashed it under the bench in the visitors' bullpen. When the game started Bragan sat down and kept his eyes on the field. I was leaning as far over the rail of our bullpen as I could. When I saw what Farrell was doing I couldn't believe it. He took the cap off the can and sprayed it up and down Bragan's shoes and pants legs. Then he took a match and threw it on him. Poof! Bragan did the damndest dance I have ever seen. Chief Nok-a-homa, the Indian who sat out in the teepee and did a few war whoops whenever the Braves homered, would have been proud.

Bragan was a product of the Branch Rickey system with the old Brooklyn Dodgers, and had come up through their farm clubs. He could really get on your case. He had a way of talking out of the side of his mouth, like Humphrey Bogart, and he could dust you off equally well with a sarcastic line or with your basic seaman's vocabulary.

One day, after the Braves had moved to Atlanta, the team was in a wretched slump, and Bobby and Del Crandall had gotten into a shouting match at the end of a road trip. So Bobby decided to call a clubhouse meeting to clear the air. He just started moving from locker to locker, and as he faced each player he would curl his lip and say, "Bleep you." And on to the next one.

Finally, he was a few feet away from Eddie Mathews, who seldom made trouble, but didn't suffer insults, real or imagined, lightly. When Bobby got to him, Eddie's fists were curled. Bragan paused, looked at his eyes, said nothing, and moved on to the next locker. No one ever accused Bragan of being stupid.

Each manager loses in his own way. Sometimes, in his own several ways. Some swear, some sulk, some suffer in silence. When Alvin Dark managed the Giants, he once picked up a clubhouse stool and threw it against a wall, unfortunately catching a finger in a hinge and ripping off the tip of it. When he showed up in a bandage the next day, the players started calling him "Lefty." Alvin also quoted the Bible a lot.

Silent, stern Walter Alston once stopped a bus and challenged his entire team to a fistfight.

After his New York Mets lost a doubleheader, one of the games in twenty-three innings, Casey Stengel took off his clothes, stood in the middle of the locker room, and leaped straight in the air. When heads swiveled in his direction, he shrugged and said, "I just wanted to see if I was still alive."

And when Fred Hutchinson was managing the Reds, teams that followed them into a town could always tell if the Reds had lost by the number of light bulbs and chairs that had been smashed in the visitors' clubhouse.

In my time, the manager who was most respected by the players was Hutchinson. The one we most liked to be around was Stengel, and the one we most liked to analyze was Gene Mauch.

Eddie Kasko was with the Cardinals in 1957 when Hutch was the manager there, and pushing the Braves for first place. "He sent up Del Ennis to pinch-hit one night in a tight spot," recalled Kasko, "and Ennis had that real big bat—the U-1 model. He swung at a two-and-oh pitch and popped it up.

"Coming back to the dugout, he was swinging that bat like a cane, walking along in that slow, shuffling sort of walk that he had. You could see that Hutch was seething, and he was trying hard to control himself.

"Just as Ennis stepped down into the dugout, he flung his bat toward the bat rack, and out of the corner of his eye Hutch saw it go by. He wheeled around and grabbed it and, man, you should have seen the players on the Cardinal bench scatter. Hutch took the bat and began beating it against those concrete steps.

"Then he threw it to the floor and began stomping on it, and you know what? The damned thing wouldn't break. Finally, Hutch picked it up and gently handed it back to Ennis. 'Here,' he said, 'keep it. It has good wood in it.'"

Fred Hutchinson was the hero of some of baseball's favorite essays on fury and indignation. In his time he wrecked more chairs than Duncan Phyfe built. He was seldom misunderstood. He was never patronizing, not to his players or to the batboy or to reporters, not necessarily in order of importance. He was a big bear of a man, restless, with curly hair and sad eyes. He was not a phrasemaker, but he had the knack of saying a lot in a small space.

In the winter before the pennant race of 1964—that great race between the Cards, the Reds, and the

Phillies—the story broke that Hutch was ill with cancer. It was in June that the word spread that he was dying. We heard it from the Cincinnati players. "He started to smoke again and to take an occasional drink," said one. "He knew he wasn't going to whip it and he figured, what the hell, he might as well do the things he enjoyed doing."

He turned the team over to Dick Sisler in August. He would still visit the ball park and his picture would be in the paper the next day. His friends winced at the photographs of the drawn, gaunt face.

He was in the clubhouse on the last day of the season, the day the Reds lost the pennant. Dick Sisler nodded in his direction and told reporters: "I'm only sorry we couldn't have won it for that gentleman there."

Hutchinson overheard him. "I'm only sorry," he said, "they couldn't have won it for themselves."

I never played under Casey Stengel, but I played against him, and I am reasonably sure we would have gotten along. I can still see Casey marching out to the mound with his hands jammed in his back pockets, or punching the air with a fist in the dugout, or sprawled on the bench like Cleopatra on a barge, regaling his writers.

It was a tossup whether Stengel's most memorable achievement was winning ten pennants with the Yankees, or finishing tenth three times with the Mets, and making them the greatest failure story in history.

He had one of those rubbery faces that make a fellow look as if he could swallow his nose. His legs were so lumpy it looked as though he were smuggling walnuts in his stockings. The week that Casey retired from the Mets, at seventy-four, *Look* magazine ran a picture of him stalking away from some umpires after arguing about a call. The umpires were all laughing.

In his heyday with the Mets, Casey came to Florida one spring with his hair dyed a strange, youthful shade of henna. It was a wild sight, that hair, above that wrinkled, cartoon face. The Mets players could hardly wait to tell you about it.

"Have you seen Casey?" they braced each visitor. "He looks like Dorian Gray's UNCLE."

He had his faults. He could be rough and impatient with young players, and cruel in his opinions. Of Jimmy Piersall, who had a history of odd behavior, he said: "He's great, but you gotta play him in a cage." Bobby Richardson was straight as an arrow, and Casey didn't know what to make of it: "He doesn't smoke, doesn't drink, doesn't run around with girls and doesn't stay out late, and he still can't hit .250."

But Stengel believed in the miracle of being young. "I'll tell you about youth," he said. "Look how big it is. They break a record every day."

I especially liked what he said when he turned eighty-one, and a reporter asked what his plans were. "To tell you the truth," he said, "what I'd like to become is an astronaut."

12. The Men in Blue

MANY YEARS AGO, when the world was young, an umpire named Jocko Conlan called a strike on Richie Ashburn, a career .300 hitter then with the Phillies.

"Where was that pitch?" Ashburn snarled, in the ballplayers' traditional retort to a call that went against them.

Conlan, who had the look of a leprechaun, did not answer, at least not directly. What he said was, "Okay, *you* umpire. *You* call the next pitch."

Ashburn, startled, never moved his bat as the next one popped into the catcher's mitt. Over his shoulder, he peeked at Jocko and said, tentatively, "Strike?"

Obligingly, Jocko threw up his right hand and called a strike. Then he marched out and dusted off home plate and finally poked a finger in Ashburn's chest. "Richie," he said, "you have just had the only chance a hitter has ever had in the history of baseball to bat and umpire at the same time. And you blew it."

Sports is not a perfect society, so the day is still distant when it will be run on an honor system in which the players call their own pitches. In fact, the 1979 baseball season, when the regular umpires went on strike, may be as close as we ever get.

Let's face it. Umpiring is not an easy or a happy way to make a living. In the abuse they suffer, and the pay they get for it, you see an imbalance that can only be explained by their need to stay close to a game they can't resist. They are like the fellow who cleans up after the elephants at the circus, and whose complaints are greeted with the suggestion that he quit. "What?" he replies, "and give up show business?"

The sad truth is that baseball has never shown a great deal of heart in its treatment of the veteran umpires. The minimum pay for that position is $17,500, rising to a top of around forty grand. Some players probably pay their tailor more than most big-league umpires make.

You picture an ump walking to the mound when Nolan Ryan or Tommy John or Phil Niekro is pitching, and they turn their backs and tell him to leave a message with their answering service.

Clearly, the umpires feel underpaid in a job that requires them to make judgments on performers earning up to a million dollars a year. Their expenses are high. They accept insults as a matter of course. Injuries are common. Crowds are seldom more amused than when an umpire gets hit by a foul tip on an important part of his body.

And the life they lead is so lonely, they are never in danger of running into Margaret Trudeau or Bianca Jagger. They do not mingle with the players, fly on the same plane, or sleep in the same hotels.

Meanwhile, ballplayers collect thirty-three dollars a day for meals alone, and most of them sleep until noon.

Insulting the umpire is a pastime as old as baseball itself. In organized baseball's first recorded game, in 1846, a New York player named Davis was fined six cents for cussing the ump.

It was Tom Gorman, among the best of my time, who spoke for all the men in blue when he said: "Nobody ever says anything nice about an umpire, unless it's when he dies and then somebody writes in the paper, 'he was a good umpire.' Oh, once in a while a player will tell you that you worked a good game behind the plate, but when that happens, it's always the winning pitcher who says it."

Yet the umpires have a special role in the structure of baseball. To many fans, their lasting image of the sport is the Norman Rockwell drawing of the four umpires huddled under an umbrella, one holding out his hand, testing for rain.

At one time the top names in umpiring was Paparella, Passarella, Donatelli, Dascoli, Guglielmi and Secory. All of which moved Walker Cooper, the hard-bitten Cardinal catcher of the 1940s, to a wry complaint. "Every guy that gets off the boat," said Cooper, "has an indicator in his hand."

Mostly they were frustrated players who never got beyond the low minors. Today they are more likely to be the products of umpiring schools, who paid their dues in the college, amateur and minor-league ranks.

My impression is that umpires today are regarded with more respect than in the past, and television is at least partly responsible. Instant replays have supported their decisions a dramatically high percentage of the time.

The good ones last twenty years or more, and it helps if they have a sense of humor, and a little discretion. "Sometimes," I once heard Tom Gorman say, "when a game gets close and tempers are short, you hear things from the dugout and you holler at 'em to shut up, and if they don't you walk over to the bench. Now, when you've committed yourself that far, you gotta chase somebody. You don't want to hurt the club so you pick maybe a guy who pitched the day before and isn't gonna be called on again that day.

"So one particular day in Ebbets Field I'm gettin' it pretty good from the Dodger bench, and I finally walk over there and somebody has to go. So I point in just a general direction and I say, 'Yer outta here, John Van Cuyk,' because he'd pitched yesterday, you see, and I'm doing them a favor.

"Chuck Dressen is managing in Brooklyn then and he says, 'Who you want out?' And I repeat, 'Van Cuyk.' and Chuck says, 'That's great, but you'll have to yell a little louder because I sent him back to the Texas League last night.'"

On another occasion, Gorman was umpiring a game involving Leo Durocher's New York Giants. It so happened that Tom called a close play at first base against the Giants, and Durocher stormed out of the dugout and demanded: "Why, Tom, why?"

To distract him, Gorman said the first thing that came into his mind, which was: "Your first baseman had the wrong foot on the bag."

Well, that stopped Leo, and he went back to the dugout, trying to decide for himself just exactly what went wrong in his argument with Gorman. Then it dawned on him, and he rushed back out to the field. "Look, Tom," he said, "you've been umpiring in the big leagues for five or six years now. You mean to tell me that nobody ever told you that it didn't make any difference which foot the first baseman has on the bag?"

As a class, umpires are tireless storytellers, and one of the best was Jocko Conlan, who was five-seven, left-handed, and as Irish as Finian's Rainbow. Jocko added a lot of rich pages to baseball's anthology of humor. Some of his National-League squabbles with Frank Frisch and Leo Durocher were like vaudeville acts. He threw them out of the games many times, but only for just cause.

Once, when Frisch was managing the Pirates against the Giants on a stifling day in the Polo Grounds, he called for time and walked down to home plate from the third-base coaching box. "Jocko," asked Frank, "put me out of the game."

"What for?" asked Conlan.

"Because," said Frisch, "I can't stand this heat and I can't stand those .225 hitters I got. Besides, my feet are killing me. I want to go home and sit by my petunias."

Conlan, honorable man that he was, refused.

The first time I ever met Jocko, he called a strike on me and I stepped out of the box, making small animal noises. "That was no strike," I moaned.

"The next one is," he said, mildly.

I don't remember whether it was or not, but I swung anyway. You didn't take chances with Jocko.

One of Jocko's fondest memories was of the day he outsmarted a bloodthirsty crowd at Ebbets Field. It so happened that Bobby Bragan, who later managed the Braves, was then a young catcher for the Dodgers, and he was on first base when Pete Reiser tried to stretch a double with two out against the Chicago Cubs.

Reiser was out on a close play at third, and since the slower Bragan had not yet crossed the plate Conlan ruled that the Dodger run didn't count. Durocher charged out of the Dodger dugout and kicked dirt on Jocko's pants. Jocko kicked back. Beer bottles began to fly.

"Get out to second base or you'll be killed," yelled Charlie Grimm, the manager of the Cubs, but Jocko stood his ground. Police finally quieted the crowd.

After the game, the police wanted to give Jocko an escort to the nearest subway, but he felt that such a move would only encourage more serious fan reaction. So, suddenly, a man stepped through the exit gate from Ebbets Field wearing a tan suit, straw hat, bow tie, and two-toned shoes. It was Conlan, who walked safely past a mob of three thousand fans, looking for a guy in a blue suit.

Jocko had a temper you could fry fish on. He was unorthodox in his approach to his profesion. No one could ever say of Jocko that he didn't want to become involved. If Charlie Dressen had listened to him in 1951, Bobby Thomson might never have hit that historic home run for the Giants. As Dressen motioned to his bullpen, Jocko shook his head. "You're bringing in what? Branca? A fast-ball pitcher?"

Years later, Dressen did listen to him. In Milwaukee, Charlie was about to remove pitcher Bob Hendley. Jocko wandered out to the mound. "Whaddya wanta make a change for?" he asked. "He's pitching good." The astonished Dressen listened, and maybe, just maybe, he remembered that fateful day at the Polo Grounds in 1951. Charlie changed his mind. Hendley stayed in the game and threw a shutout.

13. Big League, Little League

I AGREE WITH Yogi Berra, who once said that Little League baseball is a very good thing because it keeps the parents off the streets.

Sure, parents get in the way. That's why they're parents. But as a father of a former Little-Leaguer, I think there are a number of things you can do to help your youngster if he is not in the starting lineup. You can invite the kid who is playing in front of him over to your house the night before a game, and serve him a rotten meal. Or you can volunteer to drive the car pool that day, and just not bother to pick that boy up.

Listen, it is hard not to get involved when your child is out there, fulfilling your hopes and dreams. My youngest son was the one who took after me. I was proud of him. In their championship game one year he struck out three times. And in the final inning, with the bases loaded, he let a ground ball go right through his legs to let in the winning run.

It was a great feeling for me, and I know he felt the

same way, as we walked to our car together while the other parents threw eggs and garbage at us and broke in our windshield.

If you don't care to take the game quite so seriously, that attitude is all right, too. You have to remember what the country was like before we had Little Leagues. Berra, the great Yankee catcher, who later managed the Yankees and the Mets, recalled: "When I was a kid we didn't have no lighted stadiums. We didn't always have nine to a side. We'd play with four kids, two on a side, and sometimes if we had only three we made that do, too. One would pitch, one hit and one shag. We'd do it for hours."

Possibly the greatest tribute ever paid to Little League baseball came in September of 1964, in Houston, on a night when the Phillies were in the process of blowing a pennant. A baby-faced rookie named Joe Morgan had beaten the Phillies with a bloop single in the last of the ninth. By the time Gene Mauch, the manager of the Phillies, got to the locker room he found several of his players bellying up to the buffet table, stuffing their faces.

"WE GOT BEAT," screamed Mauch, "by a guy who looks LIKE A LITTLE-LEAGUER." So saying, and with a mighty sweep of his arm, Mauch cleared the table. Barbecued spareribs, cold cuts, watermelon slices, potato salad all went flying, spattering the street clothes hanging in the nearest lockers. "Boy," said one player, "the food sure goes fast around here."

Let me assure you, there is nothing wrong in being a Little-Leaguer or even looking like one. The endurance of the sport depends on the very young.

On his last visit to Yankee Stadium, his voice reduced to a hoarse whisper by the cancer that was killing him,

Babe Ruth urged the parents of the country, "Start him when he's young, teach him to play baseball when he's four years old." How Babe arrived at that age isn't clear, but no doubt he just considered three to be too immature.

When Ty Cobb, his own days numbered, took a final look around him at the game he loved, he, too, made a plea to young America: "Boys," he said, "strive to master the lost arts of a great game. Unless you dedicate yourself to that task now, as the old-timers die off one by one, they will have vanished forever."

Ruth and Cobb and the guardians of the game knew something the critics cannot understand: that there was never a game more ideally suited than baseball to the soaring spirit, the boundless energy of the eternal child. "With a bat and a ball and his imagination," Branch Rickey once said, "a boy is a complete team."

Today, of course, Rickey would have amended that statement to read, "a boy . . . or a girl . . ."

No one ever spoke more lyrically about the game than Rickey, the man who invented the farm system, discovered Dizzy Dean, brought Jackie Robinson across the color line and never took a drink in his life, even though he once managed the St. Louis Browns. Rickey understood kids and knew why they were important to baseball. He also knew why baseball was important to them. "Leisure is wonderful in creative hands," he said. "It accounts for great architecture, great paintings, and great music. Leisure, however, is a damnable thing in the hands of an adolescent."

Added Rickey: "Baseball is a romance that begins when a boy is very young; it brings a diamond into his vision where the bases are fixed and the outfield is endless."

My own four kids—Leann, Steve, Sue Ann and

Bobby—grew up around ball parks. Like all kids, they had their heroes. After every game they wanted to go home with a different player.

When I was a preteen, we made do with a lump of something that passed for a baseball, and maybe a broom handle for a bat. We could always get up a game and there was never a problem finding a vacant lot—Rickey's endless outfield. In the forties and early fifties, America was still rich in vacant lots, the diamonds of our boyhood dreams. The great urban problems, the crisis of the inner cities to come, would change all that.

Today it is far easier to find a mini-stadium than a vacant lot. Kids thrive on the scale-model big-league world around them: bleachers, scoreboards, press boxes, p.a. systems. They cultivate the mannerisms . . . the tap of the bat to knock dirt off rubber-cleated shoes, hitching the belt, rubbing rosin on their hands, spitting bubble-gum juice across the plate.

I have no interest in getting into the question of whether Little-League baseball does more good than harm, if there is such a question. I like what Doug Rader, who played third base for Houston and San Diego, once said about his boyhood in Northbrook, Illinois: "When I was a kid my dad, and a few of the other dads, maybe four or five of them, helped out with out neighborhood team. We had a little park across the road from a tavern. They'd dump all the equipment and say, 'Okay, you boys get together and choose up teams and play.' Then they'd go across the street and have a couple of beers and let us play. Every hour or so my dad would stick his head out the door and walk to the edge of the road and rub his hand across his shirt a few times—you know, flashing me the hit-and-run sign, or something. That's how we practiced. The kid who has the ability, the desire, if he plays it will surface. You can't force it."

Personally, I think Little League is valuable because it reminds us that the Parkers and the Winfields and the Reggie Jacksons are getting paid millions to play a game that small boys play for free. Which is one reason I find it hard to give kids advice, and so do most big-leaguers. The kids will learn soon enough that they have to find a style of their own.

For example, Pete Rose doesn't recommend his base-sliding technique, which is usually head-first, but he thinks it is a safer way to slide, on the theory that you are less likely to break your belly than your ankle or your leg. Also, you usually get your picture in the paper.

When someone asked Doug Rader what advice he would give a kid, he suggested that they eat bubble-gum cards. "Not the gum," he said, "but the cards. They have lots of good information on them."

Players are not always comfortable offering advice to youngsters, usually for reasons that are well-founded. Henry Aaron was asked once if he would like to teach the art of hitting to young players. "I'd like it very much," he replied, "but I wouldn't teach 'em to do it my way. I'd try to help a young player with his own style—not mine.

"I've got a hitch in my swing and I hit off the wrong foot. I've done it the wrong way my whole career."

Mike Marshall, who made his reputation as a relief pitcher who could work every day, urges kid pitchers not to experiment with trick pitches. What he won't do is tell them how HE did it. "On national television one season," he said, "I demonstrated how to throw a screwball. I specifically warned that no youngster under the age of fifteen should attempt to place his arm in this position because of possible injury.

"Immediately, I was deluged with letters from kids saying how they were working on their screwball and would I please tell them more." He wouldn't, and he didn't.

If there is one serious piece of advice I could give to kids, it would be this: *swing the bat*. Little League develops pitchers and discourages hitters. A ball is easier to throw than to hit at that age—at any age, actually. Nothing kills interest like failure. The kid who keeps striking out considers himself a failure, and he looks for something else to do.

Mike Marshall is right. A manager should not let his kid pitchers throw a screwball or a curve ball. Not only because of the risk to a young arm, but because such pitches take the fun out of the game for the kids who can't hit them.

I would tell a manager something else: No matter what the score, or the situation, let your hitters swing on a three-ball and no-strike count. Chances are he'll get a pitch he can handle, and if he does why shouldn't he swing? He's there to have fun. And a bat is no fun unless you swing it. Trust me.

In one respect, the Little Leagues achieved something that the big fellows never have: a really international World Series. An English writer, Brian Glanville, of London, once commented on this obvious American conceit: "It's very quaint. One team in the United States plays another team in the United States and is declared 'World' champion. We used to call the game 'rounders,' you know."

For years, the Little League World Series was regularly won by teams from Mexico, Taiwan, and Japan. There

was a memorable scene in 1958, when a band of
ragamuffins from Monterrey won the championship for
the second year in a row.

The Mexican pitcher, a five-six beanpole named
Hector Torres— who later made it to the majors as a
shortstop—walked halfway to home plate as the final
game came down to its last out. Mexico led, 10-1, over
Kankakee, Illinois, with the bases empty and two away.

Torres doffed his cap and bowed low to his catcher,
Carlos Trevino. *"Te dedico este bateador,"* he said. The
hitter, not understanding Spanish, didn't know he had
been insulted. Torres had said to his catcher: "I dedicate
this batter to you."

It was a lovely gesture, and I am saddened to note that
never in my entire career did a pitcher dedicate a hitter to
me.

I owe a debt to Little-League baseball, and the debt
should be acknowledged here and now. I was sitting by a
pool with Merle Harmon in Anaheim, taking the rays,
when Merle answered a call from Dennis Lewin, of
ABC, in New York.

When Merle returned to his seat, he grinned and said
ABC wanted me to fly to Williamsport, Pennsylvania, to
telecast the Little League World Series with Keith
Jackson.

I really didn't want to go. The Brewers had just
arrived for a series against the Angels, and this was my
first year (1973) of sharing the play-by-play with
Harmon. I didn't feel in a position to be asking for
favors. Also, working with a network, any network, was
not one of my obsessions. I was not then, or now, a goal-
oriented person.

Merle talked me into it. "You never know where it

might lead," he said. I flew across the country to Williamsport without even knowing what I would be paid—one thousand dollars, as it turned out. I did the Series with Keith and rejoined the Brewers.

A year later, ABC asked me to fly to New York to audition for the color spot on their Monday night baseball package, which would begin the next season. With Bob Prince, who was to do the play-by-play, I watched a silent videotape of a World Series game and recreated the action. They must have liked what they heard. I have been doing it ever since.

I guess that makes me another graduate of the Little Leagues.

PART V

Touching Some Extra Bases

In which he describes some of the great players he admired, and some whose paths he crossed, and some who were just his kind of dustball. And a few stories straight from the Hot Stove League.

"The basic idea behind this book was to cover my career and just talk about what a great guy I was. I don't see how we can miss."

14. A Few of My Friends, and Then Some

WHEN A TEAM he was managing ended its season in winter ball, Doug Rader made a point of saying goodbye to one of his pitchers in the clubhouse. He told the fellow, a kind of nutcake, that he intended to request his services at Hawaii, where Rader would skipper San Diego's top farm club the next season.

The pitcher shook his head. "The way my arm feels right now," he said, frowning, "I don't even know if I'll be playing next season."

Rader jabbed him in the chest with a finger. "I don't care if you can throw or not," he said. "Every team needs a sick individual on it, and for me you're *it*."

Known in his playing days as the Red Rooster, Rader did not mean sick-sick, as in unhealthy. He meant goofy, off-the-wall, unpredictable, *weird*. It is a role Doug played on every team that employed him. As I did.

For the most part, Rader—the ex-Padre, ex-Astro, lifelong snowflake—was correct. But more and more today's teams are making an effort, a conscious one, I think, to get along without that kind of free spirit. The teams I see now, in my role as a broadcaster, can best be described as well-behaved, well-dressed young men building a base for that day when their arms or legs give out.

I can sum them up in two words: basically boring.

That remark is not a complaint, mind you, just a comparison. The teams of my day were less colorful than those of Babe Ruth's day, but the gap wasn't nearly as wide. We specialized in miscellaneous characters and that-was-burlesque humor. Hardly a flight took place that did not produce a scuffle, some tipsy barbershop harmony, or the occasional scream of a hostess darting up the aisle.

You never doubted the truth of the stories you heard, and an explanation was seldom required. No one ever explained what Turk Farrell was doing one night chasing Jim Owens through the halls of a Philadelphia hotel, both of them naked as newborn babes. They had been members of the famed Dalton Gang with the Phillies, later traded to Houston.

Farrell claimed that Owens had stabbed him with one of those desk pens you dip in an inkwell, and he had a blue dot on his bare hip to prove it.

In the 1960s, the cutting personal reference was as much a part of the game as hitting into a double play. A young catcher who had a low opinion of a veteran player's intellect didn't hesitate to let him know it: "Norm," he told him, "if it wasn't for baseball you'd be selling apples on a corner."

When a rookie infielder, a bonus baby, found himself in a terrible batting slump, an old hand advised him to switch to a lighter bat. The rookie said, yeah, with a lighter bat he could get around on the ball faster. The veteran said, "No, but it'll be easier to carry back to the dugout after you strike out."

I still hear that kind of affectionate cruelty in the bantering among the players of the 1980s. These players are smarter. I am not sure that they are better educated. And I would be reluctant to say that they love the game less than the players did when I broke in. But there is no doubt in my mind that they take themselves more seriously. Big money has that effect on people. It is like making out your will.

Today's players are more settled, more secure in their planning. Most of them have already picked out other careers. They have investments. They want to be seen and treated as responsible people. When the players board a plane, you see so many three-piece suits it looks like they have evacuated the offices of E. F. Hutton. You get the impression that management now picks a roster with the idea of getting the best possible team photograph.

When I was making around ten thousand dollars a year, you would begin to think about an off-season job in September. You thought in terms of unloading a beer truck.

Baseball has gone through such cycles before. The teams may go back to looking for players out of the Gashouse Gang, or the stick-it-in-his-ear school. Baseball people are great copycats. They will all try whatever wins for someone else. If one club finds a guy with hair all over his body and one eye in the middle of his forehead, and he eats glass and hits .400, soon you are going to see a lot of hairy, one-eyed glass-eaters around the league.

For now some of the fun is gone, and you don't have

to hunt long or far to understand why. When even the
fringe players are knocking down a hundred grand a year,
and more, you are not encouraged to cut up and take
chances. In the past, it wasn't just the scrubs who horsed
around, it was the stars, Mantle, Mays, Aaron, Spahn,
who had the most laughs.

Of course, the conditions are not as favorable. You no
longer have the wooden floors in the clubhouse, where
you could nail a guy's shoes to the deck. Even the old
bullpens are gone. Now they are all in the open, so the
fans—and the manager—can see whatever is going on.

We used to run a closed society out there. Most of the
people in the bullpen didn't care about starting. At least,
we said we didn't. When a regular came down just to
visit we chased him away. I mean, we protected our *turf*.
It was like driving the snakes out of Ireland. Once, with
the Phillies, Chris Short slipped down to the bullpen to
hide from Gene Mauch before a game. He settled
himself in a wheelbarrow and took a nap. While he slept,
the rest of us tied him to the barrow, working like rodeo
cowboys, using the ropes and chains the ground crew
kept to drag the infield. When he woke up, and
discovered he couldn't move, Chris yelled and cursed
and carried on something fierce. We finally let him out
fifteen minutes after the game had started.

A statement ought to be made about baseball humor.
At its liveliest, it is crude and shameless and irreverent.
It is army humor, with more sweat. For a few hours every
day nothing exists outside the ball park. You are thrown
together in this tight, remote, womanless (most of the
time) world, and whether or not you like each other a
bond is forged.

The team is everything. You are glad to belong, to be a

part of it, speeding along with it, or stumbling, as the case may be. Your body may be on a bus or a plane or in a hotel, but your mind is in the locker room, and the laughs grow out of this experience.

Two examples: In the early 1960s, a writer for *Sports Illustrated* heard that John Bateman, a catcher for the Houston Astros, was one of the funniest men in the big leagues. He followed the team for a week or two and kept asking for examples of Bateman's wit. The players assured him that the supply was endless, but nothing popped quickly to mind.

At last, one night behind the batting cage, an outfielder named Howie Goss approached the writer. "I've thought of a story that typifies Bateman's sense of humor," he said, "but I'm not sure you can use it."

"Don't worry about that," the man from *Sports Illustrated* said, whipping out his pad and pen. "I can fix the language."

Goss shrugged. "Well, one day X (the team's most popular player) was sitting on the crapper"—the writer's pen stopped in mid-stroke—"and Bateman called out, 'Hey, kid, did you weigh yourself before you got on there?'

"X said, no, why, and Bateman answered, 'In case you fall in, we want to know how much shit we have to fish out before we get to you.'"

The writer put his pad back in his hip pocket, gave a feeble laugh, and walked away.

A story out of Seattle a few years ago, when an expansion team was trying to survive there, captures some of the *esprit* of the bullpen. In the late innings of a losing game the bullpen was busy, as usual.

Ray Oyler, a reserve infielder, was warming up one of

the pitchers when he missed a sinker, and it caught him right on the cup. The pitch didn't bounce or tip his glove, it simply landed a direct hit. You hardly ever hear of that happening. The "twang" of ball striking metal echoed into the stands.

Oyler pitched forward, almost in slow motion, like a Tom-and-Jerry cartoon, and on all fours he started crawling toward the dugout, unable to cry out in pain or even make a sound. The players in the bullpen began to laugh, and the action came to a stop. He kept crawling. The laughter spread to the guys on the bench. Soon they were out of control. In the stands, the fans looked on, fascinated. Oyler reached the dugout, pulled himself onto a rail and threw up.

They were getting beat, and on the field people were running around the bases, and the Seattle players couldn't stop laughing. The manager, Joe Schultz, had to take off his glasses, wipe his eyes, and hide his head in the arm of his jacket.

The stadiums are bigger and fancier, the players higher paid and more secure, the fans less worshipful. But the baseball mentality hasn't changed in a hundred years.

Trust me. This is no mournful wail for a game that once was and will never be again. Memory can be a con man. Nostalgia should go back where it came from. The crackers in the ole cracker barrel were usually stale. Penny candy rotted your teeth just as fast when it didn't cost a quarter. Trains were dusty and bumpy and you were always getting a cinder in your eye.

As a product, baseball may be better than ever. I don't think so, but who knows? It is tempting to compare players, teams, and eras, and part of the fun is knowing that no one can prove us wrong. The arguments are forever. It is like judging pretty girls on a beach. The last one to walk by wins.

I am not sure when it dawned on me that the 1960s are the good old days to the young players of the 1980s. To this generation, Aaron, Allen, Mathews, Spahn, and Gibson, even Bo Belinsky, who lost more games than he won, are part of the mythology of the sport. I don't remember growing older. When did they?

It begins to sound like a singer or comic doing a Las Vegas lounge shtick when you say that, in the end, what lasts are the friendships you made. After you have blown the money and forgotten the batting averages and lost track of the wins and losses, the only thing that counts is the people.

Now I might not go quite that far. I knew some players whose friendship you would not have wished on J. R. Ewing, and who seemed to remember the exact count on every hit in their career. But I consider myself fortunate to have played on teams with men who, at what they did, were among the best, or the strangest, or the funniest who ever lived. I've touched on some of them earlier, but here they are again, a few of however many there were:

The Hammer

Henry Louis Aaron, as he is known in the *Baseball Register*, was the most underrated player of my time, and his. It may seem strange to make such a claim on behalf of the man who broke Babe Ruth's lifetime home run record, and went through the longest countdown the game has ever known.

But that's the point. Not until he collected his six hundredth homer in 1972, at the age of thirty-seven, did the press and fans catch on to what his opponents had always known: that Hank Aaron was one of a kind.

He had three things going against him: 1) He didn't play in New York or Los Angeles; 2) he was too predictable, meaning that most years he would get his forty homers, drive in a hundred runs and hit .320 . . . no surprises here; 3) he lacked showmanship. His cap didn't fly off when he caught a fly ball, and after a game you never saw him eat twenty hot dogs and wash them down with a six-pack of beer.

When Henry reached the majors in 1954, Ted Williams and Stan Musial were already legends. Willie Mays and Mickey Mantle were coming into their own. Aaron had been in the league eight or ten years— certainly it was after I had joined the Braves in 1962— before his name was mentioned with any of those. We would argue his case with out-of-town writers, and their eyes would glaze over.

I asked him once if he felt slighted. He said, "What difference does it make?"

I said, "You may not believe in beauty contests, but if you're in one you want the judges to vote you purty."

He shrugged.

I was a broadcaster with the Brewers, in 1976, when Aaron played out his string in Milwaukee, and hit the last of his 755 home runs. If you were to ask me what was the most remarkable thing about him, I would not single out any of the obvious points, his endurance, his power, his wrists. He had the quickest wrists I ever saw. Baseball scouts talked about Aaron's wrists the way male moviegoers of another time talked about Betty Grable's legs.

But none of it impressed me so much as how stable Henry has been. With the possible exception of Stan

Musial, it isn't likely that anyone played twenty years in the majors and changed less than Henry Aaron. For a fellow who came out of Southern poverty, who was one of the last players signed out of the Negro Leagues, and who met his share of prejudice on the way up, Henry seemed to have no rage in him.

One anecdote followed Aaron all through his career. The story revealed something about his nature. It also revealed how hard it was for the writers to come up with anecdotes about Henry.

During the 1957 World Series, the Yankee catcher, Yogi Berra, noticed that Aaron held the bat in a way contrary to the usual baseball practice. "Hey," said Berra, from his squat, "you got the bat facing the wrong way. Turn it around so you can see the trademark."

Henry continued to stare at the pitcher's mound. Out the side of his mouth, he said, "Didn't come up here to read. Came up here to hit."

Other players would marvel when they heard that Henry actually hit cross-handed when he signed with the Indianapolis Clowns. That is like playing a piano in handcuffs. In his first day in spring training, he began rifling base hits all over the park and the manager asked why he gripped the bat the way he did. Henry said it was the only way he knew.

Henry never confused chatter with conversation. He liked his privacy and his natural caution was sometimes taken for distrust.

Once he sat on a stool in front of his locker, an hour or so before game time, sorting two baskets filled with fan mail. His attention was diverted by a mild commotion at the clubhouse door.

"You can't come in here," an attendant was saying,

loudly, to a fellow who turned out to be Leroy Nieman, the sports artist.

"I just want to make a few sketches of Aaron," said Nieman, looking past the guard and catching the eye of Henry, who said nothing.

"We got a rule," said the attendant. "You can't come in here."

Nieman unzipped a leather case and began removing a sketchbook and other implements. "Okay," he said, agreeably, "then I'll just draw him right here, from the doorway." Twenty or thirty feet from his subject, he calmly sketched away.

Henry glanced up now and then as he disposed of the letters, flipping them into one basket or the other. Several minutes passed. Then the clubhouse man reappeared and motioned to the artist: "Hank says it's okay for you to come in."

Nieman pulled up a chair and without a word returned to his work. Aaron followed each stroke with interest. After a few minutes, he craned his neck to inspect the sketch. "You're not getting me," he said, with firmness. "You're not getting me."

"Take it easy," said Nieman. "You don't hit a homer every time up. I'm not finished."

More strokes. More color came alive on the sheet. "That's it," said Henry, his voice rising. "Now you got me. You got me."

When Nieman finished, Henry asked if he could have the sketch. "I don't give my work away," he was told.

Aaron looked startled. "People usually give me things like that," he said.

"I don't," said Nieman. "If you want mine you pay for it." He has a rack of black hair and a mustache that divides his face in half, and he is not intimidated by athletes. He grinned and added, "But I'll make a deal with you."

Nieman was in Atlanta to teach art classes to ghetto kids. He offered to trade the sketch if Aaron would pose for one of his classes. Henry agreed. You can guess how the kids reacted when their model turned out to be the home run king.

Henry did not talk much, even in the clubhouse, and what you learned about his early life came from stray remarks, spaced far apart. He was one of eight children, supported by a father who worked on the drydocks in Mobile. At eighteen, he joined the Indianapolis Clowns, where the meal money was two dollars a day. The players ate mostly out of grocery stores, on lunchmeat sandwiches.

He weighed 180 when he reached the big leagues, and he weighed the same when he retired. He was a small man as home run hitters go. He lacked the muscle or power of a Frank Robinson or a Frank Howard or a Willie Mays. He drove the ball with perfect wrists and perfect timing.

People used to say that the difference between Mays and Aaron was this: Willie attacked the game; Henry got it to cooperate. He was as smooth and effortless as a swan gliding along a lake.

Not many fans ever knew that the Giants could have had Mays and Aaron in the same outfield. Both the Giants and the Braves made bids after scouting him with the Clowns. Both wanted to start him in Class C, but the Braves offered him a Class A contract, worth two hundred dollars more a month. And for that difference, the Giants lost the man who would one day hit more home runs than Babe Ruth.

The Good-bye Kid

No player was more stubborn or more talented than Richie Allen, but he made up for it by being misunderstood.

Allen played for the Phillies, twice, the Cardinals, Dodgers, White Sox, and Oakland. Atlanta owned his contract at one time, but he never reported. He was described as a rebel, a militant, a truant, and a night walker. He was accused of having a drinking problem, an attitude problem and a keeping-track-of-time problem.

My kind of guy.

In truth, there was nothing wrong with Richie Allen's heart, or his instincts, but he felt a powerful resistance to having his mind made up for him. If he was pushed he tended to push back.

In baseball, this is the quickest way I know to be labeled a troublemaker. Once the label is attached it is hell to get off. Allen was the classic example of the guy who felt free only while he was playing the game. The rest of the time he wanted the world to go away. His clock started when the first pitch was thrown.

The Phillies signed Richie out of high school, at seventeen. He had the biceps of a heavyweight fighter and a thirty-inch waist and he could crush a baseball. He was just a kid, but so strong that people forgot to treat him like one—until he reached the majors. The wrong time and place.

I understood that part of him. We sat and talked and drank far into the night when we were teammates in Philadelphia, and he told me things I don't think he shared with many others.

His mother drove him to the airport, in Pittsburgh, when he caught the plane for his first trip to spring training. He was from the town of Wampum, in the same area of Pennsylvania that produced Joe Namath.

All the way to the airport, his mother gave Richie instructions on how to act. She had raised eight kids by doing day work and taking in laundry and sewing on the side. When you heard Richie talk about his mother, it was a hard image to square with all the headaches he had caused his managers.

"She kept telling me to remember my training at home," he said. "She told me to be sure and change my underwear every day. She told me to be careful what I ate. She also said she had packed a Bible and she handed me a slip of paper with instructions on what verses to read."

Richie had never been on a plane before. "I was scared stiff," he said. "The weather was rough. He knuckleballed all the way to Florida. Then when I got off in Clearwater I saw in the terminal that there were separate doors for white and colored. I had never seen this before and I was confused and frightened. If Bobby Del Greco (then a Philly player) hadn't come along and helped me, I probably would have gone back home."

He didn't join the team at its hotel in downtown Clearwater. He was taken to the home of a black woman and given a room. "After a while," he said, "they felt I might have been lonesome and they sent me company. It was Marcelino Lopez, a Cuban pitcher. We were great company for each other. He didn't speak English and I didn't speak Spanish."

In baseball, reputations are made or ruined in incidents that are small and sometimes silly. It isn't hard to pinpoint the exact moment that things started to go wrong for Allen. He was in his second season with the Phillies, and the team had landed at the airport in Los Angeles.

Frank Thomas, a veteran outfielder, large and a little klunky, flipped a quarter at Richie and said, "Hey, boy, take my bags!" He was only joking and meant no harm. But Allen was only twenty-two and not yet ready for that kind of humor.

That was the background for what happened a few days later at the batting cage in Philadelphia. Johnny Callison yelled across the cage to Thomas, calling him "Lurch," after a goonlike character on the television series *The Addams Family*. Thomas thought Allen had said it.

He yelled back, "There's no fence around me, Fifteen [Allen's number]. You may get a meal out of me, but I'll get a sandwich out of you."

Richie sprang at him. His punches came in a cluster, knocking Thomas down, and Frank responded by striking Richie on the shoulder with a bat. At that point the other players pulled them apart.

Later, in the clubhouse, Gene Mauch announced that anyone talking about the fight would be fined fifteen hundred dollars. Which explains why few of the details leaked out. Shortly, Thomas, whose gawky enthusiasm endeared him to the fans, was traded, and the boos began to swell for Richie Allen.

If ever a town had a love-hate relationship with a player, this was one in the making. They cheered his home runs and game-winning hits. But the boos deepened with each contract fight, each newspaper blast, each infraction.

The year after Richie injured his hand, with the papers and the fans thriving on the team's turmoil, Mauch moved to restore discipline. He ordered every player to be in his position on the field at 5:00 P.M., with no talking permitted. He had also appointed Allen as his captain.

Richie saw the move as an attempt to get him to accept responsibility. So he did. He went to Gene and told him that the players resented being treated like children. Recalls Richie: "He said that for every day I wasn't in position at five he would fine me a hundred and fifty dollars. It was a principle with me. I didn't show up—and I paid."

It became a team ritual, Allen arriving late or not at all for batting practice. The management was groping for an answer. The team knew it needed a happy, or at least an interested, Richie Allen to win. He was a threat to win the triple crown any year he was healthy. He was their big man. But only one man knew what went on inside his head, and Richie wasn't telling.

As a measure of his importance to the club, it is worth noting that on the night I was traded back to the Braves, in 1967, most of the concern in the clubhouse was for how Richie would react.

While I was driving in three runs with two doubles to give us a 9-8 win over the Cubs, in the second game of a doubleheader, the writers were being handed a press release. I was going to Atlanta for Gene Oliver.

As we trooped into the clubhouse, Gene Mauch motioned to a reporter, and said: "Tell those other guys not to tell anybody. Let them whoop it up a while before I call him in."

We stood around for ten minutes, shaking hands and snapping the tabs off cans of beer, before the word came that Mauch wanted to see me. In the *Daily News* the next afternoon, Bill Conlin wrote about Richie: "Allen was feeling desolate, even though he had just struck a homer that will become legend long after Connie Mack Stadium is torn down. Rich Allen is a man, but right then he felt like crying. You could see it in his eyes.

" 'I wish they were sending me instead,' he said softly. 'I wish they were sending us both. He was the best friend I've got on this club and now they're sending him away. That's the thing that bugs me about this game. You make a friend like him and then he's gone.' "

I know. Reading those words, you almost expect someone to lower his head and say, "Wherever he is, he'll be better off. He's at peace now."

Bo Geste

When I joined the Phillies in the spring of 1966, I knew Robert (Bo) Belinsky by reputation. *Everybody* knew Bo by reputation. You could not dislike him. He was a gassy guy, as Bo himself might put it, and probably did.

He was a man for all seasons: bon vivant, pool hustler, dog fancier, ladies' man and occasional left-handed pitcher.

It was often said of Belinsky, but never by Bo himself, that he had squandered his talent, had a great arm but not the discipline to use it and, finally, had thrown away his career for all the women he loved. Bo did not see things quite that way.

"I have never considered myself a great talent," I heard him say once. "I think I have gotten more publicity for doing less than any player who ever lived."

He may have been right. In his first five seasons in the majors, Bo won a total of twenty-five games and was traded three times. One way or another, he was seldom out of the headlines.

As a rookie with the Angels, he reported to Palm Springs a week late, called a press conference to explain that he had been delayed by a pool tournament, and then demanded a thousand-dollar raise.

That was for openers. In May he pitched a no-hitter against Baltimore and went on to win his first six games, all but standing baseball on its ear. There was not to be a flashier, more popular debut until Fernando Valenzuela came along in 1981.

Within a month Belinsky had bought a new Cadillac and acquired, more or less in order, a fiancée (Mamie Van Doren), a business agent, a lawyer and the readership of Walter Winchell. All on an annual salary of seven thousand dollars. He might have conquered the world.

"Instead," Bo said, "the no-hitter I pitched actually cost me money. I had to buy drinks for everyone. It was like making a hole-in-one."

In unrelated adventures, he once threw a blonde out of his car at five in the morning, slugged a sixty-four-year-old sportswriter, married a former Playmate of the Year, and adopted a stray, part-cocker spaniel named Alfie.

The dog became the mascot of the Houston club and was given its own sandbox in the clubhouse. The players accepted Alfie as easily as they accepted Bo, although Barry Latman, a pitcher, asked wearily, "How am I going to explain to my wife that I got a locker next to a dog?"

For a while they were inseparable. His teammates joked that you could always tell them apart because Alfie was the one who was serious about baseball.

If much of Bo's career was a con, it was a harmless con that did injury to no one but Bo. Wherever he went he may not have won a lot of games, but he was good for the club because he kept the manager and the writers busy.

Bo was street-smart. To engage him in conversation was like catching Bernard Baruch on his park bench or Snoopy on his doghouse. He is the author of such philosophical gems as: "Happiness is a first-class pad, good wheels, an understanding manager and a little action."

He had a fine eye for caricature. It was Bo who pointed out that Philadelphia fans "would boo a funeral." Hawaii "is where the goodies are." And when Houston threatened to ship him to its top farm club, he shrugged: "Oklahoma City is nice, if you bring enough Alka-Seltzer."

The few times I caught Bo, he still had the lively arm and enough stuff to win. What he didn't have was the frame of mind, the intensity you found in a Spahn, a Gibson, or a Koufax. He enjoyed the cheers, but didn't need them as a steady diet.

Whether Bo was overrated in the romance league, I can't say, but I saw him in action and can assure you that he did not believe his own publicity. "If I did everything they said I did," he confided, "I'd be in a jar at the Harvard Medical School."

In Los Angeles, Bo was often in the company of such beautiful women as Mamie, Ann-Margret and Tina Louise, when he was not in the company of Walter Winchell, the famed gossip columnist who had taken him under his wing.

That era is gone forever. The line between sports and the arts has been so blurred that the two sides are no longer so enthralled with each other. Babe Ruth once made the Broadway scene, and Hollywood swept up Bo, but it doesn't happen that way anymore.

Bo still had the telegram Winchell sent him, after he had been quoted on a road trip as saying that he knew his Hollywood friends would drop him if he stopped winning. Winchell printed the wire in his syndicated column and possibly sent copies to Mr. and Mrs. America and all the ships at sea:

"DEAR BO:

"YOU DON'T KNOW ME VERY WELL YET, KID. I'M THE GUY WHO PREFERS TO BE WITH LOSERS. I'M THE GUY WHO WROTE 'THERE IS NOTHING AS LONELY AS A LOSER'S DRESSING ROOM.' I WOULD LIKE IT VERY MUCH IF YOU NEVER WON ANOTHER GAME SO I COULD CONVINCE YOU OF THAT.

"A CHAMPION IS ONE WHO GETS UP FOR ONE MORE ROUND. IF THEY EVER KICK YOU OUT OF BASEBALL FOR BEING A BAD BOY YOU WILL FIND OUT THAT I PRACTICE WHAT I PREACH: TO WIT, A REAL FRIEND IS ONE WHO WALKS IN WHEN THE REST OF THE WORLD WALKS OUT. SIGNED. WALTER WINCHELL."

It was beautiful. It was also just about the last word Bo heard from Winchell as he began his descent to the minors, the Phillies, Houston, the minors, the Cardinals, the minors, the White Sox, and out of baseball.

I doubt that he left the game with any serious regrets. Baseball was never his passion, it just paid his motel bill.

If he made no other lasting contribution to the sport, Bo destroyed most of the universal theories about sex and baseball.

As Bo remembered it, managers were always telling him not to engage in indoor recreation on nights before he pitched. They recommended that he rest and save himself for after the game. But Belinsky had a problem. He had no interest after the game. Neither the spirit nor the flesh was willing.

Besides, he had rejected the night-before theory after his no-hitter with the Angels. He was still looking for the girl who had left his bed that morning. "This was some kind of good-luck girl," he recalled, his dark eyes glowing. "But she disappeared from the picture. I'd met her at a steak house. Here I was with an ordinary secretary, probably—no flashy gal in any way, but a very lean, beautiful gal. And this was how I trained for my no-hitter, and it came in."

Bo never found her, proof of which is that he never had another winning season.

Horseman, Pass This Way

I am reminded of Inspector Clouseau, the Peter Sellers character, who was always being ambushed by his valet, Kato.

In St. Louis, I had a roommate like Kato, except he was taller and balder and less Oriental-looking. For a guy who later went straight, and became a big-league manager, Roger Craig had as much deviltry in him as the worst of us. His sense of humor ran to Halloween pranks.

No matter where we were, or what we were doing, Roger had this compulsion to scare people. He would turn over trash cans as you walked down the street, or thump the side of the car as you drove. God forbid you should have to get up at three in the morning to use the toilet. When you eased out of the bathroom, he would be pressed against the wall, on the other side of the door, ready to let out a bloodcurdling scream. Or he might throw a wastebasket across the room.

Even when you knew it was coming, and braced yourself, the experience was still hard on the nerves. At such times I would ask myself if this was any kind of life for a grown person.

But it was easy to forgive Craig his occasional looniness. He was bright, he had guts, he could pitch and he had once lost twenty games for the New York Mets, sixteen of them in a row, and you were inclined to give him a little benefit of the doubt. I mean, he had suffered for his art.

Craig came over from the Mets in the middle of the 1964 season, pitched well out of the bullpen as the Cards drove to the pennant, and then won the fourth game of the World Series against the Yankees in relief.

Craig's looks were deceptive. He was tall and gangly, with a long, sad, gentle face. But he was physically tough, an outdoorsman, and good company if you didn't let him sneak up on you.

On our first road trip to Los Angeles, Roger invited me to stay at his home. He owned a riding stable nearby, and the next morning he insisted that we go horseback riding. Naturally, I had no proper clothes with me, so Roger loaned me a shirt and a pair of his Levi's. Craig is six-six. I'm six-one. When we walked up to the stables I must have looked like Emmett Kelly. I caught the stable hands exchanging looks. They were thinking, "Get a load of this Elwood."

Roger picked out one of his daughter's horses for me and we started down a trail, which was actually a flood-control ditch. We found ourselves at a parking lot on one of the main streets, and we tied the horses to some cars and walked into a restaurant to have lunch.

Craig sauntered inside like he was the sheriff of Dodge City. Everyone else was wearing suits and ties and we were in Levi's with horseshit on our shoes. I never did get my wingtips clean.

We ordered a sandwich and a couple beers, then headed home. On the way back, Roger began to tell me what a great trick horse he was riding, how he could get off and the horse was trained to follow him.

With that he said, "Watch this, Uke," and he swung his leg over the back of the horse and dropped to the ground. Thirty seconds later, the horse bolted away and headed for home, his hooves kicking up small clouds of dust as the distance between us widened.

Roger did a double take and said, "Jeezus, Uke, quick, get off your horse so I can go catch him."

I said, "Your ass. Go catch him yourself. If I get off this horse I know what will happen to me."

He walked alongside us for the next two miles, bitching every step of the way.

Little Big Man

I learned a long time ago never to get into a fight with a person who comes up to your waist. You never know where their punches will land, and God forbid they should bite.

No one has ever accused Donald Davidson of not fighting fair, not in a forty-five-year career that has made him one of the most distinctive figures in baseball. No one in the sport has a bigger heart, not a player or manager—need I include umpires and owners?—and that is a lot to say for someone who stands four feet, two inches high.

With his feisty nature, Donald stands out in a crowd, especially if the crowd is on its hands and knees. In such a case he would probably pass out his business card, which is one inch by two inches and resembles a large postage stamp.

It is safe to say that among National-League players, and among the fans of Milwaukee and Atlanta, no front-office type is as well known, or as popular, as Donald.

One afternoon he strolled through the streets of downtown Milwaukee with John Quinn, the general manager of the Braves. Every few feet a friend, or a fan, would stop Donald and greet him. Quinn looked on with growing amusement, then asked one stranger, "Tell me, how did you recognize Donald in his dark glasses?"

For forty years, Davidson gave his all to the Braves, first as a clubhouse boy, in the days when Lefty Grove was their star pitcher and the team traveled by train. Then he moved up to publicist, assistant to the president, and traveling secretary. His odyssey with the team took him from Boston to Milwaukee to Atlanta. He was their link to the past. Hall of Famers, managers, owners, entire cities had come and gone. But Donald went with the franchise, like the Indian head on the team uniform.

Then the unthinkable happened. In April of 1976, Donald was fired by Ted Turner, the team's new owner, who suffered what he himself later admitted was a colossal mental lapse. It was as if someone had bought the original thirteen American colonies and fired the American eagle.

As traveling secretary for the Braves, responsible for the team's housing, Donald always occupied a suite where he served as host to the press and other dig-

nitaries. I guess what offended Ted was the fact that
Donald could have slept in a bureau drawer, much less a
suite.

But word of Donald's luxury reached Turner in a bad
mood. The Braves were in a losing streak, as they often
are. He decided that if standard rooms were good enough
for the players, they ought to be good enough for
Donald. Quite possibly, Turner didn't know that the
Braves weren't paying for those suites. They are tossed
in by hotels, grateful for the team's business.

Even if Atlanta had been paying, you had to wonder
how Turner could hand out millions to players like Andy
Messersmith and Claudell Washington, and try to reduce
the living standards of a class act like Donald Davidson.

One word led to another, as they usually do, and the
Braves and Donald parted company, after four decades.
The next time Turner saw the little man, he had been
hired for the same duties at more money by the Houston
Astros, and the wrath of the public had alerted Ted to the
size of his error.

"I guess I was wrong, Donald," he apologized.
"Even my little boy gave me hell when he heard about
it."

"It's okay," said Davidson. "You did me a favor."

The firing of a publicist, a traveling secretary, or even
a general manager doesn't usually attract much attention.
But Donald was different. Opinion was solidly against
Turner, a famous yachtsman who has won the America's
Cup and other great prizes.

But the general reaction was that Turner was probably
accustomed to tight quarters. He might even sleep in a
hammock. But he was in no position to compare himself
with Davidson. How many Hall of Famers has ever
dropped by his room for refreshments?

Had he ever been detained by Scotland Yard for looking at Buckingham Palace through binoculars from his hotel? When Donald did this in London, the British suspected that some alien ring working with an elf was trying to get information on the queen's movements.

All of which means that today Donald Davidson is smaller than life, if not more so. He is famous for his temper, his tireless spirit, and for winding up as the ironic victim of frequent jokes. One of the legends of baseball is the night he stepped into a hotel elevator with Warren Spahn and Lew Burdette.

He looked up from his key. "Punch twenty-six," said Donald, who couldn't reach that high.

Spahn exchanged cagey glances with Burdette. "We're only going to twenty-four," he said.

"Punch twenty-six, you s.o.b.," screamed Donald.

The two pitchers tumbled out of the elevator at the twenty-fourth floor, laughing, leaving Davidson to descend to the lobby. There he summoned the clerk and roared: "How many times have I told you never to give me a room above the third floor?"

In spirit and stature, if not in bloodline, Donald is related to Pearl Du Monville and Eddie Gaedel.

Created by the typewriter of James Thurber, Du Monville was a midget who became a part of baseball's library by pinch-hitting in a big-league game. The game took place in the pages of a short story entitled, "You Could Look It Up."

Thurber had a grand idea but no franchise. It was left to Bill Veeck to turn fiction into fact, for in 1953 Veeck sent Eddie Gaedel—thirty-six inches tall—to bat for the St. Louis Browns against the Detroit Tigers. Gaedel walked. The nation's sports pages the next day showed this wonderful picture of Bob Swift, the Detroit catcher, on his knees trying to provide a target for his pitcher.

Donald never swung a bat for the Braves, but it wasn't because he didn't want to strike a blow for his team. One way or another, he did.

One year, when the Braves were playing the Dodgers in a spring game at Sarasota, he was set up by the general manager of the Dodgers. Buzzy Bavasi told an elderly gatekeeper that a midget from the Ringling Brothers Circus would attempt to sneak into the park. "He'll get pretty nasty when you turn him down, and he'll make lots of threats," he cautioned. "But keep him out, and use force if necessary."

Then Bavasi hid in a passageway and watched as Donald appeared, loaded with record books and fact sheets and a brisk manner. In the argument that followed, the old fellow punched him in the nose.

The blow sent Donald sprawling. He picked up his sunglasses, gathered up his papers and then darted between the gatekeeper's legs and into the park. "You dirty bastard," he shouted over his shoulder.

When Birdie Tebbetts, then the vice-president of the Braves, and their former manager, heard that Donald had been slugged he went off to defend his honor. "Who did it?" Birdie demanded. "Nobody punches one of my men and gets away with it."

So Tebbetts was directed to the press gate. He looked at the gatekeeper, judged him to be around eighty years old, and turned around without a word.

When he encountered Donald, he said, "Thanks for getting hit by an old guy. You probably saved me from a beating."

This kind of craziness was common among clubs in

those years, and could go back and forth until the original complaint was forgotten.

Donald nursed his sore nose for several days, and his grudge for quite a bit longer. But that spring he got even with Bavasi. When the Dodgers showed up at Milwaukee's camp for a game, Buzzy walked up to the press entrance and identified himself.

"I'm sorry, sir," he was told, "but I have orders not to let you in without a pass from Mr. Davidson."

Of course, Donald needed no outside agitators as long as Spahn and Burdette were around. Once, after the players and officials had posed for a team picture, Spahn and Burdette threw him down and removed his trousers.

Donald bided his time. The next time Spahn went out to pitch, he strolled into the clubhouse, gathered up every garment he saw, including Spahn's socks, and tosed them into the shower, with the water running.

They say that when Spahn left the park that night, after he had dried his clothes as best he could, he looked like Ichabod Crane.

Clete Boyer and I once bought Donald a motor scooter, what kids call a mini-bike, for Christmas. We planned to deliver it on the appropriate day, but on Christmas Eve we sat around drinking in Clete's apartment and decided not to wait.

Our plan was to leave the scooter on his doorstep, ring the bell and hide in the bushes as he discovered his gift. Instead, we peeked into the house and saw Donald walking around. Clete checked the front door, found it unlocked and left it open. I drove the scooter right into the vestibule of the house.

His two dogs circled me, barking and snarling, followed by Donald, barking and snarling. Followed by several guests we didn't know he was entertaining. After a couple drinks, Donald settled down and we left.

The next morning, on his initial ride, he crashed the scooter into a mailbox and broke two ribs. The next time we saw Donald on the machine, it had training wheels. And that was how he kept it, when he rode around the field at spring training every year, wearing a motorcycle helmet Boyer and I had given him.

Donald is the object of endless one-liners. The players say his suits are made by Mattel. He isn't defensive about his size, the result of a siege of sleeping sickness when he was six.

He gets into situations that are not of his own making, but he grins and bears them. He was the unwitting cause, for example, of an engineering problem at Candlestick Park in San Francisco.

When the stadium was completed, it featured a fine, roomy, glass-enclosed press box. There was just one thing wrong with it. The work shelf was so high, and the seats so low, you couldn't see home plate. This loss tends to interfere with one's enjoyment of a baseball game, and the working press complained long and bitterly.

After many complaints and phone calls, a city architect came out to see what could be done to correct the problem. His visit coincided, unfortunately, with the arrival of the Braves for a series.

The architect walked in, discovered Donald Davidson sitting at a typewriter, perched on two pillows, and stormed out, convinced that the entire protest was a practical joke.

It was years before they ever raised the seats in the press box at Candlestick Park.

The Big D

In a tight spot, Don Drysdale looked at a batter digging in at the plate the way he would look at a snake crawling through the kitchen door.

Not many hitters dug in against him. He was an artist whose work I enjoyed watching. He is another one whose name is called when you talk about pitchers who were mean and tough.

I used to admire Drysdale's theory about the brush-back or knockdown pitch—a part of every pitcher's basic weaponry. He would place the first one under your chin and put you on your pants. It was what Branch Rickey called a "purpose" pitch. It was meant to plant a thought, a fear. Then, when the hitter got up, dusted himself off and took his stance, the second pitch was the one that did the job.

There was a night when Drysdale was pitching for the Dodgers against the Phillies and Robin Roberts. As the night wore on, several Phillies were forced to dive into the nearest foxhole to avoid being hit by pitches. Not all of them dived in time. Gene Mauch took the target practice as a personal affront, and he ordered Roberts to retaliate when Drysdale came to bat. He wanted Drysdale to get plugged. Roberts declined. He was the kind of guy who wouldn't hurt a fly.

So Mauch looked for someone who would, and he turned to Turk Farrell, who lumbered out to the mound. His first pitch to Drysdale sailed three feet over his head. Mauch perched himelf on the top steps of the dugout, cupped his hands and yelled: "I said KNOCK HIM DOWN!"

This time the tall Dodger righthander went sprawling. As he dusted himself off, he was getting red around the ears. Don is a nice-looking guy, well groomed, and he doesn't like dirt any better than the next fellow.

So Drysdale teed off on the two-and-oh pitch and doubled to the wall. As he pulled up at second base, he yelled out to the mound: "There's your knockdown pitch, Farrell."

At that Turk turned and fired to second, trying to pick off the runner, it says here. The throw was hard and straight and caught Drysdale on the hip. "There's your two-base hit, Drysdale," he said.

As luck would have it, I heard the story from both parties over the years, and in all the important details there is no disagreement. Both, in fact, seemed rather fond of the episode, and its aftermath.

It came to pass that during the winter the Phillies traded Farrell to the Dodgers, of all teams, and the first thing he did in spring training was look up Drysdale and make his peace. Turk was six feet four and could hold his own in a bar fight. But Drysdale stood six-six and had a memory at least that long.

"Well, Don, old buddy," said the Turk, with a hearty grin, "we're teammates now. Whaddaya say? Let bygones be bygones."

"Okay," said Drysdale, shaking his hand. "And it's a good thing. I had your name in my book." He meant it, too. Drysdale pulled out a notebook, and turned to a page with a list of names on it, and there at the top was Farrell's.

There is no question in my mind that Drysdale's record of fifty-eight and two-thirds scoreless innings—six straight shutout games—was the darndest thing ever achieved by a guy who throws a ball. It is a record I doubt will ever be broken. Today it is a rarity for a pitcher to even finish six straight games, much less do it without allowing a run.

Drysdale was one of the people you would pay to watch pitch, and good enough at bat that the Dodgers sometimes used him as a pinch hitter. I liked his style even when we were on different teams, and I liked him more after we got to know each other through our work at ABC.

Don told me once that when I turned up in the Braves' lineup on a night in 1967, his manager, Walter Alston, asked him how he planned to pitch to me. He said, "Damned if I know, I've never seen him play." He was probably right. I had been in the league six years, and so seldom started against a righthander that I had never faced him.

That night I went three-for-four and walked once, one of my hits a bullet that went right between his legs. Don said he knew then that he was nearing the end of the line. He retired two seasons later.

A Dry Gibson

I caught a few great pitchers and batted against several others, although they may not have been as great as I sometimes made them appear.

But if I had to pick one pitcher, to start one game that my team simply dare not lose, Bob Gibson would be near the top of the list. If he was not in a class by himself, it did not take long to call the roll: Spahn, Koufax, Drysdale . . . take your choice. I would take him for the same reason Johnny Keane gave when he called on Gibson on two days' rest to pitch the seventh game of the 1967 World Series: "I had a commitment to his heart."

Gibson was one of the best athletes I ever saw. He had been a baseball and basketball star at Creighton, and he was another, like Aaron and Allen, whose story was familiar: up from poor. His father died three months before he was born. His mother worked in a laundry. He remembered the first home he ever lived in, a four-room shack on Omaha's north side, as the place where a rat bit him on the ear.

I don't think the man ever lived who hated to lose more than Bob Gibson. He was a quick learner who, if you gave him a week, could beat you at your own game.

However, the first time he ever let himself get talked into a celebrity golf tournament, he shot a score of 115. It was his own fault. He counted all his strokes.

In the privacy of the clubhouse, he was known as a practical joker, a fellow who would sing, strum a guitar or join in whatever was going on. But others saw him as a guy wound tight, cold to strangers and uneasy in crowds.

I used to study Gibby. He was one of those rare individuals who seemed to be driven best by anger. Different pitchers reacted in different ways. Before a big game, dry wit rolled off the tongue of a Whitey Ford. Sandy Koufax was quiet and unfailingly polite. A Ray Sadecki would go around looking for conversation, and a Denny McLain would be on the phone to his booking agent, lining up dates to play the accordion.

But Gibson did it his own way. He would be aloof, haughty, or snappish, building up a determination that was something to behold. Winning is important to every professional athlete. With Gibson the urge was overpowering. His makeup demanded it. He primed himself mentally for the big games, but if you asked him how, he could only shrug and say, "No special way. It's just in me."

On the field he was a lion, who twice came back from broken legs and in the final week of the 1964 pennant race started or relieved in four out of six games.

Unlike Allen, who liked people but whose actions confused them, or Aaron, who went about his job like a guy building a pyramid, Gibson had an electric presence, but was never comfortable with fame. He was abrupt with writers and uncertain with fans. When one asked for his autograph in a restaurant in Detroit, Bob said, sure, as soon as he finished his dinner. The guy tore up his sheet of paper and threw it on the table. Another time a little old lady grew angry and made a scene because Gibby wouldn't join her and her guests. And a small boy, in his eagerness to obtain the valuable Gibson signature, poked him in the eye with a pencil.

I heard him say often that he did not believe in hero worship and lacked the right disposition for either end of it. What he had was the perfect disposition for a righthanded pitcher.

In his middle years he developed a hard curve to go with his slider and fastball. But his money pitch was always the fast one, which sometimes rose and sometimes sank. You never knew which was coming.

I caught Gibson on a night when he struck out thirteen in Milwaukee, my home town, and he never had better stuff. It was a big moment for me, playing in front of my friends and relatives, handling one of the game's fastest pitchers.

With two out in one of the late innings, and two strikes on the hitter, he cut loose with a pitch that moved so sharply I didn't have time to raise my glove, and it smacked against my bare hand. It felt as if I had put my palm flat against a hot stove. I picked up the ball with my mitt, tagged the runner, walked away from the plate, walked into the dugout and up the runway toward the clubhouse, and then cut loose with a scream that would have Johnny Weissmuller sound like a sissy.

Gibson came looking for me. He knew what I was doing, that I didn't want to carry on in front of my hometown folks. He grinned, and nodded, and went back to the dugout. It hurt, but it was what we called in baseball a good hurt.

Leave Us Eddie Mattress

When Eddie Mattress was seventeen, it was a very good year (1949). He had all his hair and the kind of apple cheeks that old ladies and young girls like to pinch. He didn't own a car. He lived on the third floor of a boarding house four blocks from the ball park, and he walked it both ways.

What he did own was a batting average of .363 for his first summer in the baseball boondocks, down in North Carolina. The future beckoned clear and strong. Eddie would chase it to the Hall of Fame, and the most prolific home run career any third baseman ever knew. Wherever he went, glory and groceries followed him. The trail led to Atlanta and Milwaukee in the minors, and when he returned to those cities years later he brought the big leagues with him.

He is the only player I know who can make such a claim.

He was not yet twenty-one when he joined the Braves, still in Boston, an old and faded club trying to rebuild.

Among the rookies they brought in were Mathews, and a shortstop named Johnny Logan, and a young pitcher obtained from the Yankees, Lew Burdette.

That winter the team chartered a plane. They painted the sides with the name "The Rookie Rocket," piled aboard a dozen Boston writers and flew across the country to interview a dozen of their hottest prospects, the ones who would restore the Braves to greatness.

But not in Boston.

"The Rookie Rocket," Eddie would laugh about it years later, "never got off the ground. We finished last that season . . . way, way back. We were either very old or very young. We had graybeards like Earl Torgeson and Walker Cooper on the club. And kids like myself and Logan.

"We were so bad that we used to pray for rain. No kidding. The day the season ended, the manager, Cholly Grimm, let all the extra players go home early. On the bus after the game we had more writers than players.

"I hit a double in the top of the ninth to tie the game, and when I got back to the dugout everybody was mad as hell. They wanted to get home. We were playing the Dodgers, and they had already locked up the pennant, and the game didn't mean anything.

"After twelve innings the score was still tied, and the umpires called it on account of darkness. The sun was still out."

I always liked to hang around with Eddie, not only because he had a special corner in the history of the Braves. He was just a helluva guy and the biggest spender the club ever had. Nobody ever picked up a check around him. He bought drinks and dinner for everyone.

I roomed with Eddie on the road except when the team

was in Los Angeles, where he stayed with his mother. Then Bob Buhl and I moved into the suite the Braves provided for Mathews. There was always a refrigerator filled with beer.

After a game one night at Dodger Stadium, Buhl and I sat down and started popping beer tabs and telling baseball stories. The nostalgia was flowing nearly as fast as the beer, when I noted the room had a fireplace.

I said, "Why don't we start a fire and make it just like home?"

Buhl said, "Yeah, why not?" We had the air conditioner going and were feeling kind of laid back.

I threw a bunch of newspapers into the fireplace, and the cardboard from the six-packs we had already polished off. When the fire got going fairly well, I tossed in four bats that Mathews kept in the room for practice. He would swing them constantly. The bats didn't really burn that well because the fire wasn't hot enough, but for about ten minutes Buhl and I were in heaven. It was then that the sprinkler system went off. The floor we were on began to fill with smoke, and we discovered that it was a false fireplace. Shortly, the hotel manager appeared, accompanied by Donald Davidson, who took care of the problem, one way or another.

Mathews came back to the room the next morning. I had stacked his bats next to the fireplace, all blackened and smokey, but otherwise unharmed. Eddie went into a rage, but he gave up when Buhl and I couldn't stop laughing.

As a Milwaukee kid, I knew how large a role Mathews had played in what became known as The Milwaukee Story. The Braves drew two million fans in Wisconsin after they left Boston, and their success in Middle America inspired Walter O'Malley to move the Dodgers to Los Angeles, and Horace Stoneham's Giants tagged along to San Francisco, launching the expansion boom in all of professional sports.

In those years Mathews was the symbol of the Braves, the only survivor of the team that arrived from Boston, on its way to Atlanta.

On opening day of 1965, in what would be the team's last season in Milwaukee, a local group brought back most of the Braves who had played in County Stadium in 1953.

One by one the players were introduced, waving their caps and trotting out to their old positions, standing alongside the player who was the current keeper of it. When the ceremonies ended, only one player stood alone, at third base, the only player who had been a Brave in 1953 who was still with the club. And out in the bleachers a group of fans unfurled a banner that must have been sixty feet wide. It read: "ATLANTA YOU CAN HAVE THE REST . . . LEAVE US EDDIE MATTRESS, OUR HERO."

Mattress was as close as some of the old German burghers of Milwaukee could come to pronouncing his name. When he saw the banner Eddie swallowed hard, tipped his cap and looked down at his shoes as though he had never seen them before.

Of all the records he achieved in the years he spent in the home of the Braves, wherever that happened to be, Mathews cherished most the one he set with Henry Aaron: most home runs in a career by teammates (863). They broke a record previously held by a couple of fellows named Babe Ruth and Lou Gehrig.

"I'm not a crusader about race or creed," Eddie told the press, "but I think the fact that Hank is colored and

I'm white, and we set this record together, well, I think that is kind of significant."

A Long and Twisty Road

Satchel Paige was sixty-two years old, wore bifocals, and looked almost grandfatherly when the Atlanta Braves signed him as a pitcher-coach in 1968. It was an act of grace by the team's owner, Bill Bartholomay, to qualify the old fellow for his pension.

That was the only time our paths crossed, but every ballplayer was curious about the gangly patriarch who may have been the greatest pitcher who ever lived.

One day Dizzy Dean visited the ball park. Henry Aaron asked Dean if Paige could *really* throw, asking the question mainly for Satch's benefit, just to hear how Dean would react.

"Could he throw?" repeated Dizzy. "Is a pig pork? You bet he could throw. Listen. He was quick. Me and him would pitch in exhibitions and it sounded like firecrackers going off. Warming up it was like double-barreled shotguns. Boom-boom! That's all you'd hear. Cotton came out of the mitts. We'd saw the bats off . . . right at the top."

The Braves put Paige on their roster just long enough (158 days) to give him the time he needed for his pension. He never got into a game, although Lord knows he thought he could still pitch. He described his repertoire of pitches as the blooper, looper and drooper, the jump ball, hurry ball and nothing ball, and the ever-dangerous bat dodger. It disturbed him to see today's young pitchers use only their arms and not their heads. "They throw the two-strike pitch over the plate," he complained one day. "They don't waste it. Me, on a two-strike pitch, they get something from me a dog wouldn't want to hit."

Satchel spent his time that summer singing of the old days, spreading good will and jiving the troops. He was living at the Dinkler Plaza Hotel in Atlanta.

One day I got on the pay phone in the clubhouse, rang the switchboard upstairs and had them put me through to the house phone a few feet away. I asked for Satchel Paige. When he picked up the phone, I put on my best German accent and told him I was the manager of the hotel.

I said, "I vant you to get your schidt oudt of your room, ve got a chentz to rent your room."

Satchel said, "Hey, who the hell you say this is?"

I gave him a name, Hans Gruber.

He said, "Gruber, what the hell you tawkin' about? I pay my rent by the month and my rent is paid."

I said, "Look, I don't give a schidt vat you pay or who you tink you are. To me you just a wrinkled old man, and the Braves haf gone downhill effer zintz you came. So you get your schidt out of the room."

We were talking on the phone ten feet apart and the conversation ended with Satchel announcing that he was on his way to the hotel to kick my ass.

I let him hang up the phone, watched him go over to his locker and start taking his uniform off. He only dressed to pitch batting practice, so I let him get halfway undressed before I let him in on the gag. He didn't mind. Clubhouse humor, the endless pranks, delighted him.

The Phillies had Satchel in 1958 on their farm club at Miami with kids like Dick Farrell, Don Cardwell, Ed Bouchee and others destined for the majors. Farrell remembered how the younger cult tormented Satch by putting dead fish in his shoes and nailing his uniform to the ceiling. But Satch always had the last laugh.

"He would warm up by putting a silver chewing-gum wrapper on the plate and pitching for it," said Farrell. "In Columbus, Ohio, there was a knothole in the outfield fence. A hitter got five thousand dollars for a home run through it. Of course, nobody ever collected. Satch said he could hit the hole from twenty feet. The guys laughed. He missed it five times. Then the betting started and Satch hit it three times in a row."

No one knows what feats Paige might have performed in the twenty years he was barred from the majors because of the color of his skin. He was a star in both leagues, the black one and the white one. Dean and Bob Feller both called him the greatest pitcher they ever saw. In his prime, Satch slept on his suitcase in Southern towns, barnstorming for one hundred dollars a game. In 1934 he beat Dean four out of six on one tour, when Dean was a thirty-game winner in the big leagues and a World Series hero.

When Satchel gained his first fame in the Negro Leagues in 1926, Joe DiMaggio was eleven years old. By 1935 Satchel had become a legend, and DiMaggio was still a year away from his rookie season with the Yankees.

When Bill Veeck brought Satch to the majors at Cleveland in 1948, Joe was baseball's greatest star. In 1952, by then with the Browns and back with Veeck, Paige was voted the American League's best relief pitcher. DiMaggio had been retired for two seasons.

Veeck gave him his first, overdue break not only in the interest of justice. He wanted to reinforce a weak Cleveland bullpen, and the move won the pennant for the Indians. To some it smacked of a publicity stunt.

In the *Sporting News*, J. G. Taylor Spink editorialized: "Many well wishers of baseball fail to see eye to eye with the signing of Satchel Paige, the superannuated Negro pitcher. To bring in a pitching rookie of Paige's age is to demean the standards of baseball in the big circuits."

Years later, Satchel noted: "I demeaned the big circuits considerable that year. I won six and lost one."

In the office of the baseball commissioner, the birth date of Paige is listed as July 7, 1906. Chances are that not even Satch knows for certain his actual age. What he does say, with the purest of logic, is: "It must have been meant for me to be bawn when I was . . . or I wouldn't have been bawn. If there hadn't been a color line, I might have made more money and got into trouble with Sam. This way, the whole world got to see me pitch."

His every move was one of melancholy. He could Bogart a cigarette with the best of them, holding it between his thumb and index finger. His eyes were slow and sad, his face long and wrinkled. "We seen some sights, it and I," he once said, fondly, observing his face in a mirror.

It seems strange to me even now to realize that segregation was still practiced in the South when I went to my first big-league training camp, not that long ago, in 1961. The black players lived apart from the team in Florida. They were not housed in the same motels or served in the same cafés as the whites.

They stayed in rooming houses and ate their meals with families that boarded them. In Bradenton, they stayed at Mrs. Gibson's. She served the best fried chicken in town, and we made jokes about it: how they ate better than the white guys, home-cooked meals and no curfew or bed checks.

At least, we have a way of marking where we have been. And how far we have to go. It isn't generally known, but Jackie Robinson not only broke the color line, he got the blacks into the dining rooms. Even when all the players began sleeping in the same hotels—I mean in cities like St. Louis, not some pit stop in the South—it was still standard practice for the blacks to order room service, so as not to offend whites in the dining room.

One night in Cincinnati, Jackie Robinson decided to enter the dining room and ask for a table. The captain seated him, the waiter served him, and none of the diners, whatever their private feelings, walked out. As Satchel Paige said, "The past is a long and twisty road."

The Southpaw

It was Warren Spahn who changed the perception that all left-handed pitchers were a little crazy.

I'm not sure where or when the idea started, but the impression was still fairly general when Spahn came along to prove that a left-hander could act in a perfectly ordinary way, except for winning twenty games every year.

No doubt, the tradition dated back to pitchers like Rube Waddell, a legend in the 1920s, who once disappeared from a game—he was the pitcher—to follow a fire truck. He was sometimes discovered between innings under the stands, shooting marbles with a bunch of kids.

Lefty Gomez came along in the 1930s to add his own touch. Gomez could throw a lot faster than he ran, but hand or foot he liked a challenge. One day George Selkirk, his Yankee teammate, another happy soul, said he thought he could beat Gomez to the dugout, running in from right field. They bet five dollars on it.

With two out in the next inning, and two on, the batter drove a fly ball to deep center. Gomez watched it go, saw Joe DiMaggio lope after it and then glanced toward right. Here came Selkirk, racing like a sprinter. Gomez took off for the bench, and won by a stride, just as the ball settled into the glove of Joe DiMaggio, and manager Joe McCarthy looked on in bewilderment.

Then there was Warren Spahn. No one ever suggested that Spahn had an inch of craziness in him. But anyone who played on the same team would tell you he was obsessed.

The Braves joked about it for years after manager Chuck Dressen once complained, "All he thinks about is getting his twenty."

Yet Dressen knew as well as anybody what a good thing that was for a pitcher to think about, especially one who could go out and do it. When it came to winning, Warren was selfish, and not many people begrudged him. He just didn't make it very easy on a manager. He hated to lose. Hated to get rained out. Hated to miss a turn. And hated coming out of a game with such a passion that a manager got so he dreaded going to the mound to remove him. Many of them wouldn't, and instead sent their pitching coaches. In fact, that practice may have started with Spahn.

They would practically have to Indian-wrestle with him to get the ball.

I think part of what kept that flame burning inside Spahnie was the fact that he felt he had no time to lose. He was a late starter, and he never stopped catching up.

He was forty years old my rookie season. He had just won twenty games for the thirteenth time. The *Sporting News* had voted him Pitcher of the Year.

He had signed with the Braves in 1939, years before the big bonus era, and didn't collect a dime. He spent three years in the minors and three more in the army—he was the only major-leaguer to win a battlefield commission for bravery in action.

He didn't spend a full year with the Braves until 1947, when he had the first of his twenty-game seasons (twenty-one and ten). The next year Spahn and Johnny Sain pitched the Braves to their first pennant in thirty-four years, inspiring the slogan, "Spahn and Sain and two days of rain."

I caught his record three-hundred twelfth win and he went on to add forty-one more before he retired, under protest, at the age of forty-five. His snapping fastball was gone, but he could still beat them with his off-speed pitches and his control and his head.

He was a joy to catch and a joy to watch, one of those rare people who strikes you up close just as he does from a distance. Not many ballplayers do.

Spahn moved in a peculiar sort of duck walk, his shoulders swinging from side to side, in the rambling way of a good high school athlete. His pitching form was perfect. From the side, he seemed to be turning over, automatically, like one of those old riverboat wheels, with no more strain on the arm itself than on the spoke of a wheel.

Spahnie considered himself immune to the attacks of time. When the Braves decided they needed to bring along younger pitchers, he signed on with the woeful New York Mets. He was listed as a coach, but he kept wanting to work with an old guy named Warren Spahn, rather than the bonus kids the Mets kept bringing in.

The first time he pitched against his old club in Milwaukee, the Braves scored seven runs off him in one inning, including a grand slam homer by Eddie Mathews. The fans gave Spahn a standing ovation and booed the Braves, who felt like booing themselves.

He was a grandpappy age for a pitcher, and his breaking pitches no longer dipped and wobbled like a tired moth. To Spahn it was a sad night only because he didn't win.

I have always thought that one remark typified him. The night he won his three-hundredth, he was asked what it meant, how badly he had wanted it.

He looked surprised anyone would ask. "I wanted this one," he said. "I wanted the last one, and I want the next one."

15. The All-Uke Team

I AM MORE FORTUNATE than most former big-leaguers, because I have no feelings of frustration, of promise unfulfilled. I think I got everything out of my talent I could.

To begin with, I lacked speed. I had to compensate with a few tricks. One was to knock my hat off as I ran down the first-base line, to make it appear that I was really moving.

I hated to lead off an inning, especially in a park that had Astroturf. I would hit a bouncing ball to third base and they'd whip the ball to second and then to first. It really made you look bad when they practiced their double plays with nobody on base.

The one ability I did have, and tried never to lose, was the ability to laugh at myself, or at the foibles of a game little kids play for free. After a long day, moving on to another town, the fellows usually needed some comic relief.

Once, with the Braves, we were coming in for a

landing. The time when many players tighten up is when
the plane touches down, and there is this great whoosh
before the brakes grab. I picked up the intercom mike in
the back of the plane and announced, "This is your
captain speaking. Please remain seated and keep your
safety belts fastened until the plane HAS HIT THE SIDE
OF THE TERMINAL BUILDING and come to a
complete stop."

It was fun watching the blood leave their faces for a
few seconds.

That was my way of bringing the guys together, of
reminding them that man can't live by box score alone. I
meant it one night, sort of, when I said on the *Tonight
Show*: 'Winning and losing is nothing. Going out and
prowling the streets after the game is what I liked. You'd
get half in the bag and wake up the next morning with a
bird in your room—that's what baseball is all about."

In that spirit, I have been persuaded to select my own
All-Star team, an all-character team, composed of
players whose contribution to the game went beyond
winning or losing. To be eligible, their careers had to
cross mine, meaning they had to have played at least one
game in the National League in the years between 1961
and 1968. I gave special consideration to those whose
service had a distinctive and human quality, and also to
those I thought might be seriously offended by being left
out. Herewith,

THE BOB UECKER ALL-STAR TEAM

FIRST BASE—*Marv Throneberry*, Mets. The competition was hotter here than at any other position, with

the likes of Dick Stuart, Norm Larker and Gordy Coleman all in the running. A special honorable mention should go to Joe Pepitone, for his lasting contribution to the game. Pepitone is believed to be the first player to bring a hair blower into the locker room. Throneberry wins for a career that led not to the Hall of Fame, but to a Lite Beer commercial. He once was called out for failing to touch second base on a triple. When he complained, the umpires pointed out that he had missed first base, too.

SECOND BASE—*Rod Kanehl,* Mets. Led the league for three straight years in getting hit by pitches, and defined team spirit as being willing "to take one on the ass for the team." Once, as a pinch runner, he scored from second on a passed ball to give the Mets a 7-6 lead over the Phillies. Casey Stengel was so elated he told Hot Rod to stay in the game. When Kanehl asked which position, Casey said, "I don't care. Play any place you want to." Kanehl grabbed his glove and ran onto the field. He told Felix Mantilla to move from third to second, moved Elio Chacon from second to short, and put himself in at third. "That's the kind of ballplayers we want," Stengel said later. "Tell him to do something, and he does it."

SHORTSTOP—*Ruben Amaro,* Phillies. One of the slickest glove men ever to play the game, but I have included him for two reasons. Ruben hit even fewer homers (two) in his career than I did, and he is the only man I ever heard of who was drafted by both the American and Mexican armies. He deserves it.

THIRD BASE—*Doug Rader,* Astros. He was playing for Houston, in San Diego, the night that Padres owner Ray Kroc got on the p.a. system and apologized to the crowd for how lousy his team was. Rader rushed to the defense of the Padres, adding that Kroc "must have thought he was talking to a bunch of short-order cooks." The next week, Rader received angry letters from short-order cooks all over the country. The Padres turned the whole affair into a ticket promotion, letting in free anyone wearing a long white hat when the Astros returned to town. It all worked out swell in the off season, when Houston traded Rader to—you guessed it—San Diego.

OUTFIELD—*Roberto Clemente,* Pirates. One of the really complete players of his era, Roberto was also one of the great hypochondriacs. He suffered from insomnia, and claimed that sleeping pills kept him awake. The year he won his second batting title, he said he had gotten malaria from a mosquito, typhoid fever from a pig and food poisoning from a fish—all man's natural enemies. "I feel better when I am sick," he once said. Roberto was one beautiful wreck.

Frank Thomas, Pirates, Reds, Cubs, Mets, Phillies, Astros, Braves, etc. He played for eleven teams, three in one season. Known as the Big Donkey, partly because his bat had a kick in it (when it connected), and partly because he suffered from hoof-in-mouth disease. It seemed that every few months Thomas would be traded, always leaving with the same declaration: "It's nice to know that somebody wants you."

Frank Howard, Dodgers. It was a thrill to watch him play the outfield. Jim Murray wrote that at six-eight, Howard was the only player in baseball who clanked when he walked. Early in his career, you never knew if he would drive in more runs than he let in. He had one of the biggest swings in the game, and once took a mighty cut just as Maury Wills slid across the plate, trying to steal home. A gentle giant, Howard was more shaken than Wills. "Please, Maurice," he begged, "don't ever do that again."

PITCHERS—*Ken MacKenzie,* Mets, left-hander. The first Yale graduate I know of to pitch in the big leagues after World War II. Casey Stengel once brought him in from the bullpen to face the San Francisco Giants with the bases full. The next three hitters were Orlando Cepeda, Willie Mays and Willie McCovey. Stengel handed him the ball and said, "Pretend they are the Harvards." Another time, MacKenzie was sulking on the bench. "Do you realize," he said, "that I am the lowest-paid member of the Yale Class of '59?" Stengel reminded him, "Yes, but with the highest earned run average."

Honorable mention, *Masanori Murakami,* Giants, left-hander. There has to be a category for the only Japanese ever to pitch in the National League. Described as "sneaky fast," he compiled a 5-1 record in two seasons of relief, then returned to Japan, homesick for his native land. He spoke almost no English, but had a sense of humor. Or at least, the writers who covered the

Giants did. Asked to name his favorite American songs, Murakami replied, "Horro, Dorry," and "Up a Razy Liver."

Turk Farrell, Phillies, Dodgers, Astros, right-hander. Early in his career, as a member of the Phillies' famed Dalton Gang, he set a record for barro fights. A hard thrower, with a big follow-through, Turk later set a record for most times getting hit by batted balls on various parts of the body. A line drive by Henry Aaron once glanced off his forehead, but Farrell stayed in the game. He carried a gun in spring training one year in Arizona, and shot snakes as he walked from his hotel to the ball park. A Falstaffian figure, he beat his old club, the Phillies, in a game that went fourteen innings and ended shortly before 1:00 A.M., and boasted in the clubhouse: "Nobody beats Farrell after midnight."

Honorable mention, *Gaylord Perry,* many teams, right-hander. When he came to the big leagues, one scouting report said he was only a "marginal prospect" to stay in the majors. Twenty-two years later, he was gunning for his three hundredth win. Once, after Nellie Fox had singled in the winning run against him, Perry broke Nellie's bat at home plate. He confessed some of his other sins in a book called *Me and the Spitter,* but swore he had reformed and no longer threw the illegal pitch because he wanted to set a good example for the kids.

You may have noticed that my All-Star team has no catcher. There were several candidates for this honor. Some had talent, but their humor was just warped enough to keep them in contention, such as Tim

McCarver and Joe Torre. Others were not handicapped by their talent, such as John Bateman and Choo Choo Coleman.

In the end, I decided to leave the position vacant because I have been taught that it is in poor taste to give an award to yourself.

APPENDIX

The Record

UECKER, ROBERT GEORGE
B. Jan. 26, 1935, Milwaukee, Wisconsin
BR TR 6'1" 190 lbs

	G	AB	H	2b	3b	HR	R	RBI	SB	BA	BB	SO
1962 MIL N	33	64	16	2	0	1	5	8	0	.250	7	15
1963		13	16	4	2	0	0	3	0	0	.250	2	5
1964 STL N	40	106	21	1	0	1	8	6	0	.198	17	24
1965		53	145	33	7	0	2	17	10	0	.228	24	27
1966 PHI N	78	207	43	6	0	7	15	30	0	.208	22	36
1967 PHI N	18									.171		
" ATL N	62									.146		
tot 2 teams	80	193	29	4	0	3	17	20	0	.150	24	60
6 years	297	731	146	22	0	14	65	74	0	.200	96	167

Traded to St. Louis, April 1964, for Jim Coker and Gary Kolb.

Traded to Philadelphia, January 1966, with Dick Groat and Bill White, for Alex Johnson, Pat Corrales and Art Mahaffey.

Traded to Atlanta, July 1967, for Gene Oliver.

Bestselling Books
for Today's Reader

MS READ-a-thon—
a simple way to start youngsters reading

Boys and girls between 6 and 14 can join the MS READ-a-thon and help find a cure for Multiple Sclerosis by reading books. And they get two rewards — the enjoyment of reading, and the great feeling that comes from helping others.

Parents and educators: For complete information call your local MS chapter. Or mail the coupon below.

Kids can help, too!

continued on next page . . .

The Very Thought of You

"[A] masterpiece . . . this fabulous tale will enchant anyone who reads it."
—*Painted Rock Reviews*

This Is All I Ask

"An exceptional read." —*The Atlanta Journal-Constitution*

"Both powerful and sensitive . . . a wonderfully rich and rewarding book." —Susan Wiggs

"A medieval romance of stunning intensity. Sprinkled with adventure, fantasy, and heart, *This Is All I Ask* reaches outside the boundaries of romance to embrace every thoughtful reader, every person of feeling." —Christina Dodd

"In this character-driven medieval romance that transcends category, Kurland spins a sometimes magical, sometimes uproariously funny, sometimes harsh and brutal tale of two people deeply wounded in body and soul who learn to love and trust each other . . . Savor every word; this one's a keeper."
—*Publishers Weekly* (starred review)

"Sizzling passion, a few surprises, and breathtaking romance . . . a spectacular experience that you will want to savor time and time again." —*Rendezvous*

A Dance Through Time

"An irresistibly fast and funny romp across time."
—Stella Cameron

"One of the best . . . a must read." —*Rendezvous*

"Lynn Kurland's vastly entertaining time travel treats us to a delightful hero and heroine . . . a humorous novel of feisty fun and adventure." —*A Little Romance*

"Her heroes are delightful . . . A wonderful read!"
—*Heartland Critiques*

DREAMS OF STARDUST

LYNN KURLAND

JOVE BOOKS, NEW YORK

THE BERKLEY PUBLISHING GROUP
Published by the Penguin Group
Penguin Group (USA) Inc.
375 Hudson Street, New York, New York 10014, USA
Penguin Group (Canada), 90 Eglinton Avenue East, Suite 700, Toronto, Ontario M4P 2Y3, Canada
(a division of Pearson Penguin Canada Inc.)
Penguin Books Ltd., 80 Strand, London WC2R 0RL, England
Penguin Group Ireland, 25 St. Stephen's Green, Dublin 2, Ireland (a division of Penguin Books Ltd.)
Penguin Group (Australia), 250 Camberwell Road, Camberwell, Victoria 3124, Australia
(a division of Pearson Australia Group Pty. Ltd.)
Penguin Books India Pvt. Ltd., 11 Community Centre, Panchsheel Park, New Delhi—110 017, India
Penguin Group (NZ), Cnr. Airborne and Rosedale Roads, Albany, Auckland 1310, New Zealand
(a division of Pearson New Zealand Ltd.)
Penguin Books (South Africa) (Pty.) Ltd., 24 Sturdee Avenue, Rosebank, Johannesburg 2196, South
Africa

Penguin Books Ltd., Registered Offices: 80 Strand, London WC2R 0RL, England

This is a work of fiction. Names, characters, places, and incidents either are the product of the author's imagination or are used fictitiously, and any resemblance to actual persons, living or dead, business establishments, events, or locales is entirely coincidental. The publisher does not have any control over and does not assume any responsibility for author or third-party websites or their content.

DREAMS OF STARDUST

A Jove Book / published by arrangement with the author

PRINTING HISTORY
Jove mass-market edition / April 2005

Copyright © 2005 by Lynn Curland.
Cover design by George Long.
Cover illustration by One by Two.

ISBN: 978-0-515-13948-8

JOVE®
Jove Books are published by The Berkley Publishing Group,
a division of Penguin Group (USA) Inc.,
375 Hudson Street, New York, New York 10014.
JOVE is a registered trademark of Penguin Group (USA) Inc.
The "J" design is a trademark belonging to Penguin Group (USA) Inc.

PRINTED IN THE UNITED STATES OF AMERICA

12   11   10   9   8   7

*To Cindy, Elane, Gail, Holly,
Kory, Leslie, Lisa, Lynn,
Mindy, Nikki, and Tennery:
sisters I would have chosen if I'd had the chance.*

Cast of Characters

ENGLAND, 1227

Rhys de Piaget, lord of Artane
    Gwennelyn, Rhys's wife
Their children:
    Robin
        Anne, Robin's wife
    Nicholas
    Amanda
    Miles
    Isabelle
    John
    Montgomery

Berengaria, a healer

Christopher of Blackmour, Robin's page

ENGLAND, 2005

Jackson Alexander Kilchurn IV

Kendrick de Piaget, lord of Seakirk
    Genevieve, his wife
Their children:
    Phillip
    Robin
    Jason
    Richard
    Christopher
    Adelaide Anne

Edward de Piaget, earl of Artane
    Helen, his wife
        Gideon, his son
            Megan MacLeod McKinnon, his wife

Alexander Smith, earl of Falconberg, Gideon's cousin-in-law

DREAMS OF STARDUST

Prologue

ARTANE, ENGLAND
EARLY SPRING, 1227

"What are you doing here?"

Amanda de Piaget looked at the knife in her hands and swore. Damnation, could a woman not be about a goodly bit of subterfuge without these sorts of unwelcome interruptions? It had taken her the better part of an hour to linger inconspicuously outside the armory until it became empty of anyone who might trot off and report her illicit presence to her sire.

When her chance to be about her business had come, she had taken it without hesitation. She had applied herself to a thorough search of what was available and had just hit upon the perfect weapon when she'd been interrupted by the unwholesome sound of her eldest brother's voice. She took a deep, steadying breath and turned around to give Robin her most innocent look.

"I'm doing nothing," she said, hiding the blade behind her back. "What are *you* doing here?"

"I've come to see if there might be a dagger here to suit."

"Why?"

Robin blinked. "Because I'm in need of one."

"Where is your old one?" she inquired.

"Cannot a man have more than one?"

"It seems wasteful to me," she said doubtfully.

He scratched his head, as if he were actually contemplating the wastefulness of the future Lord of Artane having more than one dagger to hand.

"Don't you have business elsewhere?" she pressed. "Things to do within the keep's walls?" The sure way to distract Robin was to demand answers to questions that did not merit deep thought. It tended to confuse him.

He paused, then frowned. "I have business *here,*" he stated finally, "and that would be to look for a dagger. What I don't understand is what *you* hope to find here."

Amanda considered. There was the danger of alerting him to her scheme, but that was balanced by the potential of having him find her a better weapon than she herself might manage. Mayhap that was reason enough for a bit of honesty. She pulled the dagger from behind her back quite carelessly, as if she couldn't be relied upon to answer accurately why it found itself there.

"What do you think of this one?" she asked. "Would it suit?"

He peered at it. "Aye, I suppose I could make do with that."

"Not you, dolt, me!"

His eyes narrowed. "And what by all the saints do *you* need a dagger for?"

"To stick you with when you vex me overmuch," she snapped. "Why else?"

He looked fully prepared to retort with something nasty, but she watched him take a very deep breath, blow it out, then chew on his words before he carefully chose which ones to spew out.

"Why do you need this?" he asked calmly.

"To protect myself."

He snorted, then held out his hand. "Let me have it."

Amanda bristled. "I most assuredly will no—"

"It is unsuitable," he said loudly. "With all the portly barges come to call on you of late, you'll need something longer. And sharper. Permit me a small look at what's available."

Amanda was surprised enough at his words to allow him to take the blade from her. He poured over the offerings the blacksmith had laid out for the inspection of the lord and his favored guardsmen. Robin considered, stroked his chin, harumphed a time or two, then reached out and picked up a dagger.

"This will serve," he said, flipping it up in the air and catching it handily by the blade with two fingers. "See you how the balance is perfect? Good for an upward stab when engaged in a bit of tight, close fighting."

"And what a pretty gem in the handle," she said.

His snort almost blew her over. "By the saints, Amanda—"

"It was a jest, Robin!" she exclaimed. She took the blade from him. "I'm sure it will serve me at night in darkened passageways when there are men lying in wait for me."

His look darkened considerably. "Have any tried such a thing?"

"I manage to drive them off before they can do me any damage," she assured him.

"No doubt. But why, then, do you need a dagger when you can flay them with your vicious tongue?" he asked.

She looked at him in surprise. Then unbidden, and certainly unwelcome, tears sprang to her eyes. She blinked furiously. Damn Robin, the unfeeling lout—

But then, despite her confidence in the extent of his dimwittedness, Robin rolled his eyes and made noises of apology. He quickly found himself a sheathed dagger which he stuck into his boot, then took her by the arm and pulled her toward the doorway.

"You are more tolerable than I allow," he said gruffly, "and any man would be fortunate to call you his."

"Call my gold his, you mean," she said bitterly.

"Men are fools, sister. What you need is someone with wealth of his own and no need of yours."

"It has been four years, Robin, since the steady stream began and I have seen no man yet who has come just for me."

"Four?" he echoed. "It seems nigh onto forty!" He cast her a sideways glance. "Perhaps you can be forgiven for that sharp tongue of yours, when one thinks on what you've had to endure."

"Perhaps," she agreed, but in truth she thought her sharp

tongue the least of her worries. That she had been looking over men for the past handful of years and not found a single one to suit was what troubled her. But how was she to choose, when all she saw were men who arrived at the castle with their eyes already full of the sight of themselves riding off *from* the castle with bags of her gold clinking at their heels?

And now her father was pressing her for some kind of decision by summer's end.

"We'll find you a man worthy of you," Robin said, slinging his arm about her shoulders in a rare, companionable gesture. "And until he arrives, I'll teach you a thing or two in the lists that will serve you."

She blinked in surprise. Robin *never* offered to train anyone. Never. She could without effort make a lengthy list of men who had come seeking the like from him only to find themselves tossed out of the front gates, untrained and unsatisfied.

Her eyes narrowed. Surely he was jesting. Besides, even if he wasn't, he was set to go to his wife's father's keep within the month. That was hardly enough time to learn sword hilt from sword point. She scowled at him.

"Aren't you leaving soon?" she asked tartly.

"Aren't you a quick study?"

Well, there was that, she supposed.

"We'll start tomorrow," he said. "You'll just have to content yourself with what I have time to teach you."

He gave her a squeeze that almost broke her shoulders, then patted her back for good measure. She managed to avoid sprawling on her face, but it was a near thing. She righted herself and watched him jog off to some other pressing errand, finding herself quite surprised at his offer and very grateful. If he only knew what she was really about . . .

But he didn't, and he wouldn't. She hadn't been careful enough that morning, but she wouldn't make that mistake again.

She stood in the courtyard and looked up at Artane, hovering over her like a bird of prey. It was, in truth, quite imposing, but she loved it with all her heart. The tenderest memories she had were wrapped up in the place, memories made with her family that she loved so much it pained her. The thought of what she was planning to do, what she knew she had no choice but to do was enough to break her heart . . .

Robin appeared before her so suddenly, she squeaked. He frowned. "You *are* merely protecting yourself from suitors, aren't you?" he asked sharply.

"Whatever else might I be doing?"

"Hmmm," he said, "I suppose. Besides, for what other reason could you possibly need skill with a blade?"

What other reason indeed, she thought.

He patted her again thoughtfully on the shoulder, then turned and went about his business.

Amanda sighed. She was grateful for many things, namely that Robin had gone away before he'd thought any more. She was grateful for aid from an unexpected source. And she was most grateful that that source had stopped asking questions.

Because if he had any idea what she was about, she wouldn't find herself on that brief walk to the lists to train with him—she would find herself on a very brief jog to the dungeon, with Robin no doubt enormously pleased to be her jailor.

Chapter 1

LONDON, ENGLAND
EARLY SUMMER, 2005

Jackson Alexander Kilchurn IV stood in the underground car park of a swanky London office building with his hands up in the air in as close to a gesture of surrender as he could stomach and paused in mid-mugging to review the events of the morning to see where he'd gone wrong.

Waking up. Waking up to the unhappy sight of his father leaning over him fully dressed—his father, not he himself—bellowing that they were going to be late if Jake didn't haul his sorry backside out of bed immediately. Yes, that was a sight that should have merely inspired him to pull the covers back over his head.

Obviously, he was not at his best in the morning.

Not telling his father to go to hell. That had been his second mistake. If he'd just done that, he could have saved himself not only the annoyance of having to get up before the sun to shuttle his filthy-rich but notoriously cheap father to the airport, but also the irritation of having to listen to another paternal lecture on Jake's shortcomings, which included but were not limited to his marital state (none), his desire to follow in his father's business-empire-building footsteps (also unsettlingly missing), and his attendance at his father's London office (scanty, at best).

When his father had begun to compare him to a barnacle on the yacht of prosperity, Jake had quickly pulled up to the curb, deposited his father and his father's suitcase onto the sidewalk, and beat a hasty retreat into his car before he'd said something he might have regretted, such as "Sure, I'll take that thin manilla envelope and have it signed by whatever massive, impersonal conglomerate you're dealing with these days if you'll just get off my back."

Which he'd done just the same when his father had tossed it onto the passenger seat before Jake could lock the doors.

That had led to mistake number three: *being cheap.* Yes, that was the third, final, and potentially quite fatal decision he'd made in a morning that had gone disastrously awry. Cheapness was apparently a trait he shared with the aforementioned disgustingly rich father, but he'd think about that later, when he thought he could stomach it. Maybe he would reterm it thrift and move on.

But for now, he had to admit that he'd been cheap and had agreed to be his father's errand boy instead of shelling out the £50 for a courier—£50 that he would probably lose just the same to the thug behind him who was currently shoving a gun into his back.

Was that a gun? Hard to say. His well-worn but at one time very expensive leather jacket wasn't exactly conducive to ascertaining the true character of lethal weapons.

He quickly ran through his arsenal of deadly self-defense techniques, trying to decide which he could use without getting himself thrown in the pokey. He should have compared notes with that high-priced body guard he'd hired for his equally high-priced baby sister last year. Somebody MacLeod, he thought.

Well, a last name didn't do him much good if he hadn't either written it down or programmed it into his cell phone, and since his cell phone was currently leaving his jacket pocket for

points unknown, that last name would do him even less good.
Where was that MacLeod character when Jake needed him?

"Blimey, mate, where're yer keys?" the thug asked, sounding completely baffled. "Should be in this pocket here, I'm
thinkin'," he added as he rifled through Jake's jacket pockets
for the third time.

Jake declined to comment. It was bad enough he was getting mugged; he had to get mugged by a moron. He spared an
unkind thought for his father. If he hadn't been humoring the
man by delivering a bit of paperwork to a business partner in
this building . . . well, he sure as hell wouldn't be standing
there being groped by a ne'er-do-well. He would have been
rolling out of bed to head to his office where he engaged in his
own brand of moneymaking.

Which he would get to as soon as he gracefully extricated
himself from his current situation. He cleared his throat.
"Trouble?" he asked politely.

The thug sighed heavily. "I'm findin' meself a wee bit frustrated at the moment. Don't suppose you have anything interesting in that fancy purse of yours, would ye?"

"It's a briefcase, and no, there's nothing interesting in it."

"Didn't expect there would be. Ah, here's something." He
removed Jake's wallet from his inside jacket pocket. "Now,
how 'bout those keys?"

"Front trouser pocket," Jake instructed.

"The things I do," the man said with another heartfelt sigh,
and slid his hand into Jake's pocket.

Jake decided, once his would-be assailant began to grope
more than keys, that the time for action had come. He spun
around, to the accompaniment of a very loud rending sound
that signaled his pocket parting company with the rest of his
trousers, then clouted the thief across the face with his very
expensive attaché case. He followed that up with a fist under
the man's jaw. The man slumped to the ground.

Jake bent down to retrieve his phone and his wallet only to
find himself seeing stars quite suddenly as well. "Damn it," he
swore as he clutched his nose. Blood dripped through his fingers as he looked down quickly at his adversary, prepared to
take further action.

But the would-be thief was lying on the ground, drooling peacefully.

Jake wondered how in the hell the man had managed to get one of his joints, either elbow or knee, in the vicinity of Jake's face, then decided it didn't merit further investigation. He made certain he had taken back his goods, then removed one of the least official-looking papers from his briefcase and used it for clean-up duty. It wasn't great, but it would do. He shoved the bloody page into his pocket, then made his way across the car park to the elevators.

Several minutes and a brief detour to the loo later, he was walking into the very posh lobby of Artane Enterprises, Inc., his father's *amour du jour*. He had no idea what sort of sweet deal had been cooked up between the two, but since Jake knew nothing about AE, Inc. and did his damndest to know equally little about his father's own conglomerate, he considered himself happily in the dark. He was, after all, the mugged errand boy, nothing more.

He walked to the receptionist's desk and flashed her a smile.

"I'm from Kilchurn and Sons," he said. "I have something for the boss."

The woman looked at his nose doubtfully.

"A little accident downstairs," Jake said deprecatingly.

He was apparently only marginally successful in easing her mind, because she put her hand over her mouth as she whispered into the phone. Jake waited patiently, with a harmless smile, until another woman came to fetch him. She looked him over and scowled, obviously not liking what she saw.

"You're late," she scolded.

"Sorry."

"There is blood on your shirt and a rent in your trousers."

"I got mugged in your car park," he said easily.

She gave him a look of skepticism his father would have envied, then sighed. "Business first," she muttered, then led him briskly down a long hallway and toward a set of imposing double doors. She opened them with a flourish to let him inside, then closed them with a discreet click.

Jake found himself in an office that somehow managed to be old world and quite modern at the same time. It was probably the smell of money. No wonder his father liked this group. The place just reeked of financial success.

A sandy-haired man sat there, taking notes on a legal pad. "You're late," he said, not looking up.

"I was busy getting mugged in your car park," Jake said.

The other man lifted his head. "Is that so?"

Jake offered his torn pocket as evidence.

"And your nose?"

"Let's not talk about that."

"Hmmm," the other said as he studied Jake for a moment or two. "You're from Kilchurn and Sons."

"I am."

The sandy-haired man studied him a bit longer. "You know," he said thoughtfully, "you look a great deal like Mr. Jackson Kilchurn III."

Given that his father was not an unhandsome man, even in his early sixties, Jake had no trouble taking that as a compliment.

"I do," he agreed. "And happily so, since I'm his son."

"Indeed," the other man said slowly, as if he couldn't quite believe it.

"Don't let it worry you. Today I'm just the errand boy."

"High-priced errand boy."

"Not high enough, believe me." He handed over the manilla envelope. "Here you go."

"Thank you." The man rose as he took it, then held out his hand. "Gideon de Piaget. I run AE, Inc. I'm surprised we haven't met before. I seem to have spent an inordinate amount of time at Kilchurn and Sons of late, but I've never seen you there."

"I try never to be there," Jake said. "I have three other, quite capable brothers who are soldiering on, doing the family name proud. They mostly live at my father's offices in Manhattan, but they do make the occasional appearance here in London to put in their obscenely long hours for the firm. I'm quite thankful for that, as it leaves me free to pursue other quite inappropriate interests."

"Hmmm," Gideon said, looking faintly interested.

"Just a bit of dabbling in gems," Jake admitted modestly. Actually, that dabbling took him all over the world in search of the unusual and exquisite, which in turn left him able to create one-of-a-kind pieces that fetched prices even his father found outrageous. All that left him with neither time nor desire to put in the eighty a week that employment at his father's money machine required. Not that he ever would have anyway. He couldn't stand the thought of all those hours and nothing but paperwork to show for it.

Gideon's fascination with inappropriate interests was apparently evaporating. He sank down into his chair, his attentions fixed on the documents in his hands.

Jake sat as well, briefly. He didn't want to be hanging out in some corporate box, no matter how luxurious; he wanted to be slogging through some mosquito-infested swamp in search of a forgotten mine where he might find a cache of something rare. In fact, he had just such a trip planned for the next day—if he could get out of AE, Inc. and over to his father's office to finish his task before he died of corporate asphyxiation.

He was on his feet almost before he knew how he'd gotten there. Gideon just turned another page and kept reading, so Jake assumed he wouldn't mind having his things perused.

To Jake's surprise, Gideon's office wasn't filled with important but impersonal pieces of art a decorator would have chosen. It was filled with quite lovely pastoral scenes that were no doubt geared to make one feel as if he needed to spend pleasant afternoons on a little hill in the Lake District. Nice, easily digested paintings that demanded nothing and offered peace.

Well, except for the one dominating the wall to Jake's left.

Jake's pacing ended abruptly as he came face-to-face with an enormous photograph of a castle. He was accustomed to seeing castles, having lived in England for well over half his life, but this was different.

It wasn't that the place wasn't huge; it was. It wasn't that it wasn't imposing; it was. It wasn't that it wasn't stark and unforgiving; it was that as well.

It was that it looked so . . . familiar.

But he was quite certain that he'd never seen it before.

Artane . . .

The name whispered across his soul, sending a violent

shiver down his spine. He never shivered, not even when facing down spiders the size of his head in the depths of South American jungles.

He wondered, briefly, if that stray blow to his nose had damaged his good sense as well.

"Artane," Gideon said absently.

I know, Jake thought with a gasp, like a drowning man gulping in his last breath of sweet air before he surrendered to the pull beneath him.

"The family seat."

"I beg your pardon?" Jake managed with enormous effort, unable to turn away from the photograph. "Your family seat?"

"Yes, actually," Gideon said. "Have you never been?"

"Never."

"Why not?"

"I'm not sure." But if it had anything at all to do with his violent reaction to the place, maybe he was grateful for it.

"You don't have much of an American accent. Have you lived in England long?"

Jake happily turned his back on Artane and leaned against Gideon's sideboard. "Years. My father sent me to Eton when he learned I was enjoying my pricey New England boarding school a little too much."

"Did you enjoy it?"

Jake was ready to blurt out his standard answer of *it was hell,* but found himself unsettled enough by his recent encounter with photography to have to scramble for something else.

"It was fine," he managed finally.

"Did you go to University here, as well? I assume you live here now."

"I did and I do."

Gideon gestured to the castle behind Jake. "You should make a visit."

"I don't really have time—"

"Married?"

"No time for that either. In fact," Jake said, straightening and rubbing his hands together purposefully, "I don't really have time for much at all. I've got to be going, if you're finished . . ."

"There are rumors that it's haunted," Gideon continued, as

if he hadn't noticed Jake getting antsy. "Artane," he added, as if he thought Jake might be unsure of which castle he was referring to.

"Interesting," Jake said, looking for the closest exit.

"Of course, I will admit that Artane doesn't have ghosts like they do at other castles," Gideon conceded. "Seakirk, for instance."

"How unfortunate," Jake murmured sympathetically, moving toward the door.

"But we have the occasional odd thing turn up at odd hours."

Jake didn't believe in ghosts and he certainly didn't believe in anything else he couldn't see—unless of course it was the rumor of a bit of sapphire or opal in some obscure third-world country that would require him to don his fedora and hike through malaria-infested jungles or leech-plagued swamps—but even so, he couldn't deny that just looking at Artane gave him a feeling of déjà vu that was altogether unsettling. All the more reason to get the hell out of there while he had his sanity intact.

Obviously he'd gotten up too early that morning. It had taken a toll on his common sense.

"Artane has been home to de Piagets since the beginning of the thirteenth century." Gideon continued, apparently oblivious to Jake's discomfort. "Quite a decent lot, on the whole."

"How nice."

"We have a fabulous collection of medieval artifacts," Gideon went on. "I come from a family of pack rats, it seems. Books, swords, jewelry. If you're interested in old, it's there for the asking."

"I have to be going now," Jake said, wondering how rude it would be if he just grabbed the appropriate paperwork from Gideon's hands on his way to the door.

"We've resorted to tourists," Gideon said. "My father isn't thrilled about it, you know, and he isn't open all that often, but you do what you have to in order to satisfy the Inland Revenue. And we have AE, as well. Several other interests globally. I'm hoping the venture with your father will add to that."

"Well, if it has anything to do with making money, you can

be sure my father won't come to the party unless he plans to take quite a haul away," he said shortly. "Now, if you don't mind—"

Then something Gideon had said registered in his busy brain.

"Jewelry, did you say?" he asked.

"Vats of it. Are you into that sort . . ." Gideon paused, then looked at Jake in surprise. "You aren't any relation to Kilchurn Ltd., are you? Importers of the rare, the unique, and the ridiculously expensive?"

"We're not ridiculously expensive," Jake said evenly. "Considering what I have to go through to procure the rare, unique and equitably priced, as well as all the design time—"

"You design it as well?" Gideon asked, with mild disbelief. "You don't look like a designer."

"I'm a full service shop," Jake said dryly. "Acquisition, accounts receivable, and security. I have fewer problems when people think I'm just the bodyguard."

"I suppose," Gideon said with a smile, tapping the papers on his desk. "All the more reason for you to go north. You'll go mad for the rubbish piled in heaps against the walls in the vault. You might even find something useful."

"No," was out of Jake's mouth before he could stop it.

Artane . . .

"No," Jake repeated firmly. "I can't."

"My father has to sign this," Gideon said.

"Send a courier."

Gideon looked at him and Jake could have sworn the man's nose twitched, as if he smelled something suspicious.

Damn it.

"No," Gideon said slowly, looking at Jake quite seriously, "no, I don't think so. Either you go, or the deal's off."

Jake felt his jaw slide south. "I beg your pardon?"

"I just have the feeling there might be something in my father's hall that you need to see." He paused, then smiled briefly. "Call it Fate."

"I don't believe in Fate."

"My father can put you up," Gideon continued, as if he hadn't heard. "Or you can stay at my wife's inn."

"She runs an inn?"

"She owns an inn," Gideon corrected. "The Boar's Head. Very quaint. Very sixteenth century. I'll ring them and have them set a room aside."

"I need—"

"A reservation? Don't worry. I'll do it for you." He handed Jake the papers. "I assume you're going home to get cleaned up?"

Jake glared at him. It wasn't very polite, but he couldn't help himself. "Damn you," he muttered.

Gideon laughed. "I'll have all the details over to you in an hour. Give my love to my family. Enjoy your stay at the inn."

Jake looked at him narrowly. "Why do I feel like there's something more going on here than simple altruism?"

"As I said before, I'm a big believer in Fate, and Fate's telling me you need to see my father's hall."

Jake gritted his teeth. He didn't have time for Fate, not when high-powered buyers were waiting for goods he was supposed to bring home in less than a week, goods he was going to have to do some ferocious bargaining to get.

That same breath of sea air whispered over his soul, bringing with it a longing so intense, a joy so sweet, that he caught his breath. He, Jackson Kilchurn IV, a take-no-prisoners kind of guy, thought he just might have to sit down. He drew his hand over his eyes and then rubbed them for good measure.

"Not enough sleep," he announced.

Gideon rose and came around the desk. He clapped a hand on Jake's shoulder and led him the rest of the way to the door. "It's been a pleasure. Ring me when you return and let me know how you found things. Perhaps I'll take some of my hard earned sterling and come visit your shop."

"I'll try not to sell you paste," Jake said sourly.

"You'll have a smashing time," Gideon promised, sounding pleased. "Expect directions within the hour."

"Thank you so much," Jake grumbled.

"My pleasure." He held out his hand and shook Jake's. "Best of luck in my father's vault."

"That much of it I'll enjoy," Jake said as he left Gideon's office.

He made it unmolested to his car and returned with all haste to his flat, fully intending to go immediately to bed and forget the unsettling and quite unwholesome events of the day.

Instead he found himself pacing in front of his expensive double-hung windows and pausing every now and again to stare at the equally expensive Georgian manors across the street. But instead of being soothed by their symmetry, he found himself being overwhelmed by the vision of a grim-looking, stone bird of prey, crouched on a bluff by the sea, looking out over the beach as if it dared anyone to come and try to conquer it.

It was just a castle.

Then why did the mere sight of it threaten to shatter his quite manly and jaded heart?

Almost an hour to the minute from when he'd left Gideon's office, a discreet tap sounded on his front door. Jake accepted an equally discreet manilla envelope from a well-dressed lad who demurred when Jake offered him a tip. Obviously Gideon paid his people well.

He opened the envelope to find that it contained only a handful of papers. One was directions to the Boar's Head Inn. The other was directions to Artane. The last was a brief note from Gideon.

Jake,

My father is expecting you and has invited you to make free with his vaults. Apparently, he purchased one of your more expensive baubles for my mother a pair of years past and finds himself delighted that you're deigning to grace him with your august presence. He has a magnificent chef and the scenery is not to be missed. Let me know how you find the old pile of stones.

Gideon

Jake took a deep breath and let it out slowly. He found himself being driven inexorably north.

Against his will.

Without choice.

But driven just the same.

There had better be a damn good reason for it. He shoved all the appropriate paperwork into his briefcase, then, with a sigh, picked up the phone to have his assistant change his plans.

Chapter 2

"What are you doing?"

By the saints, was no one capable of asking anything else? Amanda was growing enormously tired of that question—especially since she'd been hearing it for days from anyone who had breath for speaking. Unfortunately she hadn't had, and still didn't have, the breath for a vigorous answer. She hunched over with her hands on her knees and drew in her breath desperately. Robin bounced in place next to her, not even giving in to a noticeable change in his breathing.

"She's training," he said easily. "What does it look like?"

"It looks like the most sizable piece of foolishness you've ever combined," Nicholas snapped. "By the saints, Robin, she looks fair to falling into senselessness!"

"I . . . do . . . not," Amanda gasped.

"She does not," Robin agreed. "She's doing quite well. For a wench."

Amanda swung at him, but he jumped aside easily. She turned her irritation on her next eldest brother. "I . . . am . . . training," she wheezed.

"So one might think," Nicholas said. "But what I want to know is why? What need could you possibly have to run about in lad's clothing, muddying boots that cannot be yours, following Robin in his exercises in torture?"

Amanda was almost grateful for the chance to stop engaging in Robin's exercises in torture and spar with a different brother for a change. She heaved herself upright and took a final deep breath. "I have determined that knowing a bit of something useful might be . . . useful."

Nicholas put his arm around her shoulders and pulled her toward him. "How it could possibly serve you, I cannot fathom." He looked at Robin sternly. "You should be vowing to find lads to guard her, not driving her into the dirt in an effort to teach her things she does not need to learn. 'Tis a man's duty to protect the woman he loves."

Amanda closed her eyes briefly. It was truly a pity she and Nicholas were of the same family. Nicholas was, and she could admit this freely even though she had known him for as long as she'd had decent memory, a superb lad with impeccable manners and a shining sense of chivalry.

"Anyway, she isn't capable of learning these things, given that she is but a woman—"

Amanda elbowed Nicholas in the belly and he released her with a grunt. There were times she fancied that she might love him, but those notions were quickly dispelled when he opened his mouth.

"I have men to guard me," she said archly, "which you might have marked if you could pull your attention away from your polished glass long enough to look."

"There is truth in that," Robin agreed, "though I don't know how you manage to find lads patient enough to follow you on your endless trips to the seashore." Robin shook his head. "Sand in their boots, salt in their hair, sunburnt necks and backs of ears—"

"Look at her," Nicholas said with a snort. "Reward enough, I'd say."

Amanda refused to be placated by that olive branch. She turned her nose up at Nicholas. "I see them fed Cook's most select and choice pasties, things other men could only dream of tasting—things I will not recommend find their way to your trencher in the near future." She took Robin by the sleeve. "Let's be off. I daresay I prefer your company to his at present."

Nicholas made sounds of horror. "See you?" he exclaimed. "You've damaged her, Rob. When she begins to find you more to her liking than me, there has been grave damage done to her finer sensibilities—"

Amanda left him babbling behind her. She marched determinedly away, dragging an unresisting Robin with her. Of course he wouldn't resist. She was for the lists. In his mind there was no other place a man with any sense would find himself. She stopped in the middle of the field and looked up at her brother.

"Well?" she asked. "What next?"

"Knife work. Until you build your strength, we'll content ourselves with something less heavy. Given that you are of the fairer, weaker, softer sex and need coddling—"

Amanda drew the knife he'd chosen for her, not caring what weapon she had in her hand as long as it was a weapon and it was pointing toward Robin. She jabbed toward him purposefully. He only yawned, apparently unimpressed with her attempt. He was, as he would have readily agreed, the master, and she but the student.

And as he began to drill her first in defensive moves and then in offensive, she had to admit he was everything he always claimed to be. She had seen him humiliate numerous men in the lists, of course, and a handful in less civilized circumstances, but it was one thing to watch; it was another thing entirely to participate.

The afternoon wore on very slowly.

But she did not yield.

The sun was sliding west when Robin finally called peace. He nodded approvingly at her.

"You're a right fiercesome wench, Amanda," he said. "I can't remember the last lad I had charge of who had your persistence. But nonetheless, I think we'll stop for the day. Not that I couldn't continue far into the night," he added. "I feel quite energetic still."

And he looked it, damn him. But just the same, Amanda took the compliment willingly; she also took the chance to cease. She shoved her damp hair out of her eyes and accepted a cup of water from Robin's page.

"My thanks, Christopher," she said, giving him a smile.

"Enough of that fetching of water," Robin boomed. "Christopher, lad, take that sword I had made for you and let us be about a moment of work whilst Amanda rests her womanly self."

The poor lad looked as if he were destined for a trip inside Hell's mighty jaws. He swallowed with difficulty, put his shoulders back, and drew his sword. Amanda buried her smile in her cup. She would have to pull the boy aside and give him a few final words about her brother's vile sense of jest. She had tried, over the past pair of years since Christopher's arrival from Blackmour, to ease the torment of being Robin's page, but there was only so much she could do. Her brother was impossible. How could she remedy that?

She waited whilst Robin went about his instructions, then followed him and his page back to the hall once they had finished. She entered, let her eyes adjust to the faint light, then saw her family was congregated in a cluster of seats near the fire. Her father, Rhys, looked up from his ale and sighed at the sight of her.

"Robin," he said patiently, "someday you will walk in with Amanda looking quite like a squire and find a suitor here whom she might like to impress."

"And why shouldn't she impress them thusly?" Robin asked, casting himself down into a chair next to his wife. "She's a goodly wench. Quite useful about the castle. Good chatelaine and all that. And she might actually be able to guard your back in a pinch. Besides if a man cannot keep from soiling himself at the sight of Amanda in hose, then the saints preserve him when she really begins to show some spine."

Their father coughed to cover what Amanda could tell would have been a hearty laugh. "Aye, I suppose you have that aright." He looked at Amanda with twinkling eyes. "The saints only know what the poor man would do did you pull out a blade in truth and point it in his direction."

"I'm sure there would be prayers involved," Amanda said

dryly. "Now, if you will all excuse me, I'm off to resume my identity as a girl."

"But we'll be at it again at first light," Robin reminded her. "Don't let your frillies and such deter you from your labors."

She waved in answer and continued on her way up the stairs. She trailed her hand along the cold stone of the wall as she did so, wondering how many times it was she'd done the like in the past. Too many to count. Artane had been finished when she'd been a young girl and she'd spent all the years since roaming its pleasant passageways and rooftops. And now, never to run through the front doors into the great hall, never to smell the smells from the kitchen, never to feel the sea breezes on her face from the roof?

It didn't bear thinking on.

So she concentrated, as Robin continually demanded that she do, on exactly what was before her.

Dressing, then supper.

The rest would come later.

Supper was pleasant, if for no other reason than Amanda was afforded the company of her own sweet kin and for that she was grateful.

Until they gathered in her father's solar, that was.

She should have been accustomed to it after all these years. The discussions had been light ones, when the first men had come to seek her hand. The family had sought and found faults, laughed at foibles, and dismissed the lads out of hand.

But now things were different.

"'Tis grave, the situation in the north," Rhys said, for what was no doubt the hundredth time. "I don't know if we can hold our borders with what strength we have ourselves."

"An ally is what we need," Robin said wisely, nodding ever so slightly toward Amanda.

Had she found him tolerable company that day? Amanda glared at him as he sat sprawled in his chair with the ease of a man who had found his heart's desire and had no fear of his father wedding him to someone unpalatable.

"And we all know that lawlessness has increased—" Rhys continued.

Amanda pursed her lips. She had no more use for ruffians than the next woman, but she had no liking at all for this conversation, for she knew the direction it was taking. Rhys, Robin, and Nicholas would begin stroking their chins and examining each of their allies in turn, seeking fatal flaws. Then they would turn their jaundiced eyes upon the lords in the north who had, for whatever reason, remained aloof to the de Piaget charm.

It would be at that point that her younger sister Isabelle would plead pains in her head that could only be alleviated by an immediate retreat to her bed.

Nicholas would suggest that perhaps her father send his youngest two lads, John and Montgomery, to squire with the lords needing appeasement, that said lords might see what marvelous things Artane produced.

Robin would suggest that perhaps the finest export they might possess would be someone of marriageable age and tractable mein, and could not that person perhaps see her way clear to allow herself to be betrothed to one of the fools in the north and thereby assure them all of security far into the future?

Anne would elbow him gently in the ribs, Gwen would make noises of protest, and the rest of the males in the family would stroke their chins even more, as if the very voicing of that idea was the most miraculous and inspired thing to ever be uttered inside Artane's hallowed walls.

Of course Isabelle wouldn't be there to offer an opinion, and Amanda's opinion wasn't one to be voiced in polite company, so she would take herself and her sour thoughts and seek escape on the roof.

But tonight she chose a different path. She sat calmly and listened, nodded politely when her name was mentioned, and did her best to look as tractable as possible.

And all the while she thought of how this might be one of the last times she would sit in that family circle.

But if she was wed to some oaf from another keep, she would likely never see her family again, so perhaps she would be no worse off if she fled with her virtue—and her sanity—intact, than she would have been had she acquiesced to her father's plans.

Or so she told herself.

In the end, she was forced to close her eyes, lest the tears that threatened to leak out escape in truth and give her away.

Finally she did rise, excused herself, and fled. She wasted no time in dashing up stairs and down passageways and up more stairs until she exited the southeast guard tower and made her way along the parapet to her favorite brooding spot, where she could stand and look out over the ocean. A pity she wasn't closer to the water, else she might have heaved herself into it and spared herself the irritation of choosing someone to wed.

"Mandy?"

Amanda looked over to find her younger brother Montgomery walking along the roof toward her. She was as little surprised to see him as she had been by the topic of conversation below. Montgomery had been her devoted shadow, her most loyal champion and fiercest defender from the time he'd learned to say, in his most possessive of tones, "Manee, mine!" to anyone who tried to take her away from him. She had loved him for it and missed him whilst he'd been off squiring for Lord Pevensey this past year. Fortunately for him, Rhys had been loath to let his youngest lads be trained by anyone but him and a year had been the length of their torture.

Amanda suspected hers would go on for decades.

Montgomery was now a lad of ten-and-five, but still boy enough that she could put her arm around his shoulders and reach up to ruffle his hair affectionately.

"Have they chosen for me yet?" she asked lightly.

"Nay," Montgomery said. "They were deciding upon a final date for your decision when I left. Robin was for a date a month hence."

Damn him. She would slip something foul into her his porridge at her earliest convenience.

"Father says by the end of the summer," Montgomery continued.

"He's said that before."

"I believe he means it this time."

Amanda had no doubt of that. All the more reason to put her plan in action whilst she could. At least she could count on her family not being nearby whilst she was about her bid for freedom. Her mother, father, and sister Isabelle were set to travel to

France to visit her paternal grandmother who was finally beginning to feel her age. Robin and Anne would be off to Fenwyck
in a month for their yearly presentation of their son to Anne's
father. Nicholas was heading for Wyckham where he was going
to attempt, yet again if anyone was curious, to fix the roof of his
keep. The little twins were going with him. Her other brother,
Miles, was due home in a month's time.

All of which left her a fortnight after the bulk of her family
left to make good her escape before Miles returned to super-
vise her. She could manage that. Indeed, she had it planned
down to almost the very moment of her flight—

"What?" she said, looking at Montgomery. "What did
you say?"

"I'm not going with Nicholas," Montgomery said, looking
torn between happiness and misery. "I am fond of him, as you
know, but the thought of leaving you behind, unprotected—"

"You're not going?" she said incredulously. "But . . ."

"But?" Montgomery looked at her in surprise. "But what?"

"Nothing," she said, smiling through gritted teeth. "Nothing
but that I'm glad you'll be here to see to me. Very kind of you."

"And John," Montgomery added.

"And John," she echoed weakly.

Damnation. Her plans befouled, and so quickly! Montgomery continued to tell her of the tasks he and John had been
assigned in Rhys's absence, but she heard little of it. By the
saints, what was she to do now? How would she manage to escape them? They would sew themselves into her clothing.
John would spend his time reminding her that their sire had
left him in charge. Montgomery would want to know what she
was doing five-score times a day.

By the saints, 'twas a catastrophe.

Well, for now, perhaps the best she could do was get herself down from the roof before she threw herself off it. She
would worry about the details of her escape later, when she
was safely on the ground. She sighed deeply and looked at
Montgomery. "Is there possibly any kind of sweet below?"
she asked. "Or are the kitchens secured for the night?"

"I imagine you could charm something from Cook," Montgomery said.

"I'll smile; you use that silver tongue of yours," she

suggested. "No one could resist such a potent combination of de Piaget charm."

"Mandy, you have hit upon the perfect way to win you a husband. You smile, and I'll plead your case."

She turned him toward the guard tower and pushed. "Aye, but the lad would meet my vile tongue eventually, and be sorely disappointed in what he'd bought himself. Better that he see what he's getting from the start. But I'm not above trying that strategy to have one of Cook's sweet pasties. Off with you."

She followed him down to the great hall. What she said was true: she would find a suitable lad, but then lose him thanks to no one but herself—

But to find a lad, one who would love Amanda, not Rhys de Piaget's very wealthy daughter . . . ?

Impossible.

She stepped out into the great hall and took another step closer to leaving it forever.

Chapter 3

Jake gripped the steering wheel, turned the wipers on high and peered into the driving rain, wondering if he'd lost his mind as well as his way. He should have left London earlier. He should have checked the weather report.

He should have gone to the Bahamas.

The wheels of his very rare, very expensive-to-fix 1967 Jaguar slipped and slid on the pond that had at one point been the B6499. He should have known better than to have taken a B road. It was, after all, his hard and fast rule: nothing over £40,000 on less than a well-recommended A road. Jake wished heartily that he'd taken his own advice. He wished he was driving a Range Rover, one that had been seasoned on all kinds of rugged Scottish terrain, one that would have been undaunted by a little bit of wet masquerading as a small river.

Night fell.

It was as if the sun had been suddenly extinguished, like a light that had overstayed its welcome and was keeping young children of exhausted parents awake. Jake rolled the window down and looked out, hoping beyond hope to see some sort of landmark. He couldn't see a damn thing and he felt as if someone had blindfolded him and spun him around a dozen times.

His sense of direction was normally quite good, but now he found himself without a clue as to where he was, which direction he was going, or if he was even on the right road.

And his foray out into the night air left him with nothing but a very wet head.

He pulled that wet head in, slowed down, stopped, then considered. He could go forward and hopefully find the road terminating onto something more substantial, or he could turn around and try to find his way back to the A road he'd blistered down so cavalierly.

He suspected continuing on might be foolhardy.

But he didn't like to retreat.

He tried to make heads or tails of his map but it was quite dark in the car and his damned mechanic had neglected to fix the map light. Too tricky. Too temperamental.

Too useful, apparently.

Jake tossed the map into the passenger seat, cursed enthusiastically, took a purposeful grip on the steering wheel, and plunged himself back into the fray.

Conditions worsened.

So did his language.

And at some indeterminate point in the evening, his car slipped, slid, and came to a graceful and quite final stop in front of massive wrought-iron gates. Jake eased off the clutch, then gunned the engine just for good measure; that only accomplished a deeper easing into the mud.

He cursed a final time, then got out of the car and waded through the ankle-deep mud toward the iron gates. He banged a time or two. To his complete surprise, they opened, apparently by some remote-controlled mechanism. He entered, more hesitantly than he would have liked, but the weather was dreadful and the whole evening smacked of something supernatural.

If he believed in the supernatural, which he did not.

He trudged up the way to the front door, finding himself not in the least bit surprised that said front door found itself inserted into a castle. He squished up the steps, took a deep cleansing breath, and knocked on the door.

It creaked open, after a time, and light fell on a very proper, very butlerish gentleman of indeterminate age.

"You rang?" the man asked.

Jake shoved his sopping hair out of his eyes. "My car is stuck in the mud in front of your gates," he said. "If I might use your phone?"

The butler looked him over, apparently found him less than threatening, and took two precisely measured steps backward. He made Jake a little bow. "Seakirk's hospitality is always open to the stranded traveler."

Jake froze halfway across the threshold. "Seakirk?" he asked.

The butler lifted a single, silvery eyebrow. "Yes, sir. Have you heard of the keep?"

All right, so he'd heard of Seakirk, and not just from Gideon. At Eton, he'd been befriended early on by one Alistair McKinnon, son of a Scottish laird, who had dragged him numerous places in search of the old, musty, and sharp. Well, that and the odd Scottish artifact that Alistair had felt compelled to pinch and return to its rightful place on the proper side of the border, but that was another story entirely.

Alistair had wanted to go to Seakirk, and had even tried numerous times to get inside the gates, but had found himself firmly rebuffed each time. He and Jake had remained friends over the years and Jake was periodically updated about Alistair's progress in his eternal quest to investigate Seakirk's nooks and crannies. Rumors of ghosts and incredible artifacts had only made the challenge more irresistible.

"Heard of the keep?" Jake echoed. "Oh, only in passing. But I understand you have quite a collection of medieval weapons here."

"That we do, sir."

"How nice," Jake said.

He stared at the butler.

The butler stared back at him.

All right, so the first move was his. He was no wuss, but this was Seakirk after all. He stepped inside the hall and allowed the other man to shut the front door behind him. It closed with a very ominous click.

Too late to turn back now. Jake looked at the butler and attempted a smile. "My car is mired," he began. "If I could use the phone—"

"Unfortunately, I fear it is too late for anyone to come out now," said the butler. "You are, of course, welcome to stay the night."

Jake couldn't help the very long pause before he managed an answer.

This was Seakirk after all.

"Sure," he said finally. "Thank you. I'll just run and get my bag from the car."

"I will see to it, sir," the other man said with stiff formality. "I will also ring down to the village first thing."

"I appreciate it," Jake said sincerely. He held out his hand. "I'm Jake Kilchurn."

"Worthington," the other man said, discreetly overlooking Jake's hand. "Come this way, Mr. Kilchurn. I'll show you to your room for the night."

"I'd like to pay my respects to the owner—"

"The master is away," Worthington said. "As is the mistress. As are the children. It is," he said without a trace of humor, "very peaceful."

Jake very much doubted that any number of rambunctious children could cause Worthington to lose his unflappability, but he'd been wrong before and suspected he might be wrong here as well. Honestly, he didn't care. He was just grateful for a bed and a way to get his car hauled out of the muck in the morning.

He followed Worthington obediently across a very medieval-looking great hall with fireplaces set into the walls and a raised dais at the back. A large table stretched the length of the dais, with very old, apparently very well-cared-for chairs pushed up behind it. Banners hung behind the table, and the rest of the hall was filled with tapestries of equal quality.

Jake continued to watch the amazing parade of antiques as he followed Worthington up the stairs and down the hallway to what was apparently the guest room. An enormous canopied bed with thick, velvet bed curtains sat prominently against the wall, accompanied by other heavy pieces of furniture.

Gems he could identify in a low-light jungle loaded with spiders and snakes crawling happily around him, and he could certainly pick out the age of the odd sword or weapon, thanks to Alistair's nose for it, but antiques were not his forte. He did have eyes, however, and that was all it took to realize what he was looking at was very old and in amazingly good condition.

"Nice," he said sincerely.

"The master does not slight his guests," Worthington said.

"Isn't he afraid some stranger's going to make off with his nice antiques?"

Worthington looked at him for a long moment, then chuckled.

It was, Jake decided, a very unwholesome sound.

"Make off with?" he echoed. "No, sir, the master doesn't worry about that. He has a very unique security system."

Jake looked around. "Cameras in every room?"

Worthington only backed out the door. "The chamber is ensuite, of course. Refresh yourself and I'll bring up your bag. And as for my lord's retainers, why they're ghosts, didn't you know?"

Jake laughed, but it sounded quite hollow, even to his own ears. He waited until Worthington had shut the door before he permitted himself a really good shiver. Whatever the rumors were and however true they might or might not have been, one thing was for certain: Seakirk gave him the creeps.

He went to the bathroom, feeling entirely observed while he was at it, then returned to the bedroom a new and more realistic man. He didn't believe in ghosts. It was probably just a good way to drum up business for Seakirk.

Though given that Seakirk's lord was a recluse and apparently had no need for business to be drummed up on his behalf, the rumor was rather unsettling.

Worthington's discreet tap on the door a few minutes later almost sent him through the roof. He took a deep breath, then went to answer the door. He accepted his overnight bag from the butler and learned that there would be something appearing on the table downstairs quite soon. He watched Worthington back out of the room and disappear behind a rapidly closing door.

How long was it before he could politely go downstairs, and what would it do to his own image of masculinity if he just bolted there now?

Deciding there wasn't anyone around to pass judgment on

him if he did the prudent thing and caught a good place at the table early, he left the room and headed down to the great hall himself.

Dinner was excellent.

It was also much too short.

Jake expressed what he hoped was an appropriate amount of appreciation. Worthington was, as was apparently his custom, quite unmoved by either the flattery or the speed with which Jake wolfed down his meal. He merely stood at attention, not a silver hair out of place, and waited patiently.

Jake did the sensible thing and toyed with the remains of a lovely chocolate mousse as long as possible. "Does the family have quite a few children?" he asked conversationally.

"Triplet boys, seven years old," Worthington said with nary a flinch. "Two more lads and then a wee girl."

"Good grief!" Jake exclaimed. "The poor kid."

Worthington only lifted one eyebrow. "Young mistress Adelaide Anne is the loudest of the lot."

Jake descended with him into comfortable silence for quite some time. "When do they return?" he asked finally.

"On the morrow, perhaps."

"Then I should leave you to your peace and quiet. I appreciate the meal."

Worthington nodded and began to clear the plates. "I do have an assignation, sir, so I do appreciate that."

"An assignation?" Jake asked, smothering a smile. What an old-fashioned term for it.

"A discreet pint down at the pub with a certain Mistress Adelaide," Worthington confided carefully. "She owns an antique shop in the village."

"I like antiques."

"So I see by your pristine automobile," Worthington said in admiration. "I will have it seen to in the morning. I placed a tarp over it and flashers behind it for the night, lest anyone damage such a marvelous piece of history."

"It is a great car," Jake agreed. "I appreciate the effort."

Worthington nodded and Jake rose to head upstairs. He found himself with a sudden lack of desire to retire. Not that he thought that bedroom was haunted, but it was dark and stormy outside and a little company didn't sound all that bad.

Then again, Worthington, poor man, probably did need his evening out. Jake had the feeling that when the crew returned, not all those immaculately groomed silver hairs would remain in their places.

"My lord does have a rather interesting smattering of artifacts," Worthington offered suddenly, pausing on the way to the kitchen. "Through there, in the library. Of course, those are just the more ordinary things. If you're truly interested in a bit of history, I can show you his lordship's private collection."

"How do you know I'm not a thief?" Jake asked, quite frankly surprised that Worthington was so forthcoming with His Lordship's private things.

Worthington only smiled.

"I know," Jake said with a sigh. "Ghosts."

Worthington put the plates down on the end of the table. "Follow me, sir."

Jake followed him obediently up the stairs and down a long hallway. He was ushered into a very nicely appointed study, complete with an enormous plasma television in the corner of the room that had to have cost the same amount as a small BMW. Apparently that wasn't the real treasure, because Worthington opened a door at the far end of the study, flicked on the lights, and stood back.

"Here we are," he said.

Jake looked inside and caught his breath. "Wow," he said, in genuine appreciation. It was the reaction he generally had at the end of a long slog to a mine where he didn't expect to find anything and then found clusters of fine quartz and corundum instead.

He looked down the hallway, a hallway long enough that he wondered if it might not run the length of the castle. It was filled with all manner of weapons, suits of armor, and other paraphernalia of war. There was a doorway on the right and Jake looked back at Worthington, who motioned him to go on. Jake opened the door and peeked in.

"More wow," he managed.

"Enjoy, sir."

"I think I will," Jake said.

The hallway had been impressive, but the good stuff was evidently in here. Swords, knives, spears, armor, shields; and all of a decidedly medieval bent. He noticed Worthington leaving, then noticed little else for quite some time as he happily made himself at home puttering about in history. He marveled at the depth and breadth of the collection, at its age, at its level of preservation. ·

Amazing, and nothing but.

Time passed.

Though he couldn't have said how much time had passed before he saw it.

It was an enormous broadsword laying in an open, velvet-lined case, beckoning to him with all the seductiveness of a Siren. Jake walked over to it and reached his hand out to touch before he thought better of it. He traced his fingers over the word *Artane* carved into the crossbar of the hilt.

Artane again.

He shouldn't have been surprised.

But what in the world was one of Artane's swords doing here at Seakirk? Maybe Seakirk's lord roamed a bit in his travels to find the old and the unusually well kept. Jake reached out to run his finger along the blade—

"Better not."

He spun around in surprise.

There was no one there.

He suppressed a shiver and turned back to the sword. He stretched out his hand again.

"Bloody fool," someone behind him muttered, "can't he take a bit of friendly advice?"

"I'd say not," said another voice. "They never learn, do they? Let him cut hisself, then, and be the one to clean up the mess."

Jake shook his head, hoping that a good shaking would either clean out his ears or clear away what seemed to be a colossal hallucination. He decided that discretion was the better part of valor, so he put his hands in his pockets, his imagination on notice, and his attention on something besides a sword that seemed determined to warn him not to touch it.

He continued to peruse Seakirk's treasures unmolested and unaccompanied by comment until he found himself standing in front of a desk. He stared up at the familial portrait there. A woman was there, beautiful, with long, blond hair. A younger version of the woman was seated before her on a stone bench, only the younger girl's hair was dark. A man stood next to the woman, dark haired and gray eyed. No doubt he was her husband. Three young men of various ages either sat on the bench or lounged on the ground before the bench.

And in the background was a castle. Part of a castle. Enough of a castle that Jake knew that it wasn't the castle in which he was standing.

Artane . . .

Jake closed his eyes. What was it with that place that he found it in front of him at every turn lately?

He took a deep breath, opened his eyes, and stared up at the portrait. He could only assume that the family seated in front of that majestic castle belonged to it. A lord of former times with his wife and children? Lucky man, then, because the woman was indeed beautiful, with her hair cascading over her shoulder in a long, straight sheet of pale yellow. Jake leaned up on his toes for a better look.

"Aye, she was fair, that Lady Anne," came a voice from directly behind him.

Jake fell over onto the desk. Fortunately for him, it wasn't boasting the usual deskly accoutrements and he only knocked over an empty bud vase. He righted it carefully, giving himself time to get a grip on his wildly overactive imagination.

His retainers are ghosts, didn't you know?

Worthington's words came back to him, along with half a dozen other unbelievable rumors he'd heard over the years. He pulled out the desk chair and sat down. Not because he needed to, of course, but because he thought he might hang around for a little and see what kind of conversation he might eavesdrop on.

"Aye, Anne was fair," another voice conceded, "but I meself preferred the Lady Gwennelyn. The hair dark as midnight, the eyes the color of the sea, her skin like alabaster—"

"As if you'd ever gotten close enough to alabaster to see its color," another voice interrupted with a snort. "Stephen, you great horse's arse!"

"And you've no room to be lusting after the Lady Anne,

Colin of Berkhamshire," the one named Stephen exclaimed. "What with you wed, and happily too."

"I'm not lusting after her," Colin of Berkhamshire said in offended tones. "I was merely pointing out that for a woman, she was tolerable fair. Not that I spent all my time mooning after her, as you did after the Lady Gwen. *I* spent my time improving my swordplay in the lists, as a real man should."

"My swordplay was perfectly adequate!" Stephen exclaimed. "And at least my eyes functioned properly—"

The ring of steel was so clear that Jake had to turn around just in case he was about to get his head chopped off. And what he saw would have knocked him off his feet, if he hadn't already been sitting down, that is.

There, in that weapon-stocked gallery, stood three men in chain mail, looking as if they'd just stepped off a Hollywood set. Two had drawn their swords and were looking at each other as if they had every intention of killing one another. A third stood to the side with his arms folded over his chest, listening to the other two fiercely argue the merits of the ladies they had apparently chosen to champion.

"Anne!"

"Gwen!"

"Mindless dolt!"

"Blind, smelly pile of refuse!"

Jake listened, open-mouthed, as the insults continued, and descended into points and body-parts heretofore unexamined and insulted.

And then the swordplay began. Jake, wisely to his mind, got off his chair and crouched down behind it. He considered himself a man's man, but these men were ghosts after all. Who knew if the swords were real or not? Besides, it wasn't as if he could trot out any of his more lethal moves on this crew. He doubted he could even touch them.

Then again maybe they could touch *him*, so hiding under the desk might not do him any good when they really started going at each other. He decided to worry about that later. For now, at least he had some kind of cover.

The battle heated up, and so did the insults. Complaints were made about the closeness of the quarters. Speculation was offered about the possibility of a stray swordhaft smashing the glass of His Lordship's fine display cabinets and what sort of retribution that might entail. Other names were put forth, apparently women who had lived at Artane over the years and were considered quite fine looking, by other ghosts who seemed to appear out of nowhere.

Those other women were, however, regretfully dismissed as quite stunning but not up to the quality of the first ladies of Artane who, Jake surmised after a good quarter hour of eavesdropping and ducking to miss stray sword swings, were simply beyond compare.

He began to wonder who would win out in the end: Gwen or Anne, Anne being the woman in the picture above him (again something he learned thanks to a particularly pointed sword jab in her direction) and Gwen, who he learned through rather colorful language was none other than the mother of Anne's husband, Robin, who had been lord of Artane sometime during the middle of the thirteenth century.

Jake grabbed a quick look over the edge of the desk at Anne again. He couldn't deny that she was beautiful, but he wondered just what Gwen had looked like to inspire such loyalty.

And he wondered, with even more curiosity, why it was he was hunkered down behind a chair, watching ghosts fighting each other over women who had been dead for centuries, and viewing it all as if it were as normal as a quick trip to the Mini-Mart for some pork rinds.

Obviously, he'd been up too long.

The battle raged on without signs of abating. Then the third ghost, who had remained out of the fray, spoke. It was a single word, but its effect on the battle and the accompanying commotion was immediate.

"Amanda."

Colin of Berkhamshire hesitated, then put his sword point-down on the floor, leaned on it, and stroked his chin. "Aye, well, you have a point there."

Stephen of Burwyck-on-the-Sea rested his sword on his shoulder and looked off into the distance. "Aye, I would have to agree."

The dozen or so other ghosts who had been observing the argument put away daggers and other gear and also stared off into space as if recalling a particularly pleasant memory. Murmurs of approval were given without hesitation.

Stephen sheathed his sword and rubbed his hands together. "Robert, I believe you have settled the argument."

"Again," Robert agreed.

"Her hair," Colin said with a sigh, fingering his own sweaty locks.

"Her eyes," Robert disagreed.

"Her face," Stephen said, dashing a stray tear from his own eye. "By the saints, she had a face that could—"

He paused. Everyone else paused as well, as if they contemplated just what her face could do. Jake waited, then cleared his throat.

"What?" he prompted, from behind the chair. "Her face could what?"

Every man in the room turned to look at him. Jake would have said the hairs on the back of his neck stood up, but he was past that now. His curiosity, as it generally did when on the hunt, had gotten the better of him.

"Her face?" he prompted. "What could it do?"

The ghosts looked at each other.

Then they, as one and if on cue, made motions by the side of their heads that said more clearly than words just what they thought of him. Of course, that didn't stop several from looking at him, shaking their heads, and muttering uncomplimentary adjectives as they walked through walls and otherwise exited the chamber. Jake rose, banged the back of his head on the front of the desk, then straightened with a curse.

"Well?" he demanded of the first three, who were still standing in a manly cluster, comparing battle notes.

"Saints, man," Colin said, shaking his head, "have ye lost what little wits are left ye?"

"Apparently so," Robert remarked sadly.

Stephen only looked at Jake suspiciously, as if he found him not only crazy but capable of making off with His Lordship's finer bits of weaponry under his shirt.

"Well," Robert said, putting up his sword, "I'm for Conyers. What of you, lads?"

"I'll stay here abouts," Stephen said, with another pointed look thrown Jake's direction. "To look after the place whilst His Lordship is away. Colin, what of you?"

"I'm for home, of course," Colin said briskly. "Alienore will be expecting me."

Robert shook his head. "Don't know why you come here, Colin. Berkham is a fair distance, wouldn't you say?"

"He comes because Kendrick is here," Stephen said. "Well . . . um . . . because Kendrick was . . . well . . ." He trailed off and looked perplexed.

Colin scratched himself contentedly, then put away his sword. "'Tis a bloody long commute, I'll give you that, but after all these centuries, I'm in the habit of it. Besides, my lady craves a bit of peace during the days, you know, from all the training and improving I'm still about. Once a warrior—"

"Always a warrior," Robert and Stephen finished together.

Colin looked offended, but Jake suspected that wouldn't keep him from returning the next day, for whatever reason.

Jake wasn't sure he wanted to know the reason.

So he watched the ghosts make their way out of the room, listened to their talk as they left His Lordship's study, and stood where he was, rubbing the back of his head, as silence descended. And he wondered about what he'd heard.

Wondering was bad.

It usually got him into trouble, or landed him in places he would have been smarter to stay out of. And it always began with the rumor of something really fabulous, such has "Hey, Kilchurn, did you hear about that huge cache of emerald in Brazil? Deep, deep in Brazil?"

Which invariably, he had found, involved big spiders and hikes through uninhabitable forests.

But, despite himself, he couldn't help but wonder what Amanda had looked like.

Probably better not to know.

He checked the bedroom but found no ghosts behind curtains, or large rodents in armoires.

Amanda.

The name whispered across his mind as he climbed into bed, and he couldn't help but think about her. A woman who had lived centuries ago, if his hallucinations in Seakirk's museum were to be trusted as reliable purveyors of truth, who caused grown men to grow silent and others to cease fighting amongst themselves.

He wondered if there might be some sort of portrait of her at Artane. It was tempting to ask, just so he could see for himself if she was worth all the good press.

Well, it might be enough of a mystery that getting himself to Artane would be worth the solving of it.

It was very late the next morning when he gripped the steering wheel of his recently liberated Jag in much the same way he had the night before, only it was a headache now that left him clinging to stability, not the condition of the road.

He'd had a terrible night's sleep, with dreams full of things he hadn't understood, and noises he hadn't been able to recognize. It had been a heavy sleep as well, heavy enough that he hadn't been able to rouse himself from it until late in the morning.

He'd descended to find his car, squeaky clean and in perfect working order, waiting for him in the courtyard. Worthington had provided an ample breakfast, but Jake hadn't done it justice. All he'd wanted to do was get out of that ghost-infested, dream-disturbing keep and to Megan de Piaget's comfortable inn where he could crash for the rest of the day before attempting the trip to Artane.

He almost ran into the Range Rover before he saw it. He cursed the driver and continued on his way, cursing himself as well. He wasn't in the habit of complaining, but his head was killing him. It was all he could do to keep his eyes open against the glare of the sun.

And then, quite suddenly, the sun was less of a glare than a blinding flash.

And then he felt himself beginning to spin. It all happened so fast that the only thing that was clear to him was that he was going to die.

Oh, and that his car was going to be completely totalled.

The spinning, rolling, flying sensation took forever. In fact, it went on much longer than it should have. He decided that he really was going to die when the spinning stopped and the ground came up to meet him. Hard.

And then he knew no more.

Chapter 4

Genevieve de Piaget grabbed at the dashboard of the Range Rover and gasped. "Kendrick, look where you're going!"

Her husband was busy staring back at a black Jaguar that had just passed them along the soggy track that the spring zephyr had left behind. It was a nice Jag, even she had to admit. One could not be married to Kendrick de Piaget for any length of time and not have come to some slight appreciation of a finely made car.

But when such appreciation left her distractable spouse almost plowing her and her six children into a stone wall, she had to draw the line.

"Forgive me, my love," Kendrick said, flashing her a smile and putting the car back onto the road.

"That was a nice '67," she remarked casually.

"Aye, it was indeed," he agreed, not sounding nearly as impressed as he should have been by her correctly identifying the black rocket they'd just passed. "I wonder if that man had been at the keep."

"Well, we'll know soon. Maybe he stopped by to visit."

"Perhaps," Kendrick agreed, but he didn't sound convinced.

"I think, Gen, that I'll drop you and the wee ones off and do a little hunting, if you don't mind."

"Really?" she asked, surprised. "Is something wrong?"

He shook his head. "Not at all. I just have an odd feeling. I'm never one to ignore odd feelings, you know."

"Dad, I want to come," Phillip said from the very back of the car.

"Me too," came the chorus from Robin and Jason, followed closely by an echo from five-year-old Richard and three-year-old Christopher.

The baby, sweet Adelaide, only cooed happily.

"Nay, lads," Kendrick said, "you'll help your mother. I'll return straightway and we'll repair to the lists. Nothing like a bit of tramping about in the mud to really make a man feel as though he's done a fine day's work, aye?"

Apparently the consolation prize was enough, though Genevieve suspected Kendrick wouldn't make it without at least one lad in tow.

She found herself deposited with most of her children inside the front door, watched a quick game of rock/paper/scissors to determine who would ride shotgun with his father on the adventure, then prepared for the unenviable task of unpacking from their trip.

It didn't take all that long to at least have things back in the rooms where they would need to be put away eventually. Genevieve was soon sitting with her baby girl in the rocker near the roaring fire Worthington had prepared in the great hall. Genevieve sat and nursed her baby with her toes happily warming against the blaze. She loved to nurse, mostly because it forced her to sit and be still, which was at times quite difficult with five rambunctious boys to ride herd on. She stared into the fire and gave herself a moment or two to contemplate the twists and turns her life had taken. Who would have thought that eight years ago when she was broke, without job or home, and only the lifeline of an inherited castle in England to hang on to, that she would one day be happily ensconced in that castle with a wonderful man and a beautiful family?

Kendrick had spent the last eight years being a father, running his estate, and training up his lads to follow after him.

He'd written a book or two on medieval weaponry and tactics of war that had found their way onto scholarly bookshelves. But she knew that he secretly longed for more.

He wanted to go back home.

Why he hadn't, she didn't know. Perhaps it was complicated. Perhaps he was afraid to go to Artane, where he'd grown up, and find it so changed that it would break his heart.

After all, several years had passed between his youth and his current state of mid-life.

Perhaps he wasn't quite sure how to introduce himself to Artane's current lord.

She couldn't say. But she did have the feeling he was ready to do something about it now. He'd puttered, he'd made money, he'd spent countless hours with his family, but there was something missing. They'd driven by Artane several times—on the A1, actually, where they could see Artane in the far distance—but they'd never gotten close enough for Genevieve to have any idea what the place truly looked like outside of the pictures she'd seen.

The front door opened and shut. Kendrick and Phillip came in and Phillip went immediately to the kitchen to see what was in the fridge. Genevieve looked up and smiled as Kendrick cast himself down in the chair opposite her.

"Find what you were looking for?" she asked.

He sighed. "I need to call the authorities, though I imagine I won't be the first one to do it."

Genevieve looked at him in surprise. "What happened?"

"The Jag rolled and burst into flames."

"Rolled," she said, stunned. "Here? Near here?"

"Keeney's field," he said. "It looks as if the driver took the curve too fast and rolled down the embankment."

"Oh, Kendrick!" she exclaimed. "How horrible."

"Aye," he said, looking into the fire thoughtfully. "I didn't see any body, though. Not thrown from the car, not burning up in the car, not screaming for aid." He chewed on his words for a minute or two before he looked at her. "There was a flash. I saw it from a great distance."

"And what do you think that means?"

"I daresay I don't know," he said with a half smile. "I'm speculating."

"You don't look nearly as worried as you should," she chided.

He stretched and smiled. "I've lived too long to be worried. Besides, we live in a very odd part of the country. There are all manner of peculiar happenings hereabout."

"Don't I know it," she muttered.

He laughed and rose before he leaned over and kissed her briefly. "I'll notify the bobbies and see to the lads. Enjoy your time with your wee one. She's growing too quickly."

"She looks like your mother already."

"A happy combination of you and my dam. What a beautiful lass she will be."

She watched him walk off toward the kitchen and was unsurprised to find him surrounded by a pair of men who hadn't been there but a heartbeat before. It was nothing new, that ghostly garrison. She had her own little collection of men who seemed to think that letting her poke her nose outside the hall door without them in attendance was tantamount to a national emergency. She'd grown used to it and, worse yet, her children had grown used to it. Even her sons' friends had grown used to it, which did nothing to dispel those pesky paranormal rumors that swirled around Seakirk like a mist that wouldn't dispel no matter the amount of sunshine.

She spared Kendrick one last look before she turned back to her baby. Whatever he was up to, he would tell her in time. For now, she would concentrate on the sweet little girl in her arms and let the other inhabitants of the keep take care of everything else.

Chapter 5

Amanda stood at the entrance to the great hall and chafed. She chafed at being confined to the hall by virtue of the press at the doorway. She chafed at the delay that Robin was placing upon her by not leaving when he said he would. And she chafed at the seams of John's best tunic as it rubbed her raw under her gown.

Damnation, but she should have chosen one of his older, more comfortable tunics instead of the cleanest, one which was obviously only clean because it had never been worn.

She waited impatiently as Robin's company made their way with exquisite slowness down the stairs and onto the horses. Robin was coming and going to and from the great hall in his usual fashion of not knowing any direction save up and down. She wondered how it was he managed such a reputation for ruthlessness when he could scarce find his way to the stables.

He scowled at her as he passed. "I do not like this."

"Like what?" she asked politely.

He made a noise of impatience at her and continued his fruitless search for meaning and organization. Amanda stood to the side and watched the goings on, trying to be as patient as her own impatient nature would allow. Her sister-in-law was standing by her horse, swaying. Amanda didn't envy her the journey to Fenwyck not only for the distance but because Anne was still quite ill from her coming child. The only reason they were traveling in such haste was that she had ceased heaving for more than a single day. Poor woman. First the torture of having to endure Robin as her husband, then the misery of carrying his child.

Not that Amanda had anything but fond feelings for Robin's progeny. His first son was possibly the most perfect lad ever created.

Anne's doing, obviously.

Amanda jumped as she found her brother standing in front of her.

"I wish you wouldn't do that," she groused. "Always popping up where you aren't expected . . ."

"I don't like this," he said, for what was surely the dozenth time that morning. "I wish Nick were here."

"He'll return soon," Amanda said confidently. "I'm sure of it."

"And I'm not. I know Wyckham's condition, as do you. He'll be there all summer, doing work he could easily employ stone masons to do for him."

"No one does it as perfectly as he can."

Robin cursed. "So he tells me, but that doesn't aid me now. What am I to do? I need to go now, but I cannot leave you here alone."

"I'm not alone," she said. It would have been far easier if she were. "Besides," she added, wishing she could just give Robin a good shove toward his horse without seeming overanxious to see the back of him, "Miles should be home soon."

"Miles is a child."

"He's ten-and-eight, and hardly a child. Think on yourself at that age. Were you not formidable?" Flattery might work. Indeed, she had never known a time when flattery hadn't served her where Robin was concerned.

"I was formidable at five," Robin snapped, "and Miles is still a lad."

"I have guardsmen aplenty," she said, suppressing the urge

to scratch viciously at the chafing of John's finest tunic. "I will
be fine."

"Stay inside the hall."

"I'll be fine."

"Stay inside the hall," he repeated, enunciating each word
slowly and quite carefully. "I'll have your word."

"What if the hall catches afire?" she asked sweetly. "Am I
to remain inside then? Besides, think on all my recently acquired skills. I will be well protected. Indeed, 'tis almost as if
you were here defending me."

He scowled.

She smiled her most innocent and accommodating smile.

He heaved a great sigh and loped down the stairs. And just
when she thought she might be able to breathe and manage a
discreet scratch, he turned and fixed her with a steely gaze.

"Watch your back," he said seriously. "And don't go outside the gates. I vow, Amanda, you've truly no idea of your
worth, and I speak of more than your dowry."

And then he smiled at her, the charming smile he reserved
for his wife, their mother, and others whom he truly loved.

Damn him. She had vowed that she simply would *not* weep.
Not when she planned, not when she prepared, and certainly
not when she left. Somehow she was unsurprised that it was
Robin who caused her to do so now. She would be glad never
to see him again. He was, without a doubt, the worst brother
ever spawned, full of irritating habits and undesirable charac-
teristics that she would be overjoyed never to be subjected to
again.

"Go," she said, in a choked voice, blinking furiously. "Go
whilst your bride retains her meal where it should reside. I
will be quite safe on my own until you return."

He gave her one last, searching look, then turned and tromped
down the remaining few steps. Amanda watched him quite solic-
itously help his wife into her saddle, give his men his final orders,
then mount up himself. She forced herself to wave to him and
Anne cheerfully when in reality her own gorge was easily as
close to the surface as Anne's had to have been.

She would never see Robin again. She could scarce believe
her . . . her good fortune, of course.

She waited until Robin had exited the gates before she put her plan into action. A quick look back inside the hall revealed Montgomery and John at the high table, as usual, haunting it in hopes of finding something useful left behind. They had already said their good-byes to Robin and were presently arguing over who should be in charge in his absence. They wouldn't miss her for a good hour.

Ample time to be on her way.

She took a deep breath, faced her fate, and walked swiftly down the stairs. The time for tears was past. She'd left missives for each of her family members, explaining what she was doing and vowing to let them know when she found her future. She'd wept all the tears she had to weep. Now all that was left was to be about her plan.

The chapel was her destination and she gained it without trouble. No one had questioned her early morning visit there with the large bundle under her arm, nor did they stop her now as she made her way there with empty hands. After all, piety was a virtue to be prized in a woman her age, one so well into her dotage that only many prayers would rescue her from her unwedded state.

She slipped inside the door, made certain she was alone, then quickly stripped off her gown. She rolled it into a bundle and stashed it in the saddlebag she had hidden behind a saint's shrine for just this occasion. She checked to see that her knife was in her boot, tucked her braid into her tunic, and donned a cloak with a hood she pulled close round her face. With that, she left her family's chapel for the last time.

She made herself continue over the threshold, despite the almost overwhelming temptation to stop and have a final look. It was only a building. Besides, she wouldn't miss the cold floors on winter mornings.

But she would miss the warmth of her family gathered there with her.

"Damnation," she said, digging the palms of her hands into her eyes angrily. She would never achieve her goal if she continued to stand about and blubber like a silly maid. She had things to do, new cities to visit, guileless men to meet.

All of it locked safely in her future.

She slipped down the step to the courtyard floor then made her way quickly to the stable. She walked inside as if she had business there. It was only when she began to saddle Jasper, her father's most uncontrollable horse, that things began to go awry.

"Oy, what ye doin'?" demanded a stable lad. "Don't suppose ye should be in here, should ye?"

Amanda turned and looked at him.

He gaped at her, then seemed to find himself unable to decide if he should shout for aid or bob and scrape. Amanda took his hand, slapped a gold sovereign into it, closed his fingers around it, and continued saddling her horse. The lad made many noises, as if he truly strove to find something useful to say.

Amanda led the stallion out of the stable, leaving the boy babbling behind her. The stable master was nowhere to be found, likely only because Robin had driven the poor man to the cellars for something to shore up his strength. Amanda spared her brother a kind thought, swung up into the saddle, and rode out the inner barbican gate. Men stared at her, she could tell, but no one gainsaid her.

She wasn't sure if she should be relieved by that or troubled. Perhaps her disguise was better than she thought.

Or perhaps Robin had men lying in wait for her to exit the gates so he could lock her in the solar until Nicholas returned.

She rode toward the outer gates cautiously indeed.

But Robin was not loitering outside them, so she proceeded, unmolested. She made her way through the village and far enough out into the countryside that a turning had to be made.

North it would be until she was past keeps where she might be recognized. Then she would turn south and travel to London. She put her heels to Jasper's side and he sprang forward as if he'd been bred for just that moment in time. She laughed in spite of herself. She might be leaving her family, but at least for the moment, she was reveling in speed.

Perhaps that joy would last.

Then again, perhaps not.

A shout went up behind her, very far off and very faint. She looked back over her shoulder. Damnation! She dug her heels into her mount's side. He needed little encouragement to turn his simple run into an all-out gallop. The faint cries of anger behind her turned into shouts of alarm, but she ignored them. She could manage the horse and she could manage her fate. She needed no aid in either.

And she would be damned if her future was to be interfered with by two young lads with too much chivalry and too little sense.

She hazarded a look behind her to find her brothers falling farther and farther behind her. At least it was but the two of them, not the whole of her father's guard. Then again, she supposed the latter was only a matter of time.

She swore again. What was she to do now?

Well, she had no choice but to continue on and leave her brothers to fend for themselves as best they could. The twins would never outride her. She had pinched her sire's finest horse, one that not even he cared to ride outside the gates lest it throw him and be off without a backward glance. Jasper's speed was only matched by his endurance. He could have been to Edinburgh before she knew it if he hadn't unexpectedly slowed.

He trotted up to something in the grass, then leaped over it easily. Amanda was startled enough that she turned him around to see just what he'd bypassed.

A man, lying facedown.

She came to a halt.

Jasper went still.

Even time seemed to slow.

Amanda slid down off her horse before she thought better of it, to the accompaniment of howls in the distance. She looked up to see her brothers flying toward her, each of them hollering and making motions for her to get back up on her horse. She ignored them and took a step closer to the man. He was, she had to admit, finely fashioned.

And, as Fate would have it, wearing nothing but what greatly resembled those flimsy Scottish trews.

She would have studied that particularly interesting bit of clothing more closely, but instead she found herself with her face, and the rest of her, suddenly upon the ground, with her brother flattening her there. Jasper whinnied in distress and she supposed it was only by some saint's protection that she did not find herself flattened by him as well.

"Off," she gasped through a mouthful of grass.

"Are you daft?" John demanded. "My best clothes. That devil horse. A strange man in the grass who might be just waiting there for you to lean over so he might more easily slit your throat! What are you thinking?"

"Get off me," she wheezed.

John heaved himself up with a grunt, but didn't have the courtesy to help her up. He leaned over to study the unmoving man, completely ignoring the fact that he'd done more damage to her than an unconscious man ever could have.

She lay, crushed, on the ground next to the man and stared at the back of his head, wondering what he looked like. She stretched out her hand to touch his limp one that lay in the grass.

And the shock of it was almost enough to steal her breath again.

She squeaked as she found herself quite suddenly hauled to her feet and held there by Montgomery's hands under her arms. She managed to breathe in and out, though she wasn't quite sure she would be doing it very deeply any time soon.

"Can you stand?" Montgomery asked.

"No thanks to John," Amanda said. She took an unsteady step away from Montgomery and tested the extent of the damage. Nothing broken, nor permanently crushed. She brushed off John's clothes, then pushed him out of her way. "Move, you unchivalrous oaf. A knight does not crush his lady under himself and then not aid her."

"You're not my lady, you're my sister," John grumbled, "and you've less sense than a mewling babe. This man could have done you a serious injury."

"John, he's senseless!"

"So he appears," John said, turning to study the man, then stroking on his chin in an unsettlingly good imitation of Robin at his most speculative, "but what is he really?"

Amanda rolled her eyes, leaned over, and felt the man's throat. There was life there in him, and he breathed still. She straightened and looked down at him. It was obvious he'd been robbed. No man, well, other than a Scot of course, would have gone about dressed so scantily. It was summer, true, but summer did not mean an end to rain or to chill.

Nay, something untoward had happened to the man before them. It was only right that they execute a rescue.

But hard on the heels of that thought came the realization that if she aided this man, she would be giving up her own chance for rescue from her string of unsuitable suitors.

Home.

The thought whispered over her like a cool sea breeze. She struggled against it for a moment or two, but the images of her home, the feeling of safety and belonging, all combined together into something she could not fight against.

Tears rolled down her cheeks and she did nothing to stop them.

She looked down at the man again.

"I owe him nothing," she whispered. "I don't have to take him home. I can leave him here and continue on my way, keep on with my plan to flee."

The man didn't reply.

Neither, she noticed after a moment or two of complete silence, did her brothers.

She turned slowly and looked at them. They were staring at her, the both of them, slack-jawed and wide-eyed. She chewed on her lip and looked at them, wondering what she could say now to wipe that expression off their faces.

Montgomery was the first to recover. "Continue on your way?" he asked.

"Keep on with your plan to flee?" John echoed incredulously.

Amanda found, for the first time in her life, that she was without a single useful thing to say. She attempted a smile, but that failed completely.

And her brothers continued to look at her as if she had just plunged daggers into their chests.

"I would have given you clothes if you'd asked," John said in a low voice.

"I would have filched John's clothes *for* you, if you'd asked," Montgomery said.

She looked at the two of them, their earnest gray eyes brimming with tears, their faces wearing identical looks of dismay, and she felt the magnitude of what she had been trying to do catch her with full force.

By the saints, what had she been thinking?

Well, she'd been thinking she would have to leave them just the same when she wed. She had thought the brief notes she had left behind would have seen to the business of her good-byes, leaving her free to flee without any unpleasant and uncomfortable encounters.

But this, this having to face her youngest siblings was far more dreadful than she would have imagined.

She closed her eyes and sank to her knees.

If this was the reaction of her brothers, who in truth had done little but worship her from the time they'd realized she would tramp about in the mud with them and not complain of it on her clothes, what would the rest of her family have said?

What would her mother have said?

She put her face in her hands and wept.

Arms went around her. She hugged her brothers and found nothing to say in her defense.

"How could you?" John asked reproachfully. "How could you leave without telling us you meant to?"

"I can't believe you would," Montgomery added, his voice quavering in a most unmanly way. "Mandy, how could you?"

Amanda kept her arms around them for a moment or two longer, then pulled back. "What else was I to do?" she asked, wiping the tears off her cheeks. "Find myself carried off to some keep by a man who wanted me for naught but my dowry—"

"Like every other woman in England," John noted.

"Not me," Amanda said, delivering a friendly slap to the back of his head where it might inspire him to keep his thoughts to himself. "I would likely never be allowed to come back home anyway. Far better that I leave when 'tis my choice, go where I willed it, than to be little better than a prisoner."

Montgomery cleared his throat. "We could find you a man, couldn't we, John?"

John nodded quickly. "I'm sure we could."

"I've been at market for four years and seen not a man

I would wed without a knife to my throat. Who will you find that I haven't already met?"

Montgomery looked about him until his gaze fell on the senseless man lying next to them. "Here is a man. What is amiss with this one?"

"Other than we haven't a clue who he is?" Amanda asked.

John shrugged. "He's not covered with the pox—"

"John!" she exclaimed. Then she actually felt herself begin to smile. "You are impossible."

Montgomery put his arm around her. "You aren't really going to leave us, are you?"

"I cannot now. I don't know if you two would survive it."

"We wouldn't," they said together.

By the saints, she was doomed. All her planning, her preparations, her agony of heart, all for naught. And now she would have to go retrieve the letters she'd left behind. For one thing, Robin would likely never recover from all the sentiment she'd dribbled all over his missive. The others would think she had lost her senses with all the pleasant things she'd had to say. Aye, she would certainly have to collect those when she returned to Artane.

She sighed deeply and rose.

"Very well, my lads, let us be off before we find ourselves robbed like this poor fool." She looked down at the man. "But we cannot leave him here."

"Nay, we cannot," Montgomery agreed. He knelt and turned the man over carefully.

The man didn't change so much as his breathing.

Amanda wished she could have said the same.

It wasn't as though she hadn't seen a fine-looking man or two during the course of her life. Even her brothers were, she had to admit, extremely handsome. Every one of them. She had even marked the occasionally passable suitor. But this man was easily the equal of any Artane lad, and that was no small compliment. She leaned on her brother's back where she could have a better look.

The man stirred briefly. His eyes opened and he focused on her.

And time stopped.

It was the same feeling she'd had when she'd first touched him.

Overwhelming sweetness, breath-stealing joy, heart-wrenching longing.

By the saints, who *was* this man?

Then his sea-green eyes rolled back in his head and he became as senseless as before. Well, except for the fact that this time he had begun to snore.

Amanda leaned so hard on Montgomery that he had to catch himself with his hands on the ground before he went sprawling.

"By the saints, Mandy," Montgomery said with a laugh, trying to right himself with her on his back, "get off me."

Amanda righted herself with a scowl. "My apologies. I lost my balance."

John grunted. "Indeed. And apparently you had the same effect on him."

Montgomery slung his arm around her companionably. "Or perhaps John's finest tunic and one pair of unpatched hose are what did the poor lad in."

John shot her a faint look of irritation. "Why do you always have to filch my clothes when you're about your adventures? Can't you fashion some of your own?"

"Yours fit best," she said evenly.

"Why can you not use Montgomery's?"

"His aren't as clean."

"I don't suppose I should begrudge you the wearing of them," he grumbled.

"I don't suppose you should. You've no idea how it feels to be trapped inside a keep."

"Ha," John said with a snort. "You should try squiring for Pevensey. You might as well be a prisoner in his dungeon for all the liberty you have. I couldn't be happier to be home where I can roam at will."

"And torment me at your leisure," she added.

He smiled and the charm of it, as usual, left her wondering why it was she wanted to do him so many injuries. "Aye, that as well."

"And what of him?" asked Montgomery, gesturing at the man. "How do we get him home?"

"We'll put him on my horse and I'll ride back with you, Montgomery," Amanda said. "Your mount will never feel my weight."

"And what," asked John as he pulled the man up into a sitting position, "are we going to do with him once we get him home?"

"We'll worry about that later," Amanda said as she watched Montgomery take hold of the man's lower half.

"Dungeon," John said with a grunt.

"Solar," Montgomery suggested as he helped John heave.

"He might be an outlaw," John said through gritted teeth.

"He's too clean to be an outlaw," Montgomery huffed.

Amanda had to agree; the man was, outside of a bit of dirt in his hair and some blood here and there, remarkably clean. She stood by and watched as her brothers got their quarry settled over her saddle. She hesitated, then looked at the lads.

"I think I should ride behind him and keep him balanced. We'll offer him the courtesy of our hall when we return, but watch him carefully, lest he prove to be false."

"I don't think Sir Walter will like this," John warned. "He'll demand that we lock him away until we know who he is."

"I daresay that's true," Amanda agreed, but chose not to think about it. She had far more overwhelming things to think on.

Her ride that morning had produced two moments of complete giddiness, when she thought her soul had crossed from joy to madness.

The first had been at the peak of Jasper's speed, when she thought he might fly if asked.

The second had been when the man had opened his eyes and looked at her.

She rubbed her hands over her face, took a deep breath, and accepted Montgomery's boost onto Jasper's back. Perhaps she had traveled fully to madness, leaving good sense and caution behind. Perhaps she had been trapped in her father's keep for too long.

Perhaps she should have continued her flight and ignored a stranded, obviously in-need-of-aid traveler.

She put her hand on his back and felt a shiver go up her hand, as if she'd touched something she shouldn't.

"Dungeon," John said, to no one in particular.

"Dungeon," Amanda agreed, though she was having second thoughts about who should be going in.

Considering all the impossible things she felt just looking at the man, it just might be the safest place for her.

Chapter 6

Jake woke up with a start. He sat up just as suddenly, then realized that that was an extraordinarily bad idea. He clutched his head in his hands until it stopped pounding long enough for him to think straight. He'd been in the car. The last thing he remembered was the spinning that had gone on endlessly. In fact, the spinning was still going on, only he was quite sure he was sitting on something solid.

So out of a very strong instinct for self-preservation, he kept his eyes closed, his fists pressed over his eyes, and decided to take his time figuring out where he was.

He simply sat for a moment. He was in a farmhouse, probably. An old stone one, likely. There was no offensive smell, but there wasn't anything that smelled like dinner on the stove either, which didn't bode well for his growling stomach. He should have taken advantage of Worthington's traditional English breakfast earlier that morning and downed some fried tomatoes and sizzling sausage.

He gingerly felt the bench he was sitting on. It was wooden, quite smooth, and gave no indication of either its origin or ownership. He put his hand back over his eyes and slowly swung his feet around to the floor, where he could rest his elbows on his knees and let his head get used to the idea.

And as he did, images began to come back to him.

One image in particular.

Eyes. Turquoise—no, aquamarine. Or perhaps a soft, pale sapphire. No, aquamarine, he finally decided. Blue-green eyes in a face that could cause angels to weep.

Man, could he ever conjure up a hallucination when he had to.

He would have shaken his head, but he knew where that would lead, so he remained still until the pounding in his head subsided a bit and he thought he could keep his lack of breakfast down where it should be. He moved his fists from off his eyes and anchored them firmly under his chin where they could do the most good in holding up his aching head. He opened his eyes slowly and hoped for the best.

Well, it was for damn sure he wasn't in a hospital. That was a good thing. The downside was, he had no idea where the hell he was.

He looked around him slowly, trying to absorb the details of his surroundings. He was, from what he could tell, in some sort of study. But it looked nothing like Seakirk's study. The glaring omissions were the big-screen TV and comfortable couch. There were wooden chairs, and though he had to admit that there were cushions on them that looked relatively comfortable, they were not of Seakirk's ilk. Under the deep window stood a desk littered with papers of all kinds.

Parchment kinds, actually.

A bookshelf stood against one wall. There were, and he could count them from where he sat, ten books. The other shelves were filled with what looked like ink pots, several wooden boxes, and other kinds of study paraphernalia allowed by a man who didn't particularly care for knickknacks.

Heavy wooden shutters were pulled back from the windows and folded against the walls. Jake almost wished they were covering the windows, for the cold was numbing. The chill came up from the stone floor as well, a floor devoid of a good, thick carpet, but instead strewn with straw. He frowned, then shrugged. It took all kinds, he supposed. He followed the floor as it led to a fireplace across the room that was unfortunately devoid of a good fire.

All in all, the place could have done with a good remodel.

Then again, if the owners were going for bona fide medieval, they had it nailed. Jake had been through enough castles to appreciate the authenticity of the place. He just wished he was appreciating it with the promise of a pint in front of a roaring fire at day's end to look forward to.

Well, the only thing he could surmise was that somehow he had been liberated from his car and brought to the closest house for a little recovery. That didn't bode well for his Jag, but he seemed to be free of injuries, outside of a colossal headache, so perhaps the Jag had escaped as well.

He got to his feet, swayed, then waited until his head cleared. He patted his pockets and then realized something quite unsettling.

He was standing there in his boxers.

No wonder he was so cold.

Good grief, what had happened to him? He speculated quickly. Maybe he'd been robbed. Maybe he'd been abducted. Maybe he'd been robbed, then abducted.

Or maybe he'd just been taken in by some kind soul— hopefully that stunning woman he'd hallucinated—who had taken his clothes to give them a good cleaning and would soon be handing them back to him with his keys and his wallet. He would then leave the house and find his Jag in pristine condition outside.

It could happen.

He took a deep breath and crossed the room to the door. He was feeling great. He would feel even better when he was back in his car and on his way. Maybe he could call the earl of Artane and apologize for the delay and thereby buy himself another couple of days' recuperation in the Boar's Head Inn. He seemed to be sadly lacking in sleep hours of late.

And he could trace the beginning of that directly back to his father, damn him.

Jake took a hold of the door handle and pulled. It didn't open. Not good.

He tried again, to no avail. He then realized that he had been locked in. And for some reason, that was a very unhappy confirmation of his worst fears.

Fortunately for him, he had collected a wide variety of rather unsavory skills during his long and illustrious career as hunter of gems and other items requiring difficult and semi-legal acquisition. Thad, a man whom he had hired as a guide on his first trip into the depths of South America in search of the perfect bit of sapphire, had taught him a few of the more innocuous things he himself had learned in a special operations unit he wouldn't talk about. Jake had been tempted to push Thad for some answers until Thad had given him a password to use while they camped, just in case Jake had to get up and pee in the middle of the night. Apparently, Thad didn't wake up well.

And his camping buddies didn't wake up at all unless they warned Thad first that they intended to move.

Jake smiled at the memory now, but at the time he'd wondered just what in the hell he'd gotten himself into, hiring a man with such a short, pointed résumé. But he'd gotten his sapphire, he'd earned a very lethal friend, and he'd learned how to pick any lock in front of him silently and with a minimum of tools.

He wasn't silent now, and it took the liberation of a very rustic shutter hinge to help him, but he got the door open eventually. Too bad Thad hadn't been all that up on medieval-type locks, otherwise Jake might have been able to leave the window-covering intact. At least Thad wasn't around to give Jake that look that said oh-so-clearly what a pansy he was if he couldn't get something open with a wish, a prayer, and a bit of bent, rusty wire.

Jake stepped out into the hallway. It looked a bit like Seakirk, but this place was definitely in need of a little of Worthington's spit and polish. And some central heat. Jake rubbed his bare arms as he followed his nose to the left. Dinner was that way, and dinner had to mean hosts and that meant an explanation and perhaps some directions to the inn.

The torches that burned in sconces along the hallway were real, with real flames and very real smoke. Jake shook his head. Cheap was one thing, but this was taking frugality to an entirely new level. What was wrong with a good space heater or two?

He came to a circular staircase and descended it silently, no mean feat considering his lack of balance at the moment. The stairs widened at the bottom of the flight and then, quite suddenly, he was out into a great hall.

And out, apparently, into the middle of a costume ball.

He stood stock still and gaped. He could feel his mouth hanging open, but couldn't do a damn thing about it.

Massive logs crackled in the fireplaces set into the walls. A long table sat near that fire with mailed knights eating enthusiastically and talking just as animatedly. To his right on the dais was another long table, covered with a cloth and a decent amount of food and boasting a handful of quite impressively carved chairs. Only three of those chairs were occupied at the moment, two by young men and one by a woman.

That woman.

The one with the blue eyes.

Jake retrieved his jaw, but only partway. He tried shaking his head, but that only left him clutching the table to keep his feet. His vision began to blur, but not so much that he didn't notice the two young men leaping to their feet and bellowing in dismay. Before he could ask them to quit shouting, he found himself grabbed by the arms and slammed back against the wall.

"Hey," he said in irritation, "what the hell—"

A knife at his throat effectively cut off everything else he had to say. He attempted a brief struggle, but found the knife to be quite sharp, so he ceased.

This was not good.

Jake listened to the babbling going on around him and tried to decipher it. It was difficult, but he wondered if some of that might have been due to the blood thundering in his ears. He closed his eyes and listened for several minutes.

Well, what he could say with certainty was that they were speaking French, or perhaps some dialect of it. Unfortunately his French, despite years of it at Eton and more study of it at Cambridge, was not what it should have been. It was serviceable, however, and he would make use of it, once he had the chance to sit down and listen in peace.

But that would come after he'd extricated himself from his current less-than-comfortable situation.

He could have escaped, he supposed. After all, picking locks wasn't all Thad had taught him, in return for a few one-of-a-kind baubles for the wife he adored. But that would mean Jake would hurt the people he liberated himself from, and he wasn't quite ready to do that yet. No, best he wait and see what was up—and where he was.

It would, of course, give him ample time to look at the woman in front of him and try to catch his breath.

He opened his eyes and stared at her. Her long, dark hair was held back from her face by a circlet of silver. Whoever she really was probably didn't matter. In the game these people were playing, reenactment or whatever, she was the princess and played the part to within an inch of her life. Her posture was regal, her profile noble. She spoke with authority and in a rich, melodious voice that left him wanting to do something that would require her to speak some more.

The argument escalated.

The woman glared at the older man, with the young men standing behind her and nodding, until the older man took a very small step back.

And then Jake found her turning to him.

And he lost what breath remained in him.

He didn't suppose there were words in any of the smattering of languages he knew that could possibly describe her. To call her beautiful just didn't do her justice. She was flawless, like a stone of perfect clarity that had been cut by a master gemsmith at the height of his powers. Jake could only stand and admire her, mesmerized by the facets of her face, her hair, and those eyes that simply defied description.

She stood several paces away from him, surrounded by the three men she had successfully argued with, and many others. She spoke to him, but he didn't have a clue what she'd just said. If he just could have had a few days to get his ear accustomed to what he was hearing, he wouldn't have had any problems.

Perhaps another language might work in the meantime. He considered Gaelic, but what she was saying sounded nothing like any of the pithy phrases he'd learned from Alistair or Alistair's testy grandmother, phrases of which from the latter had usually included dire warnings about his state of bachelorhood and more dire warnings about what would happen to a man who plundered her stew pot uninvited one too many times. No, Gaelic would not do here.

The woman before him asked him several questions.

He couldn't begin to string two words together in answer.

The lads flanking the woman, who looked enough like her that he assumed they were brothers—and twins at that—twirled their fingers near their temples in a sign that reached across cultures. He agreed heartily. And just in case he really was losing his mind, he trotted out several possible explanations for his current situation before he lost his remaining brain cells.

He'd fallen in with a band of gypsies. Maybe that exquisite bit of aquamarine he'd paid pennies for and vowed never to cut into gems really had been hexed and he was suffering the penalties of one who had dared cut it into gems. He'd gotten several stunning pieces out of it and had suffered no regrets, though he had to admit he was beginning to regret it now.

Alternately, maybe he was being held captive by this woman in order to become her love slave.

Then again, maybe he really had rolled his car and he was now in a coma, living out the most outlandish of medieval fantasies.

He considered the last and found it to be the most realistic. Who knew what kind of drugs they gave you while you were comatose and what kinds of very real hallucinations those drugs produced? After all, hadn't he gone to bed after looking at what had ostensibly been a band of medieval ghosts arguing over the beauty of several medieval ladies? All of that just had to be filtering into his damaged brain. It made perfect sense.

Of course, there was that quite sharp bit of steel pressing up against his neck, but maybe that was some sort of hospital tube bothering him subconsciously.

Either that, or he really had been captured by a band of gypsies and heaven only knew what they wanted from him.

Suddenly, the older man barked out an order. The woman protested, but Jake realized that she just might be overridden when he saw several mailed soldiers rise from one of the tables near the door. He suspected that wasn't to make him feel more at home.

The time for action had come. He went into Thad mode, as Thad himself modestly termed it, and first slumped to throw his captors off guard before he disabled the two holding him against the wall. Others were either dodged or disabled just as easily, and he honestly tried not to leave any casualties behind him, though he had to admit that the chain mail they were wearing was not within his realm of experience. It was entirely possible that several of the men who tried to stop him would be nursing broken bits of bodies in the next little while.

Shouts went up behind him as he sprinted across the hay-strewn floor and jerked open the massive front door. He leaped down the steps and was halfway across the courtyard before he felt himself beginning to slow. It was as if someone had suddenly poured molasses into his veins, molasses and a sense of inevitability that sank down into his very bones. He'd never felt anything like it before.

He slowed to a stop.

The evening sun was in his face, but that wasn't much trouble because it was what loomed behind him that he had to worry about. He studied the courtyard beneath his feet. It was dirt, though he could see a finely laid cobblestone swath that wandered down toward the barbican a goodly ways off. Whatever castle this was, apparently no expense had been spared in its construction.

He gathered himself together and turned slowly, looking upward as he did so.

A castle rose up before him, stark in its simplicity, massive in its proportions, unforgiving in its martial superiority. It was a place of refuge from war, shelter from the elements, comfort for the weary traveler.

Artane . . .

Of course. And he had a nagging suspicion this wasn't the same Artane that the determined tourist might find lurking in the back of the National Trust brochure.

It figured.

He looked at the front door. Souls spilled out of it and down the front steps, all watching him as if he'd truly lost his mind. He looked back at them in like manner, because it was for damn sure one group of them had lost its mind and he liked to believe it wasn't him. Unfortunately he seemed to be the one out of his element, so it was probably best to assume he was the one really out there.

The woman started toward him, the woman whose face could likely change the course of wars.

"Amanda!" her brothers shouted, before they pulled her back into the crowd.

Amanda.

Of course. He found he was even less surprised to discover her identity than he was to realize in which courtyard he stood. No wonder the ghosts had waxed rhapsodic about her. He would have too, if he'd had the wherewithal to do so.

Fortunately for his unperspicacious tongue, someone clunked him over the head with something very hard and he descended quite happily into oblivion before he had to do any more searching for pithy phrases to describe the most beautiful woman he'd ever seen.

Chapter 7

A *manda* crept into the shadowy kitchen, wincing at the
sound of swearing she could hear wafting up from the
dungeons. The dungeons were found, conveniently enough,
behind and under the kitchens, in the seaward wall. She supposed that in the height of summer they might be not uncomfortable, for the sea breeze that blew in might be pleasant and
perhaps even warm. But a fierce storm raged outside and that
dungeon with its opening only protected by iron bars driven
deep into the stone had to be less than hospitable. She shivered, from more than just the chill.

She had the feeling they were making a horrible mistake.

She hadn't been allowed to watch as the guards tossed their
prisoner into the hole. She'd managed to get close enough
during the wee hours of the morning to hear him working on
the lock that kept him inside his cell, but unfortunately for
him, her father's guards were not ones to be caught sleeping at
their posts. The man cursed them each time they whacked his
questing fingers with whatever they had to hand, until he finally gave up trying to unlock the bolt. He had resorted to
merely cursing.

He'd been cursing for quite some time now.

The cadence of his cursing didn't sound like that of an uneducated peasant, but the words certainly sounded like a poor imitation of peasant's English. He had cursed in several other languages she hadn't understood, and she was not uneducated. One of her father's garrison knights said some of the words sounded like the Gaelic one of his own father's retainers spoke. Amanda had come to the conclusion, quite early that morning, that the man they had locked up in her father's cellar was no peasant, but perhaps a great Scottish lord who had little interest in the language spoken south of his home.

Unfortunately, trying to convince her very sleepy brothers of any of this had earned her nothing but more snores. Sir Walter had been likewise unresponsive to her attempts to gain entrance to the garrison hall, where she could confer with him privately.

All this had left her with only one choice.

She would have to liberate the man herself.

Soot from the hearth in her father's solar had covered her face well enough, and John's most patched and stained hose had been her next choice—though in truth she had seriously considered choosing something less disgusting from his trunk. He would have deserved it, the wretch, for having slept through her heartfelt, guilt-ridden recitations on the evils of having imprisoned a man unjustly. John had scratched, belched and rolled over again to descend once more into pleasant slumber. Aye, he deserved whatever was missing from his trunk.

The final addition to her disguise had been a handful of Nicholas's clothes wrapped around her middle, under her tunic. She might look like a kitchen lad, but she was definitely a well-fed one. Surely, her brother wouldn't begrudge her his clothing. It wasn't his best, but it was serviceable and would certainly keep the prisoner covered.

All of which had left her about her self-appointed mission, using her best skills of subterfuge and disguise to make her way through the kitchens, past Cook, who only yawned at yet another filthy lad about his morning's labor, and down to the dungeons where her next task was to use the guards' dungeon keys in the most appropriate place.

The guards jumped to their feet when her foot touched the ground. She assessed them quickly. There was no wine at their elbows, damn them, so she couldn't liberate the keys from their drunken fingers. And the men were frowning, never a good omen.

She considered what means she might use to convince them she should be obeyed, then decided on a direct command.

"Give me the keys," she demanded.

They blinked. She could almost see them considering from whom they might receive the most trouble if they obeyed her—Sir Walter now or her sire when he returned.

"I am chatelaine here," she announced, then she paused. "Presently," she added, wanting to be truthful. "Until my mother returns."

They hesitated, then shook their heads, almost as one.

"Too dangerous," said one.

"We've firm orders to keep him where he is," said the other.

Amanda gestured at the cage in frustration. "Does he sound dangerous to you?" she asked. "Nay, he does not. He sounds irritated. For all we know, he is a lord from across the border who will bring his equally irritated clansmen down upon us for not treating him with the respect he should have been accorded from the first."

The guardsman on the right shifted. "Aye, well, I've a cousin who wed with a Scotsman and I must admit that I've heard this man make sounds akin to what that Scot makes when he's all in a snit."

"See?" Amanda said. "That proves a great deal."

"But the rest of the time he's blatherin' on in the peasant's tongue," said the other. "And so poorly that not even me, with my fair bit of learning, can make heads or tails of it."

"All the more reason to see him go," Amanda said firmly. "We'll release him and set him outside the gates. He'll go his way and that will be the end of it."

The guards hesitated. Amanda walked forward and relieved the one on the left of his keys. When he squeaked in protest, she gave him the look she gave her brothers when they had pushed her too far. The man looked horribly indecisive, which gave her time to turn around and unlock the bolt that kept the bars securely closed. She dropped the lock onto the floor and opened the grillwork—

And found herself suddenly jerked inside the cell itself with an arm across her neck.

Damnation, when would she find sense? Perhaps never, now that she was going to die. She was a fool. Beguiled by a handsome face . . .

The guards set up a cry. Amanda swore. There would be hell to pay now.

"You idiot," she said to the man holding onto her, "now we'll *both* find ourselves locked up. And here I came to free you. Ha."

"Go home," he said.

At least that's what she thought he said. By the saints, the man could not manage even a simple phrase without mangling it. Perhaps next time she would listen to her father's steward, her father's garrison knights, and the more logical part of her mind. The man behind her might not have been a starving peasant, but she had serious doubts about his being a lord. Surely even a poorly educated Scottish laird could have mustered up more coherent French when pressed than this one.

"Help," he added.

"Aye," she said, in exasperation, "that had been my plan. I even brought clothes with me for such an event, you great horse's arse."

He grunted, but seemingly had nothing to say.

Amanda pursed her lips. Perhaps he was merely a Scottish clansman, lost on the wrong side of the border. She stood there with his arm across her neck, leaned back against him, and gave that more thought. Perhaps he was a Scottish clansman who had been robbed and left for dead on her father's land. That, too, was possible.

But where had he been going? What business had he been about? Where was he from in truth?

Well, wherever he was from, he was chilly. She stroked his forearm across her throat absently. She couldn't help but have some bit of sympathy for a man who had been trapped in this bloody place for the whole of the night, cold, hungry—

He sneezed all of the sudden.

"Exactly," Amanda said.

He lowered his arm far enough for her to ease herself away from him. She pulled Nicholas's clothes from beneath her tunic and turned to face him.

"Here," she said. "Take these."

He accepted the clothes with a look of surprise, then hesitated, as if he wasn't sure what to say.

"Thank you?" she prompted.

"Thank you," he repeated, his pronunciation of that, at least, without flaw.

The guards were still making noises of alarm. Amanda turned her back on the prisoner to give him some privacy and made motions for the guards to be silent.

She waited, tapping her foot as she stood there in that very chilly dungeon and listened to the man dressing behind her. When he stopped making noise, she turned to find him wearing her brother's clothes. He was, however, quite still.

He was staring at his shoes.

Not that she could blame him. Unfortunately, the only shoes she'd been able to find were the slippers that Nicholas wore—under very loud protests, of course—to court, or when royalty descended upon Artane. They looked exceptionally ridiculous on the muscular man in front of her, but they looked equally as ridiculous on Nicholas, so perhaps there was nothing to be done about it. At least when Nicholas wore them, he was dressed in his finery. The man in front of her was dressed in rugged work clothing; dainty shoes were not a good addition.

And then he looked at her.

And Amanda wondered how it was she could be so warm in such a chilly place.

She was, as she desperately reminded herself, quite accustomed to the sight of very handsome men. There wasn't a man in her family that didn't cause women of all ages to either blush prettily at their winks, or fan themselves after the men in question had passed. She was unimpressed by a handsome face, unaffected by pleasing features, completely unmoved by strength of arm.

But somehow, despite her indifference to all those things,

she found herself being quite undone just the same. There she stood in her father's uncomfortable dungeon, freezing and burning at the same time, staring into darkened eyes, and all she could do was wish desperately that she hadn't used so much soot on her face.

He reached out and touched her arm.

She tried to ignore that. It wasn't as if she hadn't touched men before. Indeed, she'd slapped several. But never in all her days had the mere touch of someone else's hand on her person left her so unsettled.

And there she was, on the verge of sending him away.

He slid his hand down her arm until he had enclosed her fingers with his own.

He pointed toward the open door.

Suddenly, the spell was broken. She had expected him to leave. Indeed, hadn't she come down here for just this purpose? Then why did it suddenly seem like the worst idea she'd ever had? And given how many ideas she'd had over the course of her life which had turned out to be quite bad ones indeed, that was saying something.

Before she thought better of it, she pulled him along behind her, ignoring the protests of the dungeon guards. Cook hardly looked up from the stirring of her pot, and the kitchen lads were too surprised to squeak.

The great hall was a bit more difficult. Her brothers were there, yawning and scratching. Sir Walter was hastily pulling his tunic over his head and bellowing for his squire to hand him his sword. But even he fell silent when he saw her with her baggage in tow. Sir Walter's men were scrambling to put themselves in some sort of defensive position. Amanda glared her open-mouthed brothers into submission but found the way blocked by Sir Walter and a contingent of his more intimidating lads.

"My lady," he began, "I must insist—"

"I insist, as well," she said firmly, pulling her stranger behind her. "A terrible mistake has been made."

"Aye, those shoes with that tunic," John muttered.

"Be silent, you fool," Amanda snapped. She turned back to Sir Walter and took a deep breath. "This is no peasant." His language aside, of course. "If we cannot offer a man of his obvious nobility a place at the table, then we must allow him the use of the gates. To hold him prisoner is to bring nothing but ruin down upon our very deserving heads."

"*Oui,*" the man behind her said, his rich, melodious voice sounding every inch the educated, cultured lord.

A pity he couldn't seem to spew forth any other phrases that might make him sound less an idiot. Amanda almost turned to tell him as much, but the fight was in front of her, not behind.

"Let him go?" Sir Walter said doubtfully.

"What else are we to do?" Amanda asked. "Hold him here until his folk come seeking him and then lay siege to the castle in return for the insult to their lord? If you are bent on keeping him in the dungeon, best kill him now and toss his body by the wayside, so his people may find him there and think ruffians are responsible. And then you, Sir Walter, will have his blood on your hands, not I."

Sir Walter hesitated, a sure sign he was near to being bested. But he was, after all, an old and wily warrior and had not earned his reputation for relentlessness in battle for naught.

"And if we release him, how will we know he will return to his folk?" he asked. "Insult has already been done to him. It is possible he will lie in wait outside the gates, ready to take his vengeance."

"With us safely inside," she asked, "what does that matter?"

Sir Walter smiled pleasantly. "My thinking exactly. So, my lady Amanda, you are in agreement that until your elder brother or your sire returns, you will keep yourself within the gates? For safety's sake?"

Damn the man. The glint of victory in his eye was all too plain. She scowled at him, but saw no way to accomplish her desire without giving up something in return.

"I will not go outside the gates without an escort," she conceded. "But I also will not be kept prisoner in my own home. Not even for this man's sake will I go that far."

Sir Walter was no fool, and she supposed he knew he would get nothing else from her. He nodded in satisfaction.

"Done."

"Harumph," she said as she pulled the reason for her loss of freedom along behind her. Men parted to allow her passage, but her brothers followed immediately, like a wake that could not be outswum.

"At least those are Nick's clothes," John said clearly. "And he won't miss the shoes."

"Shut up, John," Amanda said, wrenching open the front door. She pulled at her captive, but he wouldn't move. She turned to look at him.

There was, she had to admit, a look of genuine regret in his face.

"He's under her spell already," Montgomery said matter-of-factly. "Another one felled without a stroke."

"He's anxious to go home," Amanda said flatly. She looked at the man and nodded down the stairs. "This way," she said.

He wouldn't move. He pointed at her. "Amanda."

"Aye, well, that would be my name," she said briskly. "And yours?"

He stared at her blankly.

"He's daft," John noted, sounding rather disappointed by that discovery. "Perhaps that is why he was robbed. He was too big a fool to run."

"Perhaps 'tis merely because we don't speak his language," Montgomery said. "I'll try Scots." He said something to him in what Amanda could only assume was Gaelic. Lord Pevensey had many Scottish retainers, lads he imported from over the border who didn't care if they served an Englishman or not. Montgomery was forever muttering in it, though he was the first to admit that he didn't know as much as he might have had Lord Pevensey given him but five heartbeats peace to breathe now and then.

The man looked at Montgomery in astonishment, then replied.

Amanda looked at her brother. "Well, what did he say?"

"I think," Montgomery said hesitantly, "that his name was Jake."

"Jake," Amanda repeated, the name feeling foreign and strange on her tongue. She looked at the man. "Jake?"

"Jackson Alexander Kilchurn," he said slowly. "IV."

"Kilchurn," she repeated. "IV."

"Jake."

"Jake."

John sighed in exasperation. "Just call him 'dolt' and be done. I for one would like to return to my bed!"

Amanda would have delivered the slap he deserved aside his head instead of to the empty air if he hadn't been so quick. She contented herself with a look of warning before she turned back to Jake.

Jackson Alexander Kilchurn IV. If that wasn't a Scottish name, and one made for a lord not a peasant, she didn't know what was. Aye, they would have made a mistake by confining him.

Even if that confinement would have meant she might have been able to see him now and then.

"A horse, then," she said, "and he'll be on his way." She looked up at Lord Kilchurn. "You're ready to go home?" she asked.

"You're ready to go home," he repeated, flawlessly.

"An imbecile," John grumbled. "And he looked so fierce . . ."

Amanda hissed for him to be still. She looked at Lord Kilchurn and found that he had offered his hand.

She paused.

That sweetness washed over her, the same feeling she had had the past pair of months every time she looked at her home, the same feeling she'd had when she first touched the man standing before her.

Home . . .

She felt, for the first time ever, as if she might have met someone she could be fond of. She could certainly spend many years looking into those beautiful eyes and finding herself not unhappy. That she was escorting him out of her father's front gates shouldn't have surprised her.

Poor lordly imbecile that he was.

He rubbed his head suddenly, as if it pained him, then waited for her to take his hand.

She did.

And to keep herself from making a complete fool of herself, she led her stranger to the stables, her brothers trailing along behind her, Sir Walter and his men trailing along behind them. Jake spent a goodly amount of time looking at his shoes as he walked, shaking his head as if he either couldn't believe he sported something so completely repulsive or he couldn't fathom that anyone would put those colors together and call it fashion. Amanda shared his opinion thoroughly, but refrained from comment.

She stopped at the entrance to the stables and waited until the stable master had come out. He bowed politely.

"Aye, my lady? Are you thinking to exercise your sire's finest again today?"

She looked at him archly. "I am a very good rider, Master Otto."

"Too good, I'd say," he replied, but with a polite nod. "Who will you have today?"

"Have we not some mount about who might bear this lord hence to his home?"

Master Otto looked Jake over, then nodded and retreated into the stables. He came out several minutes later leading a tall, black horse with a white blaze down his nose. The animal looked good-natured, but not overly polite. Amanda recognized him as one her father had bought a month or two ago. She'd never ridden him, preferring to see what sort of demon horses she could liberate from her father's stables. Perhaps Jake would find him to his liking.

Master Otto invited Jake to mount.

Jake stared at him blankly.

John made "I-said-as-much" noises that forced her to elbow him in the ribs. He coughed and fell blessedly silent.

"Montgomery, tell him he may take the horse."

"I don't know how to say horse in Scots," Montgomery said.

"Then say, 'Get up there and ride off,'" Amanda suggested. "Say anything!"

Montgomery said something. Jake considered, then shook his head with a smile. He made walking motions with his fingers.

"As I said," John muttered. "He's hopeless!"

Amanda could hardly believe her eyes. Was it possible

this man, this handsome, powerful-looking man, could not ride? She stared at him in shock and a bit of dismay. Perhaps he was as John had said: a simpleton let loose from his village when someone failed to attend him closely enough.

But, by the saints, he was so handsome. She could hardly bring herself to believe he wasn't what he seemed.

Perfect.

Beautiful beyond belief.

"Show him the gates," John prodded, "before he forgets how to use his feet."

Jake sighed.

With regret, if anyone had noticed.

As if he might have liked to stay.

"Tell him to go, Montgomery," John said pointedly. "Before our sister swoons any further."

Montgomery sighed and said something to Jake. Jake replied, haltingly. Montgomery looked at Amanda.

"He said, and 'tis but a guess at that, that he's sorry to have to leave the table so quickly but stew stirred too much turns to mush."

Amanda considered.

Very well, so he was an imbecile. "Tell him he is free to go but to have a care. Ruffians abound, as he well knows. Can he find his village?"

Montgomery and the man attempted conversation for quite some time before Montgomery turned back to her.

"He hopes he can find his village. As I said, Mandy, his language is very weak. But he promises to be wary and thanks you for the hospitality of your cooking fire." Montgomery paused. "It sounds to me as if he learned his words at the cooking fire of an ill-humored Scottish grandmother."

Amanda blinked. "I daresay."

John blew out his breath and walked away.

Amanda gestured toward the gates in front of her. "There you are," she said to Jake. "Off with you, then."

He turned toward her. The next thing she knew, he had taken her face in his hands and was scrubbing off the soot. She stared up at him in surprise, then wished she hadn't. Daft though he might have been, and incapable of intelligible speech, she had to admit that he was quite magnificent.

And his touch made her tremble.

He smiled once more, then walked away.

Amanda stood amidst the activity that was normal fare for her father's home, and watched Jake for as long as she could. He stood taller than the groups of peasants as he made his way to the front gates and out. She watched until she couldn't see him anymore.

He did, she noted with something akin to satisfaction, turn himself about several times to look back at her.

When she could no longer see him, she turned but found her way blocked by Sir Walter and his men. She knew the steward didn't care for her roamings along the walls, and she was quite certain she could have told him to take himself and his men to the devil quite happily, but it had been a most tiresome morning already, and that, added to the intrigues and difficulties from the day before, and the trials leading up to that, had left her with great pains in her head.

She ignored the pain in her heart.

"I will take my ease in my chamber," she said regally.

"As you will, my lady," Sir Walter said, with a little bow.

She walked sedately inside the hall, giving one after the other of her younger brothers a shove when they tried to waylay her, and continued on to her chamber.

Then she bolted for the roof.

By the time she reached the west wall, Jake was leaving the village. She watched him until he was nothing but a speck in the distance. And then came the point when she wasn't sure if she was actually watching him or seeing motes in the morning air.

Well, that was that. She was better off. He was beautiful, but lacking in wit. Her father never would have approved. Far better that she watch him leave before her heart was involved.

All the same, perhaps she would do well in a few hours to have herself a ride outside the gates. It wouldn't do to let a guest find himself assaulted by ruffians. And, as her father would be the first to say, lawlessness in the north was on the increase.

Aye, she would make certain Jackson Alexander Kilchurn IV hadn't been waylaid again.

Chapter 8

J*ake* walked along a dusty track, contemplating the twists
and turns of Fate. He also contemplated the twists and
turns of his pointy-toed shoes, but that was but a distraction
from the irritation of tights that chafed. He decided, at one
point, that Fate had a very vile sense of humor. As did Gideon
de Piaget, whom Jake would repay for his current straits as
soon as he possibly could.

That was assuming he could find Gideon to repay him.
Jake scratched his head, but that didn't provide him with any
decent answers—and answers were certainly what he needed
at present.

He stuck his hands in his pockets only to realize he didn't
have pockets, damn it, he had tights. He scowled. If he managed to get home, he would definitely have to find something
else to wear right away or no one would ever take him seriously again. Not that anyone would, if they ever caught wind
of where he'd just recently been.

Not that anyone would have believed him anyway. He
wasn't sure he really believed it himself, except that the facts
were almost beyond dispute.

There was the business in the great hall the night before,

with everyone in their medieval costumes. Weird, but that could have been just a fluke. But waking in a dungeon? Twenty-first century Englishmen didn't put other men in holes under kitchens and leave them there for indeterminate lengths of time.

The language was another problem. He hadn't had all that much chance to familiarize himself with it the night before; the men sitting outside his cell had been remarkably uncommunicative. Still, what he had heard from them, and what he'd heard from Amanda had brought him to the unmistakable conclusion that she and her family spoke French. But it wasn't modern-day French.

Then there was the English he'd heard spoken amongst the guards and in the village to consider. He'd lived in England for more than half his life and he'd grown quite accustomed to, if not proficient at, a variety of accents. What he'd been listening to for the past twenty-four hours belonged in some Anglo-Saxon tutorial at Cambridge, not in the environs of Artane.

Artane.

And medieval Artane, at that.

He shook his head. Who would have thought it? It was no wonder the place had given him the willies, when this was what it had had in store for him.

He paused. And what had it had in store for him? Besides a trip back into the past?

Amanda.

If he hadn't recognized her as the woman that group of medieval ghosts had waxed rhapsodic over, he might have just thought she was a beautiful woman and called it good.

Then again, maybe not.

She was, in all honesty, far beyond anything he'd ever expected.

He stopped and stared into the distance, past trees that looked just like trees in his day, and wondered. Was it possible? Was he hallucinating? Was it a reenactment society gone mad, reenacting far beyond what their club charter allowed? Were they Artane fanatics who had permission from Artane's earl to take over his castle and turn it into a slice of the past?

Not likely.

But the thought that he actually had traveled to a different time was just as unlikely. Things like that didn't happen. He lived in a modern, rational time with modern, rational occurrences. That paranormal stuff was just mumbo-jumbo made up by people with too much time on their hands and a driving need to measure things on little instruments of their own making. His world was cold, hard reality; rocks, minerals, things that could be touched, cut, dug out, and put in pockets. He didn't believe in Fate, time travel, or . . . er . . . ghosts.

He shifted uncomfortably.

All right, so he'd seen ghosts. There was probably a logical explanation for that as well. In a way, that was reassuring, to think that existence didn't end at death.

But time travel?

No way.

No way at all, which was why he was going to start looking for familiar landmarks such as roads, phone boxes, or tracks left by Range Rovers on their way to the local market for snacks. The very *last* thing he was going to look for was something that screamed "Get in me, I'm a time-travel machine."

He scowled. His '67 was probably just such a machine. Unfortunately, after its last flight, he suspected it wouldn't be good for driving, much less allowing him to warp time to his will and pleasure. And that assumed, of course, that it had any sort of time-traveling capabilities—which he most certainly doubted it did.

So, having no other alternative, he kept on walking.

He came to a point where he wondered why he hadn't asked for a doggie bag back at the castle. He saw trees to his right and paused to look at them. Was there at least water there? It was worth a look.

He wandered over, found a little trickle, and didn't bother to check the source before taking a long drink. The water was clear and so sharp it almost burned his mouth. It wasn't particularly cold, but he hadn't seen any glaciers around either, so maybe that wasn't a surprise. He drank until he was satisfied, then sat back on his heels and looked around him. It was a pristine little glade, with no sounds of traffic, no sounds of civilization, no sounds of modern man to disturb the peace.

But there was, quite suddenly, the sound of loud conversation in a language he didn't speak.

He looked up and saw men come to a stop across the little stream from him. They were dressed, and he used that term loosely, in ratty tights and tunics. It made him realize just how nice the clothing he was wearing was.

Jake jumped to his feet, only to have the ruffians stop still. He stared at them. They stared back at him.

Then they pointed to his shoes and burst into laughter.

He did what any red-blooded male would have done in that situation.

He flipped them the bird.

Apparently that translated well, whatever the century.

The men snarled in unison and Jake looked around him quickly to judge the terrain. Too rocky. He turned and made tracks for a nice flat surface where he might stand a chance, one against eight.

Without warning, he tripped over something in the grass and went down. Damned shoes. When he managed to scramble back up to his feet, he found himself surrounded by half a dozen or so men who looked as if they hadn't seen a bathtub in thirty years.

Jake held out his hands, palm up, to show them he had no weapon. He would have turned out his pockets, but again, he had no pockets to turn out.

They made motions for him to take off his clothes.

"Shove it," he suggested.

They discussed that for a moment or two, then growled and attacked. Jake was outnumbered, but not outmaneuvered. He dodged, he spun, he made himself as impossible-to-catch a target as possible. And when it came down to a choice between him and the men attacking him, he got down to business.

He left two unconscious on the ground with what he half hoped weren't broken necks and was well on the way to taking out a pair more when out of the corner of his eye he saw something coming toward him at great speed. He elbowed another thug in the throat absently as he watched the rider approaching.

It was Amanda.

He took a fist to the belly during the time he took to gape at her, flying toward him on two thousand pounds of Belgian as easily as if she were riding a bike. He noticed a knife coming toward him, but was too distracted to avoid the full impact of it. Amanda ran through the group of thugs, scattering them like leaves. Jake clutched his arm to stop the bleeding and watched as she wheeled around and came back. The horse reared, an impressive sight in itself, and when he came down, Amanda slid off his back and landed on the ground in a crouch, a wicked-looking dagger in her hand.

Jake wondered if it would be unmanly to fan himself.

Apparently the remaining ruffians didn't think so. They paused to make noises of appreciation. Amanda said something to them that made one of them snort.

Jake slapped that one on the back side of the head.

Amanda pulled a knife out of her boot at the same time the thug turned to deal with Jake. Jake found two knives coming at him at the same time. He avoided the stabbing one and fumbled with the sheathed one. He avoided another stab and looked at the dagger he was holding. Amanda shouted something at him. He frowned at her. It was obvious she had just given him a weapon, but he wasn't sure he could use it. His hands? Yes. But a knife, no, he wasn't at all sure about that. After all, one didn't just go about stabbing people met casually on the road.

Then again, these guys weren't exactly elderly Brits with picnic hampers looking for a likely spot for a snack. They had weapons and looked to have every intention of using them. In fact, one of them was taking on Amanda, mercilessly. Jake would have jumped to her rescue, but he found himself suddenly too busy trying to avoid becoming a pincushion for the remaining men.

And then, just as suddenly, shouts went up from nearby. Jake watched in surprise as Amanda's brothers leaped off their horses and dove into the fray. They had swords and seemed to know how to use them. They were taking on the largest of the group, seeming to take great pride in irritating him as much as possible.

That left four for him. Jake took out one immediately, leaving him in an unconscious heap on the ground. The remaining three were a bit more difficult. He was good with his hands, and he was used to facing thugs with knives in dark alleyways in countries where a little murder for the sake of moneymaking wasn't that big a deal, but these guys were desperate. He received a nick or two more than he would have liked, and he had certainly done more damage to them than he was comfortable with in return, but in the end, three more were down. That left the big one and Amanda's guy.

The boys seemed to have no trouble letting Jake take over. The only problem was, the biggest thug had a sword and Jake had only his bare hands.

He dodged a vicious thrust and looked at the lads. "Help her!" he exclaimed, jabbing a finger Amanda's way.

"Why?"

Both brothers asked that, in unison, and he had no trouble understanding.

"Because she is a woman!" he exclaimed in his best schoolboy French.

Apparently that translated fairly well because the boys looked at him as if he had just voluntarily plunged his foot into the biggest pile of sexism ever deposited on English soil.

One of the lads made a dismissive motion with his hand. Jake would have followed that up with a stern lecture on protecting the weaker sex, but he suddenly found himself with his own problem coming at him in a fury.

He rolled, he spun, he dodged. He finally kicked the sword out of the man's hands and from there the fight was quite brief. An underfed peasant was no match for a modern man who'd eaten well his whole life. When the other man was down, Jake paused for a moment. Amanda's brothers were standing there gaping at him. He smiled briefly, then looked to see how Amanda was doing.

And it was, he had to admit, a spectacular performance.

She scored several hits on her opponent, eliciting an equal number of curses. Jake would have kept track of both, but he was an old-fashioned kind of guy and he couldn't just stand there and let Amanda fight when he could do something to defend her.

But when he started forward, one of the brothers, he certainly couldn't have said which, grabbed him by his good arm and stopped him. The teenager shook his head with wide eyes.

"She needs help," Jake said firmly. "Either you do it," and here he pointed to them so they wouldn't misunderstand, "or I will."

They shook their heads vigorously. They pointed to Amanda and made motions that he had no trouble interpreting to mean their deaths at Amanda's hands if they interfered.

Well, they might be afraid of her, but Jake wasn't. He tapped the thug on the back, leaped aside as he spun around with a knife in his hands. He waited until the man had exhausted his repertoire of moves, then grabbed his wrist and plunged the man into unconsciousness by means of a fist under the chin.

Jake looked at the fallen bodies, alive or dead as was the case, and realized that there would certainly be an inquest—

If they'd been in modern-day England, that was.

He wasn't sure what the procedure was in the current day. What he did know was that they didn't want to linger where they were, just in case the little party at their feet had friends.

"Go," said one of the twins.

"Excellent idea," he muttered. He was on the verge of wishing the three of them a nice trip back to the castle, when he chanced to look to his right.

Amanda.

All right, so he had spent his life being mesmerized by color, by things that sparkled, by the rare and exquisite. He'd been known in the past to become quite overwhelmed by the sight of a perfectly cut gem, to drool over unusual formations of quartz, to gaze motionlessly at finished pieces under bright lights.

But never in his long and illustrious career spent chasing things that dazzled him had he ever seen anything like the woman before him.

She was, as he had noted before, quite beautiful. Her face was perfectly proportioned, her skin flawless, her figure pleasing. But as ideal as all those things were, what he couldn't look away from was the fire in her eyes. No wonder men had been singing her praises for centuries. He wondered what man had been lucky enough to capture her heart.

He found, quite suddenly, that he wished it could have been him.

She took a step closer to him, a wildness still in her eyes, her knife bared in her hand. He held up his hands in surrender.

"Whatever it is, I didn't do it."

She leaned down suddenly, cut a long strip from one of the

filthy tunics of the vanquished at his feet, then stuck her knife
back into her belt and approached with cloth in hand. He realized immediately what she intended, and he didn't have the
heart to tell her that the very last thing he wanted was that filthy,
bug-infested rag anywhere near the flesh wound he sported
down his arm.

Not that she would have understood him if he'd tried.

So he ignored the sting and the potential for infection as
she quite expertly tied a tourniquet around his arm. She didn't
bother to try to speak to him.

He supposed he couldn't blame her. If she thought him
anything but a complete idiot, he would have been surprised.
She did make the effort to point at her horse.

Jake sighed. There was more to face than the impossibility
of getting on a horse. What was he going to do with his future?

He rubbed his chin and took a step away to give it some
thought, only to step quite firmly on the body of a fallen ruffian. Well, that was something to think about. He looked back
at Amanda and thought some more.

Stay or go?

All right, so he could stay at least for a while—only because
it was foolhardy to try to traverse unfamiliar country without
any preparation, maps, or other directional devices. He needed
to know where he was, and he needed to know the language, he
needed to know enough to get him across the country with some
ease.

But the real reason, he had to admit, was that even though
he knew she could never be his, walking away from Amanda
of Artane without looking a bit more would be like finding a
vein of something really spectacular and not sticking around
to see where it ended.

"Let's go home," he said, in his clearest French.

She studied him for a moment or two, then nodded and
walked over to her horse.

Jake was then faced with his next problem: how to get back
to the castle. He was in good shape, but Amanda's horse was
high-jumper huge. He turned to judge the boys' horses and supposed one of them might be manageable. Before he could fully
decide if he could actually heave himself up into the saddle, one

of the boys had shoved reins into his hands and hopped up without effort behind Amanda.

Damn him anyway.

Jake looked at the horse and wondered how it was you went
about introducing yourself to a beast you wanted to befriend
so you didn't make a fool out of yourself in front of the most
beautiful woman you'd ever met.

Brother Useful, as Jake promptly termed him, appeared
and held his cupped hands out. Jake got the picture. He put
one foot in the boy's hands, then swung up onto the horse's
back with as much grace as he could muster.

Which wasn't much, but at least he didn't enjoy an immediate return to *terra firma*.

He thanked Amanda's brother in Gaelic. The boy smiled
and nodded, then pointed to himself.

"Montgomery," he said.

"Montgomery," Jake agreed. "Thank you."

Montgomery shrugged with another smile, glared at something nasty-sounding spewed by his brother, then trotted off to
his own horse, which he mounted with ease born of years of
practice. It was then that Jake realized that a horse was quite a
bit more shifty than even his beloved '67. But before he had a
chance to give that too much thought, they were off.

Well, Amanda and her brothers were off.

He was left behind, wondering where first gear was.

Montgomery looked over his shoulder and whistled. Jake
grabbed at the horse's hair and decided that it would be in his
best interest to just let the horse do its thing until it stopped.
He applied all his energies to just hanging on.

He hung on until they had bounced their way back inside
the castle walls. Fortunately for him, the horse seemed to
know when to stop. Amanda and her brothers dismounted expertly. Jake managed to get to the ground somehow, and given
that he landed there on his feet and not his head, he thought it
might be good enough.

The older man from the night before appeared suddenly,
scowling fiercely. Jake guessed that this was not her father.
One, they looked nothing alike. Two, Amanda was polite, but
not deferential. In fact, the deference went the other way. But

Amanda did eventually nod and walk away toward the castle.
Jake watched her go until she disappeared inside.

Then he turned to the animated conversation going on between the older man and the brothers. Jake had the feeling,
based on the way all three would periodically gesture at him,
that they were discussing his fate. He decided that he wouldn't
be spending any more time in the cellar and was digging
through his inadequate stores of Gaelic for words to that effect, when the older man folded his arms over his chest and
looked at Jake sternly. He pointed to the boys.

"Hear them," he said, nodding to the lads. "Learn you."

Or words to that effect. Jake decided that first on the list,
after ditching his fairy shoes, would come a crash course in
medieval lingo.

He nodded to the older man, then looked at his tutors.
They listened to a long list of instructions from the older
man, then watched him walk away. They consulted with each
other, then turned and looked at Jake with grins and twinkles
in their eyes.

Wonderful.

His induction into the Middle Ages was about to begin and
he had two fifteen-year-olds as his guides.

He could hardly wait.

Chapter 9

Amanda put her thumb into her mouth and sucked on it, cursing as best she could around it. What had she been thinking, to see to the enormous pile of mending in that basket? She was quite certain Sir Walter had obtained every piece of cloth that might have had even the most minor of rents in it to foist off on her. She looked at her basket of finished bits and decided, based upon the meagerness of its contents, that the se'nnight had been completely wasted, though it had certainly kept her occupied, out of the great hall, and far away from Jake.

Which she was quite certain had been the purpose.

And she had no one to blame for that but herself, given that she had agreed to Sir Walter's demand that she stay upstairs until he had ascertained Jake's true intentions—which she could do just as well as he could. Aye, and given that she was likely more capable than Sir Walter of judging Jake's character, there was no reason not to be about the task immediately.

So she tossed the poorly mended tunic into the finished pile and hurried to her chamber, where she changed into her training clothes. She braided her hair, put on her boots, and took a moment or two to make her plans before she went out into the passageway. If anyone were capable of finding out all there was to know about Jackson Alexander Kilchurn IV, it was she. She had spent years honing her skill not only of subterfuge, but investigation. How else was a girl to learn what she needed to about a suitor if she couldn't observe him, unobserved herself?

She made her way quickly and quietly down to the great hall. She peered around the edge of the stairwell. Jake sat at the high table with her brothers. Montgomery and John were blathering on about this and that, without ceasing, one jumping in to carry on the tale whilst the other paused for breath.

But instead of being irritated, as most men would have been, Jake merely sat there, stroking his lips with a finger, as if he fought not to smile. And when Montgomery finished John's favorite jest for him, Jake actually laughed.

Amanda considered. Her brothers were notoriously hard on visitors. That Jake could tolerate them, nay, even appear to enjoy them was something indeed.

She watched him as he stretched for his cup, then winced. He rubbed his arm gently, then said something to Montgomery. Montgomery nodded and the three of them rose and made their way from the great hall.

Interesting.

Amanda filched a hunk of bread from the table and walked to the front door. Were they going to the healer's house? She suspected so. Montgomery had told her, at various times during her confinement upstairs in the solar, that Jake had a most curious method of tending to his wounds. Amanda had her own notions on the methods most healers employed, but then again, she had grown up with a woman as Artane's healer who had had her own very strong thoughts on the matter.

Amanda sighed. 'Twas no wonder she drove all men away. Her opinions were too strong and her tongue too quick to express them.

She peeked out the door and saw the threesome making their way across the courtyard in the direction she'd anticipated. She stood there and watched thoughtfully until they entered the small house. She had forgotten how tall Jake was, or how handsome. Sir Walter had made her take all her meals upstairs, so she'd only had brief glimpses of him from a great distance as he followed her brothers to the lists.

She had forgotten, indeed.

Well, that was of no import in her present business. She made her way quickly across the courtyard and paused at the doorway to the healer's quarters. She eased the door open and listened.

"Wine?" said Master Erneis. "Again, my lords?"

"Jake wishes to soak his arm in it," Montgomery said earnestly. "'Tis his way of healing. Quite new and exciting, wouldn't you say?"

Amanda suspected she knew precisely what Master Erneis would say, and that wouldn't include praise for new and exciting methods of healing. The man was certainly capable, but he wasn't overly imaginative.

But she listened as the healer provided what was asked for and made noises of interest at the list of herbs that Montgomery and Jake managed to fashion between themselves.

"Thank you, sir healer," Jake said clearly.

"He means he'll return on the morrow for more," Montgomery added.

"Aye, thank you," Jake said. "I am grateful."

Well, at least he was no longer a fragrant rose, a village gigolo, or a braised swine rump, all of which he'd been at some point during his first week—according to her brothers and thanks to their tutelage. It was little wonder Jake had reportedly given up speaking for a few days.

But the saints only knew what he would be now that he had taken it up again: a peasant; a disinherited son; a ruffian with handsome manners and no scruples.

Or a lord who had been waylaid and now sought refuge at her home?

She was almost afraid to find out.

But she could hardly bear not knowing.

She heard footsteps coming toward the door and she leaped backward and hid herself behind the firewood stacked along the wall. She waited until her babbling brothers and their charge had headed toward the stables before she raised up and looked over the wood. She watched them go, Jake with wine and herbs in hand and her brothers still wearing his ears down to nubs.

Were they on to a lesson in riding, then?

She slipped along the wall, hiding behind shrubberies and other kinds of vegetation that could be found inside her father's walls. She eased toward the stable doors, then stopped suddenly when she heard Jake's voice. His language was, remarkably, much improved. She was still marveling at that when she heard the unmistakable sound of breathing behind her. She whirled around to find three of her guardsmen standing there, each with their hands over their mouths, as if that might stifle the noise. Amanda put her hands on her hips and frowned at them.

"I'm not leaving the keep," she said.

They nodded as one, but didn't move.

"My gratitude, lads, for the aid, but I'm about a bit of investigation and don't need a cluster of men following—"

The sound of Jake's voice right behind her sent her scurrying around her men. She made certain she was well hidden, then held her breath.

"Amanda's guardsmen," Montgomery said. "They follow her everywhere, but I don't see her here. Do you, John?"

John grunted. "I do not, but she's sure to be nearby. Come on, Montgomery, let's take him to the armory. He'll need a sword of some kind if we're going to train with him later. I still think he needs lessons in horsemastery."

"He doesn't want to ride a horse," Montgomery argued, "not with his arm and all."

"His arm is fine," John said. "Isn't it, Jake?"

"It is better, John," Jake said easily. "Perhaps later."

"Don't you *want* to learn to ride?" John asked incredulously. "How can you not want to ride?"

"I don't think 'tis that he has no desire." Montgomery defended Jake. "I daresay he will when his arm is better. Fortunately for him, the wound is to his left arm. We'll be about training him with his right straightway."

Amanda listened to them discuss how best to begin Jake's training until their voices faded away. And once she could look around her men and see that they were gone in truth, she came out from her hiding place and considered. She could follow her quarry to the armory, she supposed, but what would it serve her? She had her doubts that Jake would reveal any of his true self to her brothers. If he had some great secret, did it follow that he would confide in two lads of uncertain discretion?

It most certainly did not.

She continued on slowly toward the lists, wondering mightily about their guest.

"My lady?"

She turned to look at Robert of Conyers, a guardsman her father had imported from an estate near her great-grandmother's in France to captain her personal guard. Robert was fierce indeed, but he had been nothing but kind to her, leading her men to follow her on all sorts of ridiculous adventures without complaint.

"Aye, good sir?"

"Are you about more investigating, or . . ." He paused and looked at her uneasily. "Or . . ."

"The lists," she announced. "A bit of training there. You needn't come, of course. I'll be safe enough."

He nodded and he and the other two men made her low bows and walked away. Of course, they would regroup near the lists, she knew, and watch her just the same, but at least she would have the illusion of privacy. She made directly for the lists before they changed their minds.

She hadn't begun to actually be about her work of running when it began to rain.

Somehow, she was unsurprised.

It matched her mood perfectly. She wasn't one to allow circumstances to trouble her, or events to depress her, but for the first time in her life, she felt rather hopeless. All her planning, all her schemes and dips into her reserves of courage, all for naught. Her freedom had been snatched before she'd managed to truly have a taste of it. And now she was back where she started: locked in the cage of her beloved home, loving it and hating it at the same time, with marriage the only key available to set her free.

By the saints, a small rest was sounding better all the time.

She outran that tempting thought until she was drenched and she didn't think she could put another foot down. She hunched over with her hands on her thighs, gasping for breath. Robin would have been impressed that it had taken twenty trips around the lists and not just one to wind her so. She would have to write and tell him, though he likely wouldn't believe it unless he saw it himself.

Then she realized, with a start, that someone else might have seen her feat.

A man stood leaning casually against a wall, having conveniently located himself under an overhang that the less sturdy of Artane's guardsmen were wont to use when inclement weather threatened, watching her. He held something folded over his arm. A cloak? Perhaps he was trying to keep it dry for her. Perhaps he was trying to keep it dry for himself.

Or, finally, perhaps she should continue to drive herself into the ground in a manner worthy of one of Robin's more legendary bouts of list-running until her head cleared itself of these damnably foolish thoughts. The man had probably brought something to sit himself upon should he encounter a less-than-hospitable bit of bench.

She came to herself enough to realize that she was gaping at him whilst panting. She quickly straightened, lest he mistake her breathlessness for something it wasn't.

Not that he wasn't breath-stealing.

He turned to hang up what he'd brought, which she could now see was indeed her cloak, on a bracket put there for such purposes, then came across the muddy field toward her. Amanda reminded herself of all the reasons he was unsuitable.

He couldn't wield a sword.

He couldn't ride a horse.

He could barely speak her language.

But, by the saints, he was enough to make her cast those reasons to the wind. Not only his face, but his broad shoulders, his easy gait that was so different from Robin's swagger. This man padded toward her as if he were an animal on the hunt.

She felt decidedly like the prey.

She would have fanned her suddenly warm cheeks, but it was pouring with rain and that should have been enough to cool them.

Jake came to a halt before her and smiled gravely. "Finished?" he asked politely.

Finished? Ah, but she suspected she might never be finished—looking at, listening to, wondering about the man in front of her. But looking was all she could manage at present, and there was no sense in not doing a thorough job of it, so she applied herself immediately to the task.

He stood there, not three paces from her, with his hands clasped behind his back. If she'd been a woman given to it, she would have cast herself fully into a vat of lust. Nicholas's oldest clothes did little to hide Jake's fine form. If she hadn't known better, she would have thought herself facing a nobleman of unimpeachable lineage and limitless power and influence. He carried himself just as her brothers did, with confidence and ease. And if his bearing wasn't enough to weaken her knees, the stark beauty of his face would have been. He looked at her from sea-green eyes that seemed to sear her where they looked, as if he strove to burn her into his memory.

And then, as if he knew the depths of lustful depravity into which she'd tumbled, he smiled.

Just a little smile.

But it almost felled her where she stood.

She grasped frantically at the shreds of good sense she still possessed. No matter the seductive beauty of the peasant before her, he was not for her. She was still trapped in her father's larder until the appropriate dinner guest arrived to demand her as his main course, and, damnation, the rain was increasing, not abating.

"Finished?" she managed, finally. "Ah, nay, I am not."

And with that, she did the most sensible thing she'd done all morning.

She ran away.

She realized, after a time, that she had a companion for her labors. Amanda was acutely aware of Jake loping alongside her so easily, as easily as Robin himself would have. She looked at his feet and was faintly surprised to see boots there. Worn ones, but still serviceable. Perhaps someone had taken pity on him and given him something besides court shoes. Boots were a vast improvement over Nicholas's footwear.

"May I join you?" he asked, as politely as before.

"It seems you have already," she managed.

He only smiled.

It almost undid her.

She made her circuit five more times. It fair killed her to stop, given that Jake wasn't even breathing hard and she didn't want to look weak beside him, but she suspected it might kill her to go on. Besides, she'd already worn herself out that morning—no small feat in itself. She was due a rest.

"I am finished now," she announced, gasping for breath, clutching her side, and wishing she had a place to sit down that didn't require walking to reach it. She pushed her dripping hair out of her eyes and looked at him. "And you?"

"I am here to . . ." he seemingly searched for words, "to be company."

She couldn't answer. She shivered instead, and it had little to do with the rain.

By the saints, she had to find some control over her galloping feminine sentiments. She would be begging him to wed with her soon if she did not.

"Wait, if you will," he said, pausing to retrieve the cloak, which was indeed hers.

She stood on the side of the lists in the rain and trembled as he put her cloak around her shoulders. He hesitated, then reached out and pulled her braid free. Then he stood back and smiled again, that little smile that spoke of secrets that only she would be allowed to have part in.

She felt her forehead.

She had a fever. She was certain of it.

"I must go in," she said weakly.

"As my lady wishes."

She nodded, then walked quickly back, even though she would have greatly preferred to have limped there. Jake accompanied her silently. She found that to be almost as devastating as running next to him had been. She was desperately aware of him and found herself without a single weapon to fight it.

By the saints, she needed a rest.

She ran up the steps to the great hall, then paused at the door and looked at him.

"I've many important things to do," she said importantly.

He made her a low bow. "As my lady wishes."

By the saints, could the man muster up no other words? She scowled at him and strode into the great hall and back to the stairs, where she could flee up them in peace. She wasted no time tromping up them and preparing to be about her important tasks.

Now, if she only had something important to be doing.

She tidied the chamber she shared with Isabelle—something that took very little time, as Isabelle had taken most of her belongings with her and Amanda had few things of her own. She walked over to the window, sank down upon the stone bench there, and stared out at the rain.

She sighed, sparing a wish for her life of a fortnight ago, when things were simple and all she had to fear were a few overanxious suitors.

She rose and walked to the door before she could think better of it. The saints only knew what sort of mischief her younger brothers were about. Best that she stop them from engaging in it whilst she could.

Or so she told herself.

She honestly couldn't have been less interested in what Jake was doing.

She walked down the stairs and stopped at the bottom when she heard her brothers' voices. She peeked around the wall's edge, much as she had done earlier, and saw her brothers and their student sitting at the high table. They were talking, unsurprisingly, about food.

"Eels?" Jake asked. "Under sauce?"

"You daren't eat them any other way," John said. "Passing foul, though at least here Cook can manage a decent sauce. At Lord Pevensey's keep, the sauces are worse than the meat."

Amanda was suddenly quite grateful she'd grown to womanhood in a place where the food was edible.

"And the king's supper?" Jake asked. "It is better?"

"It had best be," Montgomery said with a laugh. "Though I daresay Henry wouldn't go into a rage over it. Not like King John might have."

"Henry III," Jake said slowly. "He is the king now?"

Amanda scowled. Of course he was the king. Who else?

She continued to listen to Jake, in his suddenly vastly improved French—far improved over what he'd used with her—question her brother as to the events of the day, the state of the king's armies, the condition of England in the glorious year of Our Lord 1227. It occurred to her suddenly, with the same sort of suddenness that made her realize she was almost asleep on her feet, that Jake was far more intelligent than he let on. And her brothers were too stupid to realize it.

He was not at all what he seemed. She couldn't decide if she should be frightened or intrigued.

She jumped suddenly when she saw that he had turned and caught sight of her. Her brothers, sitting not-so-innocently behind him, were grinning.

Damn them.

Amanda walked briskly across the great hall. A pity she'd already exhausted herself in the lists, else she would have gone there straightway. She supposed she could have retreated back upstairs and made for the roof. But that was too wet.

She considered the armory. Nay, too tempting to pinch something to use on any of the three souls behind her who were calling for her to leave the lists be and torture them no longer with her pounding.

She slammed the hall door home with great energy. She looked across the courtyard and espied the chapel. Aye that was the place for her. She had several things to repent of whilst she was there: lying; subterfuge; too much swearing . . .

And, most importantly, lust.

Chapter 10

Jake rolled his shoulders as he jogged in place, trying to work the kinks out of his neck and the chill from his bones. Historic homes were drafty in the twenty-first century, but at least most had been modernized with some sort of heating system. Artane in the Middle Ages was just the raw deal—and it was only June. Heaven help him when it was December . . .

He shook his head. He wasn't going to be there in December. At least not at medieval Artane.

He swung his arms back and forth to warm up and walked over to the window seat before he had the chance to give that too much thought. He pulled the shutters open and was rewarded with a blast of air. Medieval window treatments weren't exactly energy efficient.

He shook his head in wonder. It was amazing, this adventure he was having. Amazing and almost unbelievable.

But he did believe it. If his surroundings weren't evidence enough, he had many, many conversations with fifteen-year-olds to prove it. Fortunately for them all, his travels had forced him over the years to pick up key phrases and a good accent in short order. Add that to all those years spent conjugating the past pluperfect in French, and he'd rewarded the lads with success in brushing up his speaking skills. That was all good and fine, but it didn't do much to answer the question that had kept him up at nights over the past week.

Why was he here?

What possible reason could Fate have had to plunk him down eight centuries out of his element, short of some paranormal experiment gone horribly wrong?

Amanda.

He stared out the window, scenes from the past few days spent out of his own time passing before his eyes. Amanda soaked to the skin, running around a dirt field, running as though running hard enough might distance her from things he couldn't begin to guess. Amanda descending upon his attackers like a Fury, her hair streaming behind her, her eyes flashing. Amanda dressed like a boy with soot covering her face, come to spring him from the brig with clothes and a friendly hand.

Amanda.

He turned away from the window abruptly. He was here because of some weird cosmic quirk, not because Fate had a hand in it. Amanda was not for him. He had nothing to offer her. He might have been a ruthless businessman, a damned good designer of very expensive baubles, and a master gem hunter, but none of those things would do him any good in medieval England. They certainly wouldn't be enough to win him the most beautiful woman he'd ever seen.

No wonder men were still singing her praises eight hundred years later.

Well, there was no point in thinking about it. He would take a moment or two and be grateful he wasn't in the dungeon, then get on with his day.

He looked over his dandy medieval digs. He had a bed at least. John and Montgomery had decided that he would do best to stay with them at all times—lest he wander off and call some high-ranking noble a piece of roasted tripe under sauce—so he found himself bunking in their room on a cot that one of them had no doubt slept in five or six years earlier. Jake didn't complain about his feet hanging off the edge ten inches. Again, it was better than the breezier accommodations belowdecks. The company was better as well. The twins were, well, he hesitated to use the word *fun,* but entertaining wasn't too far off the mark.

His own brothers, Charles, Theodore, and William, were a

miserable trio. They were each fourteen months apart and, as a cluster, several years older than he. He had arrived on their scene, unwanted and irritating, only to be followed several years later by a baby girl who had been spoiled in utero. Personally, Jake couldn't stand the lot of them. His brothers were selfish, ungrateful, and greedy. His sister was selfish, ungrateful, greedy, and stupid. They hated him, the whole crew, which didn't bother him.

Or so he'd always told himself.

Now, with two younger brothers shadowing him, he wasn't so sure that he hadn't missed having brothers who liked him.

They seemed to like hanging out with him. He knew this because they said as much when they thought he couldn't understand them, discussing his virtues (his height, his potential for hefting really big swords, and his apparent immunity to Amanda's charm) and discounting his flaws (his poor French and his obvious inability to hop on a horse at a dead run), but in spite of all that, he passed muster with them.

All in all, medieval England had turned out to be a good place. He still had no idea what in the hell he was doing there, but maybe there was no real reason. Just a mistake. And one he would have to rectify very soon.

Maybe tomorrow.

Today, he thought as he flexed his chilly fingers, he would ditch those de Piaget brothers and spend the day with someone he shouldn't.

He was walking a fine line and he knew it. Amanda would be marrying someone else and it certainly wouldn't do to get in the way of that. But how could he be so close to her and not indulge in a little admiring? It would be like getting to examine the Crown Jewels at close range and walking away instead. He couldn't do it.

He had a wash with water that was just this side of icy, dried his face on his sleeve, and set out from the bedroom. He would go keep Amanda company for the morning. The morning wouldn't hurt.

He made his way to the great hall, helped himself to some rather edible porridge left on the table, then went on his little explore.

He visited the lists, the infirmary, the garden, and the stables. He left the stables and wandered across the courtyard, nodding and smiling to those he passed. He even attempted a few innocuous greetings and got real answers in return. Life was good.

He paused in front of the chapel. He couldn't imagine Amanda sitting still long enough to meditate, but he'd been wrong before. He stepped up a single step, opened the door, and went inside. He didn't have to look far before he saw a woman sitting on a bench in the front, straight-backed and regal.

Amanda.

He shut the heavy door behind him as softly as he could and leaned against the door frame. He wondered if he would ever get used to the sight of her. A woman who ended arguments eight hundred years into the future, and there he stood, just ten feet from her. Spooky. And he wasn't one to indulge in paranormal musings.

She was perfectly still, with her head bowed, that cascade of long, straight dark hair hanging down her back. It was difficult to reconcile the woman in front of him with the one he'd seen in previous days, riding like a madwoman, outrunning her demons, executing rescues against men half again her size.

He jumped a little when he realized she was looking back at him over her shoulder. He smiled.

"Sorry," he said.

She studied him for a moment or two longer in silence, then tilted her head toward the empty place on the bench beside her. An invitation, or the flaring up of a kink in her neck? Jake decided on the former. He hopped up the aisle and plunked himself down next to her before she changed her mind and fled the scene.

She regathered her stillness about her and sat with her head slightly bowed, her eyes closed. He stared at her, unable to look away. She was, simply put, breathtaking. And if she'd just been beautiful, it would have been enough. But she was tough and apparently outspoken and gutsy. Her brothers were wrong.

He wasn't immune at all.

She looked at him suddenly from under her eyelashes. "Aren't you praying?"

"I should be," he said fervently.

She laughed.

Jake felt like he'd just taken a body blow.

Amanda clapped her hand over her mouth, then dropped her hand back into her lap and bowed her head. But she was still smiling. Jake wondered how it was that a single sound of mirth from a woman he scarcely knew could render him feeling like a fourteen-year-old with his first serious crush. Only he wasn't fourteen. And this was most definitely not a woman he could have.

He sat there for quite some time, just allowing himself the pleasure of sitting next to her, and pondering the complete improbability of it. He stole looks at her, because he couldn't help it. Finally he had to speak, because he couldn't help that either.

"What are you doing?" he whispered.

It took her a moment or two to answer. "Repenting."

"Repenting?" he echoed. "Do you really need to?"

She looked at him fully then. "Always."

"What a troublemaker."

"If you only knew."

He couldn't imagine. The only trouble she probably caused were fights over who got to sit next to her at dinner.

"Do you do it often?" he asked.

"Which? Repent, or do things that merit it?"

"Either. Both."

She smiled. "I am here every morning, if that answers your question."

It did. Perhaps he should be taking a closer look at his own life. A little chapel time wouldn't be such a bad thing for him either. Was it wrong to dredge up vices with if it meant getting to spend time with Amanda of Artane?

"Your French is more improved even than yesterday," she remarked.

"It is."

"My brothers think you still struggle."

"I like to be . . ." he searched for the right word in his still not stellar vocabulary, "underestimated."

"Why?"

Why indeed? It was his father's favorite ploy to gain advantage with business adversaries.

"It gives me time to study things," he said, "before I commit to a plan."

Or something to that effect, he hoped. He was beginning to wonder if he was overestimating his verbal abilities.

"I have brothers like you," she said thoughtfully. "Like you, yet still not."

He gave up any pretense of praying and shifted so he could see her better. "How many brothers do you have?"

"Five."

"Five? You poor girl."

She smiled again, and again the sight of it almost knocked him off the bench.

"Aye," she said, "I would have to agree."

"And what are the names of these tormentors?"

"Montgomery and John, you know already. Then there is Miles, Nicholas, and finally Robin. Robin is the eldest and the worst of the lot."

Robin. Jake realized with a start where he'd heard the name and realized with equal shock that he wouldn't have to see Robin to recognize him. Or his wife, Anne, or their four children.

"How many children does Robin have now?" Jake managed.

"One, but Anne expects another babe in the winter." She looked at him closely. "Are you unwell?"

Jake smiled, though he suspected it had come out a bit sickly. All right, it was one thing to nip back a few centuries as casually as you might dash out to the store, but it was another thing entirely to have seen Robin's future.

Then another thing occurred to him and he wondered why it hadn't before.

"Your brother is Robin. Ah, I mean, you're Robin's sister."

She was giving him that look again, the one that said she had known he was a loser but she now was going to give renewed thought to him being crazy as well.

"I'm sorry," he said, rubbing his hands over his face, "I think I'm missing some sleep somewhere."

"Perhaps you lost it in the dungeon."

It was his turn to smile. "No doubt."

She fell silent and the silence grew. Jake didn't doubt what was on her mind. She would have questions. He wasn't sure he could deliver the answers.

She studied him for a moment or two more before she continued. "I am curious about several things—"

"How about we go walk on the beach and I'll tell you what you want," he said. *Well, most of what you would want,* he added silently. "You do have a beach nearby, don't you?"

"Of course."

He jumped to his feet, then held out his hand for her. "Then let's go. Unless you have other things you need to be doing?"

"Nay," she said. "My curiosity is all that needs to be satisfied today."

And then she very carefully put her hand in his and let him pull her to her feet.

It was literally all he could do not to pull her into his arms. He wanted to wrap one arm around her waist, bury the other in her hair and kiss her until they both were dizzy from lack of air.

She shivered.

Maybe she felt it too.

"Food," she said suddenly, pulling her hand away. "I'll fetch food."

"Good idea." Something to do with his mouth that didn't involve kissing her.

He walked with her down the aisle, his boots scuffing the new stone. He looked at the woman walking next to him, admired her medieval gown, and found absolutely nothing odd about that. He was losing it quickly.

But in his defense, there was much to like about Amanda, above and beyond the woman herself. He honestly couldn't remember the last time he walked with a woman who wasn't after him for some superficial reason. Amanda wasn't asking him about his portfolio or if she could just have one itsy-bitsy peek into his vault to see if there might be something there she might like.

Then again, Jake had no gems in his vault even half as spectacular as the one walking next to him so even if she had asked, she probably would have been unimpressed.

"—wait?"

He blinked, realizing they were halfway across the courtyard and she was talking to him. "What?"

"I'll fetch food. Will you wait for me here?"

Wait?

Wait to kiss her. Wait to tell her to kiss her life good-bye and come with him. Wait to feel himself hit the ground again, because he was almost certain he was still spinning in the Jag that had sent him here.

"Yes," he managed. "I will wait."

She smiled at him again, then turned and ran up the steps to the keep. Jake looked around for something to sit down on, but found nothing. He settled for planting his feet a manly distance apart and trying to pretend he didn't feel as if he'd just been punched in the gut for the third time that morning.

He knew he was swimming in dangerous waters, but he couldn't help himself. He couldn't help himself and he didn't want to. She couldn't be his. But he could pretend for a day or two.

What could it hurt?

He didn't want to think about the answer to that.

Chapter 11

Amanda stood in the kitchens and held a basket whilst Cook filled it with all manner of food for hungry souls stranded on the shore. She didn't want to be clutching a basket as if it were all that held her upright; what she wanted to do was sink down onto that bench over by the fire and see if she could warm up. Yesterday, she had been certain she'd had a fever. Today it was the chills.

Chills when he touched her.

Chills when he looked at her.

Either she was on the verge of becoming gravely ill, or there was something else amiss with her that she couldn't identify.

"Here ye are, milady," Cook said, covering everything with a clean cloth and giving it a fond pat. "Enough for you and the fine lordling. Can ye carry drink as well?"

Amanda nodded and accepted a bottle of wine. She hefted the basket, took a firmer grip on the bottle, and made her way through the great hall and to the door.

"Mandy, where are you for?" Montgomery called from behind her.

"Nowhere," she threw over her shoulder as she opened the door. "Go see to your swordplay."

Of course, she wouldn't be able to dismiss her guards that easily. She could already see them forming ranks down at the inner bailey gates. She walked down the stairs to find Jake in the same place she'd left him. He immediately reached up and took the basket and wine from her before her foot touched the courtyard floor.

"A beautiful day," he said. "A perfect day to go to the beach."

She could only nod. If she opened her mouth, she would only babble something unintelligible, so she clung to silence as if it were all that could save her, and walked with Jake down to the gates.

Jake seemingly shared her desire for quiet, for he said nothing until they were outside the main gates and had turned toward the shore. He looked over his shoulder a time or two, then handed her the basket and bottle.

"Hold this," he said quietly. "We're being followed."

Amanda looked back to see no one but her guard. She smiled. "Them? Those lads are my guard."

"They're dressed very casually for men pretending to guard you," he said with a frown.

"They're supposed to look like ruffians. At least a few of them are. You'll note there is the odd man here and there, dressed in his knightly gear."

He studied the men for a moment or two more in silence, then relaxed and took back their burdens. "Are they with you all the time?" he asked finally.

"Unless I've managed to elude them by disguise."

He smiled. "How can you possibly disguise who you are?"

"Soot from my father's hearth."

"How effective is that?"

She laughed in spite of herself. "Not very, unfortunately. I did manage to escape the day we found you senseless in the grass, but that was by far my most memorable outwitting."

He reached up to tuck a strand of hair behind her ear. "Poor girl," he said softly. "It must bother you to have your freedom curtailed that way. How long has it been going on?"

"Years," she said, surprised that he would understand something that her father and brothers seemed to understand not at all.

The caging of Amanda of Artane.

She might as well have been a prisoner in the Tower of London for all the liberty she had.

He offered her his arm. "Come on. If nothing else, maybe today can feel a little like freedom."

She took his arm and hiked over the dunes and down to the seashore, finding, as seemed to be the case always, that even touching the man was too much for her poor self. She was excruciatingly aware of his every movement. If she could have stopped him, taken his burdens away and put them down, then gone into his arms and stayed there forever, she would have been content.

She felt her forehead surreptitiously with the back of her hand. Still no fever.

Maybe she was losing what little wit remained her. Was this how it felt to descend into madness? She'd known Jake less than a fortnight. It was impossible to love someone in less than a fortnight. Then again, Anne had loved Robin from the start, from the day when he first put a worm down her gown. Jake had been far more courteous than that. How could a woman not appreciate that sort of chivalry?

Jake found a likely spot and set his burdens down. Amanda sat, took off her stockings and her shoes, and sighed in relief at the feeling of her bare toes on the sand. Jake laughed at her.

"I wish I could do that, but it wouldn't be modest."

"One of the few times that being a woman has its advantages," she said archly. "So I will enjoy my toes dipping into the water and not feel a bit sorry for you."

"Don't. I've waded in the surf enough in the past that not doing so today won't hurt me."

He had spent time near the sea? Well, all the better for him because today she didn't want sand between his toes distracting him from the answers she had to have.

And there was no time like the present to begin. Perhaps he would answer poorly and she would have reason enough to cast him out the gates and never give him another thought. Perhaps, but in the deepest place in her heart, she hoped not.

"Shall we walk?" he asked, holding down his hand for her.

She allowed him to pull her up, then she tucked part of her skirts into her belt so she could more easily cool her feet in the surf.

Then she found herself with her hand in Jake's and somehow that didn't lend itself all that easily to her wading in the water, for then she would have had to let go.

And somehow letting go was the last thing she wanted to do.

"You said you had questions," Jake said suddenly. "There are some things I cannot answer, but—"

"Cannot, or will not?" she asked.

He paused, then smiled. "Will not."

"You're a spy," she stated. "John thinks you're feigning ignorance of language, swordplay, and other knightly skills because you're here at the behest of some king or other."

He shook his head. "I'm not a spy."

"Montgomery thinks you're a fairy."

He smiled. "Does he? Why is that?"

"Because he thinks you have skills far beyond what a mere man would. That business with the ruffians a se'nnight ago has convinced him beyond all doubt."

"Do fairies do that sort of thing?"

"You tell me."

He laughed. "Amanda, do I look like a fairy?"

"I've never seen one, so I can hardly judge. They hide in the grass, so 'tis said. I've even heard that you can be staring at an unassuming field and have one appear before you, fully grown, where nothing but weeds grew but a moment before."

Jake stopped. It wasn't a sudden thing, but it was as if time had ceased to be and he was stopping because of it.

Then he turned quite slowly and looked at her.

His face was very pale.

"Oh?" he asked quietly. Very quietly.

His stillness was almost frightening, as was his grip on her hand. "Aye, so 'tis said," she replied, trying to free her fingers from his. "I know nothing of it for myself. 'Tis merely a tale of the sort a father might tell to amuse his children at night. There is no truth to it."

He closed his eyes briefly, then opened them and looked at her with a smile.

And the sun shone again, the waves resumed their ceaseless noises, and she found she could breathe again.

By the saints, who *was* this man?

He took her hand in both his, stroked it gently as if to apologize for crushing it before, then turned them both forward again to continue their walk.

She walked with him for some time before she dared speak again. She stole a look at him to make certain he had regained his color before she spoke. "So," she said easily, "you aren't a fairy."

"No, I'm not," he said, just as easily.

"Then what are you?"

He looked at her from under his eyelashes, the same way he'd looked at her in the chapel that morning, as if they had spent a lifetime together already and shared so many confidences that just a look might revive that camaraderie.

"I am just a man."

"You cannot wield a sword, you cannot ride a horse, and you couldn't speak two coherent words in my tongue a fortnight ago."

"True."

"And now you speak as easily as if you've known my language all your life. But you still cannot ride. I suppose you don't need a sword, but I still do not understand why you cannot use one."

"It is a very long story," he began.

"Then begin it," she said tartly. "Perhaps at the beginning. Perhaps by telling me where you are from."

He walked in silence for a moment or two, then looked at her sideways. "London."

"See," she said, "that was easily done."

"But I wasn't born there," he added with that smile that just begged her to ensconce herself in his arms and stay there for days on end.

She blew the hair out of her eyes. "You're making this difficult."

"But you are so magnificent when you're annoyed."

She was halfway to demonstrating a bit of that annoyance when she realized he was only teasing her. At least she thought he was teasing her. With the way he was watching her, with such frank admiration, she decided that she wasn't sure of anything at all.

"This would be easier if you wouldn't look at me thusly," she said.

"How am I looking at you?" he asked.

"As if I amused you."

"You do. But that's only part of it." He shook his head with a rueful smile. "Only the very smallest part of it. And to say more would be saying too much. Perhaps another question?"

She had to struggle to bring another to mind. "You weren't born in London. Where were you born?"

"Not in England."

"Unsatisfactory."

"It's the best I can do."

Amanda tried a different tack. "Why were you senseless in the grass?"

"Honestly? I'm not sure. I was traveling and the next thing I knew, I was waking up in your father's study."

"Why were you here in the north?" she asked. "What is your business?"

She realized, with a start, that she was starting to sound like one of her suitors, interrogating her sire about the exact contents of her dowry. She pursed her lips and vowed to remain silent.

For a moment or two, at least.

"I was in the north," he began, "because I was coming to Artane to deliver a . . . missive to Artane's lord."

"My father?" she asked in surprise.

"Mmmm," was all he answered.

A lie, there. She scowled at him. "And your business?"

"I am a . . ." he searched for the word, "a merchant. I buy and sell gems. I design things for very wealthy patrons."

She blinked in surprise. "A merchant?"

"A merchant," he repeated, sounding not in the least bit horrified by the fact. "I'm a very good one, if that matters."

"A merchant," she said softly. "I see."

And so she did. No wonder he had no sword skills.

By the saints, she wished she hadn't asked.

She pulled her hand away from his and clasped it together with her other—so hard that it pained her.

"Amanda?"

She looked up into his beautiful face and wondered why it was Fate seemed to despise her so. The man before her was so handsome, so pleasingly fashioned, so full of confidence and surety—all the things her father would have insisted upon. And not only that, he was amusing, he humored her brothers, and he could have kept her safe with his hands alone.

A merchant.

She could scarce believe it.

"Is there something wrong?"

"Nay," she croaked. "Nothing. Nothing at all."

None of it made any sense to her. Even if he were a merchant he had to have some skill. Many of the merchants she saw coming through her father's gates had very large swords and they knew how to use them. They had horses pulling their carts, or they rode into her father's gates on the fine horses their industry had purchased them. They spoke her sire's language, and had fine manners that made most of them quite welcome at his table—especially the ones who had lovely things that pleased her mother.

"Amanda?"

She forced a smile to her lips. "Perhaps we should eat. I daresay Cook has sent lovely things."

"Hmmm," was all he said.

By the time they had returned the way they had come, John and Montgomery were already assaulting the supper basket. Amanda gave John a healthy shove with her foot.

"You weren't invited here, and you certainly weren't invited to make free with our meal."

"We were hungry," John said, continuing to eat even as he rolled to dodge another kick.

"Besides," Montgomery said, helping himself to drink, "we wanted to know when Jake was ready for another lesson in swordplay."

"Unless he doesn't need it," John said, looking knowingly at Jake. "Spies usually have great skill, but feign ignorance. It keeps others in the dark about their true identities—"

"Be silent," Amanda said, aiming another dig at him before she sat down in his place. "He isn't a spy. Didn't he tell you as much during all those long hours spent at table?"

"He's a fairy," Montgomery breathed.

"Nay, not that either, you foolish child," Amanda snapped. "He isn't a spy or a fairy. He's a bloody merchant."

But even as the words were coming out of her mouth, she regretted them. Not only for herself, but for Jake and her brothers. John and Montgomery looked at Jake as if he'd just sprouted horns. She put her hand over her mouth and wished she could disappear.

"A merchant?" Montgomery asked, sounding devastated.

"A seller of goods," John said, shaking his head in disbelief.

"Actually," Jake said, sitting down and helping himself to wine, "it's worse than that. I buy and sell gems."

"Gems," John gasped. "For baubles?"

"Very expensive baubles," Jake said. "And the finding of those gems for those pretty baubles takes me all over the world." He smiled pleasantly. "I enjoy it very much."

John and Montgomery had fallen silent, seemingly too horrified by the tidings to do aught but stare at Jake and ignore the food they still held in their hands, food they had been previously stuffing into their mouths as quickly as good sense had allowed.

Of the four, only Jake ate. And he ate with the gusto of a man who was not troubled in the slightest by what he had to do to earn his daily bread.

Amanda felt shame stain her cheeks. By the saints, when would she learn to check her tongue?

"You must be quite skilled," she offered, when she thought she could speak without weeping.

He looked at her from clear green eyes that held no hint of anger or annoyance. "I am," he said simply.

"What of your sire?" John asked glumly. "No title there, either?"

"He can trace his fathers back to Scottish nobility," Jake said with a shrug. "But even though he has great wealth himself, he has no title."

"Did your father give you part of his wealth?" Montgomery asked.

"He did, but I've never used it. I haven't taken any of his money, outside of what he sent me for my studies here in England when I was too young to make my own way." He looked at Montgomery with a smile. "What I have, I've earned myself."

"Are you rich?" John asked.

"Very," Jake said, without so much as a hint of pride.

Amanda wondered if it might be possible to dig herself a hole deep enough to crawl into and cover herself with sand. She would have been much more comfortable thusly.

"As much as Amanda?" Montgomery asked. "Though you may not know how much she has, do you? Her dowry calls men from far and wide here to seek her out. Did it call you as well?"

Jake began to tear bread into pieces. "I knew nothing of it," he said, "and I don't care now how much it is. Her beauty and sweetness are the true prize."

Montgomery laughed and John snorted. Amanda wasn't sure if they had difficulty seeing her sweetness, or they couldn't fathom a man coming for her for any reason but her gold. Whatever the case, she wasn't even tempted to cuff them as they so richly deserved.

What she was tempted to do was weep, and she never wept. By the saints, when would she learn to curb her tongue! Jake hadn't deserved what she'd said about him, to ruin his standing with her brothers. Was it his fault he was a merchant and not a fine lord? An accident of birth, and one that easily could have been hers.

It was the ultimate of ironies. Here she spent countless days disdaining any and all who came to offer for her because they could see nothing but her title and the fatness of her purse, yet she was discounting a man for precisely the same reasons. Because of his lack.

She rose and walked away. She came to stand at the edge of the sea and let the tears course down her cheeks unchecked. She had insulted a man who had been nothing but kind to her. She had belittled a man who apparently owed his riches to no one but himself—something she couldn't say for herself. If he never spoke to her again, she wouldn't be surprised and 'twould be nothing less than what she deserved.

She, of all people. She, who disdained the men who came to seek her hand because they could not, or would not, see her and not her dowry. She was a fool.

She turned and walked farther down the shore away from the keep, ignoring her guardsmen, not caring if they surrounded her or not—not that she would have noticed either way. Her own condemnations were ringing quite loudly in her ears and she found that she had a very long list of things to shout silently at herself as she walked.

Facing one's flaws, she discovered, was a very loud business.

She had to cease long enough to shed a few more tears and it was only then that she realized there was someone walking a pace or two behind her. She sighed, then turned, prepared to tell her guardsman that she wasn't going to go much farther— only it wasn't her guardsman.

It was Jake.

He smiled. "I wasn't sure you knew how far you'd walked."

Amanda looked around her and realized that she was indeed quite far down the shore. She shook her head. "I hadn't realized."

"Shall we go back?"

She looked up at him. No one would call her a coward or accuse her of shrinking from what needed to be done. She cleared her throat. "I would ask pardon," she said, lifting her chin to give herself courage. "I insulted you, and I'm sorry for it."

"You insulted me?"

"I did."

"How?"

By the saints, could the man not recognize an apology when it broadsided him? Or was he so dense that he couldn't determine just where it was she had bludgeoned him with her cruel words? She felt her attitude of contrition begin to rapidly dissipate. "I insulted you when I called you a merchant."

"But I *am* a merchant."

She folded her arms over her chest. "But I made it seem that 'tis less than a knight. Which it is, but that was no reason to be vile about it."

He looked at her with a frown of confusion. "And that is an insult?"

"Aye," she said shortly. "Did you not notice?"

He studied her for a moment and she could tell that he had noticed indeed. But he only smiled.

"A man can only be insulted when he allows himself to be. You were telling the truth. It is what I do. I am sorry, though," he said slowly, "that I am not a knight. Or a lord, I suppose, which would be better."

"And why is that?" she asked glumly.

He looked at her in silence for a moment or two, then smiled. "Because I see you, Amanda." He nodded back toward her brothers. "They're worried about you. We should go back."

Because I see you, Amanda.

Not her purse. Not her father's purse. Not her father's title and his power and his skill with which they might tidy up their own reputations by virtue of wedding with his daughter.

Just her.

A man who saw past all that to just her. She could scarce believe it. Worse yet, she didn't deserve it. Even worse still, she suspected she couldn't have it to call her own.

Jake held out his hand. "Shall we go?"

She closed her eyes briefly, then opened them, nodded, and took his hand. She couldn't stop the tears that continued to leak from her eyes.

She walked with him back down the beach, silently, unable to muster up a single thing to say. But she did do a bit of furious thinking and the conclusion she came to was easily reached.

The man wasn't a spy, or a merchant, he was obviously a demon. He had shamed her, then paid her the highest compliment possible all within the space of moments.

By the saints her father would have liked him a great deal.

"I suppose," she said as they neared the place where her brothers were waiting, "that you will need to return to your business soon."

"Tomorrow," he agreed.

She looked up at him in surprise. "Tomorrow? But that is

so soon. Surely you need . . . there are . . . you must—"

He stopped and turned to look down at her. "I have to go. I have things to see to. And so do you. There is someone out there—damn him—who will come for you, propose marriage, and you'll live happily ever after. Someone with a title and a few skills necessary to keep you safe."

She bit her lip very hard. Damnation, where were all these bloody tears coming from? She never had any to hand when they might have rescued her from a horrible dinner with some vile suitor.

Unfortunately there she was, stout of constitution and apparently leaky of eye, and all when it would have served her quite a bit better to be neither.

"No doubt," she managed. "I'd best be getting back to the keep, then, to prepare for his arrival."

He looked down at her hand in his for a moment or two in silence. Then he brought it slowly to his lips, kissed it, and deposited it gently by her side.

"Let's go," he said.

She didn't want him to touch her anymore. Aye, that was the truth of it. She was unaffected, uninterested, uncaring.

Damnation. More reasons to frequent the chapel on the morrow.

Without Jake.

She would have said that that was a good thing, but that would have meant another falsehood and more time on her knees.

She took all her pride in her hand, looked up at him, and did her damndest not to blubber like a mewling babe.

"Must you go?" she whispered.

For a moment, just the briefest of moments, she saw clearly in his face that he was no more unaffected than she.

The longing, unreasonable though it was, mirrored her own perfectly.

He reached out, tucked her hair behind her ear again, then briefly, very lightly touched her cheek. He dropped his hand to his side.

"How can I stay?" he asked quietly.

How indeed.

She nodded, dragged her sleeve across her face, and nodded again.

"We'll go back," she said firmly, with much more conviction than she felt.

She gathered up her brothers, her guard, and her merchant, and made her way back to her father's keep.

Chapter 12

Jake stood on the steps leading down into the courtyard from the great hall and surveyed his domain. Well, actually he surveyed Rhys de Piaget's domain, but who was going to quibble with a man eight centuries out of his element? Besides, given the fact that he was getting ready to get back into his element, who could blame him for entertaining delusions of grandeur? It beat the hell out of entertaining thoughts of marrying Amanda de Piaget.

Damn it anyway.

He'd known she would react with a start when she found out just how far his lack of title went, but what he hadn't expected was her apology, or her tears. If he hadn't known better, he might have thought she liked him.

Which, all things considered, had to be yesterday's most devastating piece of news.

He walked down the stairs to the courtyard before he could give that any more thought. He had to go; she had to stay. That was the cold, hard reality. He was a merchant; she was medieval nobility. That was more of that same kind of reality.

And never the twain shall meet . . .

John and Montgomery appeared suddenly on either side of him. They looked at him glumly.

"Ready?" John asked.

"Yes," Jake said. "We'd better go while we can."

"Can't you just stay here?" Montgomery asked.

Jake slung his arm around Montgomery's shoulders and pulled him toward the stables. "I have responsibilities at home."

"Then see to them and come back," Montgomery said. "That's simple enough."

"My business is in London. I can't come back north." *Or back in time,* he added silently. He looked over his shoulder at John, who was slouching along behind them. "Coming?"

John sighed and hurried to catch up with them. "I'm here. What is the plan?" he asked.

"I need to get back to where you found me," Jake said. "There might be something there I need."

"The robbers didn't even leave your clothes," John said. "Why would they have left anything else?"

"I still need to look," Jake said. "You never know."

There were two horses, one for him and one for the twins together. Two, but not three. Jake was unsurprised. He hadn't expected Amanda to come with them. He hadn't expected to see her at all that morning—and he hadn't. He supposed he was glad she was remaining behind. Who knew what sorts of dangers lurked out in the wilds of medieval England? He wondered about the advisability of taking the boys with him.

"Are you certain you don't want a horse?" Montgomery asked, for what had to have been the tenth time that morning.

"I don't think I'll have a way to send it back," Jake said.

"But that doesn't make any sense," John said. "How are you going to get home without a horse?"

"I'll manage," Jake promised, wondering how in the hell he was going to do that. Maybe he would just zip back in time and the boys' memories would be wiped out in the process. Maybe he would vanish in a puff of smoke and they would think he was a powerful fairy and tell stories about him for the rest of their lives.

Maybe he needed to sleep on a bed that was long enough for him. He was starting to hallucinate.

"I think you should manage to stay here," Montgomery said stubbornly. "Amanda likes you. *We* like you. I think even Father would like you."

"And how does that serve him?" John snapped, turning on his brother. "He's a merchant, Montgomery. Father would never give her to a mere merchant." He shot Jake a look. "I beg your pardon, Jake."

"That's all right," Jake said, smiling easily. "I'm sure there's a really great titled guy with lots of land just waiting to come sweep your sister off her feet."

The thought left him, unsurprisingly, with an intense desire to grind his teeth.

But lest he reduce his molars to powder, he wiggled his jaw, rubbed his hands together, and took the reins of his horse. "Let's go while the sun is still shining. I'm sure it won't last."

Montgomery and John grunted in agreement and they swung up easily onto their mount's back. Jake swung up less easily, but he managed it.

And with that, they were off.

Jake felt distinctly like the blind leading the blind. He had no idea what he was going to do short of just making it back to the place where he'd landed. Once he got there, he had no idea how to proceed. Should he turn cartwheels? Recite Burns? Knock three times?

He considered the problem as he rode through the village with Artane's youngest lords. He supposed there had to be some sort of something that would indicate a gate through time, but he didn't remember any standing stones, fairy rings, or big red Xs marking any spots in Northumberland.

Worse still, who would he ask about just such a thing, in either century? He supposed he might have consulted the village midwife, or the local witch, if Artane currently possessed either. But such questions would undoubtedly get around and then he'd be labeled a certifiable whacko and who knew where that would land him.

He had very unpleasant memories of Artane's dungeon and no desire to make new ones.

Who would he have asked in his own time? Gideon? He examined his time spent with him and decided that even if Artane had odd things turn up now and then, that just couldn't mean time travelers.

Could it?

He shook his head. Gideon was far too normal a guy to have had any kind of experience with the paranormal. Surely if he had known that something really weird was going on in his ancestral keep, he would have mentioned it. Wouldn't he?

Now, Seakirk was a different story. Jake suspected that Worthington could cough up quite a few interesting details. He seriously regretted not having interrogated the butler more thoroughly. Seakirk had ghosts; could it not have time-travelers as well?

And if it didn't, surely there was some nutcase in the twenty-first century who had ideas on the whole thing. Surely he wasn't the first to find himself centuries out of his own time. People went missing all the time, didn't they? There had to be more explanations for it than getting eaten by bears.

Unfortunately, he didn't have any of those resources at present and was stuck with just his own clever self and whatever ingenuity he possessed to get himself out of his current mess.

It seemed to take an inordinately long amount of time to get to where he was supposed to be going, probably because he was spending most of his time scrutinizing for clues every patch of grass his horse stepped over.

Nothing looked out of the ordinary.

Nothing looked in the least bit time-travelly.

The boys stopped eventually and looked at each other before they looked at him.

"This is it," John said heavily. "Where we found you."

Jake sat on his horse and stared at the countryside. It looked a bit like the countryside near Seakirk, but really, how could he tell? He'd first seen it—or not, as the case might have been—in the driving rain. He'd avoided looking at it the next day, thanks to that blinding headache. He couldn't have said with any certainty what the place looked like.

So that solved nothing for him. He turned to the mystery of his clothes. Could he have been robbed, or had he just been stripped on his way through time? He looked carefully at the grass at his horse's feet and saw something sparkle all of the sudden. He dismounted as gracefully as he could and dug through the grass until he found it.

A pound coin.

He closed his hand around it and felt a shiver go through him. So, he hadn't lost his mind after all.

He had, however, lost his clothes and it was obvious by the trampling of the grass that he'd had help with that. So he had been robbed. He handed John his reins and continued his search. He made wider and wider circles, but found nothing else.

He stopped finally, looked up at the sky, and wondered what in the world thieves were going to do with his wallet, his jeans, his very expensive leather coat, and his Dr. Martens. Well, actually, he could imagine what they might do with his shoes and coat. It was his wallet that concerned him.

He hoped that wouldn't come back to haunt him.

He went back to where he'd found the coin and stood there, putting up all his paranormal antennae. He waited, but nothing happened.

So he wasn't exactly Mr. Poltergeist, but even he was beginning to suspect he wasn't going anywhere soon. He looked up at the boys to find them staring at him as if he'd lost his mind.

"What are you doing?" John asked.

"Looking for clues," Jake replied.

Montgomery shook his head. "I told you, Jake, you won't find the thieves. I think you should forget the loss and come back home with us."

"No," Jake said.

They looked less than satisfied with that answer, and he couldn't blame them. He wasn't all that satisfied either. He looked at them, trying to to come up with something useful, when it occurred to them that perhaps they were part of the problem. He hesitated.

"You know," he said, "I might be able to find what I'm looking for if you could move back a little."

The boys blinked.

Jake shooed them with his hand.

John shrugged and took over Jake's horse. Then he and Montgomery did as they were asked and backed their horses up. Jake stared at the spot of ground where he'd found the pound coin and willed himself to go somewhere. Anywhere. Forward, to the future.

Nothing happened.

He looked at the boys. They were watching him, solemn-eyed and silent.

He waited again.

It took a long time.

But still nothing happened.

The boys started to shift, as did their horses. Jake shifted as well, but he didn't have any other choice but to remain where he was, just to see what was going to happen. What else was he supposed to do? He had to get home.

The feel of hoofbeats came to him through his feet before he heard them. He looked up and saw a rider, one he recognized. In fact, he doubted he'd ever mistake her for anyone else. So she had come to see him off. For some reason, that was very heartening.

Amanda pulled up, breathing hard. He was about to thank her for coming, but she spoke before he could.

"I had to flee," she said. "I saw Ledenham coming from a distance."

Jake felt his ego being properly deflated. He might have struggled to come up with something to say to save his pride, but he was distracted by the looks John and Montgomery were giving each other.

"What?" he asked. "What's wrong?"

"Nothing," Montgomery said, looking less than sure of himself.

"Nothing at all," John agreed.

"Liars," Jake said. "Who is Ledenham?"

"One of our neighbors," Amanda said grimly, "though not a close one. His keep is on the border like ours, but inland. Past Wyckham. I'm surprised Nicholas didn't see him coming and send someone to warn us." Then she shook her hair back over her shoulder. "He's no one of consequence."

"But he is," Montgomery protested. "Mandy, he is more powerful than you allow. And wiley."

"And vile," John added. "I'd be wary of him, were I you. He's not one to offend."

"And what will he do?" Amanda demanded hotly. "Steal me away? And have the wrath of Artane as a whole descend upon his sorry head?"

"Amanda," John said seriously, "he could harm you quite thoroughly before any of us could reach you. I tell you, he is not one to have as an enemy."

"We'll protect you," Montgomery said, putting his shoulders back and smiling bravely. "Never fear, sister. He'll not best us—"

Famous last words. Jake looked behind Amanda and saw several horsemen coming their way. Amanda looked over her shoulder and swore. Jake considered his limited options, which amounted to run or fight, and came to a quick decision. He shoved the pound coin down into his boot, then called to the boys.

"When they come, I want you to ease around them and ride like hell for the castle."

"But—" John began, looking horrified.

"Go get help," Jake said. "You aren't running; you're going to get help. Let's just hope they let you do it."

They looked indecisive. Well, John looked indecisive. Montgomery looked terrified and was doing his best not to show it. Jake liked them both very much. He only hoped he would get to see more of them. He didn't like what he'd heard about the men coming toward them.

And he liked the looks of them even less when they arrived. Amanda had moved her horse so she was standing beside him. The lads backed away, then suddenly bolted. One of Lord Ledenham's men started after him but Ledenham called him back.

That told Jake all he needed to know.

He put his hand on Amanda's horse and waited for Lord Ledenham to make the first move. Ledenham looked at Amanda disdainfully.

"So, Amanda my love, you have a peasant here to tidy up after your horse. He looks to be a sturdy one."

"He's not a peasant," Amanda said calmly. "But it would take eyes far clearer than yours, Lord Ledenham, to see that."

Jake studied the man in the very bauble-encrusted clothes and saw less a man than a snake, coiled and ready to strike. Montgomery and John's assessment of this one was not far off. He was dangerous. Amanda needed to be careful.

Lord Ledenham waved a dismissive hand toward his men. "Take her. I'm finished negotiating with Artane. I need a bride and today seems as good a day as any to have one."

Jake squatted down as if to duck out of the way of the men coming for Amanda, then grabbed two handfuls of eminently fresh, steaming horse dung and flung it upward and outward.

While Ledenham's nearest guardsmen were swearing and brushing off their clothes, Jake slapped Amanda's horse on the rump. He managed to pull himself up behind her as the beast leaped forward.

No small feat.

Apparently desperation was a good teacher of horse skills.

"Fly," he shouted, and they did.

For himself, all he could do was hang on for the ride and hope that he'd neither misjudged their adversary or his own riding skills.

"You're mad!" Amanda shouted over her shoulder.

"Probably," he shouted back. "Sorry about your clothes."

She laughed. He would have been glad she appreciated his sense of humor if he hadn't been concentrating so hard on just staying on the horse.

And all the while, he braced himself for the feel of an arrow in his back.

Amanda looked back over his shoulder. "Still there, but falling behind," she said, then urged her horse to greater speed.

They overtook the boys a hundred yards outside the village. Jake bellowed for them to hurry, which they did, sending farm life and villagers scattering with equal dispatch.

They thundered across the drawbridge and up the way to the inner bailey. Amanda shouted for the gate to be drawn up, but Jake suspected that wouldn't happen in time.

What did happen, though, was that the portcullis slammed home with a resounding clang the moment the boys cleared it. Amanda's horse skidded to a stop in front of the stables. Jake slid off, then leaned over with his hands on his thighs, sucking in air. He saw Amanda dismount in much the same fashion. He straightened, then took her arm and pulled her toward the keep.

"You can't stay out here," he said.

"My father's guards can—"

"I'm sure they're wonderful, but please go inside."

She hesitated, then nodded with a sigh. "As you will," she said and walked away. She hadn't taken five steps, though, before she turned and looked at him.

"You stayed."

He smiled. "So I did."

She stared at him silently for a moment or two, pursing her lips as if she considered what, if anything, she should say. Apparently, there was no good comment for a merchant who had promised to leave but was now going to be underfoot for an indeterminate amount of time. She merely looked at him again for a long moment, then turned and walked back to the house.

Jake watched her go, noticed peripherally that the boys had taken the horses away, and then after dunking his hands in a horse trough and wiping them on his clothes, stood in the midst of Artane's courtyard and contemplated life and its mysteries.

It took quite a bit of time, but left him no wiser.

What in the *hell* was he going to do now?

He rubbed his hands over his face and wished desperately for pockets. He thought so much better when he could shove his hands in his pockets and pace.

So, lacking the proper clothing, he settled for clasping his hands behind his back and pacing in front of the stables.

Unfortunately, it didn't provide him with any decent answers.

The truth, the unavoidable truth, was that he was stuck, and he had no idea how to unstick himself.

He didn't bother wasting time bemoaning his fate. It was in

his best interest to assume the best, to assume that there was a reason he was in medieval England, to assume that he had something to accomplish before he found an empty seat on that Paranormal Express back to the Future.

What else could he do?

The boys came out of the stable. Montgomery looked at Jake carefully.

"You're staying?"

Jake took a deep breath. "Yes."

"Good," Montgomery said, fighting a grin. "I hoped you would."

"Well, it's just for the moment," Jake said. "To keep Amanda safe until your brothers get home."

"Then you will be here a while," John said. "Who knows when they will come? Miles is due any day and Nicholas, well, Nick's keep is in sorry shape, so 'tis possible he will be there for the remainder of the summer. Robin will come home when Anne's father irritates him overmuch. That could be any day."

Or it could be in a month. And since Jake supposed he was going to be in medieval England for a while, he would have to do something about his lack of medieval skills. Skill with the sword could only be an asset in protecting Amanda. Maybe that was the whole point.

He nodded to himself. Yes, it was entirely possible that that was the very reason he was staying. It was obvious that though the boys were certainly willing, they were not completely able to keep Amanda safe. And while his skills with his hands were certainly useful in certain situations, he was sorely lacking when it came to facing many men with swords.

That could change.

If he could just find the right teacher.

He stood there for several moments, wondering where he might begin his search, when he was suddenly distracted by a commotion at the gates. He watched as the portcullis was raised a bit and a young man slithered underneath. He crawled to his feet, cursing furiously. He was quite rumpled and sweating profusely.

"'Tis Miles," Montgomery said joyously. "He's home!"

John followed his brother as they scampered over to the new arrival. Jake could hear the grumbles from where he stood. The complaints only increased in volume as the twins brought their brother back to where Jake stood.

"Damned gate," Miles was saying. "I had to dispatch Lord Ledenham and his men before I could even get to it. The louts were littering it like so much refuse." He continued to grouse about his exertions, the lack of aid offered him in those exertions, and the heat, then stopped in front of Jake. "And who is this?"

"Jake Kilchurn," Montgomery supplied promptly. "He saved Amanda this afternoon."

Miles looked him over. "Where is your sword?"

Jake looked at Miles, sufficiently knighted and apparently a little jaded, and decided he'd just found his new tutor. He clapped a hand on Miles's shoulder and smiled.

"It's a long story. I'll tell you later."

Miles shrugged. "As you will." He looked back toward the gate. "Ledenham will no doubt be heading home to lick his wounds, but 'tis best we remain inside for now." He looked at his brothers. "Is it possible there might be something left to eat inside, or have you lads laid siege to the larder?"

He slung an arm about each of his younger brothers, then walked off toward the great hall with them. Jake watched them all go, feeling heartened. Then Miles stopped, looked over his shoulder, and frowned.

"Aren't you coming?"

Jake nodded, more pleased that he cared to admit.

Having brothers, even borrowed brothers, was not a bad thing at all.

He caught up with them and went in to the great hall where he was included in their foray into the kitchens. He joined the lads for a late lunch and gave final thoughts to his plans.

Medieval skills were definitely the order of the day, and Miles was his answer, at least the answer to the only problem he could manage to solve at present.

He would protect her, and then he would go home.

That he might not be *able* to get home was a thought he just wouldn't entertain. He had a pound coin in his shoe that said he could. He would just have to wait until the right time, or until he'd done in the past what Fate had sent him there to do.

He applied himself to his meal, leaving the rest of his future to be dealt with in time.

Chapter 13

Montgomery of Artane knew how to keep his own counsel. Even Lord Pevensey had noticed it and that man noticed little beyond what arrived upon his supper trencher. Once, he had actually looked up from his feasting to remark to Montgomery that he wasn't nearly as stupid as the other lads and that he certainly knew how to hold his tongue.

Montgomery had taken that as high praise.

He sighed in pleasure, partly from the warmth of the fire and partly because he would never have to wonder again what Pevensey thought of him. Montgomery had managed to endure that year at Pevensey's keep only because he knew his father wouldn't force him to stay longer, not after he'd learned what a useless master Pevensey was.

It hadn't been time completely wasted. Montgomery had learned a thing or two about warfare, learned how to hold his tongue, and learned that he loved his home best of all.

No wonder Amanda didn't want to wed.

Montgomery stood with his back to the fire, warming his hands and other important parts of himself, and considered his sister. She was a capital chap, unafraid of mud and vermin, unafraid to hoist a sword or ride like a banshee. How could a lad not love her best of all?

She had changed, though, in the past year. She didn't laugh as much. When she rode, she rode as if she sought escape. When she fought, she fought as if she practiced for the heat of battle. Montgomery had despaired of her ever being happy again.

Until Jake had arrived.

Never mind that the man was a merchant. Montgomery knew there had to be more to him than that. After all, didn't it take a canny wit and quick hands to keep your goods away from thieves? There was that unsettling bit of business of finding Jake senseless on the ground, but Montgomery still wasn't sure that hadn't been something unusual. If Jake had been himself, he surely would have been victorious. Montgomery had vivid memories of watching Jake cripple several of the men who had been attacking him when Montgomery, John, and Amanda had come to the rescue.

A rescue Jake had not needed.

Nay, there was no reason Jake couldn't become a knight.

Montgomery shifted uncomfortably. Very well, there were several reasons he couldn't, but those reasons were foolishness. Why did a man only have the privileges of knighthood if he were born to it? Surely a man with vigor and strength could just reach out and wrest a knighthood away from the king— and retain it as a reward for his cunning.

Besides, Montgomery liked Jake.

He liked him very much more than anyone else who had come seeking Amanda's hand.

He was still a bit confused about why Jake couldn't go home. After all, London was only a handful of days's hard ride to the south. Why couldn't he just go, take care of his affairs, then come back? Obviously, merchantry was a more complicated affair than he supposed.

He looked over to his right as Jake came down the stairs with Miles. They were deep in talk, no doubt about Jake's training. Montgomery couldn't begrudge Jake his opportunity to have Miles's expertise. His brother was, after all, a very daring warrior, ever willing to take chances no one else would. Perhaps Miles would give Jake the skills he needed to make a good showing for their father. Not that skills would likely impress Rhys de Piaget. He was, after all, the most skilled warrior in all of England, followed closely by his son, Robin de Piaget.

Montgomery felt a surge of pride flow through him at the thought that he carried that same blood in his veins. He continued to warm his backside contentedly against the fire as he watched Jake and Miles plow through a hearty meal, rise, and start for the front door. And then Jake paused, smiled, and came over to sling his arm around Montgomery's shoulders.

"I think I might need your opinion as well, Montgomery. Come with us and keep an eye on my form."

Montgomery's heart swelled within him, in spite of his attempts to look unaffected.

By the saints, he wished Amanda could wed with this man. Never mind that he had no knightly blood flowing through his veins. He was kind to Amanda, and he was kind to Amanda's younger kin. That was a kind of nobility none of Amanda's other suitors had ever shown.

For Montgomery, it was enough.

Chapter 14

The air was thick with stratagem. The two combatants leaned forward, each looking to have the advantage. They circled, paused to consider, then struck again, seeking constantly to best the other so thoroughly that the only honorable escape was death.

Amanda watched Miles and Jake facing each other over her father's chessboard and wondered who would emerge the victor. Miles was a very good player, but it looked as if Jake was equally as good. She had watched them trade insults, then bluff, all the while comporting themselves as equals.

Which, she supposed, they might have been, had things been different.

"Damnation." Miles tipped his king over with a sigh. "Checkmate."

Jake smiled. "A very good game. You're a good player."

"I should be," Miles grumbled. "My father has drilled me in it from the time I was small. He said it would make me a better knight." He looked at Jake with a frown. "I can't say as it has."

"Are you kidding? You almost had me several times."

Kidding was another of those words that left Amanda shaking her head. She caught the gist of it, though, and hoped that

Miles understood the compliment. That was one thing she could say for Jake: he was not stingy with his praise.

And he was an exceptionally fine chess player.

Miles sighed, rose, made Jake a low bow, and then came to sit next to Amanda on the bench. He put his arm around her shoulders and scowled.

"He may be a mighty chess player, but the man can't wield a sword to save his life."

"Miles!"

"That's what you think this week," Jake said easily. "Give me a month or two and see what you think of my swordsmanship."

Amanda leaned back against Miles and contemplated the mystery of Jackson Alexander Kilchurn IV.

First, why had the man been given such a lofty name if he were a mere merchant's son? Second, where had he learned to play chess so ferociously, and didn't that canny sense of warfare obviously extend to his sword arm? Third, why was it a man who was so far below her brothers in station could look so comfortable with them, grinding them to dust in her father's solar with her father's chess pieces?

And fourth, and most distressingly, why couldn't *he* have been one of the scores of men who'd come to seek her over the past four years?

"You're muttering," Miles said pleasantly. "Careful, Amanda. You're beginning to take on several of Robin's more irritating habits."

She stuck her tongue out at him, but couldn't follow it up with anything nastily said because he was wearing that very small smile he gave only to her, his admittedly preferred sister, and when he did so, she forgave anything and everything. She studied him.

"You're very cheerful tonight," she remarked.

"Why shouldn't I be?" he asked, cheerfully. "I'm home. I have you here to cook for me and mend my clothes. I've just found myself soundly thrashed in chess by a man who takes your barbs and laughs at them. Where in that list should I find anything to bemoan?"

"You don't want me mending your clothes."

"I don't want you cooking for me either," he said, with a friendly laugh, "but I'm happy just the same."

Amanda had to admit that, astonishingly enough, so was she. She was sitting comfortably in her favorite chamber in the keep, she had three of her most favorite brothers to hand, and she was basking in a very homey feeling of belonging.

"Amanda, are you next?"

She blinked when she realized Jake was speaking to her. "I beg your pardon?"

"Do you play chess?"

"I'd tread carefully there, Jake," Miles warned. "Amanda has many hidden talents and the ability to thrash us all in chess is one of them."

"Then perhaps I'd better practice on your brothers first," Jake said. He looked at Montgomery. "Do you want to play next?"

Montgomery looked as if Jake had offered him the contents of the king's treasury. He leaped up and threw himself down into the empty chair.

"Ready," he said, flexing his fingers.

"I can only hope I am," Jake said fervently, but he turned his head and winked at Amanda.

"Thrash him, Montgomery," Amanda suggested.

"Now, was that kind?" Miles whispered. "Such a nice man. So nasty of you to make sport of him."

"I'm wearing him down," Amanda said loudly. "To make my task of reducing him to rubble that much easier."

Jake only laughed and continued on with his play. Amanda watched him, finding that she couldn't look away. It wasn't so much his handsomeness, which was undeniable, or his skill with what she had always considered a game reserved for nobility, which was also quite evident.

It was that he was good to her brothers.

She watched Montgomery simply glow under Jake's attentions. Jake complimented Montgomery's strategy, fretted over the potential for his own king's demise, wondered aloud if he could possibly prevail against one so young, but so obviously skilled in the knightly arts.

Montgomery ceased to glow. He began to preen.

Jake pinned his king eventually, but it took a great deal of time and appeared to take a great deal of effort on Jake's part.

"Oh, by the saints," Amanda said. "He has that one completely won over."

"And what of you?" Miles inquired innocently.

"Me?"

"Has he won you over yet?"

"Why do you ask?" she asked with a scowl.

Miles shrugged. "He seems a good sort."

"And how does that serve me?" she asked. "He is a merchant. I, by some accident of birth, am not. There can be nothing between us."

Miles tugged on her hair. "Perhaps not. But it might at least show you that not all men are as wretched as the ones who have camped outside our front gates over the years."

"Again, what does it serve me?"

"Perhaps it doesn't," he said easily. "But I like him. I admit to being a little baffled at his lack of skills, even for a merchant, but I think those can be remedied. Given that he has, well," he paused modestly, "me, for a teacher."

"Poor man."

"Perhaps you should face me over swords, sister, and see if your opinion changes." He crossed his feet at the ankles and leaned back. "Aye, I like him well. He has traveled, you know. Many places I should like to see."

These were tidings. Amanda wondered how it was that Miles had been home not even a se'nnight and yet he knew so many things about Jake that she did not.

After all, *she* had been the one to find him.

"Where?" she asked, trying not to sound very curious.

"Italy. France. Spain. Other places I'd never heard of. All very exciting and new. I envy him."

She was unsurprised. Miles was surely the wanderer in their family. He was a handful of years younger than she yet already had been to France twice as often as she had. She understood his longing, though. There was something appealing about the thought of seeing other places, tasting new things, smelling new smells.

Though at the moment, there wasn't a new place she would have traded for an evening in her father's solar, surrounded by people she loved.

The evening progressed. John was treated to a game in much the same manner as Montgomery, only Jake was more serious with John. He gave fewer compliments yet talked to him in the manner her father's eldest guardsmen did amongst themselves, speaking and jesting together as if they were the only ones who could understand those particular conversations. In Jake's estimation, apparently John was someone worthy of his regard and trust.

Jake beat him handily, but that didn't seem to matter to John. He joined Montgomery near the fire, where the pair of them looked insufferably smug.

Jake sat back and looked at Amanda. "Your turn?"

"You'll not find me so easily bested."

"I never, *ever* thought you would be."

Miles choked on a laugh. Amanda glared at him, then rose to face Jake over the chess board.

"Ladies first," Jake said pleasantly.

"Your first mistake," she said, just as pleasantly.

She found, as the game wore on, that Jake offered her no compliments, nor was he nearly as talkative as he had been with her brothers. She might have, perhaps, even seen his brow furrow a time or two. And every time he looked at her to see, no doubt, if she was struggling as mightily as he, she gave him her best smile, the one guaranteed to have her father agreeing that she really should ride whatever horse she pleased and it would be perfectly fine with him if she tromped about in lads' clothes because they were more comfortable.

Apparently, it worked on men other than her father.

Several minutes later, Jake looked up from the board where his king stood, helplessly pinned by her queen, a bishop, and a knight.

He blinked. "I think I've been beaten."

"Then surrender."

He put his hand on his king, looked at her seriously and, with deliberate slowness, tipped his king over.

"I think I surrendered the moment the game was begun."

She had the feeling he was talking about more than just the game.

He leaned back in his chair and put his hands behind his head. "You're very good," he said.

"Strategy is my lifeblood," she agreed. "I should have been a commander of armies."

"France would have lived in fear," he said with a smile.

"My suitors certainly have."

"So, what else do you do with your time when you're not inventing strategies to baffle and bemuse those impertinent enough to try to get past your guards?"

"She doesn't sew," John supplied.

"She *definitely* doesn't cook," Miles said lazily.

Montgomery remained silent. Jake looked at him.

"What, no offerings from you?"

Montgomery shook his head with a smile. "I don't think there's anything Amanda cannot do. She rides, she knows what to do with a sword, she dances, she can forage for herbs—"

"She consorts with witches, you mean," John muttered.

"John!" Miles said sternly. "They are not witches. Berengaria was a girl at Segrave, and I can assure you that Grandmother never would have condoned witchcraft on her land. Well," he added with a smile, "not any of the foul kind."

"They aren't witches, they're midwives and healers," Amanda said, "and I do not consort with them, I visit them when they are traveling our way. I've learned several useful things that might save your sorry life, John, if ever I desired it to be saved. And besides, Berengaria lived here for many years. The only reason she left was because you had been born." She looked at Jake. "Any other questions?" she asked briskly.

He held up his hands in surrender. "Not a one. I can see you are very busy."

"And what of you?" Montgomery asked. "What do you do with your merchantry business?"

"Aye, I would like to hear of your travels," Miles said.

"And I would like to hear of the jewels," John said. "Robin has a dagger with a very fine red stone in the hilt which I think is too ornate for his use, though he seems quite reluctant to let me have it."

"He'll allow you to have it when you have the skill to take it away from him in a fight," Amanda said. She looked back at Jake. "I for one would like to see what you create for these wealthy patrons. Can you not describe it to us?"

"I can do better than that. Do you have paper and anything to write with?"

"You can write?" John asked in surprise.

"Of course," Jake said, looking equally as surprised. "Can't you?"

"Aye, but I'm a lord's son."

Jake only smiled. He accepted a scrap from the pile their father kept for lesser correspondence, as well as a feather and ink.

Amanda put away the chess pieces and returned to her seat in time to see a creation half drawn on the parchment.

"What is that?" she breathed. "'Tis magnificent."

"Just a brooch," he said modestly. "It's a spray of flowers I designed for a woman who loved different colors of gems. Right here I put citrine, then blue zircon here, rose garnet here, aquamarine here—a very unique color of it that was very hard to find and even harder to cut." He looked up at her from under his eyelashes and smiled. "It was, in fact, a great deal like the color of your eyes. Very beautiful, very rare."

Amanda wondered if anyone had bothered to bring wine with them. She was, quite suddenly, quite parched.

"Cut?" Miles asked, dragging a stool over to sit next to Jake. "What do you mean, cut?"

"Amanda, may I have your dagger?" Jake asked.

She pulled it out of the back of her belt and handed it over to him. He held it up so all could see the dark-red stone in its hilt.

"When you find gems, they don't look like this. They're dull, much duller than this one. It's the gem cutter's task to take a dull stone and turn it into something beautiful. And to do that," he said, "you have to be able to see more than what's on the surface."

He looked at Amanda for a moment or two in silence.

"Take Amanda's dagger," he continued. "This gem's not a bad stone, and it's actually cut quite well, but look here. If it could be faceted here," he pointed, "and here as well, then the fire that lies within the stone would be easier to see. Of course, I don't have the tools here to do it . . ."

He frowned at her dagger thoughtfully and Amanda could readily see how in this, at least, he knew of what he spoke.

And at that moment, there was a part of her that envied him his passion for his work.

She realized just as suddenly that she had no true passion of her own, short of devising new and interesting ways to avoid matrimony. She did have a goodly knowledge of herbs, and of languages, mathematics, and other manly subjects her father had insisted she learn. She could break a horse, tend a child, and face a man over blades and likely come away the victor if she had to.

Odd, though, looking at the small, exquisite forms that continued to flow from Jake's pen as if they took on lives of their own as he sketched them, that her life had seemed so important and the lives of others outside her gates so ordinary but a handful of days before. Now she could see how a mere merchant might be so much more than that.

How sorely she had misjudged his depths.

And how generously he had granted her virtues far beyond what she deserved.

She was beginning to wonder if everything she had believed about her place in the world and everyone else's on a lower plane was completely false.

"Amanda?"

She looked at him, dragging herself away from her thoughts. "Aye?"

"Are you all right?"

She nodded, trying to smile. "I am well. I am just . . . well, I had no idea how beautiful your wares are. They are . . . breathtaking."

"Thank you," he said simply.

Without gloating. Without an *ah, see how you've misjudged me, you disagreeable wench* look. Perhaps he was modest, or perhaps he just knew his worth and didn't need it countenanced by anyone else.

He was, as Miles had said, a goodly sort.

"Can you teach us to draw?" Montgomery asked, looking at Jake's renderings. "I would like that."

"I would as well," John admitted. "Though I think I would prefer to draw scenes of glorious bloodshed, not dainties for a lady's cloak."

Jake laughed. "No doubt. Yes, if you'd like. I'll trade you for more lessons with the sword."

"*I'll* see to your swordplay," Miles put in. "And if there's anything left of you at the end of the day, the boys can have you and you can do with them what you like."

"But where does that leave Amanda?" Montgomery asked.

All eyes turned to her. She would have cut off her own arm before she blushed, but somehow, she couldn't quite reach for her dagger to do it before she felt herself growing uncomfortably hot.

She pushed her hair back from her face, though it cooled her not one bit. "I would like to learn as well," she admitted slowly.

"Done," Jake said promptly. "Especially if we can use you as our model on occasion." He looked at the twins. "Just think on it, boys. Long stretches of time with nothing more to do than study your sister and figure out how to capture her on paper." He shuddered. "Torture."

"The torture you'll find each night begins and ends here," she said, gesturing toward the chessboard.

"Happily," he said with a smile. "Now, someone help me figure out how to clean up this ink, because I've never used a feather to draw with before."

Amanda shared a knowing look with Miles, who seemed to be just as baffled as she herself was.

"No, not that look," Jake said.

"What look?" Amanda asked.

"The one that says you think I've lost my mind. There's a logical explanation for what I don't know."

"Then give it," she said.

He smiled pleasantly, then rubbed his hands together and rose. "Montgomery, help me clean this up, would you? Then I should get to bed. We have a big day tomorrow in the lists."

Amanda pursed her lips, but didn't press him. There would be plenty of time later to get answers. She'd overheard Jake saying earlier to Miles that he planned to remain for a bit at Artane, at least until Nicholas came home. Lord Ledenham had convinced him that even with all the guards still at Artane, Amanda would do better with him as added protection.

What protection he could offer, she didn't know.

But even as that thought took shape in her mind, she knew that wasn't exactly true. The man was canny, and he would certainly be able to see to anyone if he could avoid being skewered with a sword long enough to do it with his hands alone.

And just where had he learned that skill?

So many questions.

The saints be praised she might have the time to have those answers.

She found herself wishing that Nicholas's roof might find itself quite unfinished for several more fortnights.

Chapter 15

Jake put his borrowed sword point down in the dirt and dragged his sleeve across his sweaty forehead. He looked at the castle rising up next to him and shook his head. Who would have thought that an innocent enough trip north would have ended here.

At Artane.

In a very roundabout way, of course.

He looked at the sword in his hands, then lifted it up and examined it. It was odd enough to be standing in a medieval castle; it was beyond weird to be standing there with a sword in his hands. Stranger still to be learning how to use it.

He looked at Miles. "That was better."

"Better," Miles conceded. "I only dozed off a handful of times."

Jake laughed. "You're merciless."

"Nay, I am quite soft—especially compared to my brother. Not only would Robin grind you under his heel, he would demand that you scrape yourself off his boot so he could stroll back to the hall in comfort."

"You're a good teacher," Jake said frankly. "I appreciate your help."

Miles made him a small bow. "'Twas my pleasure, truly,

and no thanks are necessary. You've kept the twins from driving me mad. That is worth a great deal."

"Right," Jake said, not believing it for an instant. Miles and his brothers seemed to share a genuine affection for each other, despite Miles's grumbles that they took up too much of his time and the twins' complaints that he was ignoring them.

Jake envied them.

Though he had to admit that, over the past week since his aborted attempt to get home, he had felt a part of that family circle.

It was a very pleasant feeling indeed.

He supposed that even Amanda had by now gotten over her horror at the fact that he was a mere merchant. He honestly hadn't expected her to feel anything else. How could she? This was her reality. In her world, a title was everything.

"Let's have a drink and a bit of a rest," Miles suggested. "Then we'll go at it again, if you wish."

"I wish," Jake said. "I've figured out which end to hold my sword by, but that's about it."

"'Tis a fine start. We'll improve upon that this afternoon."

Jake walked with him over to the well. He wondered what sorts of things found themselves in that well, but at the moment, he was too grateful for something cold to drink to give it much worry. Miles had dredged up a mail shirt for him earlier that week and though Jake was used to sweltering heat, of both the jungle and the mine kind, this exercising in a tin can was an entirely new experience in par-boiling.

He poured water over his head and came up spluttering. He shook his head.

"I don't know how you stand the heat."

"You grow accustomed to it," Miles said. "When you're in a battle for your life, you appreciate the protection mail gives. I'm surprised you don't have at least a leather jerkin. That might turn a dull knife. Perhaps."

"I've worn leather before," Jake admitted, "and I agree. It's some protection." He spared a thought for his perfectly broken-in leather coat that was now keeping some medieval opportunist warm.

"Did you lose that when your gear was stolen?" Miles asked.

"Yes, among other things."

Miles shook his head sadly. "You shouldn't travel alone. Not even the most skilled knight goes about without a man to guard his back."

"You did," Jake pointed out.

"Well," Miles said with a small smile, "I'm not exactly the most cautious of souls."

Jake laughed. There Miles stood, a medieval knight with all the skills necessary for the execution of knightly duties. He had no doubt spent many years perfecting his skills in quite rigid ways. But despite what had to be a very serious bit of self-discipline, Jake could see that Miles had a good dose of the same wanderlust he had himself. He imagined that if Miles had found himself in the twenty-first century, he would have been traveling all over the world, possibly in search of the rare, the unique, and the ridiculously expensive.

Jake smiled to himself. Too bad he couldn't have traded places with Miles. It would have solved several problems for the both of them.

"Let us make for the table," Miles said. "For all we know, Amanda will be there, waiting to display her chatelaine skills and pour our wine."

"I've known your sister less than a month and I'm positive she isn't going to be standing there with a bottle in one hand and a plate of fine meats in the other."

"Probably not," Miles agreed. "Nevertheless, we should at least take our ease for a moment or two before we return to our labors."

Jake nodded and walked with Miles to the great hall. He had almost stopped thinking about the complete improbability of what he was doing, but it caught him at odd times.

Like now, when he was crossing a medieval courtyard wearing chain mail with a sword slapping against his thigh as he walked. He squeaked a little, he sweated a lot, and he was actually looking forward to eel under sauce.

Who would have thought it?

He wondered what the people he'd left behind—or ahead as the case might be—were thinking at the moment. Or doing, for that matter. Was time passing in the same manner there? Had a month gone by, leaving Gideon's father without his paperwork and Jackson III grinding his teeth at a missed deal?

Had Gideon done any investigation into Jake's disappearance, or had he chalked it up to irresponsibility?

He couldn't have said and today he didn't care. Today he was going to continue with his plan to remake himself into a medieval knight—minus the title, of course—so he could protect Amanda until one of her older brothers got home. And then he would go home and take back up his own life.

His own dull, flat life.

He walked into the hall and the first thing he saw, once his eyes adjusted to the gloom, was Amanda standing near the high table, talking to one of Artane's servants.

And he wondered if he *could* go back, back to that life in the future when everything that sparkled was here in the past.

He walked across the floor with her brother and found that he simply couldn't take his eyes off her. And when she finished speaking, turned, and looked at him, he had the most absurd feeling of pleasure wash over him.

And then she smiled.

And he felt like he'd been winded.

"Steady," Miles murmured.

"Shut up."

Miles *tsk-tsk*ed. "You shouldn't be rude to your sword master, especially when your work for the day isn't finished."

"I'm older than you are. I can take you."

"So the little lads claim. Not with the sword, surely."

"Surely not," Jake agreed. "But with my bare hands? Definitely."

Miles hesitated only briefly. "Will you show me?"

Jake smiled at him. "Of course. Tomorrow, though, and without mail."

"Done." Miles waved an expansive hand Amanda's way. "You may moon over my sister all you like," he said loudly.

Jake gave him a friendly pat on the back that was firm enough to make him stumble, smiled warningly, then turned his attentions to the really interesting occupant of the great hall. He stopped in front of her and made her a small bow.

"My lady."

She wrinkled her nose. "You need a bath."

"Knights don't bathe," Miles said from behind Jake.

"They do in this house."

"We're not finished with our training for the day," Miles argued.

Amanda pursed her lips. "Very well, you may stink now. Bathe before supper, else you won't eat. At least not at my table."

Miles made her a low bow, then hopped around the table and made himself comfortable in a chair. Jake smiled at Amanda.

"Shall I sit downwind?"

"I'll hold my nose. Come and eat, so you'll have strength for your afternoon."

So he came, and he sat, and he ate. And the entire time he was acutely aware of her sitting next to him, sparring verbally with Miles, trying to repair the twins' bad manners.

Saying very little to him.

He finished, then sat back—as comfortably as a man can sit back while wearing chain mail—and simply watched her. She pointed a final wagging finger at John, then looked at him and frowned.

"What?"

He shook his head, unable to stop a smile. "Nothing. I'm just watching you."

"Why?"

"I can't help myself. You are without a doubt the feistiest, mouthiest, most fascinating woman I have ever had the pleasure of meeting."

"Mouthiest?" she echoed.

He made a quacking motion with his hand.

She blinked for a moment or two, then one corner of her mouth twitched. "I think I should be offended."

"It's a compliment."

"Robin says my vile tongue drives all sensible men away," she said, quite casually, looking down at her hands.

"I'm still standing."

She went still. It was that same stillness she'd had in the chapel, only this was something that covered not only her, but the rest of the occupants of the dinner table as well. Miles no longer grumbled; the twins stopped chewing. It was as if they all held their breath, waiting for whatever was to come.

"Are you?" she asked quietly, still looking down at her hands folded tightly in her lap.

"Not that it does any good," he said, just as quietly. "But for what it's worth, nothing you've said has made me run for the front gate."

She was silent for a very long time.

John belched loudly, then clapped his hand over his mouth and looked at Jake with wide eyes.

"Sorry," he stammered.

"The emotion was too much for him," Miles said dryly. "My thanks, brother, for saving us all from Jake falling to his knees and professing undying love." He rose suddenly. "Let us be about our work again, Jake. We've much to do and little time in which to do it."

Jake had to agree. He drained his cup, then rose. He would have followed Miles around the end of the table if he hadn't felt a light touch on his hand. He looked down. Amanda was looking at her fingers touching his, then she put her hand back in her lap.

"Why?" she whispered. "Why are you doing this?"

He pushed his chair back and went down on one knee next to her.

"Ah, by the saints," Miles groaned.

Jake shot him a glare over his shoulder, then turned back to Amanda. "Because anything I can do to keep you safe, I will do."

She met his gaze.

He was floored to see tears in her eyes.

"So much effort," she murmured.

"So worth it," he replied. He reached out and touched her face, looked into her turquoise eyes for another endless moment, then rose suddenly and turned. He had to shepherd Miles in front of him to get out from behind the table and out of the great hall, but that was actually a good thing, because in the shepherding he held onto Miles's shoulder and kept himself upright.

"You poor fool," Miles said as they walked down the front steps together.

"Thank you," Jake said politely. "Do you have anything else useful to say, or is that it?"

"Give me time and I feel certain I'll manage something else," Miles said cheerfully.

Jake let him have his think and while he did, he cursed

himself a thousand times and a thousand ways. He couldn't have her. He couldn't flirt with her. He probably shouldn't even stay within a hundred yards of her. She was going to marry some bloody medieval guy with gold stars on his shirt and a kingly stamp of approval on his forehead, and that guy wasn't going to be him. He was going to have to go home, get back on with his life, and make the best of it.

Make the best of life without that mouthy, feisty, amazing woman who really deserved a twenty-first century kind of guy who could let her be herself without being so threatened he would beat the spirit out of her.

Which he was quite certain Lord Ledenham wouldn't be able to do if he ever got his hands on her.

They continued on their way through the courtyard and into the lists. Miles hummed pleasantly, then came to a halt. He turned and looked at Jake.

And the look on his face made Jake freeze.

Damn it, what was it with this place? Either Fate had a horrible sense of humor, he was stuck in some kind of relentless time warp, or he was going through some kind of withdrawal from junk food. He couldn't say. But what he could say was that if he didn't stop having these kinds of déjà vu moments that threatened to knock him flat, he was, well, he was going to have something to say about it.

To the proper paranormal authorities.

Whoever they were.

He clasped his hands behind his back. "All right, Miles, spill it."

Miles considered for another eternal moment. "I have," he said slowly, "a tale you might be interested in."

If it had anything to do with the waves of Something Monumental that seemed to be washing over him, Jake knew he would be very interested indeed. "Go ahead."

"Well, you may or may not have known him, but my mother's father was very powerful," Miles said. "Her widowed mother still is. When it came time for her to wed, there was no question of my mother going to anyone not her equal in station."

"Typical," Jake noted.

"Aye, well, this is where the tale becomes interesting." Miles paused. "To you."

The way he said it sent renewed chills down Jake's spine. "I'm listening."

"I hope so. You see, my father, as you also may or may not know, was not born the immensely powerful lord he is today."

Jake really had no frame of reference for Rhys de Piaget's life, but he was willing to take Miles's statement on faith. "Wasn't he?"

"He was a mere knight," Miles continued. "But landless. Even worse, he was, and still is, related to a band of quite vile souls. All this contributed to him being looked upon not only as simply a knight, but a most undesirable one." Miles paused. "Completely, utterly, thoroughly unsuitable."

Jake felt, quite suddenly, as if the whole world had suddenly paused as well.

As if it waited with him.

"And?" Jake asked.

"And he loved my mother. The exact details are unimportant, but suffice it to say that when the time came that my mother was free to wed him, he had amassed enough skill and enough power that he went to the king and bargained for what was required to wed with my mother."

"And what was that?"

Miles paused, then smiled. "Land and a title."

Jake closed his eyes briefly as the world around him shuddered.

Land and a title.

All that was necessary for a man to offer for someone he never in his wildest dreams would have thought he could have.

Amanda . . .

"I see," he managed.

" 'Tis not only strength of arm that will win a man what he needs," Miles said with a shrug. "Buy the land and the title comes, or purchase the title and the land will be given. They are connected."

Jake turned and walked away. He shoved his hands in his nonexistent pockets, cursed, then clasped his hands behind his back and paced in front of Miles a time or two. He came to a stop and turned to look at Amanda's brother.

"How much?"

"Likely all you have."

Jake had absolutely no idea how much that might be, if he could convert modern money into medieval coin, if he could get back home to do it, or if he could manage to get back to medieval England once he did.

But the thought that it might be possible was absolutely staggering.

He took a deep breath. "I could buy her a castle, but I probably couldn't feed her."

"She doesn't eat much anyway."

Jake suddenly felt so lighthearted, so full of disbelief, so racked with a feeling of absolute unreality that he laughed. If he hadn't been not altogether sure he wouldn't have impaled either himself or Miles, he would have thrown his sword up in the air for sheer joy.

"It couldn't be that easy," he said.

"Nay, it won't be," Miles agreed. "Gold you may take to the king, but 'twill take more than gold to win her in my father's hall."

"I sense I'll be spending much more time in the lists," Jake said.

"If it is worth the effort."

Jake clapped Miles on the shoulder. "Are you crazy? This is your sister we're talking about."

"You'd best be sure," Miles said seriously.

"It is one thing to love something because it's beautiful and mesmerizing, but know you'll only have it near you for a short time," Jake said slowly. "It's another thing entirely to think you might have it forever."

"She is not an easy woman," Miles said quietly, "and I say this though I love her well."

Jake looked up and saw Amanda coming down the stairs from the great hall. She was wearing her brother's clothes, obviously off to do some bit of business she probably wasn't supposed to. One of the twins, Montgomery likely, opened the door and flew down the stairs after her. He caught up to her and she put her arm around him and hugged him as she pulled him along with her. And then she slowed. And stopped.

And looked at him.

And he knew.

Jake had to lean his forearm on Miles's shoulder to remain standing.

"Whatever it takes," he said, with feeling.

"Good. Then let us work whilst we may. We'll stop in time to bathe, else we'll have no supper. We'll be at it again at first light. I'll leave it to you to determine how you'll fetch your gold."

"It will take me awhile to put together a plan," Jake said, "but I will."

"Until you do, we'll use our time wisely."

"Evenings free," Jake insisted. "I have a chess date with your sister I won't miss."

"The more time in the lists, the better."

"Even the sun goes down."

"Briefly." Miles looked at him, then shook his head. "I hope you know what your life will be like."

Jake could just imagine.

If he had money and he had some skill, he might be able to put himself in a position to ask Amanda of Artane to marry him.

He thought he might be able to someday forgive his sorry father for sending him to AE, Inc.

The details, the what-ifs, the impossibilities and improbabilities of the situation were lurking in the wings, but he ignored them. He would deal with them later, if and when they arose for real.

Right now, he would use some of his renowned self-discipline and concentrate on what he could do something about, on the tasks that were right in front of him.

Rhys de Piaget had done it.

So could he.

Chapter 16

A *manda* started down the path toward the front gates, desperate for a distraction. She had been watching Jake and Miles off and on in the lists for well over a fortnight. Jake trained with a desperation that was almost frightening and Miles was no better in indulging him in it. They were mad, the two of them, and she could sit no longer on the edge of the lists and watch them engaging in their madness.

So she had decided that, no matter what peril there might have been from Lord Ledenham, she would take a small walk through the village. She might even veer toward the seashore if the weather were amenable. It was a beautiful midsummer's day and who knew how much longer the cloudless skies might oblige her?

"My lady, wait!"

She sighed and paused. Her gaggle of guardsmen thundered up behind her. John and Montgomery came hard on their heels, hollering her name loudly enough that most of Scotland likely heard it.

Unfortunately, that attracted more attention than she would have liked. Miles and Jake were sauntering down the way with an ease that belied the hours she knew they had already passed in the lists.

Damn them all.

She put her hands on her hips and stared at the men facing her. "I appreciate the companionship, lads, but must you all come?"

Her guardsmen only waited patiently, without comment. The twins looked indecisive, but they took heart when her guardsmen remained firm. They folded their arms over their young, manly selves and stuck their chins out stubbornly.

Jake and Miles merely continued on their way until they came to a quite easy and unremarkable halt on either side of her.

"Going somewhere?" Jake asked pleasantly.

"Aye, out the front gates, damn you."

He was apparently unimpressed by the fierceness of her response. "We'll come."

"I want to go alone."

"No doubt you do."

She scowled. "You've spent too much time with my brothers."

He laughed. "Probably. But why don't you let us come with you anyway? You'll be safer."

She blew her hair out her eyes. "Very well," she said in exasperation. "I daresay I haven't a choice."

"Are we such poor company?" he asked, his damnably beautiful eyes twinkling.

And how was she to answer that? She turned toward the gate. "Come along, then. I can see I have no choice."

"Where are we going?" Miles asked as he fell in on her other side. "To the village? Foraging for herbs? To wreak havoc on the countryside?"

"We're going out," she said crisply. "I have no destination in mind save away from the inside of the keep's walls, where I might breathe easily for a change."

"We bathed day before yesterday," Miles offered.

She hadn't meant that and he knew it. What she had wanted was a bit of quiet without people talking at her, her brothers talking continually to each other, or more discussions about the perfect balance of a sword and how that balance might best be applied to keeping one's head atop one's shoulders.

"You may come," she announced. "Silently."

And they did. They followed her through the village, silently. They followed her out into the countryside, just as silently. And when she came to a halt a short distance into her father's best grain field, they halted with her.

Silently.

A dozen men who stood in a circle, waiting for her to decide what she would do next.

And then Miles sniffed. "I smell something."

Amanda did as well and it wasn't just the wholesome smell of earth and herb. She turned herself about until she saw a strangely colored smoke coming out from the roof of a hut on the very edge of the village. The hut was, from her experience, generally uninhabited, though she supposed that the odd freeman might use it to shelter in when needful.

She started in that direction, ignoring the murmured protests of the overanxious males trailing after her. She continued on her way until she stood before the hut's door. She drew the smoke deeply into her lungs, finding it to be not an unpleasant smell, but rather a healing one. Herbs on the fire, apparently, though she couldn't have said which ones.

The door opened and before her stood none other than Berengaria of Segrave, lately of Artane, and even more lately of a place Amanda didn't know. Berengaria, who was in reality not more than eight or nine years older than she, smiled widely.

"My lady Amanda," she said, looking pleased. "You are looking well."

"And you, Mistress Berengaria," Amanda said. "You have returned from your travels?"

"For the moment," Berengaria agreed. "It matters little where I travel, for it seems that ever I must come back to Artane to feel at home."

"We are happy to have you." She peeked inside the hut. "It isn't as if you must remain outside the gates. Surely we have room enough for you in the hall."

Berengaria inclined her head. "I appreciate the invitation, but I don't think I will be lingering very long." She smiled faintly. "I have other places to visit yet." She looked at the men surrounding Amanda. "You have your keepers, I see. And your fine brothers. And—"

She looked at Jake and froze.

Amanda understood. He was an extraordinarily hand-some man. Amanda looked at him and tried to see him with fresh eyes. Aye, he was indeed quite handsome, even in cloth-ing that was older, boots that were scuffed and worn, and a mail shirt that had seen better days. He looked, if possible, like a man of impeccable lineage who had suffered a bit of bad luck and was making do with less than he was accus-tomed to.

There were times, Amanda had to admit, that she had a hard time remembering he was a mere merchant. Looking at him now, she would be even more hard pressed not to consider him an equal with her brothers.

Berengaria seemed to be under the same impression, for she nodded to Jake with the same deference she would have used with any of the Artane lads. Well, save Robin of course, but Berengaria had spent too many years at Ar-tane to do much besides smile behind her hand at Robin's grumbles.

"My lord," she said to Jake, "I think we have things to dis-cuss. Would you care for something tasty from the fire?"

"I know *I* would," Miles said, elbowing Jake aside. "If I might, Mistress Berengaria?"

Berengaria was uncharacteristically hesitant. "Of course, my lord Miles. Let me fetch you aught to quench your thirst, but there are things I must discuss alone with our fine lord here."

Miles suggested, "Discuss with him the necessity of more time in the lists."

"He has no more time to give in the lists," Amanda said tartly, "unless you've a mind to take candles out in the mud and fight during the night. Mistress Berengaria, this is Jackson Alexander Kilchurn IV. He is a traveler."

"Aye," Berengaria said with a smile. "From a long dis-tance, I daresay."

"London," Montgomery supplied.

"He's a merchant," John offered. "A very rich one."

"He was robbed," Montgomery added. "We've been look-ing after him. Amanda especially."

Amanda hated to elbow her favorite brother so hard in the belly, but what else was she to do? A substantial *oof* came out of him. Amanda made certain he was still breathing before she turned back to the conversation with no lingering remorse. She started to tell Berengaria more about Jake, but when she saw how pale Jake was, words failed her.

"Jake?" she asked. "Are you unwell?"

Jake blinked, as if he'd been suddenly woken from sleep. "A drink," he said hoarsely. "Perhaps something to drink might be nice. It's hot outside today."

"It isn't," Amanda pointed out. "In fact, 'tis quite lovely for this time of year."

"Come in," Berengaria said, standing back from the doorway. "Sit."

Jake started across the threshold, then paused. He looked at Amanda, then back at Berengaria.

"I wonder," he began slowly.

"You likely should," Berengaria said with a knowing nod. "I think I can tell you things that will aid you. But they are things which could be quite . . . well . . ."

Amanda found them both to be studying her quite seriously. She took a step backward. "I will remain without, if you like."

"No," Jake said. He reached for her hand. "No. Come with me." He pulled her into the hut with him and shut the door behind her.

Amanda was offered a stool, she took it, and waited for something to drink. It was, when it came, quite tasty and she found herself very much soothed by it.

And rather baffled by the conversation going on in front of her.

Of course, being able to hear Miles grumbling about the condition of his parched throat on the other side of the rather frail door did nothing but add to the confusion.

"You have come a long way," Berengaria was saying.

"Very," Jake agreed. "I'm a little confused at how to get home."

"Use a road," Amanda suggested, then bit her tongue. It wasn't as if she wanted him fleeing any time soon.

Not at all.

But Jake only smiled at her, then turned back to Berengaria. "Are you a midwife, or a witch?"

"A midwife, of course," Berengaria said easily. "A healer. A brewer of things that are tasty. I might have another skill or two that comes in useful."

Jake appeared to consider his words. Amanda watched him carefully choose what he was saying and that made her wonder why. Was Berengaria so untrustworthy?

Or was she?

"Have you seen the road I traveled to come here?" Jake asked finally.

Berengaria stared off into nothing for a moment or two. "I see Seakirk castle," she said slowly, "and mailed knights who told you things you hadn't known before. I see a black cart, spinning endlessly. Other things I see that I deem aren't important enough to speak of now."

Jake bowed his head, sighed, then looked at Berengaria. "How do I return home?"

"Do you want to return home?"

Jake clasped his hands together and paused for a moment or two. "Briefly," he said finally.

Amanda listened to the exchange and wondered if she was hearing things aright. Was Jake leaving?

Would he be coming back?

She looked at him sitting next to her in the dim light of the little cottage and found herself growing far too accustomed to the sensation of him sitting next to her. He seemed perfectly at ease with a woman others called a witch, yet he seemed equally at ease with her grumbliest brother, and her younger, most rambunctious brothers. Indeed, the more she thought about it, the more she realized that he was at ease with whatever company he found himself in.

Not like a great many men she had met over the long and weary course of her life who only found nobility of their same station to be tolerable.

"—fairy rings, or perhaps a clutch of rocks that seem to be a bit unusual."

"And what of the timing?"

Berengaria was smiling. "Try again, my friend, when your

need is the greatest. I have no experience with such things myself, but I have heard tales. There are many things in this world that do not come into our hands until the moment in which we simply cannot do without them."

Jake nodded thoughtfully. Amanda shook her head, wishing she'd done a better job at listening. Fairy rings? Clutches of rock?

"What are you talking about?" she asked. "Rocks? Rings?"

Jake smiled. "Places I might have lost things I need to have to get home." He handed Berengaria his cup. "Thank you very much, Mistress Berengaria. You were here at the right time."

"I try to be," Berengaria said with a smile. She looked at Amanda. "And you, my lady? Is there aught I can do for you?"

"Short of ridding me of annoying suitors?"

"Perhaps your Jackson here can do that."

"He'll need more time in the lists."

Jake only laughed and stood, holding out his hand for her. "I'm working on it. I think I'll head back there right now. Are you coming?"

"I had best do so," she said with a sigh. "I don't dare keep the little lads out by themselves, even with my guard here."

Jake thanked Berengaria again for whatever advice she seemed to have given him, Miles was allowed in for a drink and advice on how to improve his disposition, and then they were on their way back to the keep.

Amanda walked silently next to Jake for some time, until they reached the inner bailey gate. Then she looked up and swore.

"What?" Jake asked.

She pointed to the clutch of noblemen standing near the front door. "Lord Jedburgh."

"Another one?"

"Less vile than Ledenham, but no less crafty. Obviously he knows my father is gone, else he never would have come to the keep without sending word a day or two ahead of his arrival." She looked up at him. "It would have been polite."

"Maybe he isn't interested in being polite."

Miles held out his arm for her. "We'd best have you locked inside, then. Time to trot out my lord-of-the-castle mein." He looked at her archly. "How is this?"

"So like Father I tremble in my boots."

"You mock me now, but watch me at supper and see if I don't save you a goodly bit of grief," he said. He looked over her head at Jake. "Come with me, Jake, and look fierce. Jedburgh is no fool, and I daresay he will wonder why you are so near Amanda yet not wearing Artane's colors like the rest of her guard. 'Tis best you pose as one of my mates."

"Whatever you think," Jake said.

Amanda sighed, found herself guided through the press of Jedburgh's retainers, and up to her chamber.

Pleading pains in her head was not a lie, and it did excuse her from supper.

Of course, her ability to endure confinement only lasted until she heard the watchman cry midnight. She dressed in something of John's and opened her door, fully intending to have some peace on the roof. She ran into someone's back and screeched in spite of herself.

Jake turned around and smiled. "Only me."

"What, by all the saints, are you doing here?"

"What does it look like?"

"It looks as if you'll be skewering yourself on Miles's sword tomorrow when you fall asleep on your feet," she retorted.

He only smiled. "You're welcome for the guard."

"You're daft."

"And you're beautiful."

She smoothed her hand over her tunic. "Dressed for court, as usual."

"Are you dressed for a walk on the roof?" he asked.

Did the man know her very thoughts? She reminded herself to give more thought to Montgomery's contention that he was a fairy—but later, when freedom wasn't beckoning. She nodded.

He held out his hand. "Want company?"

She put her hand in his as easily as if she'd been doing it the whole of her life.

But it was no less overwhelming a feeling than it had been every time—and those times would number three, for she could call each brief touch effortlessly to mind. She held his hand and walked with him down passageways and up stairs and finally out onto the parapet. He followed her around to the seaward side of the keep and leaned with her on the wall.

"Magnificent," he said.

"'Tis, truly," she said, looking out over the sea. "I never tire of the view."

"I can see why not," he said. Then he looked at her. "But how do I choose? You or the sea. Bewitching, the both of you."

She turned her head to return his look. "Do you think Berengaria's a witch? Are you a fairy? Were you asking her questions to find out how to return to your home?"

"What do you think?"

"I think you have secrets," she said honestly. "You appear to be a normal man, but there are things about you that make no sense to me."

"Can you trust me? Will you trust me?"

"Haven't I so far?"

He took her hand again and held it with one of his, resting atop the wall. He caressed her fingers gently, then looked up at the sky. "The stars are beautiful here. You can see so many more of them here than you can in London."

"When the sky is clear," she amended. "Which is, I might add, not often."

"They are like diamonds," he said, still looking up. "Diamonds scattered through the sky like stardust."

"Diamonds?" she asked.

"A clear, icy stone that is much prized in my business," he said, looking back down at her. "Very expensive in its rarest form. But it looks a great deal like those stars."

"How can you bring something down to the earth from the sky and wear it?" she asked. "It seems impossible. Much like this," she added softly.

He took her hand in both his own and leaned his elbows on the wall. "It isn't impossible."

"You are a merchant. I am a lord's daughter."

He straightened and looked down at her intently. "And if I were something else? Someone with a title, lands, bags of money in my fists? Would that make it possible?"

She shivered. But it wasn't from the cold. "Titles, lands, and gold mean nothing to me." She looked up at him. "Nothing."

"They mean something to your father."

"Aye, they do."

"I could make this happen."

"How?" she asked, then she shook her head. " 'Tis nothing but dreaming. There is no point in even thinking on it."

"What kind of faith do you have in me?" He waved to the stars littered like dust in the sky. "For all we know, it just might be possible to pull some of that stardust down and turn it into something besides a dream, something real, something lasting. If," he said and he paused for a long moment, "if it is something you want."

She looked down. "I fear that wanting."

"Amanda . . ." he said quietly.

Damnation, where was that vicious tongue of hers, that hardened heart, when she truly had need of them? She looked up at him and savagely wiped the tears from her cheeks.

"If you've no intentions of offering for me properly, then I've no mind to answer you properly."

"And if I did?"

"Offer, then see."

He only laughed again. She was pleased to be able to provide him with such splendid amusement. But even as he laughed, he lowered his head toward hers. She closed her eyes, lifted her face, and thought she might have a bit of her own splendid amusement by having her first kiss be from this man.

Her first in what she could only hope would be a very long succession of kisses from just this man.

And no other.

He kissed her cheek. Then he kissed her other cheek.

She opened her eyes and glared at him. "Damn you!"

But then he gathered her into his arms and somehow, the feeling of coming home, of being wrapped in the embrace that had been made just for her, was enough to leave her comfortably speechless.

"I'll kiss you at the altar," he promised.

"Ha," she said, resting her ear against his chest where she might have her mouth free to more easily comment on his words. "You assume that I'll be there to receive it."

"A man can dream."

"And you think a man can pull stardust out of the sky and put it in his purse. Those are mighty dreams."

"Trust me, Amanda."

The saints preserve her, she did. She put her arms around him and held on tightly.

The saints preserve her, she certainly did.

Chapter 17

J *ake* walked around the inner bailey and enjoyed the cool. Dawn was already lightening the sky, but the sun had not yet risen. Miles would be loping down the steps soon, but for the moment, Jake had peace for thinking.

And he had plenty to think about.

He wasn't sure how long he had stood there with Amanda de Piaget in his arms, feeling something that told him that she was the right woman for him. Forget the centuries that separated their births. He'd never honestly dared hope it before. He'd never allowed himself to actually imagine himself as being allowed to want her, or to think that somehow she might be his.

He was imagining it now.

His conversation with Berengaria, as brief and sketchy as it had been, had been most instructive. Not that she was a time traveler herself—of that he was fairly certain, though who could be sure, given the way they had danced around that topic in deference to Amanda—but she seemed to have her fingers in the paranormal pie.

Either that or she had a store of old wives' tales that would shame an old wife.

To think, he might get back to the future, then back to

Artane. He might be able to buy a title and some land. He might be able to offer for Amanda.

After all, Rhys de Piaget had started with little more than his wits and a handy sword.

He walked across the courtyard, staring at the flagstones, at the cobblestones, at whatever was being used from time to time to pave the dirt. Could he do it? Could he move back in time eight hundred years and survive?

He considered his modern conveniences. All right, he loved his Jag, but it was, after all, just a car. He didn't care about ice, fast food, or, heaven help him, pints down at the pub. He wasn't opposed to camping, lack of running water, or the occasional bug in his bed. He had no lover waiting for him; no family to grieve his loss; no friends to speak of, at least none who would spend the rest of their lives pining for him. His life was his work and vice versa.

He paused. Work was something he had to admit he would miss. He would miss traveling in airplanes to arrive hours later at exotic and dangerous destinations. He would miss slogging through forgotten swamps and the absolute thrill of stumbling on something missed, something that could be cut into soaring shapes.

But could he not take that passion, and transfer it to life instead?

Besides, why couldn't he hunt for gems in the past? Men still traveled, even in the thirteenth century. He supposed that men still designed pieces of jewelry, cut gems, sold them at a profit.

He supposed the man that wed with Amanda de Piaget might also find himself too busy to worry about any of that.

To think he might actually be that man . . .

Mind-blowing.

"Did you sleep?"

Jake jumped a foot. He was almost certain of it. He spun around and found Miles standing there with his arms over his chest, grinning in a most unsettling way. Jake decided then that he liked Miles better when he was smirking.

"Yes, I slept," Jake said, shrugging off his lack of it.

"You're dreaming."

"I'm plotting. There's a difference."

"Plot later; work now."

Jake made him a low bow. "Lead on, MacDuff."

"Who?"

"Never mind. Just go."

Jake wondered, several hours later, how it was that Miles seemed to have such an inexhaustible supply of energy. Oh, to be eighteen instead of thirty-two, and have had a full night's rest on a bed that was long enough.

But who was he to complain? He'd spent an hour holding the most amazing woman he'd ever met on the roof of a medieval castle in the light of hundreds of stars. Who cared if every muscle screamed for relief and he thought nothing had ever sounded as good as a cup of sour wine and some rough, still-had-a-bit-of-the-millstone-embedded-in-the-flour-kind of bread?

Miles seemed to instinctively know that Jake was thinking about something besides the flashing sword coming at him because he pressed his advantage mercilessly. Jake found himself continually falling back until he realized he was within feet of the bailey wall. He dredged up what little skill he had, but it wasn't really enough.

And then he realized how close he was to giving up.

It surprised him.

He cursed and fought back. It was tempting to dump his sword and take care of Miles the old-fashioned way, but he knew the rules of the game and he wasn't one to cheat.

He held his ground.

And then Miles fell back a pace.

By the time the sun was standing overhead, both he and Miles were dripping with sweat, and had mutually called peace. Jake dragged his sleeve across his forehead. Miles did the same, then sheathed his sword.

"Drink. Food."

"I'm with you."

Miles paused. "That was good work."

"You just about killed me."

"I needed to."

"Apparently," Jake said dryly.

Miles started back to the keep with him. "Perhaps this

afternoon we would benefit from a change in our training. We could do more of your business with just the hands."

"If it means I can take this mail off for a few hours, I'm there," Jake said, with feeling.

"Done," Miles said, clapping Jake on the shoulder.

Jake walked back to the hall thoughtfully, surprised at how hard he had worked and apparently how little he had gained.

Obviously, he was going to have to work harder.

He spent the afternoon with Miles on the beach, which seemed, oddly enough, the most private place to be.

Amanda was under heavy guard inside the castle. Well, Jedburgh was under heavy, if not accommodating and fawning, guard inside the castle. Miles was suspicious and Jake had to admit he was too. Jedburgh was slick, but he honestly seemed to have very little interest in Amanda personally. He seemed far more interested in the weight of Artane's tapestries and the solidness of their goblets than he was the true prize.

Idiot.

Miles was a quick learner and within hours Jake found himself having deposited the sum total of all his knowledge on that sponge. It would take practice, but he doubted Miles would ever find himself backed into a corner without his sword and subsequently done in.

They walked back to the castle slowly, Miles wondering aloud just how the skills he had recently acquired might serve him in the future. Jake was so busy listening to him contemplate miraculous escapes from blind alleys in seedier parts of London that he completely missed the hoofbeats bearing down on him from behind until he had almost been run over. He leaped aside with a curse, then gave Miles a hand back to his feet. Miles hurled a hearty curse at the rider's back.

"We should do something about him," Jake said with a frown.

"We've been trying to for years," Miles said, brushing off his clothes. "That was my brother Nicholas. He's in a tearing hurry. Maybe he caught wind of our visitors and decided he'd best be coming home to take charge."

"Does he take charge?" Jake asked. The Artane brothers just seemed to get tougher as they ascended the hierarchical ladder.

"Not usually," Miles said. "He's more inclined to sit back and let others cause a ruckus. Well, unless Robin's home. Then they fight like two rabid dogs."

"Interesting."

"Oh, they love each other well, but their fists do tend to do a great deal of their speaking for them."

That was heartening, at least. Jake supposed if Nicholas said hello with his fists, he might be able to answer in like manner and not completely embarrass himself.

"Thank you," Miles said suddenly.

Jake smiled. "For what?"

"For the lessons."

"Any time. It was nice to be the one who has all the answers, for a change."

"Aye, no doubt," Miles said with a smile.

Jake walked with him up the way to the inner bailey, feeling altogether rather content with his life and the way things were going. It would take more work, but someday he might actually impress Amanda's father. Amanda's brothers seemed to be good sorts. Friendly. Willing to help when needed.

Nicholas looked to be no different from his brothers. He was standing near the stables, chatting amicably with the stable master. When he saw Miles, he came over to him, slung an arm around his neck, and gave him a manly hug with several back slaps.

"I see the keep is still standing," Nicholas said, pulling back and smiling at Miles.

"Amazing, isn't it?" Miles asked.

Jake watched Nicholas act the part of the quintessential older brother: teasing him about his lack of girlfriend and checking up on his activities over the past couple of years. It gave Jake the opportunity to size up a full-fledged medieval knight in all his glory.

It was, he had to admit, impressive.

Nicholas de Piaget was tall, easily as tall as Jake was, and Jake was a handful of inches over six feet, built, and very tough looking. If Jake had been the kind of guy to intimidate easily, he might have been intimidated. Fortunately for him, he had dealt with all kinds of men who thought they were tough, and he was not intimidated.

But this was Amanda's brother, after all, and it would behoove him to make a good impression.

Nicholas held out his hand toward him. "Nicholas de Piaget," he said.

"Jackson Kilchurn," Jake said, taking Nicholas's hand in a firm grip.

Nicholas nodded easily, then he paused for a moment and looked Jake up and down. He frowned, as if something just wasn't quite right in that vision. Then he shrugged. "So, is it Sir Kilchurn or Lord Kilchurn?"

Jake smiled. "Just Kilchurn."

"He was waylaid by ruffians," Miles said easily. "We gave him refuge."

"You gave him refuge?" Nicholas asked. "I assume he is a friend of yours?"

Miles shook his head. "He is now, but I knew nothing of him at first."

Nicholas's friendly demeanor changed immediately.

Jake understood. It was the same antennae that went up in his own life when he smelled danger.

"Let me see if I understand things aright," Nicholas said, folding his arms over his chest and looking at Miles sternly. "You gave a man you did not know refuge in the same keep where Amanda resides, protected only by you and the wee babes?"

"Actually, Amanda gave him refuge before I arrived," Miles said, apparently feeling no compunction about throwing his sister to the wolves. "But John and Montgomery were here to protect her."

Jake thought Nicholas might soon have apoplexy. If the easygoing guy the twins had talked about existed, he was buried deep.

"She also gave him your clothes," Miles said mildly.

Jake wanted to punch him.

Nicholas took a deep breath. "My ears are failing me," he said evenly, the twitch in his cheek belying his fury. "This man was allowed inside our keep and neither you, nor the lads, nor Amanda thought to make certain he wasn't a ruffian, or a spy, or a man who might want to steal Amanda and hold her for ransom." He pointed an accusing finger at Jake's sword. "He's armed, by all the bloody saints!"

Miles shrugged. "He's not all that dangerous with a sword. He is with his hands, though. You should see him, Nick."

The apoplexy neared its zenith.

"He's a merchant," Miles added, delivering the killing blow.

Nicholas made inarticulate noises of fury. Miles only stood there, either oblivious or possessing nerves of steel, and Jake knew Miles wasn't oblivious. Jake shook his head. He might have laughed if he hadn't had the underlying desire not to make an enemy of Amanda's older brother. Miles only stood there, placid and smiling pleasantly.

Nicholas glared at Jake. "Stay away from my sister," he snarled, then he turned and strode angrily away.

Jake turned to Miles. "Thank you."

Miles grinned. "How could I resist?"

"Oh, I don't know. You could have kept your mouth shut."

"And miss that?" Miles chuckled. "Never. But do not hold it against him. His roof leaks and that irritates him. He's been trying to repair it for the last pair of months. Apparently, it leaks still."

"Apparently."

Miles clapped a hand on Jake's shoulder. "You should continue to work on your swordplay. Make it much better very quickly. Your path to Amanda lies through my older brothers and Nick will not be kind." He looked toward the keep. "He doesn't like you. I can't imagine why not."

"Maybe it's because he thinks I've been plundering his wardrobe."

"Perhaps," Miles agreed. "We should go eat. Perhaps he'll even let you in the hall." He continued to laugh all the way to the great hall.

Jake wasn't so certain it was funny, but who was he to argue? He walked in to find Amanda being hovered over by her elder brother. Nicholas yelled at her for a handful of moments, she yelled back, then he hauled her into his arms and hugged her as tightly as Jake ever wished he could have.

Well, that was brotherly love for you.

Nicholas took charge of Amanda for the rest of the evening.

Jake kept as low a profile as possible. He stayed in the background and watched as Nicholas repeatedly put Lord Jedburgh in his place. Jake had to admire his skill in doing so. Jake wasn't sure where he'd learned that look, that you-bug-stop-looking-at-my-sister-before-I-crush-you-under-my-shoe look that seemed to reduce Jedburgh to a quivering bit of Jell-o, but it was effective.

After dinner, Jake sought refuge on the roof and had a very peaceful evening there until he found himself joined by Montgomery. He ruffled the kid's hair and smiled.

"How are things?"

"Unpleasant," Montgomery said, with a shake of his head. "Too much shouting. Nicholas is full of foul humors tonight."

Jake didn't doubt it. He had seemed to be extremely upset that evening.

Far more upset than a brother would normally be.

Jake had given it a great deal of thought over the past couple of hours and found that Nicholas was entirely too possessive for a man merely looking after his sister.

Entirely.

"So, Montgomery," he asked casually, "what are the marrying rules these days?"

"How do you mean?"

"I mean, are there any degrees of separation?" He looked at Montgomery. "I believe the word is consanguinity?"

Montgomery stared at him, slack-jawed, for a moment or two, then realization seemed to dawn. "Ah," he said, drawing it out for a very long time.

"Yes, ah," Jake agreed dryly.

Montgomery looked around, as if he made sure they weren't being eavesdropped upon. Then he leaned in and looked at Jake seriously. "Amanda and Nick aren't brother and sister."

It was Jake's turn to try to retrieve his jaw. "They aren't?" he managed.

Montgomery shifted. "There is a bit of a tale involved."

"I'm all ears."

Montgomery looked at his ears, then shrugged.

Jake made a mental note to not translate any more idioms word for word.

"Go ahead," he encouraged.

"Well, you see it happened this way. My eldest brother Robin belongs to both my mother and father because, well, on the eve of my mother's nuptials to the evil Alain of Ayre—and do not repeat that business of him being evil to Amanda because Alain of Ayre is her blood father, though she would feign cut his blood out of her if she could—but on that eve, well, my mother and father . . . er . . ." He stopped and looked quite miserable.

"I get the picture, Montgomery."

Montgomery nodded, relieved. "Ah, but the interesting bit is that during that same night after my mother was wed to Alain of Ayre, my father was dragged away by mates of his, encouraged to imbibe, and . . . well . . . with Nicholas's mother . . ." He stopped again and looked at Jake.

Jake nodded. "I get the picture on that as well."

Montgomery nodded miserably. "So, now you see. Robin and Nicholas share the same father, but not the same mother. Amanda and Robin share the same mother, for my mother was wed to Ayre long enough for Amanda to be born, but Nicholas and Amanda share neither."

"I see," Jake said.

And he did.

"And the rest of you?" Jake asked.

"We all belong to my mother and my father."

"Interesting."

"Many find it so." Montgomery hesitated. "So, you see, Amanda and Nicholas aren't related by blood. But there are many who have no idea about Amanda and Nicholas's parentage. So for them to ever . . . well . . ."

"I understand."

"It might be for that reason that Nick doesn't, well, seem to care overmuch for you."

"You noticed?"

"He was very uncomplimentary about your parentage below," Montgomery admitted.

"Hmmm," Jake said. "Interesting."

And it was. He was going to have to give some thought to Nicholas de Piaget. Either he was going to have to bend over backward to befriend him, or he was going to have to sidestep him. Time would tell, he supposed, which approach would work best.

He slung his arm around Montgomery's shoulders. "Let's go downstairs. It's late and I have an early start in the morning."

"Are you going to stand guard before Amanda's door again?"

"I will."

"I'll relieve you during the second watch," Montgomery offered.

Jake smiled. "If you want," he said, but he had no intention of allowing Montgomery to stand outside Amanda's doorway with strange men in the castle. He walked with Montgomery down the stairs and sent him off to bed. He took up his post in front of Amanda's room, leaning back against the wood with his arms folded over his chest.

He thought better that way.

The door opened behind him, interrupting what he was certain would have been useless thoughts anyway. He turned to find Amanda standing there, a candle in her hand.

Damn that Nicholas de Piaget.

Jake smiled. "Can't sleep?"

She sighed. "I will sleep better when Jedburgh has taken his sorry self and his lads and departed for a different pasture."

"I'll keep watch."

"You're losing sleep."

"Sleep can be made up."

"Aye, when you're abed in the healer's house because Miles has run you through by mistake."

He smiled. "I'll be careful."

She nodded, but she didn't go back inside.

Jake waited, wondering if she were gearing up to tell him that though it had been an interesting month or so, she was really in love with her brother and he should just mosey on down the road and try to get himself back home.

Assuming he could get back home, which was something he didn't dwell on too much. The thought of potentially being stuck in the Middle Ages without the woman standing in front of him to ease the pain was too much.

But the possibility of her being in love with the brother she wasn't related to was very real as well, and Jake supposed he couldn't blame her. If Nicholas was as nice as everyone claimed he was, and it was easy to tell from looking at him that he possessed all the important knightly skills necessary to make him a good catch in the thirteenth century, then she really would have been crazy not to want him.

And then she stepped out of her room.

She leaned up on her toes, pulled his head down toward her with one hand, and . . . he closed his eyes in anticipation.

She kissed him on the forehead.

He looked at her in surprise. "But—"

"Ha," she said with snort. "Now you see how it feels."

But then she smiled, took a step back into her room, and shut the door with a soft "good e'en to you."

Well, at least she hadn't started heaving. She hadn't looked displeased.

But had she looked like a woman who was in love with her brother?

Hard to say.

"Come here, my pretty wench," said a slurred voice from down the passageway.

Jake backed up against the door, trying to give himself some cover and more fully guard Amanda's door at the same time. He heard some scuffling, the sound of a woman in distress, and low laughter. He hesitated at leaving Amanda unprotected, then heard the sound of boots coming his way. Miles and Nicholas seemed to be hot on the trail of the apparent accoster.

Miles stopped and looked at Jake. "I'll stay here," he volunteered. "You and Nick go take care of our good Lord Jedburgh."

Nicholas said nothing, and Jake had no reason not to go, so he left Miles in his place and walked alongside Amanda's elder, well, brother, he supposed. The tension emanating from the man was palpable.

"How's your roof?" Jake asked pleasantly.

"Leaking," Nicholas replied curtly, not breaking stride. He shot Jake a rather unfriendly look. "Who are you? In truth?"

"Jackson Alexander Kilchurn," Jake said. "The Fourth. As opposed to my father, who is the Third."

Nicholas grunted. "A merchant."

"Yes," Jake agreed.

"My sister will never be given to a merchant," Nicholas said very deliberately. "If you think she will be, you're not only without skill, you're without wit."

"She thinks I'm without both, so perhaps she's safe."

Nicholas didn't seem to be very impressed with that answer. Jake had no better to give him, so he walked with him quickly but quietly down the passageway, following the faint sounds of a struggle. It didn't take long to reach the goings-on that were going on in a little alcove off the passageway. Nicholas cursed and started to draw his sword.

Jake put his hand on Nicholas's arm. "Are you going to kill him? What is the point of that?"

Nicholas shook off his hand. "And what do you suggest?"

"Let me take care of him. We'll put him in the stables. He'll wake up tomorrow with a splitting headache and wonder how he got there."

Nicholas folded his arms over his chest. "Be about it, then, if you can follow your brave words with actions."

Jake could, and he did. He made good use of a pressure point or two that first made Lord Jedburgh scream in pain, then pass out from the lack of important bodily substances, like air. Jake deposited the man in the hallway and pulled the terrified serving girl to her feet.

"What do we do with her?" Jake asked. "She looks roughed up, but I don't think he accomplished his main purpose."

Nicholas looked at the girl, then took her hand and gave her a smile. "Are you well, Agnes?"

"Aye, my lord," the girl said, her teeth chattering.

"The hie yourself off to bed and tell Cook that I said you were to rest for a handful of days. I will remind her myself tomorrow. I apologize for the distress of this."

"Thank you kindly, my lord," the girl said, bobbing a curtsy before fleeing down the hall.

Jake watched the exchange and marveled at the change in Amanda's brother. So he could be nice. It was no wonder Amanda liked him.

But then Nicholas turned to Jake and it was business as usual. He looked Jake up and down with a look of scorn. "Meet me in the lists in the morning," he said. "You're going to have to do better than that to have my sister."

Jake didn't bother denying his end goal. He nodded to Nick. "I'll be there."

"I'll stand watch by Amanda's door," Nicholas said. "You'll likely want all the sleep you can have."

"I've been watching half the night already," Jake pointed out.

Nicholas scowled and waved him away.

Jake went. Nicholas was right. He would need whatever help he could get.

Chapter 18

Amanda winced at the sound of sword screeching down the length of sword. There were curses, threats, and more screeching and clanging of swords. The two men fighting there looked as if they had every intention of making certain the other would leave the field in the back of a knacker's cart.

One of them was Jake. He was almost coming close to holding his own. She supposed he wouldn't last much longer, but at least he wouldn't go down having completely shamed himself.

Of course the one who would be sending him down in flames was none other than her brother Nicholas. He was fighting with a ferociousness that was generally lacking in his more nonchalant stays in the lists. Indeed, he had been in a foul humor since he'd returned to Artane.

Perhaps his roof still leaked.

The contest continued, far longer than she suspected it would. She would have assumed that Nicholas would have defeated Jake within moments. That Jake had stood this long—

"He's not bad."

Amanda came close to jumping out of her boots. She whipped around to glare at Robin. "By the saints," she exclaimed, "when did you return?"

"A few moments ago. I was drawn to the excitement in the lists."

"I wish you would announce yourself." Robin was like an unpleasant waft of cesspit odor, always popping up when a body least expected it.

She chose not to share that observation with him.

"I thought you would have heard me tossing Jedburgh out the front gates. By the saints, he is a useless bit of refuse. Now, who is that?" he asked, pointing to Jake. "Needs a goodly bit of work, of course, but he's large of stature and seemingly strong enough."

Montgomery appeared on Robin's far side. "He's Amanda's merchant."

"Amanda's merchant?" Robin looked at her with one eyebrow raised. "Is that so?"

"He's more than a merchant," she said.

"You mean he's a titled one?"

"There's more to a man than a title," Amanda said defensively.

Robin only stroked his chin thoughtfully. "Interesting."

"What will be interesting is if he manages to leave the field with his head still atop his neck," Miles remarked, coming to stand on her other side. "I trained him, you'll notice," he said to Robin.

"A passable job," Robin said, bestowing high praise. He looked at Miles closely. "How kind of you to return from points unknown."

"I wasn't in points unknown," Miles said, unperturbed. "I was having a well-deserved bit of amusement after the excruciating ordeal of being knighted by Whittenburgh."

"You've been amusing yourself for almost two years!"

"What else was I to do?"

"You could have come home sooner so I didn't spend all my time at Fenwyck being tormented by thoughts of my sister being abducted and forced to wed a lout of no character because my younger brother couldn't be bothered to return home in a timely fashion!" he finished with a shout.

Miles only smiled.

Amanda pushed them both out of her line of vision so she could concentrate on the important matter at hand—namely whether Nicholas would kill Jake before Jake could go home.

And procure that stardust he was so enamored of.

"She would have fallen for him even if I had been here," Miles said over her head. "Look you how she moons."

"She won't have much to moon over if Nick doesn't cease with his attentions," Robin remarked. "I think he actually means to do your merchant in. By the way, what is his name?"

"Jackson Alexander Kilchurn."

"Is he Scottish, then?" Robin asked. "Then why can he not fight? I don't know a Scot who isn't a credit to himself in battle."

"He can fight," Miles said, stepping in front of Amanda to more easily speak to his brother, "but just with his hands. You should have him show you. 'Tis a very useful kind of skill when you're without a blade and death is near. Indeed, I'm not quite sure why he's allowing Nick to beat on him so. Jake could kick the sword from Nick's hands and render him senseless within a matter of moments with but his hands."

Robin looked very interested. Amanda pushed them both out of her way yet again, and moved closer to the fighting. If it looked like Nicholas might truly do Jake in, she would have to execute a rescue.

Jake leaped out of the way suddenly and only narrowly avoided finding himself skewered on Nicholas's sword. Even Robin took a few steps forward at that. His arms were no longer folded over his chest and Amanda could see by the set of his shoulders that he had ceased to find this an entertaining bit of sport for the morn.

Apparently, Nicholas was thinking the same thing.

It was then that Amanda realized that Nicholas had only been toying with Jake. She should have known it, of course, but after all, the man had only been in the lists a pair of fortnights. How was he to stand against a man who had spent the whole of his life with a sword in his hands and Rhys de Piaget as his master?

In a matter of three or four blows, Jake was falling back, only managing to fend off Nicholas's attack by holding onto his sword with both hands and trying to use it as a shield.

"Why is he allowing Nicky to do this?" Amanda asked Miles in horror. "Surely 'tis not necessary."

"I daresay, sister, that Jake is allowing himself only to fight in a knightly fashion."

"And if Nicholas kills him?" she demanded.

Miles shrugged. "At least Jake will have died nobly."

Amanda watched with increasing alarm at the contest before her. Nicholas was relentless and merciless, beating on Jake's sword as if he had every intention of reducing it to shards. With one mighty blow that lacked every bit of finesse that Amanda had always seen him use and instead spoke of raw fury, Nicholas knocked the sword from Jake's hands. And instead of declaring himself the victor, he swung down with his sword, straight toward Jake's unprotected head.

"Nay!" she cried out, leaping forward.

But before she could reach Jake, a sword had come from nowhere and stopped Nicholas's in its downward arc.

Amanda stared, open-mouthed, at Robin who now stood between Jake and Nicholas.

She thought she might have to dredge up a few nice things to say to him in thanks.

"Stand aside," Nicholas snarled.

"I will not," Robin said calmly. "Nick, your passions have gotten the better of you—"

Nicholas slapped Robin's sword from his hands and brought his sword down again, but this time it was Robin's hand that stopped him. Jake, quite wisely to Amanda's mind, took a step or two back. Robin stood facing Nicholas, holding his brother by the wrist.

"Cease," Robin said clearly. "This is madness."

"I do not like him," Nicholas said, his words clipped.

"Is that any reason to kill him?" Robin asked. "Do not continue down a path you will regret tomorrow."

Amanda watched Nicholas resheath his sword with a curse, glare at Robin, glare at Jake, and then glare the most furiously at her before he turned and strode across the lists toward the hall.

"Interesting," Miles murmured.

"Be silent, you fool," Amanda snapped, giving him a shove for good measure.

"I'll say no more."

"You've said too much," she said.

"Do you ever wonder if Nicholas loves y—"

Amanda turned on her younger brother and apparently there was something in her heart that was showing on her face because, mercifully, he decided against whatever else foolish he was intending to say.

"Forgive me," he said instead. "Forgive me, Amanda. This is no fodder for jest."

"Nay, it is not," she said, feeling the hideous sting of tears begin behind her eyes.

Miles put his arms around her and hugged her. "I am an evil brother," he whispered. "Forgive me."

"Never."

He pulled back to look at her. "He loves you, you know," he said quietly. "Nicholas."

"And I him," she said, dragging her sleeve across her eyes.

"Nay," he said slowly. "I mean, he loves you."

"Dolt, do you think I don't know that? And what am I to do about it?" She turned to look for Jake who was currently retrieving his sword. "And look you there: another man I cannot have."

"Poor wench," Miles said affectionately. " 'Twill sort itself out eventually."

"I should become a nun."

"The saints preserve them," Miles said with a laugh. "You, a nun. It boggles the mind."

"Why?" she asked stiffly. "Think you I haven't the spine?"

"I think the poor sisters haven't the spine. Every man in the country would be making pilgrimages to your nunnery, just to look at you whilst you prayed. Nay," he said with a final chuckle and shake of his head, "nay, Amanda, you would make a terrible nun and a wonderful wife. Give your poor merchant a chance to make good on his promises."

"If he survives my elder brothers," she said darkly.

"Well, he's only had one of them try to kill him. Look you there. Robin is actually being pleasant to him. That counts for something."

And 'twas true. She watched her eldest brother talking to Jake and there was an ease about them both that bespoke good tidings. Miles took her hand and pulled her over to where Montgomery and John had already clustered themselves next to Jake. Jake looked at her.

"I was overconfident. There for a minute or two, I thought I could hold my own."

"You're witless," she replied promptly. "Whatever else his faults, Nicholas knows how to wield a sword. He's trained his entire life to do just that. What were you thinking, you fool, to try to stand against him!"

She realized she was shouting, but, the saints preserve her, what else was she supposed to do?

"He could have killed you!" she added, with no small bit of enthusiasm.

Robin only stroked his chin thoughtfully.

Jake, that great oaf, only smiled. And so she did the only sensible thing she'd done all morning.

She burst into tears.

Jake put his arm around her and drew her close. She wept all over his patched, inherited tunic. And as she stood there with her arms around him, drenching him with the kind of tears she had certainly never bothered to shed for any other man of her acquaintance, she realized that she might very well indeed love him.

Poor fool that she was.

"You've been at this how long?" Robin was asking.

"Less than a month," Miles supplied promptly.

"We began his training," Montgomery added brightly. "I think we did a marvelous job, don't you?"

"Marvelous," Robin conceded.

"We even had to teach him to speak when he first came," John put in. "And he couldn't ride, could he, Mandy?"

"But he can fight, can't he, Mandy?" Montgomery asked. "We saw him vanquish eight ruffians with but his hands as his weapons. It was very exciting."

"So Miles reports," Robin said, sounding quite interested. "I can see, Master Kilchurn, that there is much we should discuss. If my sister would cease with her attempts to rust your mail, we could repair somewhere more comfortable and have speech together."

"Go away, Robin," she said, wishing her eyes weren't blinded so she could have seen him to have given him a shove as well.

"She never weeps," Montgomery said in hushed tones.

"Never," John agreed. "She must be powerfully undone."

"Watching the spectacle of Nick trying to do Jake in must have been too much for her," Miles said. "I say we leave her to the drenching of Jake's mail and go ourselves into the house for something strengthening. When she's finished, she can bring her love in."

I do not love him was on the tip of her tongue, but she couldn't even muster up the energy to spew it out.

"I'm Robin, by the way," Robin was saying. "The eldest of this rabble. Come with me and I'll introduce you to my lady, Anne. Then we'll repair to my father's solar and talk. Privately," he said pointedly.

Amanda listened to her younger brothers make their protests, but she knew they wouldn't prevail. Robin was very much like their father in that when he determined his course of action there was nothing that would stop him. A trait he apparently shared with Jake.

"I will be in the solar as well," Amanda sniffed.

Robin looked prepared to say her nay, but she supposed she looked undone enough that she frightened him into acquiescing. So when Robin started off across the lists with Jake, Amanda went with them, followed by her younger brothers.

She distracted herself whilst the men ate by seeing to Anne, making certain her sister-in-law had food and drink enough. She tended Robin's son, Phillip, for a goodly part of the afternoon, finding his two-year-old's chatter to be a welcome diversion from the strain of the morning.

And all the while, Jake and Robin spoke pleasantly together at the high table.

As equals.

Amanda finally turned Phillip over to his mother and sent them both upstairs for a long-overdue nap. Jake and Robin had been eating for most of the afternoon so instead of further decimating Artane's larder, they moved to Rhys's solar with a bottle of wine and a basket of things to soothe and sustain them, should their speech exhaust them. She followed them, then made herself as inconspicuous as possible on a stool in a darkened corner.

"Chess?" Robin asked.

"Absolutely," Jake agreed.

They settled down to a game, drawing lots for white, and immediately commenced battle.

Amanda chewed on her fingernails in a most uncharacteristically womanly fashion. She was not accustomed to fretting thusly. She would much rather have been out in the lists with a sword in her hands, or moving stealthily about the castle, leaving her suitors scratching their heads as to her whereabouts. Sitting was not her preferred activity.

Not at all.

She put her hands in her lap and cursed herself. What did it matter if Robin found Jake to his liking? It wasn't as if it mattered. It wasn't as if Jake could offer for her. And it wasn't as if she would accept if he did.

She sighed. Damn, more time on her knees for lying.

She focused her attentions not on the cold chapel floor that would greet her come morning, but on Jake and Robin sitting before her at the chess board, battling with their wits and not their swords.

Jake won the first game.

Robin won the next.

And so it went, far into the afternoon. Amanda excused herself periodically, to the accompaniment of yawns from the other occupants of the chamber, which left her wondering if she was beginning to lose her charm. She brought more food and wine, and received grunted thanks. She hovered anxiously but was ignored. She frowned. Jake was starting to behave like one of her brothers.

She wasn't sure that boded well for her.

Robin sat back, after the shadows had grown long and the chamber had been lighted with a torch and several candles. He tipped his king with a satisfied sigh.

"The game is yours, Kilchurn," he said. "And gladly so. You play very well."

"So do you," Jake said magnanimously.

"I think we are most evenly matched," Robin continued. He

shook his head. "I can hardly believe you are but a merchant, but I suppose even in merchantry, you must rely on strategy."

"I do," Jake said with a nod. "Especially in my business. People are quite taken by gems and there are some who will resort to bloodshed to have them if they think they can sell them for a large profit."

"And your business is in London?"

"My shop is in London. My business takes me all over the world."

Robin leaned forward. "Dangerous locales?"

"Of course. As often as I can manage them." He smiled at Robin. "You have traveled?"

Ah, Robin's second favorite thing to discuss, or perhaps third, after his swordplay and the intricacies of battle and before the delights of being a husband and father—though she supposed he didn't discuss the latter two all that much. At least with strangers. She heard the occasional comment which was inevitably filled with pride he couldn't disguise and deep and abiding affection for both his lady and his son.

"Venice," Jake was saying with a contented sigh.

"Nay, the isle of Sicily," Robin corrected. "Hot sun, delicious food, drinkable wine. Long stretches of strand just made for a man to lie in the sun in his altogether and have a well-deserved rest."

Amanda sat on the bench under the window and listened to them argue in a friendly fashion the delights and detriments of all the locales they had both visited, and as she did, she had a great longing rise up in her to see such places for herself. She should have dressed as Miles's squire and gone with him on a few of his journeys. Maybe there was something to be said for being a merchant, if that was the content of his life. Especially a merchant who carried himself as Jake did.

The evening wore on. Jake sat with her eldest brother, laughing and talking as if he'd known Robin for years and had always found himself in Robin's closest circle of companions.

If Jake only knew how truly unheard-of that was. Amanda herself had never found her sweet person taken into Robin's confidence. She suspected no one found themselves there save Anne and Nicholas. Aye, Jake should count it a compliment indeed.

She realized, quite suddenly, that she was being observed by both men. Robin was stroking his chin. Jake was leaning back in his chair, looking at her with a small smile, his hands behind his head as if he had not a bloody care in the world.

"What?" she demanded. "Am I to be scrutinized now, like a bloody battlefield?"

"I'd say you were the prize," Robin remarked.

She glared at him. "Do you realize how many nights I've sat here being discussed by you, father, and every other bloody male in my family as if I were a mare to be sent to market? I have sentiments of my own! Tastes of my own! I might like to actually love the man I'm to marry."

"Well, do you?" Robin asked.

"Do I what?"

"Do you love him?" For good measure, Robin nodded casually in Jake's direction.

Amanda gritted her teeth. "And why should I say as much when he hasn't revealed any of his heart?"

"Haven't I?" Jake said, looking surprised.

"I've seen no bended knee, no fistfuls of flowers, no sonnets, no lays to my beauty and sweet temperament. How am I to know how you feel?"

"My grandmother's doing," Robin whispered loudly. "When I was about the wooing of my sweet Anne, I was subjected to all manner of that sort of foolishness." He looked forlornly at his hands. "I fair ruined my poor fingers, placing them at all hours and in all positions upon a lute, merely to satisfy a womanly fancy."

"You can be certain 'twas not your lute playing that won you the day," Amanda pointed out tartly.

Jake folded his arms over his chest and smiled. "Name your price, Lady Amanda, and I will gladly pay it."

"Fool," Robin said with a smile. "You've done it now. She'll have you at all sorts of labors, day and night, without ceasing, just to please her."

"I can think of worse ways to pass the time," Jake said.

Amanda sighed and put her face into her hands. "'Tis impossible," she said wearily. "Naught but a dream."

"She dreams of you," Robin noted. "A promising sign."

Amanda heard someone stand, then felt herself being pulled to her feet. She looked at Jake who stared down at her gravely.

"I know what I must have to offer for you," he said. "How can I ask you to be mine, when all I have is my heart in my hands and no title to my name?"

She sighed. "You cannot. I suppose I must content myself with knowing that the thought has occurred to you."

"From the moment you rescued me from the dungeon with soot all over your face," he said seriously.

"I hope you've thought on what wedding this wench will mean," Robin said. "Never another moment's peace, I daresay."

"I've had enough peace," Jake said with a smile. "I think I could do with a bit of turmoil."

"You'll have it," Robin assured him. "Now, let's be off to bed. If you intend to make any respectable showing before my father, we'd best be at it at first light."

"You're very generous," Jake said.

"You've no idea," Amanda said. "He rarely trains anyone. His squires, aye, but very, very few grown men."

"Then I am extremely honored," Jake said. "And grateful."

Robin rose and walked toward the door. "Come along, you two. I'd best see Jake to bed lest Nick decide a little murder in the dark would be good sport. I don't know what troubles him so. You'd think he would be pleased at the thought of seeing you finally wed so he could be about his own nuptials." He looked at Jake. "He spends all his time tormenting Amanda's suitors. I've no idea why. I think 'tis much more rewarding to torment Amanda herself."

"Aye, you would," Amanda said, suppressing the urge to roll her eyes. Robin was, as others had no doubt noted as well, a canny warrior, but when it came to matters of the heart, he was a dolt.

Jake and Robin both walked her to her chamber. Robin watched with interest as Jake kissed her very chastely on the forehead.

Damn him.

Robin did shake his head at that. "You should kiss the wench, Jake. See if wedding her's going to be worth it."

"I'm saving myself for the ceremony," Jake said, with a wink thrown Amanda's way.

She slammed the door on the pair of them. Fools, both. She crawled into her bed, pulled the covers up over her head, and cursed them to oblivion.

Temporarily, in Jake's case.

She closed her eyes and prayed with all her heart that he might be able to manage what he planned to do.

She didn't want to think what would be left of her heart if he couldn't.

Chapter 19

"**I**s this right?"

Jake looked down at Montgomery's artwork, which he had to admit had promise—what he could see of it through the sweat that was dripping down into his eyes. He was trying to learn everything Robin of Artane could teach him about sword-play and satisfy Montgomery of Artane's desire for art lessons. Concurrently. He wondered how many boys had learned to draw in the lists.

Not many, he suspected.

Montgomery was drawing Amanda as she stood on the side of the lists, hugging herself and looking quite anxious. Montgomery's rendering was actually quite good.

"Just remember what I taught you last night about perspective," Jake said, "so you can make the lists look like they're receding into the distance behind her. You're doing very well."

"My thanks for taking the time to look," Montgomery said.

"My pleasure," Jake said, with feeling. And it was his pleasure—anything for a break in the action.

"Another drink?"

Jake had to blink a time or two more to convince himself that it was Robin asking him that question and not someone out of an exhaustion-induced hallucination wondering about his state of thirstiness.

And, heaven help him, it was only noon.

He nodded. "Yes."

"Then have one. And you'd best remind Amanda that you live still," Robin said, resheathing his sword with gusto. "Before we begin again," he added.

Jake nodded and dragged his sorry backside over to Amanda, but he didn't dare sit down on the bench there. He might never get back up.

"How do you fare?" she asked, looking worried.

"Very well, thank you."

Robin came over and slapped him heartily on the back. "Aye, he's a rock. Let him have another look at his prize, then we'll be about our work again. We'll eat in another hour."

"Absolutely," Jake said, thinking privately that Robin of Artane would have been the answer to many of the social ills of the twenty-first century. *Act up and this man has you at his mercy for a week.*

Everyone would have behaved perfectly. Jake was certain of it.

Amanda handed Jake a cup. "If it eases you any, he's being very hard on you. I daresay he wouldn't be if he didn't believe you could bear it."

"I'm flattered," Jake said, downing his cup of watered-down wine and feeling quite flattered. Now, if only he didn't feel quite so flattened, he would have been doing just fine.

It had been two solid weeks of dawn to dusk tête-à-têtes with Robin de Piaget in the lists. Jake ached in places he hadn't known he had muscles, as well as in all the places he'd been certain he did. He went to bed every night shaking with weariness and rose before dawn to start the process all over again.

Medieval boot camp was hell.

Robin, on the other hand, looked so damned perky each and every day that it had been all Jake could do not to slug him. He appeared each morning, fresh as a daisy, and retired each night looking as if he'd been out riding casually, seeing to the less taxing matters of the realm.

At the moment, he was humming, smiling, and rocking

back and forth between heel and toe with his hands behind his back, looking for all the world as if he'd just hopped out of bed and was waiting for his valet to fix him eggs Benedict on cold toast.

It made Jake want to go take a nap.

He had no trouble admitting that he was nowhere near Robin's league when it came to swordfighting. He could definitely keep up with the twins now and keeping Miles at bay was possible—for a brief time, at least. Robin hadn't pulled out any of the stops yet, and already Jake knew he was in deep trouble. He could have practiced with Robin for a year and still not been his equal.

Then again, he suspected, based on one small bit of sparring in the lists, that Nicholas wasn't Robin's equal either, though he doubted either man discussed that very often.

Nicholas had been incognito for the better part of the past two weeks. He appeared for meals, watched Jake with a quiet, deadly sort of scrutiny, then headed for parts unknown while Jake headed back to the lists with Robin.

Amanda had spent her time either praying for him in the chapel or sitting on that bench against the wall as if her life depended on her keeping good watch.

He wondered sometimes if it did.

He took another swig of his wine, then looked at Robin. "Does anyone win against you?" he asked.

"Not a soul," he said modestly. "My father, perhaps, when he's feeling spry."

Amanda snorted. "He can still thrash you when it pleases him. He fears to injure your enormous ego, so he doesn't please very often." She looked at Jake. "Robin is famous for the hours he has spent in the lists the whole of his life. You cannot compare yourself to him."

"I never would," Jake said, with feeling.

"You'll manage well enough," Robin said, setting down his cup. "You have a knack for this business. With enough training, you'll see to my sister well enough."

Jake looked at him seriously. "Will it be enough?"

"It had better be, hadn't it?" Robin said pleasantly. "Let's be about our work. We've much left to do this day."

Jake put his cup down, gave Amanda his most gung-ho

smile, and tried to match Robin's bounce back out onto the field. When that took too much energy, he simply walked and left the bouncing for another day.

And then he had no more time for the analyzing of his stride because Robin was again about the business of making him over into a medieval knight and Jake wasn't about to waste any time on distractions that could be examined later—say in a year or so when he'd recovered from Robin's school of sword mastery and torture.

But the thought came to him, at some point during that very long afternoon, that he should try to go home.

Soon.

The feeling didn't leave him that afternoon, or the next day, or the next. He put it on the back burner until a week later when he couldn't ignore it any longer.

He and Robin were having a breather in the middle of the field when Jake broached the subject.

"I should leave," he said.

Robin looked at him in faint surprise. "Now?"

Jake wondered how much he could tell Robin, how much he *should* tell Robin, given that he'd told Amanda nothing of his background. He considered for a minute or two, then decided that honesty was the best policy. In the past three weeks, he'd grown to have an enormous amount of respect for Amanda's eldest brother, not only for his skill as a warrior, but for his level-headedness. Amanda thought he was dense, but Jake suspected that was a sham Robin perpetrated for his sister's benefit. Robin de Piaget was far shrewder than he let on. Jake thought that if Robin could get past the shock of Jake's birth date, he might have no trouble believing quite a few more things.

"I need to go now," Jake said.

Robin resheathed his sword and studied Jake. "I think there are many things you haven't told me."

"There are."

"Are you going to tell them to me now, or after you have returned from your journey to London?"

"Some now, others later," Jake said.

Robin nodded. "Fair enough. Have you shared these things with Amanda?"

"No, I haven't. And I think it would be best if she didn't know anything until I returned." *If I return* was his next thought, but he didn't entertain it long. He would come back if he had to move heaven and hell to do it.

"When will you go?"

"This afternoon." The words were out of his mouth before he gave them thought, but when he heard them, he knew they were the right ones. He would have to go. He almost felt as if even the elements were set to converge for the express purpose of executing a bit of time-travel with him as the traveler.

"I hesitate to interrupt your training," Robin said slowly, "but I can see you are determined."

"The time is right," Jake said. "But I would like it if you would come with me, at least into the countryside. I'll explain on the way."

Robin studied him for several moments in silence. "Montgomery thinks," he said very seriously, "that you are a fairy."

"I'm not a fairy."

"Then how does a man find himself three miles from Artane, without clothing, without sword skill, without horse skill, without a knowledge of the local tongues, and with no better explanation than that he was robbed?"

"I have a good answer for that."

"Do you? I'm anxious to hear it." Robin paused and frowned. "You know my sister will be grieved."

"I can't marry her until I have a way to," Jake said. "Your father isn't going to give her to a merchant, is he?"

"Nay, he will not." Robin sighed. "I see there is nothing else to be done. But you leave me, my friend, to listen to her weeping for hours on end until you return."

"Keep her in the lists. She won't be crying if she thinks she can cut you to shreds."

Robin laughed. "Aye, you have that aright. Nothing would please her more." He paused, then smiled. "She had a sword made for you, you know. It was finished last night."

Jake blinked. "Did she?"

"She did. 'Tis a plain one, of course, but markings can be added later. When you have secured the king's favor."

Jake was stunned. "I don't know what to say."

"Say, 'You have excellent taste in blades for a wench,' kiss her, then be on your way before she takes your sword and clouts you over the head with it."

"Good advice," Jake said with a smile. He looked at Robin. "Thank you. You have been a good friend and a peerless teacher."

"I haven't finished with you yet."

"I'm honored by that as well. I will be back to continue."

"Do," Robin said simply. "Else you leave me with that irascible woman's complaints for the rest of my days."

Jake walked with him back to the great hall, wondering how in the world he was going to tell Amanda what he was up to. He didn't see her in the hall, so he went upstairs to the boys' room to get what little stuff he had together. He left the mail shirt lying on the bed. He would use it again when he got back, but it certainly wasn't anything he would need in the future. Out of necessity, he kept the clothes Amanda had found for him. The pound coin in his boot felt oddly out of place, but it might serve him later. At least he could use it in a phone.

He stood for a moment, looking at the bed that was too small, and smiling at the sight. It was hard to believe that he had slept on that blasted thing for almost two months.

Harder still to believe that he had found his heart's desire eight hundred years in the past.

He steadfastly refused to entertain the thought that maybe, just maybe, he wasn't the one she was supposed to marry. No, he would tidy up his affairs in the future, make preparations for his life in the past, then get on with it.

He sighed, then turned to head for the door. He almost jumped at the sight of Amanda standing there, silent and watchful.

She had a sword in her hands, sheathed, point resting on the floor.

"I didn't know you were there," he said with a smile.

She wasn't smiling in return. "You're leaving today," she said quietly.

"Robin told you?"

She shook her head. "I knew."

"I will return."

"Aye." She took a deep breath. "This is yours."

He crossed the room and put his hands over hers as she held the sword.

"I don't know how to thank you," he began.

"Do not," she said sharply. "Do not thank me. That makes it sound as if I'm giving you a gift of parting, which I am not."

"I will return," he said softly.

Tears began to roll down her cheeks. She dragged her sleeve across her face. "Damnation, but I am a blubbering fool. I do not care if you come back."

"Liar," he said with a smile. "You'd better plan on some chapel time tomorrow."

She looked up at him, her cheeks tear-stained. "I do not care," she said desperately. "I tell you, this thing between us is mad—"

He kissed her. He really hadn't intended to, not until he'd managed to get himself, by medieval standards, in a position to ask her to marry him. But he just couldn't help himself.

And once he started kissing her, he found that he just couldn't stop.

If he hadn't been lost before, he was now.

When the sword boring into his ribs finally became uncomfortable enough that he couldn't ignore it any longer, he lifted his head and took a few deep breaths. Then he looked down at her.

"It isn't madness," he said. "I will come back."

Her eyes swam with tears. "I hardly dare hope."

"I will come back. I will wrest a title from the king and I will satisfy your father's demands."

She gave him one last searching look, then put her arms around him and hugged him tightly.

"Hurry," was all she said before she released him and ran down the hallway for points unknown.

Jake suspected she had headed for the roof. He didn't dare follow her because if he did, he would never dare leave.

He looked at the sword she had shoved into his hands. It was beautiful, with a place for a gem to be set into the hilt. That place was empty. He suspected he might have something in his vault at work that might fit there.

He took his sword in his hands and made his way down to the great hall. Miles was waiting for him.

"Ready?"

"Yes," he said.

"Robin's at the stables." Miles looked at him serenely. "You'll hurry about your business."

"I'll do my best."

"Amanda will be impossible to live with until you return."

"Poor you."

"Exactly," Miles said with a small smile.

Jake found Montgomery and John waiting with Robin outside the stables. Montgomery gave him an impulsive hug and John clasped hands with him in a manly fashion.

"Soon," Montgomery said. "We'll see you soon."

"If the fairies let me go," Jake said dryly.

Montgomery's eyes widened and his mouth hung open. Jake reached over and ruffled his hair.

"I was joking, Montgomery," he said. "I'll be back soon."

Montgomery nodded, but Jake suspected he would be digesting the fairy thing for quite some time to come.

He mounted, with surprising ease if anyone cared, and followed Robin down the cobblestone path, through the gates, and through the village. It was only after they had left the village behind that Robin reined in and looked at him.

"Very well, we have reached the countryside. I am ready for whatever it is you have to tell me."

Jake handed him the pound coin he'd taken out of his boot before he mounted. Robin took it, studied it, then looked at Jake.

"Interesting."

"Look at the date. Those numbers there."

Robin studied it, then looked at Jake. "2005?"

"The Year of Our Lord 2005."

Robin shook his head. "I don't understand."

"You're going to have to take some of this on faith," Jake said. "Think about it after I'm gone." *Assuming I go,* he added to himself. "Before I found myself outside Artane's gates, I was living in the year 2005. That's where the coin came from. *When* it came from."

Robin was silent. He merely looked at Jake and waited patiently.

"I was living in the year 2005," Jake continued. "I was traveling in a . . . a horseless cart, at great speed, when I slid off the road. I remember spinning, then the next thing I knew, I was waking up in your father's solar and the year was 1227."

Robin looked down at the coin, then fingered it for a bit. Then he looked back at Jake. "Go on."

"That's why I didn't know your language, or how to ride, or how to wield a sword. In my time, I am a gem merchant, but in my day that isn't a business for a peasant. I have studied many years to learn my craft and I have made a great deal of money in that business. It is a very skilled profession and I have made pieces of jewelry for royalty. I have traveled the world to find things that others simply could not."

"Do you live in London?"

"Yes, the London of 2005."

Robin considered, then smiled faintly. "Is it still crowded, noisy, and filthy?"

"Yes," Jake said. "And bigger than you can imagine."

Robin looked up at the sky for several moments in silence, then back at Jake. "This coin is a mystery I will have to think on." He paused. "I could dismiss this as the rantings of one who is mad—and I likely should—but I have watched you for the past three se'nnights."

Jake waited.

"And I daresay you aren't mad. But," he added seriously, "this is very hard for me to believe." He held up the pound coin. "Even this."

"I understand."

"I assume any other proof you might have had was conveniently stolen."

Jake nodded. "Or inconveniently, it might be argued."

Robin looked at the coin again, then put it into a bag at his belt. "I will keep this safe for your use when you return. I will endeavor to keep my sister from killing herself in the lists. And I will think on what you've said." He rubbed his hand over his face, then took a deep breath. "And how will you return to London? Your London?"

"I think there is a gate where I was found. A gate through time."

"In the grass?"

"Where else?"

Robin pursed his lips. "It sounds suspiciously like one of the tales my father's healer used to tell to the lads when they were small."

"Those tales had to come from somewhere."

Robin grunted. "I daresay. Well, let us be off to your gate and see what it has in store for you. I daresay I've seen odder things than this."

Jake sincerely hoped so. He rode with Robin to the place where he had found the pound coin, where Lord Ledenham had tried to ambush them, where Berengaria told him he might find a portal.

He dismounted, took his sword off the saddle, and handed the reins to Robin.

"Thank you, my lord," he said formally. "For the training. And for the friendship."

Robin reached down and clasped his hand. "Come back," he said simply.

Jake nodded, took his sword in his hand and walked away. He felt nothing, and wondered if he might look like the biggest jackass in history—and he had a lot of history to compete with. He stopped for a minute, wondering how he could possibly explain to Robin that the gates weren't working without sounding like a complete madman, then gave up. Maybe he was going to be stuck in the Middle Ages, without money, without means of making money, without means of asking Amanda's father for her hand in marriage. He wasn't a defeatist by nature, but he was looking at some pretty impressive odds stacked against him.

Damn it anyway.

He took a deep breath, sighed, and turned around, fully intending to tell Robin—

But Robin was gone.

Jake looked around him. The trees were different. There was a stone fence not fifty feet from him that hadn't been there a minute before.

He could hardly believe it. He'd made it.

But was it 2005?

He was tempted to indulge in a little panic over the possibility that it might not be. It was also tempting to stand there for an endless moment and wonder about the complexity that was Amanda of Artane. Would she wait? Would he return to the proper time—if he returned at all? Would Rhys give her to him or tell him to take a hike?

He shook aside his thoughts. What he had to do now was find a phone and get on with his future. He would—hopefully—have all the time in the world to think about it while he was standing again in Rhys de Piaget's study trying to convince the man to give away his daughter.

He took a moment to get his bearings, then struck out for the east. It took him little time to run into a cluster of cottages.

Modern cottages.

Jake jogged toward them, trying to come up with a good story as to why he was carrying around a medieval broadsword. Re-enactment society seemed the most logical choice. Maybe he had fallen asleep on his sword and been left behind by his mates. That made perfect sense.

He stopped at the first likely house. An elderly man came to the door, looking quite unsurprised by Jake's outfit.

"You silly re-enactment buggers," he said, opening the door. "No pockets for your mobile?"

Jake laughed. "Exactly. Mind if I use your phone?"

The old man shook his head. "Don't mind at all. Don't suppose you have any coins to pay for the call in those nonexistent pockets of yours, do you?"

"Have a Good Samaritan moment," Jake suggested.

"Bugger that," the man said cheerfully, and went back in to whatever he was watching on the telly.

Jake made a mental note to send him something nice for his wife who was commiserating with him about the odd things that happened when a body was unfortunate enough to live so close to Scotland.

When Jake heard that, he supposed he could have just hoofed it to present-day Artane, but he just couldn't bring himself to land on the modern earl's doorstep in hose and a tunic. Maybe he had lived in England too long. He was beginning to suffer from a decidedly British sense of propriety.

He stood in front of the phone for a minute or two. It was a thirty-year-old phone, but was it a thirty-year-old phone or brand new? The faint noise from the telly gave him no clues. He took a deep breath and took the plunge. He picked up the phone and called his office. His assistant probably wouldn't still be there this late, even if the year was right, but—

"Kilchurn, Ltd.," said an unfamiliar voice.

Jake heaved a sigh of relief that came straight from the depths of his gut. Then he frowned. "I'm looking for Penelope Cleary. Is she available?"

"I'm sorry, this is the service. Ms. Cleary had a collapse and is in hospital. We're the answering service she engaged before she left. Can I help you?"

"Really?" Jake asked, surprised. "Why—oh, never mind." There was no point in trying to get details out of an answering service. He would get to London and find out the details to-morrow. "This is Jake Kilchurn. I'm stuck here in Northumberland and I was hoping Penelope would arrange a car, or find me a bank—" Well, he wasn't exactly sure what he'd been thinking. Too much time-travel and not having his assistant waiting by the phone had thrown him.

"Where are you?" the service asked. "We'll have a car sent immediately."

"How nice." Jake obtained the address from his host, then relayed it to the service and hung up. He popped his head into the salon. "I'll just sit out front."

"Suit yourself," the man said.

His wife, however, apparently couldn't bear the thought of Jake sitting outside without something strengthening. He waited for his car in the comfort of a folding chair with a little folding table in front of him, laden with tea and cookies.

He wasn't sure he could say he missed eel under sauce, but he wasn't sure he wasn't going to miss Tesco cookies, either.

It was quite dark when a black Mercedes pulled up in front of the house. Jake called his thanks inside, having long ago deposited the tea things inside the kitchen, and walked toward the car. The chauffeur got out, along with another man in a dark suit. Jake wondered if the police had come to make certain he was really who he said he was. It occurred to him then that he should have asked inside for the date. Who knew how long had passed since he'd been in the past?

"Mr. Kilchurn?" the dark-suited passenger asked.

"That's me," Jake said cheerfully. "I don't mean to trouble you both—"

"No trouble at all," the man said, taking Jake by the arm.

Very firmly by the arm.

Jake looked at him, startled. "Hey—"

The sting of a needle was only the briefest of sensations before complete darkness descended and he knew no more.

Chapter 20

Amanda ran along the perimeter of the lists, wishing there was a bit of rain to perfect the misery of her morning. Instead there was nothing but blue sky above and what promised to be, for a change, a beautiful summer day.

She cursed, just on principle.

It seemed like the only thing she could do. Her choices for other activities were sorely limited. She couldn't walk along the shore. If she did, she would be faced at each step with the ghost of Jackson Kilchurn, his twinkling eyes and easy smile. She couldn't go to the chapel. There too, she would have his ghost sitting next to her, stealing looks at her from under his eyebrows whilst he should have been attending to his eternal welfare.

If she hadn't been so desperate to outrun her traitorous heart, she would have stayed away from the lists as well. She could scarce watch Robin and Miles train without seeing Jake there as well, trading parries and jests with Robin, driving himself with a ferociousness that even Robin had admired.

So instead, there she was, running as if her very soundness of mind depended on it.

Robin swung suddenly into place beside her. She jumped, as she always did, and gave him a glare. Damn the man, would he never cease with this suddenly appearing without warning?

"Save your breath," he advised cheerfully. "You'll need it for another lap or two."

She saved her breath, but made a search for something truly nasty to say to him. Unfortunately, she was distracted by the fact that she'd already made five laps about the lists and apparently that was taking a toll on her poor form. Or that could have been worry that Jake would never return.

It was hard to say.

She ran with her brother in companionable silence for quite a while longer before she managed to spit out the words she'd been chewing on since Robin had returned very late the previous evening. He had come home, quite silent, gathered his wife and his son, and gone straight to bed without comment. His look had warned her that he had much on his mind and she would be wise to leave him be. So she'd chewed on her questions and her curiosity for the whole of the night only to drive herself to the lists at first light. She should have known Robin would appear later rather than sooner.

She looked sideways at Robin. "He left, then," she said.

"Aye."

She waited, but Robin seemed content to simply bounce along, serene and humming in an annoyingly off-key fashion. She finally smacked him in the belly with the back of her hand.

"Dolt, give me tidings."

"I didn't think you cared."

"Perhaps you shouldn't think so much."

Robin smiled and slowed to a walk. He didn't look at her, however. He seemed to find the distant blue sky to be quite fascinating.

"Aye, he left," he said, finally.

"But you brought back two horses."

He shrugged, but continued his study of the sky. "He managed to find another way back to London and didn't need the mount."

She put her hands on her hips. "Well? How? Did he cast his lot in with others? Did he walk? Did he sprout wings and fly?" By the saints, Robin could be closed-mouthed!

Robin looked at her. "Aye," he said.

"Aye what, you imbecile," she exclaimed. " 'Aye' is no answer!"

"I'll let him tell you about his mode of transportation when he comes back," Robin said, reaching over to ruffle her hair. "You'd best be about your training and then off with you for some stitching and other womanly work. You mustn't let your skills slide south, you know."

"You are infuriating," she stated.

"I know," he said pleasantly. "Now, are you up for another bit of a run, or shall I have Christopher fetch our swords?"

"Swords," she said promptly. "It would give me great pleasure to cause you a bit of irritation as well. Perhaps in the form of a great, gaping wound in your belly."

"By the saints, Amanda, you are possessed of foul humors today," he said with a laugh. "I think you might actually provide me with a bit of sport this fine morn. Christopher! Fetch us the tools of death, lad!"

Amanda was tempted to try to inflict some of that on her sibling, but then he would be unable to answer her questions and she thought if she vexed him long enough, he might give her a better answer than aye.

Aye?

That told her nothing.

"He'll return," Robin said easily.

"I don't care if he does."

"Ha," Robin said, "of course you do, you cruel girl. You want him back and then you'll spend years punishing him for going away."

"It does me no good to have him," she said wearily. "He has no title."

"He'll buy one."

"Father will not be impressed."

"That won't be because I didn't give him all the aid I could."

She looked at her brother and had a rare feeling of gratitude to him wash over her. "Then you favor him? In truth?"

"Amanda, I passed three se'nnights with the man in the lists from dawn to dusk. Why, by all the saints, would I waste my precious time with a man I did not favor?"

"You've done more foolish things than that," she reminded him.

He dredged up patience; she watched him do it. He pursed

his lips and spoke very deliberately. "When a man can show me his character in such a short amount of time, when he has so little to hide of himself or his motives that I can easily see what he believes, then that is a man I can vouch for."

She hesitated. "Nicholas hates him."

Robin put his hand on her shoulder. "Unlike me, Nick is very concerned that you be happy. I couldn't care less if you were miserable."

"You are a great oaf, Robin de Piaget," she said tartly, but in truth, her heart was greatly eased by his words. She certainly wasn't accustomed to living her life according to her brother's opinions, but it was somehow reassuring to know he wasn't opposed to the man she loved.

"What an affectionate wench you are," he said with a smile. "Jake no doubt looks forward with great relish to a lifetime of such kind words."

"And he'll have them," she muttered. She accepted her sword from Christopher, then paused and looked at Robin. "Tell me he didn't walk back to London."

Robin opened his mouth, then stopped and shook his head. "Amanda, he is a man of mystery and I will tell you no more than that. I think in this instance, you will simply have to trust him."

"The saints preserve me."

"Aye, well, you'll likely need their aid as well. And in the end, I daresay you will know a great deal more about Jackson Alexander Kilchurn than I do." He shook his head. "Jake. We should find another title for him than that. It hardly sounds of modern usage."

"He has Scottish ancestors," Amanda pointed out. "And you know what sorts of strange things come from the north."

"There is that," Robin agreed, taking his own sword. He pointed it at her in a friendly fashion. "Let's be about our work. I daresay we both need the distraction."

Unfortunately, the distraction of the lists could only last so long because she was, unlike Jake, unwilling to drive herself until the sun set. She called peace at noon, handed her sword to Christopher, and set off for the house for a well-deserved rest. She snatched a hunk of bread and a bottle of wine off the high table and continued on her way upstairs, ignoring protests and questions from the little lads and Miles.

She gained her mother's solar only to find her sister-in-law there before her. Anne looked up from her sewing and smiled.

"The conquering hero returns," she said.

"Ha," Amanda said with a snort. "The exhausted one, rather." She cast herself down into the chair across from Anne and leaned her head back, closing her eyes. "I daresay I could sleep for a fortnight."

"Why don't you?"

Amanda opened her eyes. "Because I fear if I sleep, he will not return."

Anne smiled. "He will. Robin thinks so."

"Did he tell you aught? Anything of his last words with Jake?"

"Nothing more than that," Anne said. "And you know Robin isn't one to keep secrets, at least from me. But he said nothing more when he came home and his silence this morn told me that he intended to say nothing else."

"I don't suppose he'll change his mind," Amanda said glumly.

"Nay, sister." Anne paused for a moment. "I'm sorry, Amanda. I suppose all you can truly do is trust that Jake loves you and that he will return."

"Unless he was merely passing the time with me," Amanda said grimly.

Anne laughed and for some reason it was as beautiful as sun breaking through clouds. "Amanda, how could he possibly have endured all Robin's torture, all the humoring of the little ones, and Nicholas glaring daggers at him at all hours if he had no other purpose in mind than to idle away his days with you?"

"I suppose," Amanda said quietly.

"Besides, I saw the way he looked at you." Anne smiled reassuringly. "He isn't nearly as hard to read as Robin was when I was not his wife."

"Robin is still impossible," Amanda said darkly. "I vow, Anne, I do not know how you bear him."

Anne only smiled serenely. "You are very much like him, you know."

"I am not!"

"Aye, you are," Anne said. "Blustering to hide your true, tender feelings. It is so much easier just to show them."

"Easier?" Amanda asked. "More frightening, I'd say."

"That too," Anne agreed. She continued to stitch in a most contented fashion. She looked periodically at Phillip who had fallen asleep in a nest of blankets on the floor near her feet.

Amanda envied her her peace, but Anne had certainly earned it. She earned it anew each day by virtue of the fact that she was wed, poor woman, to Robin of Artane. Amanda wondered how she managed it. Love turned spines to mush, apparently.

She contemplated that for the remainder of the afternoon, content to merely sit across from Anne and watch her work. Anne offered her a bit of mending, but Amanda politely declined. Besides, no one wanted her to do their sewing for them. Her skills lay in strategy and subterfuge.

Indeed, she would have been better off as a man.

She slapped her hands on her knees and rose. "I need air."

Anne laughed up at her. "I told you: you should stop thinking so much."

"I should. It never serves me. I'm going for a walk on the roof. Mayhap the sea breezes will blow sense into my poor empty head."

"Will you come down for dinner?"

Amanda shook her head as she walked to the door. "Best that I don't. I'll filch something from the kitchens later. I've no mind for speaking with anyone and no stomach for pretending I'm cheerful."

"As you will."

Amanda left the solar and made for the roof of her father's castle, trying not to remember the last time she'd stood there, which had been yesterday morning as she'd watched Robin and Jake ride off through the village. She'd watched them until she could see them no longer.

Or, more precisely, she might have been able to see them longer if she hadn't been blinded by her tears.

She chose a different part of the roof, the one that overlooked the sea, and cursed herself for a sniveling fool. He was only a man. She knew many of them herself and had never found one worthy of her tears. Jake was no exception. He would likely begin to forget about her somewhere between Artane and York, and finish the chore by the time he'd reached London.

Besides, he was merely a merchant. He sold goods to earn his bread. He likely spent horrible months at sea on his travels with little to eat and no decent place to sleep so he could bargain for more gems to bring back to London and do with them what he did with them.

She sighed. Damnation. Now she was not going to be able to look at the sea either.

"How do you fare?"

She almost fell off the parapet in surprise, not only because of the voice, but whom it belonged to. She dragged her sleeve across her tear-stained cheeks, then looked up at her brother.

"Well, enough," she said. "And you?"

Nicholas paused for a moment or two, then nodded. "Well enough, I suppose."

She stood next to him in silence for a very long time. He seemed to have no more taste for speech than she did, but she supposed that was a man's habit. Finally, she sighed and looked up at him.

"You've been powerfully unpleasant since you returned."

"My roof still leaks."

"I see."

She fell silent.

So did he.

And then he spoke. "He left, then."

"He did."

Nicholas took a deep breath. "I behaved badly, Amanda. Forgive me."

She shook her head. She didn't want to discuss this, or anything else of serious import with her brother. So she put her arm around his waist, leaned her head against his shoulder and sighed. "Please, don't speak of it. Don't speak of anything, if you have any mercy in your soul."

"Amanda—"

"Nicholas, please," she said quietly. "Please."

He sighed and put his arm around her shoulder. "As you will." He was silent for several moments. "As you will," he repeated softly.

Amanda had thought her life could not worsen. Endless suitors who were unsuitable. A man she had lived with her entire life to whom she was not related but unable to have nonetheless. And now a man she could love and thought she just might love very much who had left and given only a promise of returning.

She stared, now dry-eyed, at the sea and attempted to allow the ceaseless roar of it soothe her.

Unsurprisingly, it failed.

Chapter 21

J*ake* woke to spinning. He would have groaned out loud, but he was afraid that groaning would make the spinning worse, so he lay perfectly still, concentrating on the pattern of his breathing until his head cleared.

It took a very long time.

Time traveling was apparently quite hard on the body.

He tried to ignore how perfectly ghastly he felt by forcing himself to produce the memories of his last twenty-four hours from the depths of his alarmingly foggy brain.

He remembered talking to Robin. He remembered telling Robin about himself, about where and when he'd come from, and where he intended to try to get back to. He remembered looking at the grass and wondering what it took to get back to the future he'd left behind. He remembered looking behind him and finding Robin gone.

The memories thereafter were a little more difficult to produce.

He remembered tea on a front stoop and a dark car pulling up in front of the semidetached house. He remembered the stick of a needle. And then he could remember nothing else.

Where in the *hell* was he?

"Is he awake?"

There was a pause and Jake sensed someone leaning over him. He gave thanks for what minuscule bit of survival training Thad had taught him during forced stays in hotels waiting out bad weather. It was almost easy to keep his breathing slow and deep, talk his heart into remaining on a steady rhythm.

"He's still asleep, Doctor."

"Give him another jab anyway."

"But, Dr. Andrews, that might be dangerous!"

"I don't think our wealthy patron cares, nurse. He's to remain sedated. Our duty is to see that he does."

Jake's first instinct was to leap up and fight, but he suppressed it viciously. He would wake again, and hopefully have more time to determine where he was before he acted.

A wealthy patron who didn't care if he died?

There was a prick, and then he slid helplessly into unconsciousness before he could decide if that might be his father, and why.

He woke again, foggy and disoriented. The memories flooded back much more quickly this time. He waited for what seemed an eternity, struggling to remain motionless and relaxed, until he was certain there was no one else in the room and no kind of monitor attached to him.

He was, however, attached to something else.

He opened his eyes. He was in a sort of hospital room. A garish night-light of some kind spilled out from the bathroom. He was, amazingly enough, strapped to the bed. He felt astonishingly bad, but at least this time his head was marginally clearer. Maybe they were giving him fewer drugs, or maybe his system was cleaning them out more quickly.

His eyes adjusted to the semi-dark and he determined that he was indeed in some kind of hospital-like room and, yes, he was certainly tied down. The why escaped at him at the moment, but he supposed he would find that out as well in the end.

Assuming he didn't meet his end first.

He examined his bonds and found that they were much looser than he would have assumed. Maybe his jailers had more faith than they should have had in their drugs. Maybe they wanted him to try to escape so they could shoot him and be justified.

Maybe he really did deserve to be in a madhouse, because none of it made sense and he was beginning to wonder quite seriously if he were losing his mind.

He decided he would give that more thought later. For now, the most sensible thing he could do was try to escape. He wiggled and shoved and pushed his calves down into the ankle bindings until he could get his teeth near one of his hands. He supposed he would have been willing to gnaw his own hand off, but fortunately all it required was a few good tugs that he hoped wouldn't require dental surgery down the road to repair. He reached over to free his left hand, then froze when he heard footsteps stop outside his door. He kept his right hand motionless by its former bond as the door opened and light steps came his way.

"Oh," a female voice said in dismay. "Thrashin' about he is. I'd best give him another jab whilst I can—"

Jake grabbed the needle and had jammed it into the woman's thigh before she managed a squeak. She slumped over him without so much as a peep. That was enough to give him pause, but he would work that out later, when he had the luxury of determining the strength of the narcotics he'd been given. He sat up and undid his other hand. He ripped out the IV line, then shifted far enough to get out from underneath Nurse Hatchett. He sat up and freed his feet only to find that he was missing his clothes. Well, that would be something to solve straightaway.

He got out of bed, but had to stop and clutch his head as the room spun violently. He felt like he hadn't eaten in days.

He probably *hadn't* eaten in days.

He waited until the pounding subsided a bit, then looked around to get his bearings. His medieval gear was laid out on a table, including his sword. That was a boon, at least. He turned back to the bed, secured the nurse there, then went to retrieve his clothes. He put everything on, strapped his sword around his waist, then paused. There was no sense in not knowing a little more about where he was and what he'd been given.

He found his chart, which contained lists of medications he knew nothing about.

But that wasn't what blew his mind.

It was that he'd been out for almost a month.

A month?

No wonder he felt like hell.

He put the chart down and considered as best he could with his extremely foggy brain. He could only hope that time passed at the same rate in the past. The last thing he wanted to do was pop back to the Middle Ages and find Amanda a grandmother.

He scrubbed his face with his hands, then gathered what was left of his wits about him. Escape was his first priority. He would worry about the rest when he was free of wherever he was. He retrieved the syringe. There was a bit of it still to hand. It would surely serve him at some point. He opened the door. It occurred to him that he should have put on the nurse's uniform, but he realized with equal clarity that he was obviously not thinking straight because it never would have fit. He didn't do drugs and it showed.

He eased out into the hallway, picked a direction, and sprinted in it.

A nurse tried to stop him. He treated her to the rest of his shot.

A very large bouncer-type with a billy club tried to stop him as well. With apologies, Jake dispatched him to temporary oblivion.

A doctor with a lab coat appeared in the hallway, carrying another syringe. Jake pretended to freeze with fear, even allowing the needle to come within striking distance, before he faked right, retrieved the drug and administered it without delay to the man seemingly willing to do whatever it took to make a buck.

Jake nipped into the good doctor's office, locked the door behind him, and made good use of a functioning window, pinching the man's keys as he did so.

People really shouldn't leave their car keys just laying about. It led to bad things.

He was letting himself into the car that beeped in response to the keys before he realized that he wasn't entirely compos mentis. The bobbies wouldn't come after him for being detained without cause, but they certainly could pick him up for grand theft auto.

He shut the car door, then disappeared into the night with the keys, hoping to buy himself some time before things—people or his unfortunate stay in la-la land—caught up with him. He would keep the keys for a while, then ditch them and change directions. Or maybe he would bury them deep enough that the man who so casually spoke of his demise would at least have the hassle of wondering if someone might find them and use them.

It was the least Jake could do.

He walked until dawn. By then he was almost incoherent with weariness and with the aftereffects of the drugs in his system. He found himself a likely briar patch in the far corner of a farmer's field and lay himself underneath it.

He hoped he'd wake up to thorns, not needles.

Sunlight woke him. He lay completely still as he tried to come to a conclusion about whether that was really sunlight or a very bright lamp designed to torture him.

No, that was definitely sunlight and that was also definitely a root in his back. He shifted just the slightest bit, but didn't move from his hiding place. Sunlight meant daytime and that meant potential discovery.

He was beginning to get a very minute glimpse into Thad's special ops mentality.

He let himself wake fully and quietly before he felt around for weeds he was fairly sure wouldn't kill him if he ate them. And he sat right where he was and waited the day out. It would have helped to have known where he was, but he didn't dare risk any exploration. He had obviously been held illegally, unless someone had had him declared insane, but who could have done that? No one had known where he was until he called his office.

Ms. Cleary had a collapse and has gone to hospital. We're the answering service she engaged before she left.

Jake turned that over in his mind and found two things wrong with those statements. One, Penelope was a tank, a Mercedes 850 with no dings and a frame that could withstand the broadside of a truck. A collapse was not something she would have permitted herself. The other was the idea of anyone else taking over her post. It simply wasn't possible.

So who had had her locked up?

Jake spent the morning going down the list, examining from every angle the men and women he dealt with. It was, he determined in the end, impossible that any of them could have cooked up a scheme like this.

He turned next to importers, gem cutters, people he'd haggled with in other countries. Several of those might have wanted him dead, but they would have killed him outright, not locked him up. There were the gypsies to consider, those of the aquamarine that shouldn't have been cut, but he suspected a pithy curse would have sufficed them. Committing him to an asylum was not their style.

It was late afternoon before Jake finally arrived at the mental destination he'd been avoiding all day.

His father.

It was possible, but why? Because Jake had neglected to deliver papers to Artane? Surely Gideon would have called Jackson III when Jake didn't arrive. And it was possible that such a phone call could have put events into motion. But why? What possible reason could his father have had for getting rid of his assistant and then shutting him up in a nuthouse?

Money was the only thing Jake could come up with and that seemed too pedestrian a reason, even for his very unimaginative parent.

Once it was dark, he set out again. He avoided civilization, crossed roads quickly, and searched in vain for landmarks he recognized. He ran until he could run no more, then he walked, but quickly.

The night passed.

He thought he heard dogs in the distance, but chalked that up to no food and residue of knock-out drugs.

He stopped hearing dogs, but started hearing horses, or those could have been medieval thugs, or maybe just a flock of birds.

He began to wonder, at dawn, if he really was losing his mind.

He almost gave up.

And then he saw it, in the distance, rising up from the surrounding countryside like a headstone.

Seakirk.

He ran. He stumbled. He wasn't sure how many times he fell, or how many times he drove himself back to his feet. All he knew was that he would find safety within those walls. If nothing else, Worthington would let him in and Jake would retreat immediately to Seakirk's study and have a short, pointed conversation with a few ghosts.

He made it to the gates. He hadn't lifted his hand to knock before they swung inward. He stumbled inside and they closed behind him as if unseen hands were at the helm. He supposed they probably were.

He staggered across the courtyard and up the steps to the front door. It was appallingly early, but Jake didn't care. He banged on the door with all his strength. He had to get out of the open. He was hearing dogs again and he had the feeling these were quite real. He banged again. The door opened so suddenly that he fell over the threshold and went sprawling.

He lay there for a moment, stunned and grateful. He probably would have lain there for the rest of the day with his face against that cool stone floor, but a voice brought him back to himself.

"May I help you?"

Not Worthington. Jake considered the accent, then realized it sounded like English with a sort of Norman French twang. He took a deep breath, then heaved himself with a Herculean effort to his feet. He looked at his rescuer. His first impression was of height, breadth, and dark hair. Upon closer inspection, he found that the man had green eyes, much like his own.

But in all other respects, he looked so much like Robin of Artane that Jake sucked in his breath involuntarily.

The man shut the door, then looked at Jake with a polite smile. "In a spot of trouble, are you?"

Jake thrust out his filthy, bleeding hand. "I'm Kilchurn. I need sanctuary."

The other man shook his hand and smiled again. "Kendrick, lord of Seakirk," he said. "Sanctuary is yours."

Jake would have laughed, but he'd had a rough few days.

Instead, he took back his hand and wished desperately for pockets. "Thank you," he managed. "I'm being hunted."

"Why?" Kendrick asked.

"Beats me." Jake hesitated. "This may not make you feel any better, but I just escaped from the loony bin up the street."

Kendrick looked at his sword. "Delusions of medieval grandeur?"

"Something like that."

Kendrick folded his arms over his chest in a gesture Robin had made dozens of times. Jake didn't consider himself overly sentimental, but he almost wept. It might have been tempting, after four weeks of being stoned out of his mind, to have believed that his whole trip back to the past had been an outlandish fantasy. But as he stood there, with his hand clutching the cold steel of his sword, facing a man who looked so much like Robin de Piaget that Jake could hardly stand it, he knew he hadn't lost it.

"I have a question or two for you," Jake said.

"Cheeky of you," the lord of Seakirk said with a cheeky smile. "Shouldn't I be the one asking the questions?"

"How about a trade? You go first."

"Very well," Kendrick said. "What is your full name?"

"Jackson Alexander Kilchurn IV," Jake said. "Call me Jake. I own Kilchurn—"

"Ltd.," Kendrick finished for him. "I know. I've bought a piece or two of yours for my wife. Lovely bits, those." Then he reached out and put his hand on Jake's shoulder. "You look fair to falling down. Why don't you make yourself comfortable and have a bite to eat? I take it your hunters are still outside?"

"Could be."

"I'll go see to them. Worthington!" Kendrick bellowed. "Guest for breakfast!"

Jake watched as Worthington appeared, looking no less immaculate than he had the last time Jake had seen him. He approached, then inclined his head.

"Master Kilchurn."

"Worthington."

Kendrick looked at them both with one raised eyebrow. "You know each other?"

"Master Kilchurn's beautiful Jag broke down in front of the gates whilst you and the mistress were away with the children and I offered him shelter." Worthington looked at Kendrick placidly. "I told you as much, my lord."

"Slipped my mind," Kendrick said easily, "though anything to do with a '67 probably shouldn't. You know," he said, turning to Jake, "there was a '67 burning up in a field not far from here a few weeks ago. No driver inside, though." He paused. "Very odd."

Jake listened to him talk and thought that there might be more than one odd thing going on there. He couldn't have said why, but unless there was some very weird generational thing going on, he would have bet his right arm on Kendrick being related to Robin.

"You look like someone I know," Jake said suddenly.

"Who?"

Jake took a deep breath. "Robin de Piaget."

Kendrick didn't blink. Jake wondered briefly if he was barking up the wrong tree in the wrong forest, then decided he wasn't. The similarity was too striking.

"Do I?" Kendrick asked.

"Against all odds, yes, you do," Jake said. "Know him?"

Kendrick smiled and nodded toward the table. "Eat, my friend, then we'll have speech together. I believe I'll have a bit of a look outside and see what yammers at my front gates."

"Want help?" Jake asked.

"I have retainers," Kendrick said with another smile.

"You certainly do," Jake said with a snort. "I met them when I was here the last time. They got me into more trouble . . ."

"No doubt. I'll join your shortly. Worthington, see to his comfort."

"Of course, my lord. Master Kilchurn, let me see to your luggage. Ah, you have no luggage. Breakfast, then."

"Breakfast would be superb." Jake started to follow him, then paused and looked at Kendrick. "You know, I've been drugged for a solid month. I could be hallucinating the guys following me." He paused. "I could be hallucinating you."

Kendrick clapped a hand on his shoulder. "I'm quite real, and so is that table at the other end of the hall."

Jake nodded, then walked wearily across the great hall, too tired to protest Kendrick fighting his battles for him. He sat down, put his head down on the wood, and thought he might have heard himself snore once or twice. He realized he'd fallen asleep only because Worthington gave him a discreet tap on the shoulder.

"Food, sir?"

Jake sat up straight, rubbed his eyes, then nodded. "Food," he rasped. "Then maybe a nap in a bed that's long enough."

"I will return to take you upstairs," Worthington said, then he headed back to the kitchen.

"I'm tempted to head up myself," Jake muttered to himself, "but maybe I should wait politely until someone comes to fetch me."

"I should hope so," a voice muttered from behind him.

Jake was past being surprised by most everything. He looked over his shoulder to see one of the ghosts from the study. Jake struggled for a name to put to the face. He smiled briefly.

"Sir Stephen," he said, inclining his head.

"Aye," said the ghost, "and His Lordship's most loyal retainer, if you please."

"I please," Jake said. "I won't help myself to a bed and I promise not to poach any of His Lordship's trinkets."

"Harumph," Sir Stephen said, looking unconvinced. "I'm not at all sure of you."

"If it makes you feel any better, I'm not sure of me either."

But he was sure that he was starving. He helped himself to a very large breakfast and didn't argue when Worthington showed him upstairs to the room he'd had before. He managed to get his sword and his boots off before he collapsed on the bed. His head was filled with questions, but he didn't have the energy for any but the two most pressing ones.

Who wanted him dead?

Why did Kendrick of Seakirk look so much like Robin of Artane?

He yawned hugely. The first would take some investigation. The second would take some imagination and a look at that portrait above Kendrick's desk, the one with Robin, Anne, and four children.

Was Kendrick one of those children?

After the summer he'd had, Jake wouldn't have doubted it at all.

Chapter 22

Genevieve de Piaget walked down the hallway with her baby in her arms, on the hunt for a rambunctious three-year-old who had escaped while she'd been unable to chase him. Young Christopher was almost as fast as his older brothers and that was saying something, given how much shorter his legs were. She peered ahead and saw nothing, which inspired her to hurry the more. Who knew what sort of mischief he could have gotten into?

She slowed when she saw a mailed knight standing in front of the guest room door. "Sir Stephen?"

"Not to worry, my lady," Sir Stephen said. "I've everything well in hand here. We've a rogue sleeping off the saints only know what inside the chamber here. My lord has no worries, but I've met this one before," he said with a knowing look. "Trouble."

"Nothing you can't handle, of course," Genevieve said politely.

"Of *course,* my lady," Sir Stephen assured her. "And I've the garrison waiting to aid me if need be." He nodded toward the baby. "How is the wee one?"

"Fine," Genevieve said with a smile. "Though I'm thinking she howls louder than any of her brothers ever did."

"Not our Mistress Adelaide Anne," Sir Stephen said with a vigorous shake of his head. "Why, she's simply perfect and I defy any man to gainsay me."

"Well, let's hope they don't. I would hate to see what you'd leave of them otherwise."

Sir Stephen puffed out his chest and looked appropriately fierce. Genevieve smiled to herself as she bid him a good morning and continued on her way. She probably should have asked Stephen if he'd seen Christopher, but then again, it wasn't as if her children could really get into trouble.

That was the upside of living in a haunted castle. Not much went unobserved.

Actually, there weren't many downsides. She and Kendrick had privacy when he bellowed for it. She knew it distressed her husband that they were only seventh on Britain's most haunted list, but she suspected that was only because he never let anyone who made up those sorts of lists inside the front gates. If the paranormal squad responsible could have gotten a good look at the majority of Seakirk's inhabitants, Seakirk would have leapfrogged to Number One overnight.

She continued down the hallway and made her way down to the great hall. Worthington was there, tidying up things that were already gleaming.

"Worthington, have you seen Christopher?"

"In the lists, my lady, with the rest of the rabble."

She laughed. "I suppose he's safe enough."

"Actually, His Lordship has the lad well in hand." Worthington smiled. "And how is the wee one?"

"Sleeping. It won't last long."

"It never does, my lady," Worthington said with a long-suffering sigh.

Genevieve only smiled and made her way out of the keep and across the courtyard. She'd made such a walk eight years ago, only then she had been something of an interloper at Seakirk and Kendrick had been . . . well, he'd been something less than he was today.

But the lists looked no different. There had been flowers and trees, as there were now, as well as a very large field of dirt where manly men went to do their manly duty—which duty today seemed to be learning how to heft swords and wave them about as if the wavers meant business.

Even young Christopher held a sword and made motions with it as if he thought he just might be able to do some damage.

Genevieve shivered as she walked across the lists to a handy bench that had been pushed up against the wall for just such an occasion. It was summer, true, but already there was a hint of fall in the air. She sat down and watched her husband, the captain of his guard, his sons, and a few other choice souls continue their exercises in medieval studies. She wrapped Adelaide more snugly in her blanket and cuddled her close, grateful for the warmth and for the security of living in a time when her husband didn't have to go out to battle with his sword every day.

Said husband strode over to her a few minutes later, his sword slapping against his leg. He wiped his forehead on his shirt, then sat down next to her and smiled.

"How fare you, my love?"

"Very well, thank you," she said, finding it just as chill-inducing to have him sitting next to her as it had been eight years earlier. "How are you?"

"I'm in the lists with my sons," he said. "How can I not be content?"

She laughed. "All I can say is it's a good thing we don't have six daughters."

"And you think my little Addy won't have her own sword as well?" he asked, his dusty green eyes twinkling.

"Over my dead body."

He laughed. "Sword skill is never a bad thing," he said. "You have some of it. Why shouldn't she?"

"Later," Genevieve said. "Later, when she's out of diapers." She smiled at him. "So, who's in the guestroom?"

"Somebody named Kilchurn."

"Kendrick," she said warningly, "you aren't entertaining strangers again, are you?"

"Moi?" he said, with his hand over his heart. "Allow hapless strangers into my hall where they might be terrified at night by restless spirits?"

"Kendrick . . ."

"Very well, let me tell you a bit about our guest," he said in a more serious tone. "I think he was the one whose black Jag rolled earlier this summer. Apparently he was thrown from the car."

"Where did he land?"

"In medieval England."

Genevieve blinked. "How do you know?"

"He told me that I greatly resemble Robin de Piaget."

"That would do it," she agreed with a weak laugh. "And you said?"

"I told him to have a rest and we would talk later."

Genevieve smiled. "Kendrick, how do you know he didn't know you as well?"

"Because he implied as much. He said I looked like my father. I assume he had to have known my father and that would put him in those glorious early thirteenth century years. Before my time," he said modestly.

"A bit," she agreed.

"I suppose he'll have questions for me," Kendrick mused.

"I suppose he will." She'd had questions for Kendrick as well, when she'd first met him. She reached out and took his hand. "Be kind to him."

"Why would I be otherwise?"

She pursed her lips. "Because you have an awful sense of humor."

Kendrick brought her hand to his lips and kissed it gallantly. "You seem to have survived and look what I put you through when first we met."

"You've made up for it since." She sat back and looked at him. "Has it been eight years?"

"Eight glorious years," he said, his dimple peeking out of his cheek as he smiled. "Add that to those years I waited to make your acquaintance and I have quite a tally in regards to your sweet self, don't I?"

"You do," she agreed. "Are you going to tell this Mr. Kilchurn the whole story?"

"I have no reason not to." He smiled. "You know, I've never really believed in time travel."

She snorted so loudly, the baby began to fuss. She clapped a hand over her mouth, then looked at him in disbelief. "You live in a castle filled to the brim with ghosts. You have had your own brush with ghosthood. All these things seem normal, yet time travel is out of the question?"

"We're comfortable with what we're familiar with," Kendrick said, with a shrug, his eyes twinkling. He leaned over and kissed Genevieve softly. "I'm being called back to the fray. If you're chilled, go in, my love. I'll keep an eye on the lads."

"And if not you, a dozen other of their keepers will," she muttered.

"Ah, but they are my sons," Kendrick said with a smile, "and I've an especial interest in them. They'll be safe enough."

"I know," she said. "I don't worry, really. It was just a good excuse to come watch you."

Kendrick rose, made her a low bow, then returned to the field with his most arrogant swagger. Genevieve laughed to herself and nestled her baby more closely in her arms.

A sword in this girl's hands?

Again, over her dead body!

Though she had to admit that the boys didn't seem to be suffering for it. They loved their time with their father, whether it was in the lists or hanging out in Kendrick's study reading or playing chess. She supposed they could be doing worse things than being outside, learning to do damage with long bits of steel.

She shivered again. Summer had definitely waned without her truly noticing it. Time flew, she supposed. Perhaps it was time to ask Worthington to do something about the fire in Kendrick's study where she could go nurse her daughter in peace.

Besides, it would give her a chance to get a good seat so she could watch the conversation between Mr. Kilchurn and Kendrick. She had the feeling it was going to be very interesting indeed.

Chapter 23

Jake sat in Kendrick of Seakirk's study in a very comfortable chair, mere feet away from where he'd had his first encounter with Seakirk's ghosts, and enjoyed the warmth of the fire. The castle was, unsurprisingly, as cold as a castle should be, and Jake was as grateful for a fire as he had been eight hundred years ago. Of course, the fire also helped to stave off those shivers that seemed to continually travel up and down his spine, due in part to the sight of Kendrick of Seakirk, as well as the incredible tale he was telling.

"Let me get this straight," Jake said, for the third time that night, "you were murdered downstairs."

"Nay, I was murdered in the cellar," Kendrick said, unperturbed, "not the great hall."

"And you were a ghost for how many years?"

"Several."

"Kendrick," Genevieve chided. "Tell him all the details." She sat next to Kendrick with their sleeping daughter in her arms, looking perfectly at ease with the conversation.

Then again, she'd been married to the man for awhile. Maybe she was past being surprised by anything he said.

"I told him all the details already," Kendrick said. "He slept through most of them. If he truly wants the details again, he can go downstairs and read my story in that book you made me write. He might need another few days of sleep before he takes that on." He looked at Jake. "Suffice it to say that Robin was indeed my father, as you guessed. And courtesy of events in 1260, I was a ghost at one time, but now I am not." He gave Jake a small smile. "The details of my . . . conversion are of no import here."

"That's your opinion," Jake muttered.

Kendrick shrugged. "'Tis the truth. What does my past have to do with your future?"

What indeed, Jake thought to himself. Just the fact that Kendrick could, with one nod of his head, assure Jake that he actually would make it back to the past, get himself a title, and live out his life in bliss with Kendrick's aunt. He burned to ask, *Will I become your favorite uncle or is there some other*— he had to take a deep breath to avoid an uncomplimentary term—*guy who will have that pleasure?*

But if he found out the truth, would it change what he intended to do?

Kendrick studied him for several moments in silence, but Jake didn't allow himself to wonder why. He wouldn't ask Kendrick if he recognized him. After all, the man's hall was full of ghosts. Maybe that look of "wow you just fell into my entry hall in medieval gear" really meant "my ghosts dress better than you do," not "hey Uncle Jake great to see you."

"Well," Jake said, raising his arms over his head and marveling over how much easier it was to do in a borrowed sweatshirt than a borrowed mailshirt, "I have to agree. Your past doesn't make any difference to my future."

"And unfortunately, I know nothing of time travel," Kendrick said honestly. "I daresay you aren't the only one who has done it. Indeed, I always suspected that one of my aunts was not of medieval birth."

"Did you?" Genevieve asked in surprise. "You never said anything about that."

Kendrick shrugged. "I suppose I never really connected the two until Jake arrived. But Abby was most definitely a woman ahead of her time." He looked at Jake. "She wed with my Uncle Miles. Quite a sporting wench, that one."

"To put up with him, she would have had to have been,"

Jake said with a smile. "Though I liked him very much."

"Aye, as did I," Kendrick agreed.

Jake rubbed his hands together and decided that the only way to keep himself from tackling Kendrick to the ground and beating the truth out of him was to distract himself. "I should probably make a few phone calls," he said. "As much as two days of being unconscious in your guestroom has helped, I think I need to get back to real life. My secretary is apparently in hospital."

"Drugged as well, do you think?" Kendrick asked.

"I hope not," Jake said grimly. "But I can say that she never would have gone willingly. I should try to find out . . ."

And then it occurred to him just how incredibly bad that could be. Alerting anyone to his whereabouts, that was.

Very bad, indeed.

He looked at Kendrick. "I think I have a big problem."

"How so?" Kendrick leaned forward and rested his elbows on his knees. "You told me that you were placed in the sanitarium against your will, but not who had done so. Have you any ideas on that?"

"I think it was my father," Jake said slowly. "It's just a suspicion. Who else would manage to take over my company so fully that an innocent call to my assistant would end up with me being drugged for a month?"

Kendrick stroked his chin thoughtfully. "I suppose there might be more than one answer. I have lads who might be able to do a little investigating for you."

"Could they eavesdrop for me?" Jake asked.

Kendrick grinned. "They would consider it fine sport."

"Then if you don't mind, I think I'd like to make a couple of phone calls."

"Let me round up the reinforcements."

Jake watched Kendrick rise and leave the study with a spring to his step and an off-key melody on his lips. Jake smiled at Genevieve.

"He is a great deal like his father."

Genevieve returned his smile. "I envy you having met them. Robin and Anne, I mean."

"I can't blame you." He shook his head wryly. "Can you believe this? Here we are, just your average, run-of-the-mill

Yanks, living out these unbelievable adventures. Who would have thought it?"

"Who indeed?" she asked. "But think your adventure has been a bit more interesting than mine."

"I'm not living with ghosts. I think I'll take the flesh-and-blooders over your crew."

"And I'll keep my Mini Mart," she said with a laugh. She patted her baby gently. "No, I don't think I could go back to the Middle Ages."

"Not even for Kendrick?"

"Unfair," she protested.

"What is unfair?" Kendrick asked, popping back into his study. "My handsomeness, or my skill with the sword?"

"Both," she said promptly, taking his hand as he resumed his seat next to her. "And I would have gone back to medieval England for you. Just for the record."

"And given up chocolate?" Kendrick shuddered. "You must love me well."

"I do."

Kendrick put his arm around her, then looked at Jake. "My lads are ready. Give me a list of where to send them and you'll be able to make your calls within minutes." He smiled. "Not even EasyJet is this efficient."

Jake nodded and prepared to give Kendrick his list.

He could hardly wait to see what turned up.

A n hour later, everything was in place for at least the first foray into current events. Jake picked up the phone and dialed AE, Inc.

"Gideon de Piaget, please," he said in his smoothest, diamond-buying voice.

"Who is calling, please?"

"I'm an old friend of his, from Eton," Jake lied. "I'd rather surprise him, if you wouldn't mind."

The secretary protested. Jake insisted. She finally connected him with a muttered "highly irregular" under her breath.

Jake went through two more secretaries, each more inquisitive than the last. Apparently two months in the Middle Ages hadn't diminished his ability to sweet-talk his way through the ranks to the boss. It took several minutes, but finally Gideon was on the line.

"Yes?" Gideon said shortly.

"Gideon, it's Jake."

There was silence on the other end of the phone for quite some time. "Jake?" Gideon said in a strangled voice. "Jake Kilchurn?"

"In the flesh."

"I thought you were dead!"

"I'm most definitely not, but it was a near thing."

"Where have you been?" Gideon asked incredulously. "Why, we looked . . . we thought . . ."

"It's a long story," Jake said. "I'd be happy to tell you the whole thing, but not over the phone. I just need to know what's been going on for the past couple of months. Can you fill me in?"

Gideon blew out his breath. "This is just such a shock. I'm still trying to regain my balance."

"Regain it in a hurry."

Gideon laughed, but it was a shaky sound. "Well, when you never arrived at the inn, I assumed . . . well, we assumed the worst. My father contacted your father, of course. Mr. Kilchurn III flew over immediately and began the investigation himself. He told us the local authorities said your car had burst into flames and that you had perished inside."

"No, I survived. I've just been . . ."—he flashed Kendrick and Genevieve a smile—"out of touch for a while."

"Well, we thought you were dead."

Jake considered. He had the gut feeling Gideon was on his side, and it was always best to go with his gut. He chose his next words carefully. "I've been in an asylum for the last little while," he said slowly. "Drugged. Committed against my will."

"Impossible," Gideon said, aghast.

"Very possible," Jake corrected. "It's because of that that I'm reluctant to trust anyone at present."

"I understand," Gideon said. "Tell me what you need. If I can help, I will, and on your terms."

"You should," Jake grumbled. "Fate. A trip to Artane. What rot."

"You should still go to Artane," Gideon said, and Jake could hear the smile in his voice. "I'm telling you that there are untold goodies there for a treasure hunter like yourself."

"I'll think about it."

"Do. Now, what can I do for you?"

"Do you know anyone discreet?"

"My sister-in-law Iolanthe's family tree is simply crawling with men named Discreet. Name your task and I'll have answers for you as fast as humanly possible."

"You'd better be careful," Jake said. "All I did was call my secretary and I wound up drugged out of my mind."

"I'll be careful."

"Then if you can do something else, make some quiet inquiries and see what my father's been up to. If he's had me declared dead—"

"The funeral was a month ago," Gideon said. "Didn't you know?"

Jake found himself to be perfectly speechless. Well, his father hadn't wasted any time, had he? If Jake hadn't known better, he would have suspected his father of orchestrating his entire journey back into medieval England.

But if his father had possessed any idea of what Jake would find in the past, he would have no doubt orchestrated a trip into shark-infested waters instead.

But to think that he was legally dead was unexpected.

Unexpected and unsettling. What of his assets?

What if he had no assets?

"Jake?"

"Sorry," Jake said, snapping back to the present. "That was a little shocking."

"I thought it was premature," Gideon was saying, "and there were rumors that no body had been found, but your father is a powerful man, even here."

Jake took a deep breath. "What happened to my company?"

"As far as I know, he left it be. I haven't checked lately, though."

Well, at least something was as he'd expected it to be. "You had no reason to check. Damn my father to hell." He rubbed his hand over his eyes. "Did you finalize that first deal with him?"

"Yes, more papers were provided and he delivered them to my father himself."

"I'll just bet he did."

"It's baffling," Gideon said. "He has made simply buckets of money in this deal alone. I can't imagine why he would have needed more—or needed your business, for that matter. I thought he didn't like gems."

"He doesn't, and he likes me even less." Jake sighed and dragged a hand through his hair. "I need a few more details. I need to know what's happened to my accounts, if he has power of attorney for me, if my assistant is being sedated as well, or if she's even alive."

"Did you have a will?"

"I left everything to my assistant," Jake said simply. "Penelope knew the business and would have taken care of it. Besides, it would have cankered my father."

"I daresay," Gideon said with a laugh. "I have a thought. I have a cousin-in-law who is a very good attorney. I'll contact him to resolve the legal issues."

"Is he discreet?"

"Alex is not only discreet, he's frightening," Gideon said. "Besides, he knows a few guys. He's your man."

"If you say so." Jake considered for a moment or two, then issued another careful invitation. "We should meet."

"Of course. Where?"

Jake looked over the phone at Kendrick. "How about Artane?" he mouthed.

He watched Genevieve reach over and take Kendrick's hand. Kendrick stared at him briefly with no expression on his face, then he nodded.

"I have a place in mind," Jake said, "but since I'm not sure your phone isn't bugged, I'll keep it to myself. I'll get a location and time to you soon."

"You're paranoid."

"You would be too if you were me."

"Well then, 007, I'll await your instructions. I suppose this line is secure?"

"One could hope," Jake said, with feeling. "I'll see you later."

"Welcome back to the land of the living."

"For the moment," Jake said as he hung up. He looked at Kendrick and Genevieve and smiled. "One down."

"And your father?" Kendrick asked.

"Well, I imagine he wasn't weeping at my funeral," Jake said dryly. "I think I'll wait until I have more information before I take him on." He studied Kendrick for a moment or two. "You hesitated when I mentioned Artane."

Kendrick pursed his lips, but refrained from comment. Genevieve patted his knee.

"He hasn't been back," she supplied. "Not since, well, you know. And before, he couldn't leave Seakirk."

"Really?" Jake asked, surprised. "You haven't been back?"

"I wasn't sure how I should introduce myself," Kendrick said with a straight face.

"I see."

"No sense in terrifying my great-nephew several generations removed without good reason."

"I see that too," Jake said with a smile. "But I think it might be the safest place for me to meet Gideon. If there are unwholesome elements out there gunning for me, I don't think I want to bring them here."

"Despite my security?" Kendrick asked with a smile.

"You have small children," Jake pointed out. "I don't know that His Lordship does, and if he does, they are likely of age and not so vulnerable."

Kendrick sobered. "You are taking this seriously."

"I was unconscious for a month," Jake said. "I have no choice. Besides," he said, rubbing his hands together, "I have to get on with the business of getting on with my life, and that includes turning my business assets into those of the medieval kind."

"Are you sure you shouldn't leave something intact?" Kendrick asked carefully. "Just in case?"

Jake paused. "I could just ask you if I should, couldn't I?"

Kendrick sobered. "Do you want to know?"

Jake considered it. He considered it very seriously. There, sitting in front of him, was a man who would know.

Or would he? What if Jake could go back and change time, change the events that transpired? He wasn't bound to Kendrick's version of the past—and to hell with the sacred space-time continuum. For all intents and purposes, he was dead in the twenty-first century. It was entirely possible that he could live a very good life in the thirteenth. He would certainly be a better husband to Amanda than the two men he'd seen come courting her.

Nicholas was a different story, perhaps, but Jake might be saving them both a lifetime of turmoil if he married Amanda.

Did he want to know?

It wouldn't make any difference to his plans.

"No," he said slowly, "I don't."

"You would go ahead anyway," Kendrick said.

"I would."

"Then we'll wait for my eavesdroppers to return," Kendrick said. "And after that, we'll do some more investigating. We have Internet access here, you know. You could find out many things via computer. I have much knowledge of the beast and many favorite sites."

"EBay," Genevieve said dryly. "You'd be surprised what kind of medieval gear people are hiding in their garden sheds, just waiting for my husband to hop online and buy."

Kendrick had no defense for that, so he merely grinned and shrugged. "A man adjusts to his time in history as best he can."

Jake leaned forward. "So, what was it like, watching eight centuries of history unfold before your very eyes?"

"Frustrating," Kendrick said, "given that I was a ghost and could not do as I liked to influence it. I am not accustomed to being an observer only."

"An observer only?" Genevieve echoed incredulously. "Seakirk has lived in infamy for centuries because of the terrifying paranormal presence within its walls. You don't think you influenced current events?"

"I never said I didn't influence events," Kendrick said with a twinkle in his eyes. "I just said I couldn't influence events the way I wished." He trailed his fingers through Genevieve's hair. "Had you any inkling of Seakirk's reputation when you first came here?"

"You know I didn't," she said with pursed lips, "or I probably wouldn't have had the guts to come." She looked at Jake. "I was the last direct descendent of Matilda of Seakirk available, so I inherited the castle while I was happily living a very successful life in San Francisco."

"The last available one?" Jake asked. "I'm surprised. You would think there would be plenty of them."

"There were," Kendrick began with a modest smile, "several who were quite unfortunately unable to claim their inheritance." He shrugged. "Insanity runs rampant in the family, I daresay. Save my Gen, of course, who is a woman of remarkable good sense and excellent taste."

Genevieve let him pull her close. She smiled up at him. "So very true."

Jake smiled. "So, are you ready to head to Artane?"

Kendrick took a deep breath. "Why not? I've seen photographs. It looks as if it hasn't changed all that much in the ensuing years. A few additions, but nothing too shocking. I can manage it." He looked at Genevieve. "The children will be interested, no doubt."

"Do they know?" Jake asked. "About your past?"

Kendrick shook his head. "We decided we would tell them when they reached their twelfth summer. I daresay the wee ones will learn it from their elder brothers, but that is to be expected. They are already accustomed to the ghosts, so perhaps the other tale won't be so upsetting to them."

"A trip to Artane might be very instructive," Genevieve said. "After all, the triplets do know that you're related to the de Piagets. They just don't know that the Robin, Phillip, and Jason they're named for lived hundreds of years ago."

Kendrick nodded at Jake. "We'll go with you. If nothing else, perhaps we can pass the time pleasantly in the lists. I assume since you have a sword, you know how to use it?"

"A week with your uncle Miles, then three with your father to my credit. Three weeks of pure torture."

"I can imagine," Kendrick said with a grin. "He was my sword master as well. I'm surprised he was willing to train you. He was notoriously stingy with his expertise."

"So I've heard. Repeatedly," Jake added.

"It wasn't that he was unwilling to train others," Kendrick continued. "He was just very choosey. He wasn't about to train anyone who might, whilst bragging about the identity of his master, turn out to be a complete failure. He must have thought you showed some promise."

"Either that, or he was feeling particularly charitable," Jake said dryly. "But I accept your offer. I would be very happy to get in whatever practice I can."

"We can start tomorrow, if you like," Kendrick offered.

"I like," Jake said. "If you don't mind, could I use your computer? I think I could do some poking around without being too obvious."

Or he could call Thad and have one of Thad's buddies do some super-secret hacking for him.

Kendrick rose. "The office is down the passageway. I'll show you where it is. Just let me know if you need help. Or a nap." He smiled pleasantly. "I am my father's son, after all, and my swordplay has not suffered from eight hundred years of seasoning."

"I'll just bet," Jake muttered. He thanked Genevieve for her hospitality so far and followed Kendrick to the office, where he was left to his own devices.

He was momentarily tempted just to stare out the window at the countryside and wonder what Amanda was doing at that very moment, but that wasn't useful. He couldn't control the speed at which time passed and he had no idea how long it was going to take him to get back to medieval Artane.

If he got back to medieval Artane.

That was another possibility—the possibility that he might *not* get back—that he had no desire to dwell on. Kendrick would have been a masterful poker player; he gave nothing away. Jake was left to his own imaginings and those were not going to serve him.

It struck him again, with a sickening flash, that he might have lost everything of value he possessed: his business; his bank accounts; his trust fund.

All the things he planned to use to buy Rhys de Piaget's favor.

If his father had declared him dead, who knew what else was in the works?

With an effort, he shook aside those unwholesome and useless thoughts and focused on what he could do something about, which was damage assessment. He would deal with the rest later.

He picked up the phone and placed a call to the States. Thad was a good place to start. At least Jake was certain that Thad's phone wouldn't be bugged.

And that seemed, right now, like the best news he'd had all day.

Chapter 24

Amanda stared down at the handful of papers scattered on her father's desk. They were full of attempts to draw as Jake had taught her to do. Unfortunately, they were also full of horrible mistakes: blotches; crooked lines; shapes that were not recognizable.

She took them into her hands and then, with great vigor, crumpled them into balls and cast them into the fire. She watched the flames lick at them, then consume them.

Fitting.

"Amanda?"

She spun around, feeling almost guilty about her actions. But why should she? Certainly she was within her rights to destroy whatever she pleased, especially when it turned out to be so much less than it promised to be.

Miles stared at her dispassionately. "What are you doing?"

"Nothing."

"Are you unwell?"

She shook her head.

"Waiting is difficult," he said simply.

Amanda knew if she remained, she would weep, so she brushed past Miles and ran for the roof before he had the chance to examine her more closely. She knew what he would find. He would find a woman whose heart was broken, who had waited in vain for a man who had obviously changed his mind about her.

Even Robin had begun to have his doubts. She knew this because he had been uncharacteristically silent about the whole affair. He trained with her still in the lists, but his cheery disposition had deteriorated as time had worn on and his frowns had increased.

It had to mean something.

Even Nicholas's mood had darkened in direct proportion to how long Jake had been away. Perhaps that had nothing to do with her. Perhaps he was anxious to return to Wyckham and finish his repairs before winter.

Perhaps he merely waited to tell her that she had been a fool and deserved her heartache.

She didn't think overmuch on that.

What she had been thinking on, almost constantly since he'd gone, was Jake. She had wondered, at first, if he hadn't been waylaid. Even Robin had suggested the like. But Amanda had seen him, even without his sword. She had no doubts that unless he'd been shot in the back with a crossbow at close range, there wasn't a man in England who could best him if Jake could avoid being skewered on that man's sword.

Had he forgotten about her?

Or had he changed his mind?

She'd tried for days to convince herself that the latter wasn't true. But now, after so much time had passed with no word, no message, no indication that he loved her still, she had to concede that he had indeed changed his mind.

Which left her where she'd been at the beginning of the summer.

Ready to flee.

She walked along the parapet wall and looked out over the countryside. She was no longer tempted to cast herself into the sea. Again, the sea was too far away, but that wasn't the reason. She knew that if she'd tried it, she likely would have injured herself seriously enough to ruin her life but not seriously enough to cause her death. She leaned her elbows on the rock wall and stared, dry-eyed, at the sea before it.

It gave her no pleasure.

It certainly gave her no peace.

"Amanda?"

Amanda closed her eyes briefly, prayed for strength, then turned to look at her brother. The one with whom she shared no blood. She tried to smile.

She failed.

Nicholas took a step closer to her, then stopped and leaned against the wall. He hesitated, then looked out over the sea.

"The summer has waned."

"Aye," she said hoarsely.

He was silent for quite some time. It gave her ample opportunity to look at him and struggle to see him with different eyes.

He was beautiful. Even she could admit that. His fair hair only made the gray eyes he shared with Robin all the more startling. And to be sure there was not a more pleasing set of features in all of England. His form was manly and powerful, surely something any maid would have counted herself quite fortunate to gaze upon all her days. If it had just been the outward appearance that Nicholas called upon to recommend him, he would have been far and away the most desirable man in England and France both.

But not only was Nicholas beautiful, he was chivalrous, skilled, noble, and kind. Indeed, he was the embodiment of all knightly virtues.

And he made her laugh.

She closed her eyes briefly. There had been a time or two—more than that if she were to be entirely truthful—when she had fancied that she loved him. She had wondered, at night in the quiet dark, if there might not be a way for it to come about.

For her to be his.

Had she not in her heart of hearts wondered if Nicholas might be willing to relinquish all to have her? His title, his lands, her gold—all because she was more important to him than those worldly things.

Because if he wed her, he would most certainly be stripped of everything he had.

It was, in truth, impossible.

And so had seemed any chance of her finding a man to love.

Until she'd seen Jake lying senseless in the grass.

It was unfair perhaps to compare him to Nicholas, but they were much alike in temperament, and not unequal in the beauty of face and form. Jake had made her laugh as well. He had stolen her breath and loved her in spite of herself.

Or so she had thought.

"Amanda?"

And now this. She looked away. It was all she could do not to break down and sob.

He covered her hand with his own. "Amanda, I must speak."

"Oh, please do not," she begged. "Nicky, I beg you."

He put his hands on her shoulders and turned her toward him, looking down at her with serious gray eyes. "Amanda, I will and you must listen. If you bear me any love at all, you must."

"You know I do," she said miserably. "But there is no purpose in this."

"He is not returning, Amanda. It grieves me to be the one to force you to accept it, but you must. Whether it is from his own will or something else, the truth is still he is not coming back." He paused. "Damn him to hell."

Amanda smiled in spite of herself and the tears that coursed down her cheeks. "Ah, Nicky."

Nicholas looked down at her seriously. "Wed me. Wed with me instead and I will make you forget him."

"If I were," she took a deep breath, "if I were to wed with you, Nicholas de Piaget, it would not be to forget him."

Hope filled his face. She'd never seen him look so desperately, so painfully hopeful in her life.

"Then you love me?"

"Does it matter?"

"Aye."

She would have turned away, or gone into his arms, or bolted for the door, but he held her where she was, damn him.

"I love him and I cannot have him. I love you and I cannot have you. What am I to do?"

"Wed with me," Nicholas said fiercely. "Wed me and let the king go to the devil. There is no consanguinity between us."

She closed her eyes and let the tears trickle down her face

unchecked. It mattered not if there was no blood relation between them. They both claimed Rhys de Piaget as their father
through adoption and that was all that would matter to the
court and to everyone else in England with an opinion on the
matter.

Not that she cared about the opinions of others. If disfavor
with the king and other nobles had been the extent of her troubles, she would have told them all to go to the devil and wed
with Nicholas just the same. But the trouble lay deeper.

Deep within her heart.

Damn that Jackson Kilchurn to hell. He did not deserve her
affection or her regard or any of her time. Nicholas did. A pity
she couldn't give it to him.

She opened her eyes and looked at Nicholas, ready to tell
him he would find someone else, that he really didn't love her,
that he would be so much happier with someone else—

Anything but the fact that she, in the end, could not love
him as he wished.

She took a deep breath. "Tomorrow. I will give you my answer tomorrow."

"As you will," he said, looking less than satisfied, but perhaps he knew better than to press her.

There was something to be said, she supposed, to living
with a person for the greater part of your life.

"I must go," she said, easing past him carefully and hasten-
ing for the door. She slammed the guard tower door behind
her and ran for her bedchamber. She slammed that door as
well, then threw the bolt home.

She stood there with her chilly hands pressed against her
cheeks, desperately unhappy and terrified by the choice she
had been making for the whole of the day. But what else could
she do?

She could not marry her brother.

She would not wait for a man who wasn't returning.

She had to run.

Evening was falling when she slipped down the stairs and
through the great hall. Preparations for supper were commenc-
ing. None of her family was there, which allowed her to continue quickly on her way to the stables. She wore John's worst
clothes under her dress so that she might more easily discard

her identity in a stall and leave as just another peasant. Assuming she could get a horse out of the stables without question.

She made her way inside without incident. The stableboy she had given a sovereign to during her last escape was there, but he quickly turned his back and busied himself with mucking out a stall. She flipped another coin in front of him and continued on her way.

Her first choice of course was Jasper, but she knew he would not serve her. He would be marked as he left the gates and if he were marked, she would be marked as well. Nay, she would have to choose a lesser mount and hope he would suffice her.

She shut herself in with one of her father's older, less spectacular bits of horseflesh, stripped off her gown, and donned a patched cloak. It took her even less time to saddle her horse and turn to let him out of the stall.

She jumped when she saw Montgomery there, looking at her over the wooden door.

"What are you doing?" he whispered.

"You know what I'm doing," she said grimly.

"Mandy, do not," he begged. "I will do anything—"

"Give me your silence," she said. "Vow it."

He balked.

"Montgomery, I am for Seakirk Abbey. I will be safe there. You may come visit me there. But I will not realize my dream," and here she had to take a deep breath to give herself courage to spew out the rest of her line, "of being a sister of prayer if I cannot leave today. Before things worsen here."

He clutched the top of the door with white fingers. "But, Mandy, nay—"

"Nicholas has offered for me," she whispered fiercely. "What am I to do? Ruin his life as well? Allow me the pleasure of ruining my own and leaving his be."

"But Jake—"

"Is not returning," she said shortly. "Now, your silence, Montgomery. Vow it."

He closed his eyes briefly, then nodded.

"Say it."

He took a very deep, shaky breath. "I vow it," he whispered. She opened the stall and pushed past him. But then, suddenly, she turned and threw her arms about him and hugged him so tightly he squeaked.

"I love you," she whispered, then she turned and pulled her horse along behind her.

She left the keep as nonchalantly as she could, unwilling to draw attention to herself. Not a soul called out to her. Not a soul sought to stop her.

She had, at best, the whole of the night to travel.

Nicholas would think she was praying in her chamber. Anne wouldn't trouble her for the same reason. Robin seemed to avoid her except when he met her in the lists and he wouldn't be expecting her until sunrise, so she was certainly safe there.

And Montgomery, hopefully, would be as silent as the tomb.

She rode quickly, without pausing, until sunrise. Even then, she only paused to water her horse, then continue on. She had no choice. They would know now that she was no longer in her chamber. They would never suspect her destination, so perhaps she had more time than she thought.

But there was no point in taking a chance.

So she rode as hard as she dared, making better time than she had dared hope. Two days only had passed before she saw it in the distance.

Seakirk Abbey.

The first rays of the sun were coming over the hill and alighting upon the bell tower. Surely that was an auspicious sign.

Surely.

It was her only hope.

Chapter 25

Jake dragged his sleeve across his sweaty face and had a moment of déjà vu so intense that he swayed. It was hard to believe he wasn't standing in Artane's lists, facing Artane's heir, and getting the crap kicked out of him. He blinked and looked at his current swordmaster who stood there in biker shorts, an NBA tank-top, and high-tops. Kendrick, not Robin.

Though when it came to the matter of swordplay, Jake really couldn't tell the difference.

But at least this time he was in sweats and high-tops, not patched tights and boots that almost fit. He wiped more sweat off his face and smiled grimly at Kendrick.

"When did you first pick up a sword?"

"I was three," Kendrick said. "I might have been two. For all I know, I was an infant when I first held one. Honestly, I don't remember a time where I wasn't with one to hand." He smiled. "I have a few years practice on you and, as I said before, I am my father's son."

"No kidding," Jake said, with feeling.

"You'll make it," Kendrick said. "Sword skill is a good thing to have. It doesn't matter the century; the ability to kill a man with a single thrust is always in fashion."

Jake snorted, dragged his sleeve across his face a final time, then lifted his sword. "Okay, I'm ready. Let's keep going."

"With pleasure," Kendrick said. "Now, as I was saying before, you want to keep the sharp end pointed away from you toward your enemy. This is very important."

"Shut up," Jake said, taking up a fighting stance. And it occurred to him as he sparred with Amanda's to-be-born nephew, that he was becoming used to the work. Admittedly, he'd been sore and quite weak initially, but after several days of good rest and exercise, he was almost completely back to himself.

That same had given him, along with a chance to recuperate, answers to several important questions.

Was he dead? Legally, yes.

Were the accounts his father knew of closed? Yes, quite.

Was his business in probate? Yes, with his father's lawyers frantically trying to find a way to change Jake's will so Penelope would get nothing and Jackson III everything.

And Jake's trust fund? In Jackson III's back pocket.

Had his father been behind his incarceration? Absolutely.

Were III's goons still looking for him? Furiously.

Jake knew this personally because they'd been at Seakirk the afternoon before. Kendrick had allowed the men in the gates and gone so far as to meet them at the door and invite them in. Kendrick had also allowed several of his own lads into the great hall for a little display of paranormal action that had left even III's hardened punks shaking. Kendrick had ignored any and all activity going on around him, apparently giving the men the impression that they were out of their minds.

They had left, unsatisfied and undone.

Jake knew that his window for action was approaching and wouldn't be open long. He would have to have everything perfectly planned and execute it with like perfection or he was, as one of Kendrick's eldest sons continually said, "Toast, dude."

Gideon's brother-in-law was set to arrive at Seakirk that afternoon with a briefcase full of legal maneuvers that would make even the most hardened businessman feel the specter of jail-time looming over him. Alexander Smith was apparently not one you wanted to face over any kind of conference table. Jake was very grateful to have the man on his side.

And speaking of sides, Jake had to jump sideways to avoid having his ribs tickled by Kendrick's blade.

"Nice," Kendrick said approvingly. "But real knights don't jump; they anticipate."

"I was distracted."

" 'Distraction means death,' " Kendrick quoted. He smiled. "My father."

"That sounds like your father."

Kendrick rested his sword on his shoulder and looked at Jake thoughtfully. "What was he like? As a young man?"

"Quite a bit like you, actually," Jake said honestly. "He was very funny, though I don't suppose he meant to be. Impossibly earnest. Very confident."

"Arrogant," Kendrick corrected.

Jake shook his head. "Very cognizant of his abilities. And considering his abilities, I think he was actually quite modest. He couldn't help being the best in England."

Kendrick laughed. "He indoctrinated you well, I see."

"I suppose," Jake agreed with a smile. He paused and smiled again. "I left him with a lot to think about, but he didn't blink. He was, for the short time I knew him, a good friend. He was very generous with his time, very protective of his younger siblings, and very much in love with your mother." Jake smiled at Kendrick. "If I could have chosen a brother, I would have chosen Robin de Piaget. He was a good man. Still is, depending on your perspective." He shivered. "Time is a strange thing."

"It is," Kendrick agreed. He paused. "Thank you for that. 'Tis not necessary to know, but welcome just the same."

"My pleasure," Jake said, then he jumped as Sir Stephen materialized nearby. Damn it, would he ever get used to it? Probably not, which was why he was better at time-traveling than living with ghosts.

He shook his head at the improbability of either.

"What is it, my friend?" Kendrick asked.

"The lawyer is approaching," Sir Stephen said. "Shall he enter?"

"Aye," Kendrick said, resheathing his sword. "Come, Jake. We'll await him inside."

Jake followed Kendrick into the house, laid his sword on the high table, and gratefully had a drink of cold, clear water. He supposed that might be something he would miss at some point. Medieval castle water wasn't bad, but it couldn't have been all that great or they wouldn't have made so much of it into ale or wine. He finished his glass and poured more. Nice, but not necessary.

Well worth the trade.

The door opened a short time later and a tall, well-built, dark-haired man walked in, dressed in jeans and a polo shirt. The only concession to lawyerishness was the briefcase he carried. Worthington led him to the high table.

"Alexander, Earl of Falconberg," he intoned.

Jake blinked. "I thought your name was Alex Smith."

Alex held out his hand to Jake. "Falconberg's my alter ego," he said. "Call me Alex. You're Jake, I assume."

"I am."

Alex turned to Kendrick. "My lord," he said with a deferential nod. "I feel quite privileged to be inside Seakirk's gates."

"One of the chosen few, my lord Alexander," Kendrick said with a smile. "Come and take your ease with us. Worthington, something strengthening?"

Jake sat and watched Kendrick and Alex get acquainted. Falconberg wasn't all that far south, he supposed, and he wondered why the two had never met before at some sort of nobility function.

Kendrick's boys ran over and around their father, finally obtaining enough of his attention that Kendrick excused himself briefly to give them a friendly wrestle. Jake was left with Alex at the high table.

"Gideon says you have an interesting story," Jake said, helping himself to more water. "And that you're related somehow?"

"His wife Megan is related to my sister Elizabeth's husband Jamie," Alex said with a smile, "through a rather convoluted family tree. We're a happy bunch in spite of it though." He pushed his briefcase back a little, had a drink, then turned to face Jake. "You seem to have yourself quite a legal tangle here to unravel."

"Are you good at tangles?"

"They're my specialty," Alex said. "We'll begin unraveling in a minute. First I want to know where you got such a nice sword." He nodded at Jake's blade, lying on the table.

"A woman made it for me."

"Not many women these days have a good eye for blades," Alex said conversationally. "She must be something."

Jake paused and wondered what he could say that wouldn't sound as if he'd lost his mind. He hadn't actually talked to Alex yet; they had conducted most of their business via fax and Thad's secure e-mail connections. He had given Alex all the details he could without giving him the most critical one of all, which was why he needed to get himself back into the land of the living so he could travel back in time.

To that woman who did indeed have a very good eye for a blade.

Well, there was no time like the present to lay all his cards out on the table.

Jake took a deep breath. "You know that my father had me declared legally dead, and when I showed up awhile later had me committed against my will."

"So I gathered from your e-mails. He sounds like a great guy."

"He's a real prince," Jake agreed. "But I probably should explain where I was during those weeks before he had his goons pick me up and medicate me."

"That might be useful," Alex agreed.

"You're not going to believe this," Jake said slowly, "and if I hadn't lived it, I wouldn't believe it either." He paused, but Alex only continued to look at him with that polite expression of mild interest. Well, there was no time like the present to just plunge right in. "I ran off the road and woke up in 1227."

Alex's expression didn't change. "I see."

Jake waited, but Alex said nothing more. "Thirteenth century England," Jake said slowly and distinctly.

"I heard you."

"Well?" Jake demanded. "Aren't you going to question my sanity?"

"Well," Alex said slowly, with a smile, "that *is* an awfully medieval looking sword over there."

"I went back in time," Jake said, trying again. "To medieval England."

"I understood the first time," Alex said.

"And you don't think I'm nuts?"

Alex smiled. "Where do you think I got my title?"

It took a moment or two to take in the full import of those words. Jake felt his jaw sliding south. He supposed he should have been used to the impossible by now, but apparently there was still room for surprise. "You're kidding," he managed.

"My sister is married to a medieval Scottish laird who no longer resides in medieval Scotland," Alex said with a deep smile. "I was wandering around on his land, foolishly ignoring his warnings that I might find myself in another century if I weren't careful. I took a wrong step and wound up back in the late twelfth century."

"You're kidding."

"I never kid about time travel," Alex said seriously.

"And your title?" Jake asked. No sense in not getting to the really pertinent part of the story as quickly as possible.

"It was a tournament prize of sorts," Alex said. "Along with my wife, as well."

"You fought in a tournament and won," Jake said, torn between amazement and dreadful hope.

"It's not as miraculous as it sounds," Alex said with a shrug. "I'd trained with my brother-in-law and could hold my own fairly well, even by medieval Scottish standards. I had to learn to joust, of course, and wearing mail was a royal pain in the butt. But it was doable." He looked at Jake. "I can't imagine you're just putting time in out in the lists for the fun of it."

Jake shook his head. "Not that it isn't fun, but I have a more serious purpose. There is a woman—"

"There always is," Alex said with a laugh. "The one who made you the sword?"

"The very same. And believe me, she's worth some agony in the lists." Jake paused. "I have a little problem, though."

"Let me guess," Alex said. "You fell in love with a titled woman and there's no way you can have her unless you have a title yourself."

"Well—"

"And to get a title you either need to impress the powers that be with your knightly prowess, or with a big bucket of gold sovereigns."

Jake pursed his lips. "That about sums it up."

"Been there, got lucky and didn't have to pony up any cash—which was a good thing because I didn't have any with me. Which is also a good thing because my wife's ancestral home is a money pit and I need it all now to make the repairs."

"Sounds expensive."

"It is." Alex sat back in his chair, holding onto his mug of tea. "Your father must have been greatly surprised to have you show back up."

"I'm sure he was. But he obviously had made preparations for the potential fly in the ointment."

"He has good lawyers."

Jake looked at him seriously. "How good?"

"Very good," Alex said. "Lucky for you, I'm better."

"Are you?"

"Absolutely."

"Good, because my father is the most unscrupulous, greedy man you'd ever want to meet."

"I know the type," Alex assured him, "and I've crushed more than my share of them."

Jake didn't doubt it, and he didn't doubt it because he knew. He'd done his homework as well. Once he'd gotten Alex's name from Gideon, he'd made a few phone calls and found that Alex had been, in his glory days before becoming a US ex-pat, a ferocious corporate attorney with a reputation for raiding that had earned him either unwavering loyalty or intense hatred.

Jake's kind of guy.

"Well, what do we do?" Jake asked. "Short of kidnapping him and holding him against his will—no, wait, that's what he did to me. Let's find something more original for him."

Alex grinned. "Oh, I have something in mind. There's a stockholder's meeting for his UK holdings here in our very own little London in two weeks. I say you make an unannounced visit. It's difficult to deny your existence in front of five hundred witnesses. I have a guy who can hack into his slide show and show off some pertinent documents. I always find visual aids to be so helpful in these sorts of situations."

"Some press coverage might be useful as well. Can you help with that?" Jake asked.

"Of course. I'm a full service attorney." Alex smiled modestly. "I can find a hungry investigative reporter or two. Of course, they'll still be hungry after the meeting and wonder why in the world you're liquidating all your assets to buy medieval coins, but maybe you can come up with a reason for that."

"I think I'm feeling the desire to rid myself of modern-day trappings and go be a recluse in Greenland. Or Antarctica."

"That works."

"Then tell me what to do," Jake said, setting his cup back on the table and leaning forward for business. "I need to get back to my life."

"Does she know?" Alex asked quietly.

"Amanda?" Jake shook his head. "Her brother does. She has another brother who thinks I'm a fairy, another who thinks I'm a spy, and another who just hates me for general reasons."

"Do you plan to tell her?"

"When I have a few things to show her that might get her to stop looking at me in that way she has that says 'whacko on the loose.'"

Alex laughed. "I understand that look." He paused. "You don't want to bring her back here?"

Jake shook his head. "She has family; I don't. Well, none I care to own. I couldn't ask her to leave that. Besides, I like medieval England. It's a good, simple life."

Alex nodded. "I have to agree. It has its dangers, just like any other century, but on the whole, it is a good place." He reached for his briefcase. "All right, here's the plan. I've got some things here for you to sign. I've had a friend of mine checking on your office. Apparently everything's been locked up and still untouched, so you may as well start making plans for what you're going to do there. As far as the rest of your assets go, I've drawn up documents that will get them legally transferred back to you. I can't say what's left of the trust fund. We can try to get that back from your father, but it could take time."

"I don't have time. I also don't have but a fraction of it left where Jackson III thinks it is." He smiled. "I love the Swiss, don't you?"

"I do, but you'll still need proof you aren't legally dead," Alex said. "Even Swiss banks are going to want that. Let's set that up, I'll introduce you to our favorite coin collector, and you can go from there. Don't access your accounts, though, until we've confronted your father."

"I won't," Jake said. "I've already faced his thugs once. I don't have time to come back for round two."

Alex handed him the papers, then looked at him. "So what will you do when you go back?"

"I'll probably do some of what I do now. I don't know why I can't design jewelry. I'm a good artist. Maybe I'll paint royalty for a living, or hunt gems in faraway places that no one knows about yet." He shrugged. "I'll keep myself busy."

"And you think you can get back?"

"I'm counting on that," Jake said. He looked up from the papers suddenly. "Where did you go back? Was there a specific place, or did you just stumble onto an odd-looking patch of grass?"

"There is, if you can believe this," Alex began with pursed lips, "a fairy ring near Falconberg. In fact, my brother-in-law Jamie could give you an entire list of places you might try. I seem to remember there is something definite near Artane. That must be how you returned."

Jake nodded. "I know the place. In fact, I don't think I'll ever forget it."

"Then you won't need Jamie's map," Alex said. "But if it doesn't work, let me know and I'll check out alternate routes."

Jake felt as if he were booking a flight and trying to decide the best way to avoid long layovers. He sincerely hoped he wouldn't be having any of those during a plague-ridden time in England. There were much worse things than cold stone toilet seats and no ice in medieval drinks.

Kendrick returned, rumpled and perspiring, to sit down on the other side of Alex. "Boys," he said, with feeling.

"We're having a boy," Alex said with a smile. "In October, actually."

"Your first?"

"Our first baby together," Alex said. "We have a pair of adopted children as well."

Kendrick wiped his brow. "I wish you good fortune, then. Lads are marvelous, but you'll find them to be as fine a workout as time spent in the lists."

Jake left Kendrick and Alex to the discussion of Scottish versus English training and how that might be compared to the raising of young boys, and concentrated on the papers in front of him. He signed them all, then he pushed them away, sat back, and contemplated his immediate future.

Well, his immediate future was taking too damn long. He'd already been away from Amanda for almost six weeks. He had to get back, and soon.

He would confront his father, get his business back, then get on with his life. He wished there were some way he could communicate with Amanda, if only to tell her to hang on another couple of weeks.

Surely she wouldn't give up on him.

*C*hapter 26

*M*ontgomery stood in his accustomed place before the fire, but there was no ease there for him today. There was too much chaos in his home, too many questions, too many loud, raised voices for there to be any peace for him.

Especially since he knew the one thing the rest of his family didn't, the one thing that would have saved them the grief they were going through.

Robin was pacing and cursing. Nicholas was sitting at the high table, alone, with a cup of strong ale in his hands. That cup had become almost a part of him over the past se'nnight. It was not like him to drink so much, but Montgomery couldn't blame him. Nicholas obviously thought 'twas his doing that Amanda had fled. Montgomery supposed there was some truth to that. If Nicholas had kept silent about his desires, perhaps Amanda wouldn't have flown.

Nay, that wasn't true either. She would have flown no matter what Nicholas had or hadn't said.

She thought Jake wasn't returning.

It had broken her heart.

Montgomery rocked back on his heels and considered the truth of the matter. Jake had not returned, 'twas true, but had that been his choice?

Montgomery had come to believe quite completely in the past several se'nnights that Jake was indeed a fairy, come to rescue Amanda from her scurrilous suitors. No doubt Jake had gone back to his homeland to gather his belongings, but not been allowed to return. Perhaps he pined in his captive state, wishing with all his heart he could return, bringing gold with him, to wed with the woman he loved.

Or so Montgomery told himself.

But what he couldn't tell Robin and the rest of his brothers was where Amanda was hiding. He'd made the vow, but vowed in his heart that if Jake returned, he would tell him where Amanda had gone, so Jake might rescue her and bring her home.

Not that Seakirk Abbey was all that far away. But it was far enough, and Montgomery missed his sister already.

But Jake had not returned, so Montgomery was left standing by the fire, trying to stay warm, trying to keep his vow of silence, and trying not to believe that the man his sister loved had decided she wasn't worth the effort of returning.

He wanted to believe that least of all.

Chapter 27

J ake stood at the door of his vault, slid Penelope's key into the computerized lock, and sighed in relief at the reassuring *click*. He looked into the dimly lit room. The walls were a very reassuring black, the carpet under his feet a plush, creamy white. He kicked off his shoes, leaving the security of his person to the dozen very large men he'd acquired through Thad and Alex, and walked into his sanctuary.

He wandered around the room, looking at the small, glass-fronted display niches where he kept his more unusual pieces, just for the pleasure of seeing them, not for any more pedestrian reason. He paused before each one, remembering the path of creation he'd taken, what had inspired him, why he'd chosen not to sell them.

And then he stood in the middle of his vault, looked around yet again, and wondered if it was worth giving it up.

Amanda.

Her name whispered across his soul, along with a sense of urgency. He'd been home close to two months already. Two months for her to wonder if he was returning. Two months for that bloody Nicholas de Piaget to convince her he was a better choice than a no-name merchant who couldn't even heft a sword.

He blew out his breath. Unfortunately, things just took time, especially when you wanted the wheels of justice to turn in your favor. He'd tried to use the time well, spending every waking hour in the lists at Seakirk, either honing his skills with Kendrick, or the former captain of Kendrick's guard, Royce. That had passed the time usefully, at least. Maybe he would never be Robin's equal; at least he might last a little longer against him than before.

Of course, that wasn't the only thing of note lately. He'd had his confrontation with his father, yesterday as a matter of fact, and found it to be enormously satisfying.

He'd walked into a room packed with shareholders and made it almost to the podium before his father had looked up from his notes and noticed him.

Jackson III looked as if he'd seen a ghost.

Why, Jake wasn't sure. After all, III had to have known Jake had escaped the asylum. Where had his father thought he'd gotten himself to? The local pub in his altogether for a week or two of abuse?

He hadn't asked his father that, of course. He'd asked his father a few other, pertinent questions while idly watching a very interesting slide show up on the big screen. When Jackson III had turned to see what Jake found so fascinating, he'd swayed.

Jake was certain that had been a first.

Medical records, e-mails instructing a north country loony bin to keep Jake sedated no matter the destruction to life or limb, photos of a grieving father juxtaposed with an alarmingly fast takeover and emptying of accounts, Jake's assistant illegally detained under the auspices of state home heath visits by non-state employees. The visual aids had been numerous and riveting.

The photographers who had quietly followed Jake into the ballroom along with the bobbies had been in a feeding frenzy, capturing III at his most unflattering.

Amazingly enough, III had been more than willing to talk turkey.

And so they had, in a very plush boardroom in the hotel where III had obviously planned to come back and relax after his exertions before the stockholders. Jake had eaten heartily of a rather fine catered lunch, invited his quite gray-looking father to do the same, then settled for a few signatures, a few more photographs, and a few stern words of filial rebuke.

And so ended one father-son relationship.

Jake pulled himself back to the present with a sigh. He stretched, then walked across the room to get what he had come for. He pulled out several quite fine aquamarines and put them in his pocket. And then he opened the glass case above the drawers and took out the ring he'd been thinking of from the moment he had seen Amanda.

It was a simple thing. Baguette diamonds and aquamarines embedded in a band of platinum. It wouldn't get in her way when she went about her daily tasks. He looked at the size and hoped it fit because there was little hope of adjusting it once he was back in the past. He put it into his pocket, then continued his circuit of the room, pulling out of drawers things that pleased him, or that he thought might be useful in the future.

Or the past, as it were.

He also selected a handful of finished pieces, ones for whom he had a particular person in mind.

Then he chose some raw rocks. They could be finished to medieval standards, or just left as is and traded for what he would need. He put those in a large pouch he'd brought for just such a purpose, then walked to the door. He paused, then took a final look around at his life's work.

Penelope's work now. He pulled the door shut behind him and turned to look at his assistant sitting uncomfortably in his chair. He handed her the key.

"Yours," he said with a smile.

She shook her head. "You can't mean it—"

"I do."

"But, Jake, you can't leave. Not after all you've built up. To go to *Greenland!* What in the hell are you going to do in *Greenland?*"

"Fish," he said. "Freeze."

She looked at him, tears standing in her normally quite dry eyes. "You've got a terminal illness, don't you? You're just doing this so I don't know."

"Caught," he lied easily, wondering why he hadn't thought of that. "Just take the business, Penelope. I ransacked the vault anyway, so you'll find your windfall to be perhaps less than you might think."

"But—"

"You know how to run the business. You'll know how to keep it running. Or sell it and do what you want. I don't care."

"I don't design as well as you do," she said in a quavering voice.

"Rubbish," he said. "You're every bit as good as I am; you just love different things. You have plenty of gems in there to use in very nice pieces. Keep the name if you like, and transition the clients over gently. You know my style. Introduce yours slowly, and over time people will forget what was and concentrate on what is."

She looked at him for several minutes in silence. "Don't you want someone to be with you?" she asked softly. "You know. When you go?"

"I have friends," Jake said. "They'll be there."

"And you're going now?"

"In a few days."

"You won't call . . . when the end . . ."

Jake shook his head. "This is good-bye, Pen. You've been a fabulous assistant and a good friend—"

She jumped up out of the chair and threw her arms around him in an impulsive gesture he certainly hadn't expected. She kissed him quickly, then ran from the room. Jake looked at Kendrick, who was masquerading as one of the dozen bodyguards. Kendrick grinned and shrugged. Jake sighed.

"All right, guys. One more stop, then you can be on your ways."

He ran his fingers along his desk one more time, looked around his office, then followed his strongmen from the room and shut the door behind him for the last time.

He took the train north with Kendrick, watching the countryside speed by at a dizzying rate. Kendrick allowed him the peace for his own thoughts, which he greatly appreciated. He considered the jewels in his pocket and more in his duffle bag; he considered the enormous sum of money which was ready to be deposited into a discreetly numbered Swiss bank account in return for hundreds of coins of a medieval vintage; he stared out the window and considered the fact that he would never again travel at this rate of speed from London to the Scottish border.

Speed was overrated.

So were a great number of modern inventions.

Though he supposed he might truly miss a soldering iron and his nice, very expensive pinpoint torch. He seriously doubted an open fire, hammer, and anvil would yield the kind of creations he'd managed in the past.

Well, perhaps he would invent new ways of working with gems and metals. There was something to be said for progress.

All of which was merely windowdressing, given the nature of the true gem he was hoping for.

"I hope she waited," Jake murmured.

"Mandy's impetuous," Kendrick noted. "I have to admit that nothing she ever did surprised me, once I understood her character."

Jake looked at Kendrick sitting across from him, a medieval knight who looked perfectly at home in jeans and a T-shirt. No sword at his side, but even so, he gave off a definite don't-mess-with-me aura.

"Do I make it?" Jake asked.

"Don't ask me that," Kendrick said, looking out the window. "Go on with your plans, as planned. Just don't ask me about the outcome."

"There's a name for a man like you," Jake said easily.

Kendrick looked at him with dusty green eyes. "What if I told you she wed with a man named Rolfe who sired ten children on her, beat her regularly, and made her life hell until the day she died in childbirth with babe number eleven? What would you do then?"

"Change history," Jake said.

"Then what does it matter what I tell you?"

Jake sighed. "It doesn't. I would go anyway and damn the consequences."

"I thought you would."

Jake laughed in spite of himself. He'd gotten what he

deserved, he supposed, for going back on his own decision to forge ahead without any details.

"Besides, you don't really want to ruin the suspense, do you?" Kendrick asked with twinkling eyes. "Where's the sport in that? Real men don't read the last five pages of a book first."

"Your wife does."

"She's not a man, she's a tender-hearted angel," Kendrick said with a smile. "Suspense kills her. You've more spine than that, haven't you?"

"If I make it, I suppose I'll remind you that I do in a million little ways, making your young life hell in payment. How does that grab you?"

Kendrick leaned forward. "Real knights don't flinch."

"I'll remember that."

"I imagine you will."

Jake laughed and settled back to watch the scenery, allowing his mind to go pleasantly blank. He supposed he might even have napped here and there. He supposed it might be the very last time he napped in a train, so perhaps it wasn't all bad.

Assuming he made it.

Assuming he wasn't going to have to spend the next five years alternately begging Penelope to give him back his business and trying to dump half a million dollars in medieval gold coins.

Heaven help him.

G*enevieve* was waiting for them at the station with the kids. Kendrick hopped in the car with her, and Jake piled several of his bodyguards in a rental, with another rental following. He would let the men go when he was sure the coast was clear— probably about three nanoseconds before he popped himself back into the past.

They drove to Artane with Kendrick in the lead. Jake was amused to find Genevieve driving, for a change. Apparently she wasn't all that confident in Kendrick's reaction to seeing the family seat after all these years.

Jake could hardly wait to see Kendrick's reaction when he laid his eyes on Gideon.

They wound their way down from the A1, through the village, and into Artane's carpark. Jake hung back as Kendrick walked up to the front gates with Genevieve at his side and his children scampering around him like puppies.

"You can't park here after six," a crusty old man said, coming out from the gatehouse. "His Lordship won't have it, I tell you. Besides, we're closed."

"I'll make sure we move the cars later," Jake said dryly.

The man folded his arms over his chest. "You need tickets."

"You said you were closed."

The old man looked at Kendrick and his family, looked at Jake, looked at the bodyguards, then scowled and scuttled back through the gates and on up to the castle. So much for being unannounced. Jake caught up with Kendrick and Genevieve as they walked underneath the barbican. Kendrick stopped once they were inside the outer walls and simply stared at the castle.

"Real knights don't flinch," Jake murmured.

"Damn you," Kendrick growled. Then he took a deep breath, looked at Jake, and smiled ruefully. "I daresay I deserved that."

"I daresay you did."

Kendrick looked at the path leading up to the inner bailey gates, then sighed and put his shoulders back. "I assume they're expecting us?"

"Well, they're expecting me," Jake said easily. "I just said I was bringing some friends. You're supposed to have your explanation ready. What, do I have to think of everything?"

"There are lists here as well as at Seakirk," Kendrick said pointedly. "I could demand a meeting with you there at dawn."

"I'll be there. But now, if I were you, I'd be thinking of a good cover story. Or you could just try the truth. Then again, maybe we should take a measure of Lord Edward's constitution first. If he looks like a pantywaist, we'll just lie."

Genevieve laughed. "Jake, you aren't making this any easier for him."

"I owe him several moments of discomfort." He put a hand briefly on Kendrick's shoulder. "Actually, Gideon's meeting us at the door and he's already talked to his dad. Apparently they have all kinds of spooky things going on here at Artane."

He smiled pleasantly. "They're not in the Top Ten, but then again, that's just the printed list. Maybe they're Number Eleven."

"If not, I could make that happen for them," Kendrick said grimly. "I know a few shades who wouldn't mind dividing their time between Seakirk and somewhere new."

Jake smiled and continued on up the way with Kendrick. It hit him, suddenly, that he was almost in Kendrick's shoes. Here he was, walking up the same path he'd walked up in borrowed medieval boots, but now he was wearing his own pair of modern, rubber-soled shoes. His jeans and sweatshirt were a far cry from tights and tunic. He paused under the inner bailey's barbican gate and looked out into the lists. They had a different look from their medieval counterpart, but take away the grass, the extra stone buildings, and that little red Mini over there in the corner, and things were about the same.

Only he knew that the family he wanted to become a part of was not inside.

He sighed and walked with Kendrick and Genevieve up to the keep. Jake climbed the steps, then waited for Kendrick to knock. After all, Kendrick had been born here, lived out the majority of his youth here. It was right that he get them inside.

"I feel as though this is no longer my home," Kendrick mused. "After all these years." He looked at Jake. "'Tis passing odd."

"Maybe they'll give you visitation rights," Jake said.

The door opened suddenly and Gideon stood there, all smiles. Until he looked at Kendrick, that was, and then his mouth hung open.

Jake understood.

"Gideon de Piaget, meet Kendrick, earl of Seakirk," Jake said. "Kendrick, meet your nephew Gideon. Several generations removed, of course."

Kendrick and Gideon stared at each other, apparently unable to do anything else but gape. Jake looked at Genevieve and smiled.

"Could be twins, couldn't they?"

"Except for the hair color, yes, they could," she agreed with an answering smile. "Spooky."

"Very." Jake looked at Gideon. "Well, aren't you going to invite us in?"

"Come in," Gideon said, stepping back, stilling wearing that look of complete astonishment.

"It's Fate," Jake said pointedly. "You know, that thing you told me about?"

"Well," Gideon said finally. "Well, I see."

Kendrick finally held out his hand. "Well met, nephew."

Gideon looked at his hand, then reached out and pulled Kendrick into a manly embrace complete with much back slapping and pounding. And then just as suddenly, he stepped back. He smiled.

"I'm sorry you haven't come sooner."

"I am too," Kendrick said. He hesitated. "Does your father know?"

"Told him last eve during his Schnapps," Gideon said with a grin. "He spewed it all over his very expensive antique carpet upstairs. I'll show you the stain."

Kendrick grinned as well and Jake shivered. He wondered, absently, if that happened often down family lines, where an ancestor and a descendant were so closely matched in face and temperament. It would have made a fascinating book.

Too bad he had other things to do than write it.

He shook hands briefly with Gideon, then hung back and let Gideon lead Kendrick into Artane's great hall. Jake trailed along behind, shepherding children when necessary, and just absorbing the sight of a modern Artane when not. He made nice with Gideon's father, accepted compliments from Gideon's mother about his jewelry, and sat at a very, very weathered high table and enjoyed afternoon tea.

The same table he'd sat at with Amanda of Artane eight hundred years earlier.

He found that it was almost impossible not to think about her constantly while he sat nibbling on cookies and sipping tea. Was she sitting exactly where he was, only centuries in the past? Was she thinking about him? Had she given up?

Please don't give up, he pleaded silently. *Just a few more days. Give me a few more days.*

"A tour," Edward of Artane announced grandly. "So you

will see that Artane has not . . . er . . . changed all that much."
He paused. "Over the years. Quite."

Jake hid his smile behind his hand. Edward had bold words,
but his hand trembled as he waved expansively, and who could
blame him? It wasn't every day that the grandson of Rhys de Piaget came to pass judgment on how generations of de Piagets
had taken care of the old pile of stones.

Jake went on the tour gladly, walking over places he'd been
before, reliving memories, wanting desperately to be back in
time walking those passageways with someone, no offense,
besides Kendrick.

"The dungeon," Edward said, pointing behind the kitchens.
"We have it walled up, of course, for security reasons, but I
understand that in the past, it was quite an uncomfortable
place."

He shot Kendrick a sideways look.

Kendrick shrugged. "I never spent the night there. Ask Jake.
I imagine Amanda tossed him in there first thing, didn't she?"

Jake snorted. "I told you as much." He looked at Edward.
"Thank you for boarding it up, my lord. It's not a nice place
at all."

"The dungeons are closed, but the cellar is open," Edward
said. "We use it as storage now, but I understand in the past—"
and here he shot Kendrick another look, "it was used for a
great many things."

Kendrick only smiled politely.

Edward looked at Jake. "We've vats of all sorts of history
in there, but perhaps you'd care to look upstairs where the
finer pieces are kept. We've housed them all behind glass, of
course, to keep the odd, sticky-fingered tourist from pinching
our history, but you're more than welcome to peruse things as
long as you wish."

"Father, why don't we let them get settled," Gideon offered. "Perhaps the rest of the tour might wait until tomorrow.
The children might like to go play outside for a bit before supper is ready."

Edward looked somewhat relieved, but not so relieved that
he didn't offer Genevieve his arm quite gallantly to escort her
back up the stairs. Kendrick trudged alongside Jake across the
kitchen.

"Well?" Jake asked quietly.

Kendrick only shook his head. " 'Tis strange, my friend, to be walking in my own home again so long after I'd last seen it."

"How does it look?"

If Jake hadn't known better, he might have seen a bit of moisture there in Kendrick's eye.

" 'Tis in tolerable shape," Kendrick said with a smile. "Tolerable shape indeed. My grandfather would have been pleased." He looked at Jake. "Have you met Rhys?"

"Not yet."

"You would like him. He was a very fair man."

"I certainly hope so," Jake said, with feeling. He followed Kendrick up the stairs, and accepted a room on the second floor.

The twins' room.

He had to go in and sit down before he fell down.

He had to get back. Soon. All these déjà vus were killing him. He put his face in his hands and closed his eyes. Tomorrow was his meeting with the coin guy. He already had his clothes. All he had left to do was pack and then make the attempt.

He wouldn't fail.

He couldn't.

A soft knock at the door had him heaving himself back to his feet. He walked over to the door and opened it to find Genevieve de Piaget standing there with a baby in one arm and a small suitcase in her other hand. He smiled at her.

"How's Kendrick doing?"

"He's already investigating nooks and crannies without His Lordship's knowledge. If we manage to get a decent meal in this place before we're kicked out, it will be a miracle."

Jake laughed. "I'm not sure Lord Edward can accuse Kendrick of breaking and entering, or stealing, for that matter. It might be Kendrick's stuff to begin with."

"I doubt that," Genevieve said. "He couldn't leave Seakirk, but he certainly had people who could. The one who painted that picture of his family over his desk, Jonathan, was one. I think he made more than one trip to Artane to retrieve Kendrick's things."

Jake looked at her thoughtfully. "How has it been?" he asked.

"Being married to a man for whom modern English is a second language?"

"Something like that."

Genevieve smiled. "Well, I've learned Norman French, if that answers your question." She shook her head with another smile. "It's been a dream from beginning to now. I don't regret it for a minute. Kendrick is a wonderful father, a fabulous husband, and a formidable warrior. I'm just happy he was kept on ice for me for eight hundred years."

"I'm certain you were worth the wait. I hope Amanda will feel the same way about me."

Genevieve nodded encouragingly. "I'm sure she will. I hope you'll find your return trip an easy one." She held out the suitcase. "Here, these are for you. Things to make your trip a little easier still. I've got to run. Baby has had a long day and so has her mother."

"Do you need help with your boys?"

She shook her head. "Gideon's wife Megan is here and she and Gideon have taken the lads on a treasure hunt."

"Like father, like sons."

Genevieve laughed. "At least the lads' hunt is a sponsored one, though I sincerely doubt they'll turn up anything nearly as interesting as Kendrick will." The baby began to fuss and she shifted her in her arms. "Gotta go. See you at dinner."

Jake nodded, then shut the door. He took the suitcase over to a chair and opened it. Inside were several articles of medieval clothing, a new pair of boots made in a very medieval-looking fashion, and a very rustic-looking rucksack to carry them in. And in the bottom of the suitcase was a little box of Godiva chocolates with a note:

For Amanda, because you can never go wrong with a box of wooing chocolate. That is assuming you make it, of course . . .

K.

Jake smiled, then packed up the gear. He would wear back the clothes he'd come forward in, and save these for a nicer occasion. Perhaps his marriage.

A man could dream.

He stashed his jewels under the bed, then with a final look at the modern incarnation of the room he'd spent so much time in, left it and went in search of supper.

*C*hapter 28

A*manda* knelt over a bench and flinched at the crack of the birch rod across her back. She squeezed her eyes tightly, but the tears rolled out from under her eyelids just the same. She wouldn't cry out. She knew that her silence infuriated the abbess no end, and she supposed that if she'd possessed the wit the good Lord had given a hedgehog, she would have wept immediately and saved herself the agony.

"Damn you, gel," the abbess said, after a particularly heavy blow, "spew out your penitence! I grow weary of this."

Amanda clamped her lips shut, but the force of the next blow wrenched a goodly bit of breath from her just the same. By the saints, if she could have, she would have risen, taken that stick away from the abbess, and clouted her a mighty blow in return.

Unfortunately she was otherwise unable to rise. And to be honest, she was beginning to doubt her ability to outlast the woman with the rod, who seemed determined to beat a confession of any kind from her.

The next blow convinced her that perhaps a confession might be in her best interest.

"Forgive me, Mother," Amanda said, through gritted teeth. "I have many vices to rid myself of."

The abbess snorted and tossed the rod across the chamber. "Finally! Too many for my poor arm, I daresay. I'll find someone else to aid you in your repentance."

Amanda dropped her head in relief when the woman left the chamber. She had no idea who would come next, but perhaps no one would have the time or desire to help her see the error of her ways. She rested uncomfortably against the bench and wondered just when her plans had gone awry.

Likely at the moment when she had ridden out Artane's massive gates.

Of course, she should have known something was amiss when she had presented herself to the abbess. The woman had recognized her immediately, which had surprised Amanda greatly. Next from her mouth had come not the words "How lovely that you feel a calling to prayer," but "How much do you bring in gold and property?"

Amanda supposed that such was a question a woman in charge of such a large abbey must ask, but it had been the way she'd asked it, as if she were a merchant weighing a bag of gold and already counting in her head how she might spend it, that had been so unsettling.

Merchants.

Damn them all, was she to be tormented by their ilk forever?

She had subsequently been deprived of her clothing and given something resembling a grain sack to wear. That wouldn't have troubled her, having spent the greater part of her life in her brothers' less-than-comfortable clothing, but this chafed abominably and had already rubbed her shoulders raw with its rough seams. She half wondered if the sisters didn't sew thistle thorns into them just to test the commitment of the postulates.

Fasting had been the next order of business. Indeed, she couldn't remember the last time she'd been given anything to eat, but she thought it might have been yesternmorn, and she was almost positive it had consisted of gruel that no one else had been willing to feed even to the hogs.

In short, she was beginning to suspect she had made a terrible mistake.

Even a life with Ledenham could not possibly be this bad.

Her wrists were untied from the legs of the whipping stool and she was hauled ungently to her feet. She swayed. She would have swayed more, but a bracing slap brought her back to her senses.

"Time in the kitchens will serve you better than another beating," a dour-faced nun said curtly. "Best be about your work whilst you have the strength." She looked at Amanda critically. "And put your hair back. Don't know why you didn't have it cut off when you arrived. Special treatment, I daresay."

Amanda tried to braid her hair, but found her arms simply would not go above her shoulders without pain so intense she gasped. A look from Sister Eunice, though, convinced her that pain was the least of her worries at present, so she did her best.

The kitchens. What a boon. Perhaps she would be able to filch something whilst she was there.

She would have shaken her head in disbelief, but that was too painful, so she settled for a silent snort of incredulity at her own stupidity. She had envisioned a life of quiet contemplation, of peace and security. What she had gotten was a place full of more intrigue than court.

Worse yet, she wasn't sure she could escape.

Or that she should even try. She sighed deeply. For once in her life, perhaps she should have more of a purpose than designing escapes from the conditions life placed upon her. This had been her choice. Was she so weak-kneed that she would shrink from the difficult?

Her father would have been ashamed of her.

She put her shoulders back—carefully—and marched on doggedly behind Sister Eunice. She had put her foot to this path; she would continue on and see it to the end.

And after she had repented to Abbess Joan's satisfaction and taken her vows, then her father could be informed and send her dowry to the church. He would have little choice, to her mind. Her commitment would be irrevocable and to refuse to honor her commitment would be unthinkable.

At least she hoped he would find it unthinkable.

She suspected that her lands and gold might be the only thing that would buy her any peace at all from the abbess.

They might as well buy something useful.

*H*er days flowed one into another until she quite lost track of how long she'd been away from home. It could have been a week, it could have been two. It could have been an eternity. She slept on a dirt floor without a blanket; she ate the dregs of whatever was on the fire—if she was allowed to eat; she worked in the garden, in the pigsty, in the stable until her hands were cracked and bleeding and her bare feet were in like condition.

She prayed quite a bit, but never, as Fate would have it, in the comfort of the chapel.

Today, her task was to serve as a carrier of foodstuffs to various places in the abbey. Amanda suspected that the reason for that was that the ground was growing increasingly cold, her feet were growing increasingly bloody, and the abbess was tiring of beating her to make her obedient.

In truth, Amanda was growing tired of the latter as well.

She limped along the stone pathways, carrying something that smelled so good, it was all she could do not to rip off the lid and eat it without pausing for breath. But she knew where that would lead, so she concentrated on her feet and not the food, and kept on her way to the abbess's cell—which was more of a luxurious solar than a cell, but who was she to judge?

She paused at the doorway, only because the door was ajar and she wasn't sure what she was going to knock with, given that her hands were full of a wooden tray laden with the afore-mentioned delicacies.

"Write this for me," the abbess commanded in a clear voice. "I don't want to sully my hands with it."

"As you will," said Sister Eunice, she of the birch rod that had a decided lack of patience.

Amanda stood at the doorway, wondering how an interruption would affect her immediate future, when she heard the most astonishing thing.

"To Ledenham," Abbess Joan began, "from me. Fill in that bit. You know how I want it to sound."

Amanda clutched the wooden tray. Ledenham? Somehow, she suspected this could not be good.

"I have the woman you want and she is being properly instructed in meekness and respect. I have not alerted those at Artane simply because I was certain that you, my good Ledenham, would wish to have the pleasure of informing Artane that you were the one to hunt down and capture—nay, that isn't the proper word. What word would you choose, Eunice?"

"Retrieve?" Eunice suggested. "Slay? Corner?"

"Oh, by the saints," Abbess Joan said in disgust, "you've little wit for this sort of business. Write 'capture' and be done with it. Say that I thought Ledenham would wish to be the one to say to Artane that he had found his miserable daughter—nay, do not write that, you twit—and 'twas for that reason that I have not informed Artane that the wench is here." She sighed so loudly, Amanda winced. "Tell him to come fetch her. Soon. Or if he thinks she needs a bit more instruction, I will be happy to provide it. And indeed, she could do with several more doses of humility. Why it falls to me to do it, I cannot fathom, but my work is never finished, it seems."

The sound of a chair scraping against the stone startled Amanda so badly that she almost dropped her tray. She hastened back the way she had come, then turned and groaned loudly as she made her way along the path.

The saints preserve her if the abbess thought she'd been eavesdropping.

And the saints preserve her from what she'd heard.

She shouldn't have been surprised. So, she was to be sold to Ledenham just the same. She could have at least been having a few last days of comfort and security at Artane. Her life there was looking far less intolerable than it had looked but a fortnight ago.

She tapped softly. "My lady?" she said. Meekly.

The door was pulled open and Sister Eunice stood there, scowling. "Took you long enough."

"My apologies, my lady," Amanda said, bowing her head humbly. "I will endeavor to make greater haste the next time."

The abbess grunted. "Set a guard over her. Well, beat her first, then set a guard over her. By the saints, I loathe these pampered lords' daughters. 'Tis such an effort to teach them what they must know to become proper nuns."

Amanda almost snorted. Indeed, 'twas only with great effort that she managed to keep her head down and her face impassive. Why, that great lying sow! She had no intentions of Amanda becoming a nun. Amanda wondered how she would escape, and if she managed it, how she would manage to walk all the way back to Artane.

'Twas a certainty the abbess wouldn't give her back her horse.

Eunice cuffed her so hard, her ears rang and she almost dropped her tray. "Clumsy gel," she said.

Amanda managed to set the tray down and escape the cell before she heard, or felt, anything else. But she had the feeling her evening would finish as it always did, with her enduring more instruction in the meek arts. One thing she could say for Eunice, though, was that she didn't have the patience for it. A blow or two and the woman was ready to be off to bed.

Amanda looked at the sky as she walked back to the kitchens. She didn't even have the strength to weep. She was a fool; she had put herself in this horrible place and she had no one to blame for it but herself.

She wondered if, by some miracle, Jake had returned to Artane.

Did he love her still?

Would he be able to pry the truth from Montgomery?

She didn't hold out much hope for either.

So she trudged back to the kitchen and prayed for a bit of privacy, if only enough to scrape the bottom of the stew pot and ease the gnawing in her belly before Sister Eunice sent for her to further her lessons in meekness.

She hadn't reached the kitchens before there were men flanking her, grim-faced men who did not touch her, did not speak to her, but walked so close to her that she knew beyond all doubt that escape was no longer a possibility.

By the saints, what had she done?

She had no answer, so she continued on her way.

And she prayed for a miracle.

Chapter 29

J ake looked over his gear set out on the bed and made certain he had everything he needed. There were the eight bags of gold, which damn well better be enough to buy him an enormous castle, a big fat title to go with it, and one quite lovely and irreplaceable Amanda of Artane.

He didn't want to consider the alternative: rich, titled, and still single in 1227.

He checked his mental list of gems, placed in several sacks and scattered throughout his clothes. He decided he would slip things in various locations on his person so if he did get robbed, at least the thugs might miss something.

He also had a few art supplies. He'd thought to perhaps take more things, something to prove his birth date, but decided against it. He wasn't sure about the state of witch-burning in the thirteenth century, but he had no desire to become familiar with it firsthand.

He dressed himself in his old medieval gear, then packed up the rest of his things. He put on his worn boots, strapped his sword belt around his waist, and looked around to see if he had left anything behind. His bed was made and a small box sat there prominently. It was for Kendrick. He was almost positive Kendrick would enjoy it.

He shouldered his pack and headed downstairs. Lord Edward was there at the table, having his kippers and cold toast. Jake accepted the invitation to join him. Lord Edward looked at Jake over the rim of his teacup.

"So, you're off this morning?" he asked politely.

"One could hope," Jake said with a smile.

Lord Edward shook his head, as if he just couldn't quite believe something.

Probably the events of his life during the past week, Jake surmised.

"I wish you good fortune," Edward said, setting down his cup. "Is there anything I can do for you?"

"You've already done a great deal," Jake said. "You were kind enough to allow me to paw through many of your treasures. That was an unexpected pleasure."

"It was the very least I could do," Edward said. "My wife so loves your jewelry and it was enormously kind of you to bring her something new as a parting gift."

"My pleasure," Jake said sincerely. And it was. Helen, the current Lady of Artane, had gushed so much the night before that Jake had been tempted to blush. Ah, that all his customers could have been so satisfied.

He looked up from his breakfast to find Gideon coming to the table with his wife Megan at his side. Jake sat back and listened to them sit and chat with Gideon's father. They seemed surreal, somehow, Gideon and his family, as if he were observing them in the right place but definitely the wrong time.

Gideon turned to him. "Your bodyguards are waiting for you at the gates whenever you're ready."

"Thank you," Jake said. "I don't think I'll need them much longer. I've left cash for them. You'll pay them once I'm safely away?"

"Certainly," Gideon said. He smiled ruefully. "You know, I feel terribly responsible for all this somehow."

"I'll be thinking kindly of you for eternity," Jake said with a laugh.

"Yes, but the primitive conditions," Gideon protested. "No mobile phones, no computers, no ability to do business all over the world from the ease and comfort of your office." He shivered. "I don't think I could do it."

"I would say that technology is overrated, but that might be too much for you," Jake said. "I admit I will miss some of the tools of my trade and the ease of getting supplies. But the trade off is worth it."

"She must be spectacular."

"She is. In every respect."

Gideon paused. "And your family here?"

"They'll survive," Jake said, and that was the understatement of the millennium. "I'm hoping for a new set of relatives in the near future."

"Well, you'll be marrying into a good bunch," Gideon said with a smile. "Sterling souls, all through the centuries."

Jake nodded with a smile. Amanda would be a Kilchurn, not a de Piaget, but hopefully her family wouldn't hold that against him.

Assuming she would marry him after all.

"Friends?" Gideon asked.

"I've said good-byes," Jake said easily. He'd called his old Eton chum Alistair for their once-a-year catch up. Penelope he'd already led astray. Thad had listened to Jake's story silently, without even so much as a change in his breathing, from what Jake could tell over the phone. He'd wished Jake good luck, told him to remember all he'd learned in Thad's Survival School, then said he would miss him.

Actually he'd said, "Later, Buddy," but Jake had translated that easily enough.

Jake applied himself to his last modern meal—without allowing himself to dwell on the possibility that it very well might not be his last modern meal—and made polite small talk with his host, Gideon and Megan, and finally Kendrick and Genevieve.

And then, quite suddenly, he knew he had to leave. It was as if he'd just heard the final call for a flight over the PA system. He stood up, thanked his hosts, and asked Kendrick if he was ready for a little drive. Kendrick nodded and walked with him out of Artane's doors.

"Weird, isn't it?" Jake asked as they descended the steps to the courtyard.

"Aye, very," Kendrick said with feeling.

"Do you regret coming?"

"Nay, not at all," Kendrick said. "It was long overdue. I daresay Gideon and I will have many fine conversations in the future about things past and present. I'll enjoy that."

"Think of me while you're doing it."

"Hmmm," Kendrick said, noncommittally.

"You are completely without mercy," Jake said with a laugh. "Aren't you going to give me one bloody little hint?"

"I wouldn't want to ruin the surprise."

"And if I don't make it?"

"Call me and I'll come fetch you. You can begin a new life as a coin dealer."

Jake shook his head. He had his own opinions on what would happen later that day, but he would do just as Kendrick did, and keep his opinions to himself.

The journey to the appropriate spot took far less time than Jake suspected, though he supposed he shouldn't have been surprised. Cars were, admittedly, faster than horses.

Kendrick stopped his Jag, turned off the motor, and looked at Jake.

"You're sure?"

"I'm sure."

"Then I wish you good fortune. Leave us a message somehow if you get lost in time. Apparently your attorney's brother-in-law is quite the time traveler."

"James MacLeod?" Jake asked with a smile. "Yes, I heard all about him. I think you should get to know him. You might like to do some traveling with him."

Kendrick shook his head with a shiver. "Surely you jest. I've already seen all the centuries between mine and yours. I've no desire to see them again. Though I must admit, I think Laird MacLeod and I might have an interesting conversation or two about them." He put his hand on Jake's shoulder. "If you become lost, find a way to leave your mark and we'll come fetch you and deposit you in the right place."

"I'm so relieved."

"You should be," Kendrick said, suddenly serious. "This is no game."

"I never said it was," Jake said easily. He got out of the car, then leaned back in and looked at Kendrick. "You'd better get the bouncers out of here. I think I need privacy to do this properly."

Kendrick inclined his head. "As you wish. Be careful."

"You too. Those boys of yours are hellions, but I think your daughter is going to give you the most grief."

"Cad," Kendrick said. "She's an angel."

Jake pursed his lips and shut the door. He shouldered his pack, patted his sword, and climbed over the fence to the field where he'd arrived. He looked around him to make certain his father wasn't going to leap out of the trees with dozens of gorillas in tow, then looked at Kendrick and waved him away.

The cars pulled away slowly. Jake watched them go, realizing that if he was extremely fortunate, those would be the last cars he would ever see.

He sighed and tromped off through the little tree break and into the clearing where he knew the gate to be. He had the same feeling of urgency he'd had before, when he'd known he needed to be at the proper place at the proper time. He gripped the straps of his rustic backpack and said a little prayer. He wondered what was really the best way to proceed.

Should he sing? Walk three times counterclockwise and mutter a druidic incantation? Alex had told him to think about where he wanted to go and the gate would take him there.

So he thought about Amanda. He pictured her so vividly that he could almost see her in front of him. He closed his eyes and wished with all his heart. He waited.

Nothing happened.

Well, he was nothing if not patient. He stood there, hoping that he wouldn't soon hear the sound of his father yelling for his goons to attack. He heard very few things, actually. A bit of wind stirring the trees. Far off traffic from the A1. The waves against the shore near the castle. And then he began to have a hard time telling the difference between the three.

But he had no difficulty at all hearing the gasp behind him. He spun around to find none other than Montgomery de Piaget standing there, clutching his horse's reins as if they were all that held him fixed to reality.

Montgomery crossed himself.

Jake took a brief moment to let out a shaky breath. He'd made it. One very large hurdle down; several more to go.

Montgomery started to back up. Jake rolled his eyes and strode forward. "It's only me, Montgomery," he said, grasping the lad by the shoulder. "Stop looking at me as if I were a demon."

"You're a fairy," Montgomery said in a strangled voice.

"I am not."

"You are too. You sprang up from the grass."

"Are you sure?"

Montgomery nodded, wide-eyed.

Jake smiled. "What are you doing out here?"

Montgomery smiled suddenly. "I was looking for you. I hoped the fairies would release you soon, and here you are."

Jake considered the very weary-looking young man, and smiled. "How well did you sleep last night, Montgomery?"

"In truth, not very well," Montgomery admitted.

"If you were to ask me," Jake began, "I would say you were sleeping standing up. I've had it happen to me. I've been so tired that one minute I was staring at nothing and the next something was there, but in reality what had happened was that I'd fallen asleep for a moment or two." He smiled reassuringly. "Happens all the time."

"I still think you're a fairy," Montgomery said stubbornly, but then he smiled. "And I feared the fairies had taken you captive and wouldn't let you return." He looked behind Jake. "Where is your horse?"

"I walked."

Montgomery nodded wisely. "No wonder it took you so long."

"Has Amanda forgotten about me?" Jake asked lightly. "Or has she ground Robin into the dirt with her marvelous swordplay?"

Montgomery hesitated. Jake looked at him, wondering suddenly if he'd taken Amanda's affection for granted.

"What?" Jake asked sharply. "What happened?"

"She isn't at Artane," Montgomery said carefully.

"Was she abducted?" Jake demanded. "Or," he said slowly, "or did she decide to marry someone else?"

Montgomery shook his head miserably. "She ran."

"She ran!" Jake exclaimed. "Why?"

"I daresay," Montgomery said slowly, "she thought you had changed your mind."

Jake took Montgomery by the arm. "Come on. Let's go home. Is Robin still there?"

"Aye, and Nicholas as well. Everything is as you left it."

Jake swung into Montgomery's saddle and pulled the boy up behind him. He thundered back to Artane, through the village, and up the way to the gates in his best Nicholas de Piaget impression. He dismounted in the courtyard and ran up the steps and into the great hall. Robin was standing in front of the fire, alternately stroking his chin and rubbing the back of his neck. Anne sat in a chair next to the fire, holding her son and speaking in a low voice. She looked up first as Jake entered and the relief on her face was clearly visible.

Jake was very glad he'd brought something especially beautiful for her.

Robin looked less relieved, but no less welcoming. "You're late," he said shortly.

"I hurried," Jake said. "What happened?"

"I've no idea," Robin said. "Amanda was troubled, as you might expect, but I credited that to her worry over your delayed return and ability to win her."

"Well, if gold will win the day, the day will be won," Jake said. He unslung his backpack. "Is there anywhere safe I can store this? It's my future."

"The solar," Robin said. " 'Tis as safe as anywhere. Follow me and we'll see to hiding it."

Jake nodded, smiled at Anne, and followed Robin to the back of the great hall.

The same great hall in which he'd enjoyed fried eggs, fried tomatoes, and cold toast that morning, if anyone was curious. He was still contemplating the complete improbability of that when he ran bodily into Amanda's other elder brother.

He looked Nicholas in the eye—grateful he could do so without having to look up at him—and smiled politely.

"My lord," he said, inclining his head.

"You've returned," Nicholas said flatly.

"I have."

"She's gone, you know," Nicholas said, in that same, flat tone that spoke volumes about the depths of his grief. "The saints only know where."

"Why did she go?" Jake asked.

Nicholas opened his mouth to speak, then shut it and jerked his head in Robin's direction. "In the solar. We'll speak of it there."

Jake had no argument with that. He followed Robin into Rhys's solar, acutely aware that Nicholas was behind him and could have stabbed him in the back at any time. Robin gestured to the heavy trunk pushed up under the window.

"That's safe enough."

Jake could hardly believe his eyes. "That?" he managed. "That thing there?"

"Aye," Robin said in surprise. "My father keeps his gold in it."

"But I could get into that in a manner of minutes!" Jake exclaimed.

"Are you a thief, then, as well as a seller of goods?" Nicholas asked.

Jake turned and looked at him with as neutral an expression as he could manage. "Being able to open a lock is a very useful skill. If we were both tossed in a dungeon, could you free us?"

Nicholas pursed his lips. "I would never find myself thrown into a dungeon."

"Then I'll always stick close to you. I have many skills that are less than savory, and I suppose opening locks is one of them." He looked at Robin as he put his backpack down on the table under the window. "My entire future is in this," he said quietly. "If I lose it, I am lost. I'm sorry, but I don't trust a simple trunk to hold what I have in here."

"Short of sinking it in the cesspit, I fear I've no other alternative for you," Robin said. Then he looked with interest at Jake's gear. "What do you have in there? Gold?"

"As well as a few other things."

"Then let's have a look," Robin said, rubbing his hands together. "Amanda can wait a few more minutes."

Jake sighed and put his backpack on Rhys's table. He

pulled out bags of gold and gems from inside the sack, then pulled other things out of his boots—where they had been digging into his ankles and shins quite uncomfortably. Robin picked up one of the bags and spilled the gold out into his hand. He was silent for so long that Jake began to worry.

"Not enough?"

"How many do you have?"

"Eight."

Robin considered. "Add this to Amanda's dowry," he said thoughtfully, "and you might come close to a small part of my own wealth." He looked at Jake from under his eyebrows and his eyes twinkled.

Jake couldn't help but smile. It was Kendrick, all over again.

"Have anything else?" Robin asked, nosing through Jake's things with interest.

"I brought something for your mother," Jake said. "And Anne." He paused for several moments, then looked at Nicholas. "In fact, I brought something for all of Artane's ladies."

"You were wise to have brought something for Isabelle, else you would have regretted it far into your dotage," Robin warned. "Let me see what you have for Anne."

Jake dug around in one of the bags and pulled out a brooch set in white gold with peridots and diamonds. An odd choice together, he had to admit, but at the time he'd liked the combination. Robin whistled softly.

"I'd best pay you for this. She'll love you far more than me if I don't."

"I wouldn't take it," Jake said.

Robin grunted. "You will and be grateful for it. But if you think wooing my lady with gems will make me easier on you in the lists, you're mistaken."

Jake laughed. "I'm only hoping Anne might see her way clear to repair the odd tunic for me now and again."

" 'Tis a certainty you don't want Amanda doing it for you," Robin said with a snort. He handed the brooch back to Jake. "Put this away. We'll put one bag of gold in the treasury, and I'll hide the rest in the stones."

"In the stones?"

"Loose stones in the walls," Robin said. "Don't fear; I'll remember where I put them."

"I'd keep them myself," Nicholas muttered. "Rob has lost more than one thing of value thusly."

Robin tapped his forehead. "I've a mind that makes other men quail and cower, feeling their lack against my superior intelligence."

"As I said, put them in the trunk," Nicholas suggested. "Or keep them on you. They'll be safer that way."

Jake gave it serious thought, then, in the end, he handed Robin most of his gold and all the gems. He kept what he thought might serve him in his search. Then he looked at Nicholas. "I did bring something for y—"

Nicholas shook his head sharply. "Many thanks, but nay. I'll see to my own bride."

Robin shook his head. "You should accept Jake's offer. He has far better taste than you do."

"Mind your own affairs," Nicholas snarled.

"I will, when you've the wit to see to your own."

Jake leaped out of the way as Nicholas launched himself at Robin. He barely managed to rescue his gems and gold before they were taken down to floor and pummeled like Amanda's elder brothers.

As Jake stood there and watched the two men try to kill each other, he wondered how old they were. He realized with a start that he had no idea how old Amanda was. Age was relative, he supposed, and to look at Robin and Nicholas was to see them as grown men with a medieval toughness that probably belied their age.

He reached out and stepped on Robin's sleeve that was close enough to the ground for that kind of stepping on. Robin glared up at him.

"What?" he growled.

"How old is Amanda?"

Robin looked at him as if he'd lost his mind. "A score and one. Why?"

Jake released his sleeve, watched the brothers go at it for a few more minutes. Well, if Amanda was twenty-one, it was a safe bet that Nicholas and Robin were at least two, maybe three or four years older than she. Odd as it was to be in the position of elder statesman, if ever there were a time to take on the role, this was probably it. He unbuckled his sword and set it aside in a safe place, then he reached in and hauled a de Piaget brother to his feet, not worrying overmuch about which one he had until he had him by the tunic.

It turned out, unsurprisingly, to be Nicholas.

Nicholas twisted like a snake and would have landed a perfect shot to Jake's chin if Jake hadn't been expecting something like it. He feinted to the left, then grabbed Nicholas and spun him back around, wrenching his arm up behind him and placing his hand oh-so-lovingly on a pressure point guaranteed to produce immediate cooperation.

"Damn you," Nicholas gasped.

"Stop it, the both of you," Jake said.

"Who are *you* to tell me what to do?" Nicholas managed, followed by a grunt of pain that Jake was quite sure had been very unwillingly given.

"I'm older than you are."

"Think you?" Nicholas grunted.

"Well, how old are you?"

Nicholas swore furiously. "What could that possibly matter?"

"Just satisfy my curiosity."

"A score and six and when I have you within reach, I will use all the skill I've gained in those score and six years to grind you into dust."

"I'm a score and twelve, and since I'm older than you both, I say we stop fighting and start worrying about Amanda."

"He has that aright," Robin said, gingerly touching his cut lip with a knuckle. "Besides, you can kill Jake later if your feelings still smart."

Nicholas went quite still. "Release me."

"Do I dare?"

"Release me, damn you to hell," Nicholas growled.

Jake looked at Robin, who grinned at him. He released Nicholas abruptly; Nicholas wrenched away. Jake supposed he could have held him and taken him down to the ground and taught him a very great lesson in humility, but perhaps now wasn't the time.

After he and Amanda were married, maybe.

Nicholas glared at him and rubbed his shoulder. "You will regret this."

"I'm sure I will," Jake said, reaching for his sword. "But later, if you don't mind."

Robin gathered up some of Jake's goods. "I'll take these; you keep the rest. Nick, don't hurt him quite yet. He might prove useful in hunting down that witless wench. Besides," Robin said with a very straight face, "he's older than you are. Show him some respect."

Nicholas looked at Jake with undisguised dislike. "I'll respect him when he can best me on the field." He stalked toward the door. "No sooner."

"He bested you in Father's solar," Robin called after him cheerfully, then shrugged and looked at Jake. "He isn't usually so sour. Of the two of us, he is definitely the more pleasant soul. I can't imagine what eats at him."

"Can't you?" Jake asked simply.

Robin paused for quite a long while. He sighed, finally. "I thought I was imagining it."

"They aren't related by blood."

"How is it you know so much?" Robin asked.

"Montgomery."

Robin dragged a hand through his hair. "That one is better than anyone I know in keeping sec—" He looked at Jake, startled. "I was nigh onto saying that he keeps secrets very well."

"Damn it," Jake said curtly. "Hide my gold for me; I'll dump the rest of this stuff, then go find him."

Robin nodded and they left the solar together. Jake ran upstairs to stash his gear in the boys' room only to find his mail shirt lying just where he'd left it.

And that, for some reason, was possibly the most heart-warming thing he'd ever seen in his life.

He smiled to himself, then went on his search.

Montgomery was milling about the lists. Apparently he was no dummy; the moment he saw Jake striding toward him purposefully, he turned tail and ran.

Jake caught him easily and turned him around by the arm.

"Whoa, little one," he said with an easy smile. "I think you might know something I need to."

"I don't know anything," Montgomery said nervously.

"Montgomery," Jake chided, "a knight doesn't lie."

"Montgomery!" Robin bellowed from a great distance. "Damn you, you witless girl, when I catch you . . ."

Montgomery gasped and tried to pull away. Jake looked over his shoulder to find both Robin and Nicholas running toward them. He was momentarily tempted to let Montgomery go, but the boy had answers. Montgomery continued to try to get free.

"Please, Jake," he pleaded. "Let me go. They'll thrash me if they catch me."

"You'll never outrun them. Best you stay with me and answer a few questions." He took Montgomery by the shoulders in a grip that was guaranteed to prevent any escape. "Now, let's talk. Why is it your memory seems to fail you at this point?"

Robin and Nicholas had stopped in front of them, with Miles and John running up within moments. Robin and Nicholas folded their arms over their chests and put on stern looks. Miles and John did the same. Jake might have laughed if he hadn't been so sick at heart. Anything could have happened to her. Anything.

"Speak," Robin demanded.

Montgomery shook like a leaf.

"We're not going to thrash you," Jake said, still holding Montgomery firmly, "but we do need some answers."

"I swore I wouldn't say anything," Montgomery said, looking as fierce as circumstances allowed. "I gave my word as a knight."

"You aren't a knight yet," Nicholas growled.

"But he will be," Jake said easily. "All right, Montgomery, surely you see the problem. If you know something about where Amanda went and you don't tell us, you are putting her in danger. Don't you think?"

Montgomery considered. "But my vow . . ."

"Or your sister's safety." Jake looked at him with a smile. "But you choose, Montgomery. We can't force you."

"Aye, we can," Nicholas said, putting his hand on the hilt of his sword.

Montgomery looked at Robin. "What think you?"

"I think you're a—"

Robin held up his hand to interrupt Nicholas's growl. He looked very seriously at his brother.

"Breaking a vow is not something to do lightly," Robin

said. "A knight has his word, his arm, and his character. But in this instance, I daresay your character has been amply demonstrated in your willingness to honor the vow you made to Amanda. But part of being a man is knowing when to . . ." he considered, then spoke again, "when to sacrifice yourself and perhaps even your honor for the welfare of someone you love."

"She's at Seakirk Abbey," Montgomery blurted out. His eyes filled with tears. "She's going to become a nun."

Jake wouldn't have been more shocked if Montgomery had told him Amanda had followed him back to the future. "A what?" he asked incredulously.

"A nun," Montgomery said, looking up at him. "I couldn't dissuade her." He swallowed with difficulty. "She feared you had forgotten her. And—" he looked at Nicholas.

"Damnation," Nicholas growled.

"Let's be off," Robin said. "Jake?"

"I'm there," Jake said. "If I might borrow a horse?"

"Of course." Robin hesitated, then slid Jake a sideways look. "A nun."

"I'm unsurprised," Jake said with a snort. "And how long has she been gone?"

"Over a fortnight," Robin said.

"And you didn't look for her?" Jake asked incredulously.

"We've been looking for over a fortnight!" Nicholas exploded. "We simply had no idea where to look. Something that might have been solved if *someone* had opened his mouth."

Montgomery wrenched away and scuttled behind Jake.

Jake looked over his shoulder. "I think you should stay here, don't you?"

Montgomery nodded, wide-eyed.

"I agree," Robin said. "But I think I should leave one of us behind as well." He looked at Nicholas. "Perhaps you should stay."

"I will not," Nicholas said. "Kilchurn and I will go. You remain behind."

"Oh, nay," Robin said, shaking his head with a small laugh. "I want Amanda rescued by someone still breathing. If I leave you two alone, you'll likely do each other in before you reach Seakirk."

"I will stay," Miles said. "You won't need me."

Robin nodded. "Aye, likely not. And Amanda's guard is here, and those lads are fierce enough." He looked around Jake at Montgomery. "I want you at Anne's side continually. If it comes to a choice between her life and yours, I hope you understand which you will choose."

Montgomery nodded vigorously. "I will give mine gladly, brother." He paused. "Forgive me. I tried to honor Amanda's wishes."

Robin pulled Montgomery forward and ruffled his hair. "You did right, Montgomery. No harm will come of it.

Montgomery smiled gratefully. "I'll go see to Anne."

"You do that," Robin said.

Jake watched Montgomery hurry off the field, followed closely by his brother and less closely by Miles, who sauntered in his usual fashion. Jake listened with half an ear as Robin and Nicholas considered supplies and gear, then followed them when they walked off the field.

A nun?

What in the *hell* was she thinking?

He parted company with the brothers when they reached the keep, then ran up the stairs to fetch his gear. Seakirk was a good three hours by car, so who knew how long it would take to reach it on horseback. Well, the sooner they started, the sooner they would be there.

And hopefully they wouldn't be too late.

Chapter 30

Genevieve stood at the doorway to Artane's great hall and watched her husband walk with his nephew. By now, she was accustomed to the sight. She wasn't sure Lord Edward was, but apparently Kendrick had given him some irrefutable proof of his identity by means of holes in the walls that even Edward had had no idea about. Genevieve had smiled as she listened to her husband relate to his, well, nephew all the things around that castle that he had taken apart in his youth and somehow put back together. Gideon and Kendrick had become fast friends and Genevieve felt as if she'd found a sister in Megan. There was something to be said for extended family and the pleasures of their association.

She sincerely hoped Jake would enjoy that pleasure.

She spent the rest of the day chasing her children all over her husband's ancestral home, or watching Lord Edward, Gideon, or a very pregnant Megan chase them as well. It made her smile to see it, but she had the feeling it touched her husband far more deeply. He was happy in a way she hadn't seen him in years.

If ever.

Perhaps it had something to do with being home.

* * *

Early that evening, she corralled her boys and put them to bed in one large bedroom, then collapsed in a chair next to the crib holding her sleeping daughter. She looked up at the ceiling and wondered about the passage of time. Had Jake made it back to Amanda's time? Had he lived out his life, loved Amanda, fathered children, then passed on peacefully?

Odd to think she had seen him that morning at breakfast and now it was entirely possible that his life had been over for well over seven hundred years.

She sat up when the door opened. Kendrick smiled and put his finger to his lips.

" 'Tis only me. Is the wee one asleep?"

"Finally," she said with a yawn.

He padded across the room and sat down nearby on a bench. "I feel as if I haven't seen you all day."

"You haven't," she said with a smile, "but I've been watching you."

"Have you? Doing what?"

"Roaming," she said. "Reliving glorious moments in the lists. Showing your boys around while making it look like Gideon was pointing out the highlights."

Kendrick laughed and took her hand. "I will have to give the triplets the truth soon enough. Perhaps tomorrow I might steal you away for a bit and show you the locations of some of my more memorable exploits."

"I can hardly wait," she said dryly.

"No doubt."

He fell silent and so did she. Until she saw the little box Jake had left them sitting on the table next to the bed.

"Have you looked in that?"

He shook his head. "Nay, not yet."

"Why not? Do you have any idea what's in it? He left it for you."

"Likely something smelly, foul, or vile, just as repayment for my treatment of him in the lists."

She laughed. "Seriously, Kendrick, why don't you look? It might be something that tells us if he made it."

"Now, where is the sport in that?" he asked with a wink.

"I say we let him season for a week or two, then check. Perhaps he's lost in Elizabethan England. I would hate to deprive him of all those ruffles and lace."

"You haven't got a curious bone in your body," she grumbled.

"Ah, but you know I do."

"Then you know something I don't," she said, wagging her finger at him. "Do you remember him? Did he get his title? Did he marry Amanda?"

Kendrick yawned widely. "I feel suddenly quite sleepy. Perhaps we had best snatch what little slumber we may before our wee babe wakes us again."

"Kendrick," she warned.

"A fortnight," Kendrick said, leaning over to kiss her. "Let us make our home here for a fortnight and think on nothing but the strand, our children, and all things pleasant. Then we will look."

"And you'll spill the beans?"

"I'll spill the beans."

"All right," she conceded. "Two weeks. What can it hurt?"

"What indeed," Kendrick murmured.

Chapter 31

J*ake* wondered at the advisability of having accepted the horse he was currently riding. It was Jasper, Amanda's mountain, and Jake knew he was definitely not equal to Jasper's potential. But the stallion was fast and that seemed to make up for Jake's lack of skill when compared to Robin and Nicholas.

And it wasn't just Amanda's brothers that he was trying to keep from falling off in front of. Though the major part of Artane's garrison had been left behind, Robin had selected three men to come with them, three grim-faced Thad-style warriors who didn't seem to have smiles in their repertoires. Jake didn't mind. Help was help, whether it was cheerful or not. But he still didn't want to look like a wuss in front of them.

They rode like the wind for the rest of that day, stopping only to water the horses and rest for a bit. By the evening of the second day, they were within striking distance of the abbey. Jake could see Seakirk castle in the distance. He tried not to let that unsettle him, as unsettling as it was.

Life was, he decided, very, very weird.

"Let us be about it," Nicholas said after they had paused for a brief moment to regroup.

"Wait," Robin said, holding out his hand. He looked over the countryside with a jaundiced eye. "I do not care for the feel of this."

"You're daft," Nicholas growled. "Let us fetch her out before another day passes."

Jake hesitated. "I have to agree with Robin. There is something that feels . . ." He searched for the right word, but came up with nothing. He shrugged. "I don't like it either."

"You're mad as well!" Nicholas exclaimed. "'Tis the countryside, you fools. How is it supposed to feel?"

"Well, for one thing," Robin said placidly, "I daresay we should be seeing a peasant or two. Have you seen any?"

Nicholas sighed heavily. "Nay. Not for the past league or so."

"And as fierce as we might be, we are only six," Robin said, "and though we go to parley with nuns, they may have men-at-arms of their own. Perhaps 'tis best we go quietly. Think you, Jake?"

"I think," Jake agreed. "And night time is a good time for leaving our horses behind and doing some scouting. It's always best to know more than the enemy than he knows about you."

"Ha," Nicholas snorted. "Even I know that, dullard that I am."

"I never suggested you didn't," Jake said frankly. "You are much of the reason I think we can overcome any, er, resistance inside. Your cunning, Robin's sword, and my hands. How can we lose?"

"To a gaggle of terrified nuns?" Nicholas asked, only slightly less antagonistically than before. "The saints pity us if we cannot rout them out."

Robin dismounted. "Let us remain here until 'tis dark, then proceed on foot and see the real face of our enemy. And let us hope 'tis only Amanda's bout of surliness we encounter, not something more sinister."

Jake didn't like the delay, but as it had been his thought as well, he couldn't exactly complain about it. He sat on a log and looked at his hands, wondering just what they would do before the night was over. He didn't want to kill anyone, but would he have a choice? And what would the consequences be?

Perhaps life in the Middle Ages wasn't so simple after all.

It was late in the evening when Robin rose. He chose one

of his men to stay behind, then motioned to the other two to come with him. Jake got up and followed him and Nicholas as they set off toward the abbey.

Jake walked, still more lost in thought than he probably should have been. He could hardly believe where he was, or that he was walking alongside medieval nobility on a rescue mission to liberate another bit of medieval nobility from the gentle clutches of some no doubt very kindly nuns.

Oh, and he was wearing a sword.

The hair on the back of his neck stood up suddenly, almost as suddenly as Robin held his hand up to stop them all. Robin started to go forward, but Jake stopped him with a hand on his shoulder. He pointed to the knight sitting with his back against a tree some twenty yards in front of them.

"Let me," Jake breathed.

"Don't kill him," Robin whispered.

"I wasn't going to. Just cover me." Jake looked for a bow or something useful in Robin's hands. "Well, cover me with something."

Robin drew his knife and grinned. "I'll manage it somehow."

Jake nodded and walked on silently. Fortunately he'd had years of experience in doing just that, though his experience had come mainly from humoring Thad on long marches through inhospitable terrain. If you had to walk, according to Thad, you had better be quiet about it.

So it was with ease that Jake crept up behind the unmoving man. It was no great stretch to realize the man was sound asleep. He beckoned over his shoulder and soon had Robin there with him.

"Where are the others?" Jake asked.

"Scouting. Let us wake this one and see if his powers of speech will avail us." He walked around to stand near the man and drew his sword. Then he kicked the snoozer awake.

The man leaped to his feet, but Jake took him down before he could produce any kind of weapon. The man squeaked as Jake knelt in the middle of his back.

"Whose are you?" Robin demanded softly.

"Ledenham's," the man said promptly. "Never liked him— oy, go easy with that knee—and don't like him now. Terrorizing hapless nuns. Beastly bugger."

"He'll likely terrorize you for falling asleep at your post," Robin said sternly. "Where are your fellows?"

"All guarding the abbey," Ledenham's guardsman said. He looked up at Robin. "Artane, are you?"

"His son," Robin agreed.

"Don't suppose you'd be needin' a new guardsman, would you?"

"I don't, but I might know someone who will in time." He looked at Jake. "I say we tie him up and if there's anything left of him when we return, we'll take him home with us. Do you have a family, sir knight?"

"Aye," the man said. "I've a sister who is one of Lady Ledenham the elder's attendants. She'd likely wish to come too, so you'd best make it look as if ye bested me fairly, so as she can."

Robin pursed his lips. "I've no need for a man who surrenders so easily."

"I'm no fool," the man wheezed. "I'd cast my lot in with anyone who wasn't Lord Ledenham, and I can't do that if I'm dead now, can I?"

He had a point. Jake hauled him to his feet. The man stood there and waited for Robin to do something to him.

"Insult him," Jake suggested.

The man took a deep breath. "Is my sister the one blonde you haven't sired a bastard on, my lord?"

Jake gasped at the words, but Robin did more than that. Jake waited until an appropriate amount of damage had been done, then pulled Robin away.

"Touchy, aren't you," he said, rolling the man over so he could tie him up.

"Well," Robin said, his chest heaving, "you told him to insult me."

"He did a proper job of it apparently." Jake gagged the man with his own tunic sleeve for good measure, then rose and looked at Robin. "It was an interesting choice of words. Not that it's any of my business."

"It isn't," Robin said shortly. He paused, almost spoke, then shook his head. "Too long a tale. We'll speak of it some night when we're well into our cups and our ladies are not within earshot."

"I can hardly wait."

Robin rubbed the knuckles of his right hand then smiled at Jake. "I've had a taste of what's to come. Let us be about our business and finish it quickly. I understand the abbey sets a poor table, but there's also the rumor that the abbess keeps everything edible for herself. I've a mind to verify the truth of that."

"Lead on, my lord," Jake said with a nod. "I'm with you."

Robin led on. Jake had a hard time finding Nicholas and their two knights as they neared the abbey, but he saw them eventually, slipping out of the shadows when several more of Ledenham's were found guarding the outside of the abbey's walls. These men were not so quick to lie down and play dead. They were dispatched, though, all to an oblivion which would include waking up with gargantuan headaches.

Jake slipped over the abbey wall with the others and dropped down onto the soft grass of what Robin said had to be the abbess's private garden.

"Quite a luxurious life for a nun," Nicholas said sourly.

"Hmmm," Robin agreed, then continued on.

Jake followed him, then stopped Robin with a hand on his arm. "Look," he said, pointing.

A cluster of armed men stood in front of a small house. Whether it was bad luck or Fate with a thumb on her nose, the men were looking straight at them and immediately set up a cry.

"Damnation," Robin said shortly. "Well, lads, let's be about this business and have it over with."

Jake knew he shouldn't have been surprised, but he was, just the same, to find one of the men coming at him as if he had every intention of killing him. Jake drew his sword and held his own, but it wasn't easy fighting at night. The only thing that aided him was the torch sitting in the sconce near the abbess's front door—and even that was almost of no use.

He realized within minutes that he was the only one still fighting. Robin and Nicholas had dispatched their opponents, as had their men, and were merely watching him dispassionately.

"Will he manage, do you think?" Nicholas asked.

"With me as his swordmaster, he had better, hadn't he?" Robin said. "Be about it, Kilchurn. The real test waits inside."

Ledenham's guardsman yelled suddenly and threw himself

forward in a ferocious attack. Whether it was skill or just misfortune, Jake had his sword up at the right angle at the right time. And the man skewered himself on it.

He gurgled out his last breath, twisted, and fell to the earth, sliding back off Jake's sword.

Jake stood there and thought he just might lose the remains of that cold supper of eel he'd just ingested a couple of hours ago. And he was neither weak-kneed, nor a coward. But there was something about killing a man you didn't know and hadn't really wanted to do in . . .

And then he found his sword taken from him. Robin cleaned the blade on the man's tunic, then shoved the sword back into Jake's hands.

"Put it away."

Jake resheathed it numbly.

Robin backhanded him. Jake blinked, then shook himself sharply.

"Thank you."

"It won't be the last time you do that," Robin said harshly. "Accustom yourself to it. Grieve in private, if you must, but do not do it here."

"Right," Jake said curtly.

Robin hesitated, then looked at Jake seriously. "When we return home, I'll introduce you to the keg in my father's cellar and we'll have ourselves speech then. Right now, think on the fact that Ledenham could be bedding your love."

Jake needed no further encouragement. He nodded curtly and followed Robin to the door of the abbess's house. They threw themselves against it and shattered the wood. He rolled to his feet only to find Ledenham hopping nimbly out the window.

Robin strode across the room to stop in front of the woman sitting at the table. Jake suspected, by her dress, that she was the abbess. He knew by her mein that she was not a pleasant woman.

"Where's my sister?" Robin demanded.

"Why, my lord Robin, she is not here," the abbess said, blinking innocently.

"Liar," Robin said, slapping his hands on the table. "Where is she?"

The abbess only smiled. "You're too late. Indeed, I suspect

His Lordship is already on his way to the chapel to retrieve his bride. His properly trained bride. You see, there was much pride to drive from her." She sighed, then shook her head sadly. "It took great effort on my part—"

Jake didn't stick around to hear any more. He vaulted out the same window Ledenham had and bolted after him. It would have helped if he could have seen him, but he had no trouble finding the abbey. Now if he'd just known which door to go in—

"This way," Nicholas said, passing him at a dead run. "Follow me."

They leaped up the steps, wrenched open the massive doors, and spilled into the antechamber. Massive iron gates separated them from the nave of the church.

"Keeps the rabble in their places, that," Nicholas growled. "Look, there Ledenham is, trying to undo the lock."

Jake strode forward, put his hand on Ledenham's shoulder, and spun him around. He leaped back only on instinct but he still wasn't fast enough to avoid the sting of a knife grazing his ribs.

"Damn you," Jake gasped.

Ledenham was quick as a snake and just as merciless. Jake spent the first thirty seconds doing nothing but leaping out of the way as Ledenham continued to come at him. He managed to get his sword belt undone and his sword tossed to Nicholas without getting himself killed, but it was close. Ledenham stopped his attack long enough to stare at Jake in surprise.

"You threw away your sword," he said, nonplussed.

"Throw away yours and we'll be even," Jake said. "Or not, and I'll still kick your ass."

Ledenham only snorted and drew his sword. Jake wasted no more time with pleasantries. He kicked the sword out of Ledenham's hands, then followed that immediately with a quick jab to the underside of Ledenham's chin. And while the man was still trying to see if he had all his teeth left, Jake took his hand and wrenched it so hard he heard the bones snap. Ledenham screamed. Jake did them all a favor and plunged him into unconsciousness. Jake looked around.

"Key?"

"I have it."

He looked over to find the abbess standing there, a triumphant smile on her face.

"Not that it will serve you," she added. "Look."

Jake looked and saw the figure laid out before the altar. He couldn't tell who it was, only that the woman was dressed all in white and lying face-down.

"Amanda?" Nicholas asked in a choked voice.

"Has she taken her vows?" Robin demanded.

The abbess shrugged. "Who's to say?"

"You'll say, you bloody wretch," Nicholas said, whirling on the woman.

The woman only continued to smile.

"Give me that damned key!" Nicholas bellowed.

"Come find it, my lord," she said, a knife suddenly in her hands. "I must protect my charges and I will, if need be."

Jake looked up. The top of the gate was above his head and crowned with spikes. He had visions of himself slipping and impaling—well, it wasn't pretty, that vision. So he considered, then looked at Robin.

"Find me some sort of utensil. Do you have forks? How about a thin spoon? Something I can bend."

Robin, who apparently knew better than to ask too many questions of a twenty-first-century man, merely nodded and left. Jake gripped the bars and stared into the nave, listening with only half an ear to Nicholas making increasingly ugly threats to the abbess and the abbess in turn vowing to find ways to see his eternal soul damned. Jake suspected Nicholas didn't care; he also suspected the abbess didn't have the power, so in reality, they were at an impasse.

Robin returned before long and handed Jake several eating implements.

"All I could find."

"They'll do."

It took him half an hour, and Thad again would have been appalled at that, but Jake finally had the gate open. Nicholas even stopped his litany of threats long enough to notice.

"Well," he said, taken aback.

"See you in the dungeon, bud," Jake said with a smile.

And for a brief moment, Nicholas smiled back. Jake suspected that he might have just caught a glimpse of why people liked him so much. But that disappeared quickly when they jockeyed for position, trying to be the first one into the nave.

"Move, damn you," Jake said, elbowing him in his mailed ribs.

"I am her brother."

"So what?" Jake said, pushing past him and striding down the aisle.

Nuns scattered like leaves. Well, all except one, who stood over the figure on the floor.

"Move," Jake suggested.

"When I'm dead," the nun said, folding her arms over her chest. "The child deserves peace. You will give it to her."

"Oh, by the saints," Robin said in disgust from behind him. "I remember a time when it was a very spiritual bit of business to come to Seakirk Abbey and be allowed in the chapel. I can see that things have indeed changed."

And with that, he disarmed the nun who had a blade hidden up her sleeve, and moved her bodily aside.

Nicholas leaned over to haul the white-robed body to her feet, but Jake stopped him.

"What if she's hurt?" he said.

Nicholas hesitated, then knelt down next to her. Jake did the same, running his hands gently over her arms and legs. He looked down and saw Amanda's fingers coming from within that white robe, but they were white and bloodless.

Hoping that he didn't do her permanent damage, he slid his hands under her arms and hauled her—and it took no effort at all—to her feet. He put his arms around her to steady her.

She cried out in pain.

The hood fell back from her head and all three of them, Jake, Robin, and Nicholas, gasped as one.

"Who cut your hair?" Robin demanded.

"I did," the abbess called defiantly from outside the gates, where she was being looked after by Artane's men. "Just today, and I did it with pleasure!"

Nicholas drew his knife and Jake half thought he was going to go after the abbess. Instead, he slit the back of Amanda's robe.

And that gasp was something entirely different.

Jake only caught a glimpse of the damage, but that was enough to keep him from stopping Nicholas as he strode angrily away. He wasn't sure how he could do anything for Amanda; he couldn't pick her up; he couldn't hold in her in his arms. He settled quickly for helping her over to a bench. He sat, then eased her down onto his lap. He wasn't sure where he could touch her back without hurting her, so he held her hands in one of his and stroked what was left of her hair—and that wasn't much.

She started to cry.

Jake winced. "I'm sorry," he whispered.

She said nothing, but one of her hands crept up and rested on his chest. She leaned against him and wept like he'd never heard anyone weep before. He wasn't sure if that was a good thing or not, but he wasn't about to stop her. So he held her on his lap and closed his eyes, listening to the goings-on around him but not really caring about their outcome. Robin and Nicholas would do whatever needed to be done and he supposed they would pick up the pieces when it was all over.

It could have been minutes, it could have been an hour: he wasn't sure. Finally Amanda gingerly dabbed at her face with her sleeve, then looked at him with bloodshot blue eyes still the color of some exotic bit of ocean in the Bahamas.

"You're late," she whispered.

"I hurried."

She shifted, but gasped in pain. "Do not be late again."

"I never will," he said with feeling. "But what in the world possessed you to come here?"

"I didn't think I had a choice."

"And now that you do?"

She looked at him again for a long moment, then put her head on his shoulder. "I want to go home."

"I'll get you there." He looked up at Nicholas, who was suddenly standing there in front of him. Or he could have been standing there forever. Jake had no idea. But he did understand the look on his face.

Resignation, if not acceptance.

Jake nodded in understanding and received a short nod in return.

"Well?" Jake asked, more than ready to move on. "The abbess?"

"She lives still," Nicholas said, "but I daresay she'll wish she didn't once I'm finished with her."

"I think we should bust her down to scullery maid."

" 'Bust her down'?" Nicholas asked.

"Turn her into," Jake clarified. "Can we do that?"

"Consider it done." He looked at Amanda. "I've liberated the abbess's chambers for Amanda's use, but I don't know how we'll get her there."

"We'll make a seat for her. Amanda, can you stand?"

"Briefly," she said, wincing.

Nicholas pulled her up, then Jake rose. He showed Nicholas how to clasp hands to make a seat, then they carried Amanda to the abbess's chambers. It wasn't as though Jake had carried Amanda before, but he couldn't help noticing that there was nothing to her.

"Have you eaten?" he asked.

"I don't remember," she said wearily. "I fasted quite often to rid myself of my vices."

"And we know those are legion," Jake said dryly. He set her down, then he and Nicholas helped her lie facedown on the abbess's very soft-looking bed.

"Ah, this is worth it all," Amanda said with a heartfelt sigh.

"I'll go look for the healer," Nicholas said.

"Wait," Jake said, looking up from where he knelt by the bedside. "Who knows whom we can trust here?"

"Not trust a healer?" Nicholas asked, aghast.

"Just bring me some wine," Amanda managed.

"And herbs," Jake added. "Do we have herbs now in England?"

Nicholas stared at him as if he'd lost his mind. Amanda turned to look at him from a single, aqua eye.

"Aye," she said. "Nicky, storm the kitchens. See if they have dried plantain or knitbone. Either will serve."

Nicholas rolled his eyes, but left the little room just the same without further comment. Jake covered Amanda's hand with his own and looked at her seriously.

"I *am* sorry," he said.

"That you were late," she asked with a faint smile, "or that I was foolish enough not to wait longer?"

"I'm sorry I didn't tell you everything I should have before I left," he said.

He felt her stiffen. "Everything?"

"Answers to all the questions you asked me."

She took a careful breath. "And those answers? Will I find them to my liking?"

"I hope so."

She looked at him for quite some time in silence. "Will you leave again?"

"Not alone," he said.

She smiled at that, a small curving of her mouth that he found utterly enchanting.

"Is that an offer of marriage?"

"Not yet."

"Haven't you decided if you like me well enough?" she asked, without flinching.

"I knew the moment I saw you that I liked you well enough," he said honestly. "But I have a few more things to put into place before I get down on bended knee and profess undying love."

"You can do that without asking me to wed with you."

He laughed, then leaned over and kissed her forehead very gently. "I love you, Amanda of Artane, and will to my dying breath and beyond."

She considered, then closed her eyes with a smile. "That will suffice me."

He waited. He looked at her hand that had curled itself around his and waited some more. And just when he opened his mouth to chide her for not returning the favor of declaring her love, he realized there was no point.

She was snoring.

He hoped it wasn't an omen.

He considered her wounds—and his—and decided they could wait a few more minutes. So he sat on the floor and held her hand. And there came a point, not long afterward, that he thought he might just fall over if he didn't rest his head too, so he put his head down next to hers and closed his eyes.

He'd done it.

He knew that the hardest part was in front of him and not

behind him, but that he had come this far and apparently had a little of the esteem and affection of the woman in front of him was nothing to take lightly.

He would manage the rest.

He had no intentions of failing.

Chapter 32

Amanda sat on a stool next to the fire in Artane's great hall with a blanket wrapped about her shoulders and knew that she had never been more grateful for anything in her life than she was for the simple fact of being home. Well, she might have been more grateful for a chair, but who was she to quibble over details?

She was sitting on a stool instead of a chair because her back was still healing and she could not bear to lean against anything. It had been that last bit of instruction from the abbess to almost finish her. Amanda remembered the start of it, but she didn't remember the end. Perhaps she had become senseless from the pain. What she did know was that for a day or two there in the abbey, her brothers and Jake had actually wondered if she would be coming home at all. She had been out of her head with a fever. She did remember, vaguely, Jake refusing to allow anyone to come bleed her and she was almost certain that she'd heard the ring of steel.

Robin was sporting a swollen eye. She hadn't asked where he'd come by that. Nicholas wasn't breathing very well and she suspected he might have a broken rib or two. She hadn't inquired as to the origin of those injuries either.

Jake was unscathed and ferocious in his protection of her. Or at least he had been until they'd returned home, he had assured himself that Anne would keep any and all leeches away from her, and Robin had invited him out into the lists for a bit of training.

She could say this for the man: he was singleminded.

Of course that applied to his attention to her as well. When he returned from his day's labors, his entire self was focused on her and nothing else; not even the chance to thrash Nicholas in chess was enough to distract him.

Indeed, she had little to complain of and very much to be grateful for.

She shifted, winced, then shifted again until she was as comfortable as possible.

"Hurt?" Anne asked.

"'Tis nothing I do not deserve," Amanda said grimly.

"Mandy, stop," Anne chided. "You were foolish to flee, but not even that justifies how you were treated." She shivered. "What a horrible woman the abbess was."

"Aye, well, she'll have her due." She looked at Anne. "Didn't Robin tell you?"

"I haven't seen him," Anne said with a smile. "He spends all his time in the lists with Jake."

"I'm sorry for that, sister," Amanda said.

Anne shook her head. "Do not be. If he were not driving your love in the lists, he would be hovering over me and annoying me with his commands that I do nothing but sit and rest. Nay, 'tis a fair trade and I'm happy to make it. But it does mean that I've heard very little about your escape."

"Then I'll give you the details I haven't been able to from my sickbed this past fortnight," Amanda said, shifting again. She wasn't sure what was more annoying: the pain of bruised muscles or the itching from healing welts. "As you know, Jake rescued me just before I was to take my vows."

"Timely," Anne said approvingly.

"Aye, well, those vows would have been to Ledenham, so 'twas timely indeed. And you know how he tended me whilst I was out of my head with fever."

"I've seen the results on Nicky and Robin," Anne said with

a laugh. "Ah, Mandy, I daresay your Jake will see to you well enough."

"I daresay. But apparently his skills do not end with his ability to fend off my brothers' best intentions. When the abbot arrived to make certain the abbey was being properly prepared for the king's visit—"

"The king?" Anne interrupted. "Here?"

"Seakirk," Amanda corrected. "I daresay Father will go to meet with him there."

"No sense in depleting our larder unnecessarily," Anne agreed.

"Nay, let him ravage Seakirk castle and the surrounding countryside. But because of our good fortune in escaping a royal visit, Abbot Bartholomew was on hand to see firsthand what our good lady Joan had been about. Jake suggested that perhaps the best way to save the woman's soul was to give her the chance to pass the rest of her days in service, true service to those sisters around her."

"What, cleaning the privies?" Anne asked with a laugh.

"Oh, that as well," Amanda agreed. "Scullery maid and cleaner of privies and stables, if I remember aright. Attended in her duties, I might add, by one Sister Eunice, she of the rather heavy, but dilatory hand." Amanda shivered. "At least I can thank heaven that 'twas Eunice who beat me most often. She hadn't the stomach or the endurance to administer more than a pair of blows."

"Amanda," Anne said in a low voice, "how did you bear it?"

"My heart was broken," Amanda said with a shrug. "What did it matter?"

"And now?"

And now? The front door opened. Amanda looked over to see Jake walking in with Robin and young Christopher of Blackmour. They were laughing about something. She despaired of ever seeing Nicholas be as easy with her love as Robin was, but perhaps that would come in time. For now, she would content herself with the sight of that man, the one she loved, drawn into the bosom of her family by her eldest brother. If Robin could see in Jake what she did, perhaps her father would see it as well.

She watched as they walked toward the fire and her heart ached within her. By the saints, she had come so close to never having even the small joys she had at present. If she had been forced to wed Ledenham . . .

Jake knelt down in front of her. "You're thinking again."

"I do it often," she said lightly.

"Can I hope it was about my great successes in the lists?"

"That, too," she said with a smile.

He looked at her seriously. "How are you?"

"Better," she said. "I'm home. That counts for a great deal. How do you fare?"

"Still on my feet and not bleeding from dozens of wounds," Jake said.

Robin collapsed into the chair next to Anne. "He's making good progress. Christopher, lad, will you fetch me wine? And for Jake as well."

"And for me, if you will, Christopher, my lad," Nicholas said. He had brought two chairs from the high table. He put them both down, then dropped into one of them. He nodded toward the other.

"Kilchurn," he said, in a not unfriendly tone.

Amanda looked at Jake with a raised eyebrow. "How companionable you are with each other."

"Amanda, it is not fodder for jest," Nicholas warned.

She looked at him and hoped that somehow he would understand that she loved him very much indeed, that he would hold a place in her heart that even Jake would never fully take away. By the bloody saints, hadn't she told him as much on their way back from the abbey?

"Oaf," she said curtly, "I wasn't jesting."

Nicholas scowled at her. "He may have bested me in matters of the heart, but he will never best me on the field."

"Never is a dangerous word," Robin remarked placidly. "Give him a year or two and he'll be your equal. Never mine, of course," he said with a modest smile, "but few have the cheek to aspire to such a lofty height. Even fewer manage it. Indeed, I cannot think of a one."

Nicholas grunted and looked at Jake. "Think twice, Jackson, before fully committing to wed with this family, for Robin, unfortunately, is a part of that family. Not only is he impossibly arrogant without cause, his favorite activity is poking his nose into your affairs."

"Amanda and I will travel enough that he won't have a chance," Jake said with a deep smile. He reached over and took Amanda's hand. "I'll survive."

Amanda sat near that warm fire, holding the hand of the man she loved, and wondered if things could improve. Her aches and pains could go away, she supposed, and Jake could trot out a title to please her father, but perhaps for the moment, she couldn't ask for anything else.

"Are you up for more?" Jake asked, looking at Robin.

Robin looked at Amanda. "This is your doing, not mine, sister. I was fully prepared to sit happily inside this evening, enjoying the companionship of my wife and son, yet it is your love who drives me back out into the lists for—"

"I'll go," Nicholas interrupted.

Amanda frowned. "Perhaps Robin should . . ."

Nicholas smiled. And it was almost easily done. "He will return unscathed, sister," he said. "Hard as it might be for Robin to admit, I do have some skill myself."

Jake kissed her hand, then rose. "I'll be back." He looked at Nicholas. "Let's go."

"By way of the kitchens," Nicholas said, heaving himself to his feet. "Let me borrow your page, Robin. And why is it you have one and I do not?"

"Because even for a young lad, Christopher has a remarkably keen eye and very sound judgment. You may borrow him, but be careful with him and try not to ruin him by having him watch poor technique."

Nicholas looked at Jake. "Do you begin to understand now why I hate him so?"

Jake grunted and pushed Nicholas toward the kitchens. "Go. If you're especially nice to me, I'll show you the infamous disarm-unsuitable-suitors-with-no-blood-spilt move I used on our good Lord Ledenham."

"In truth?" Nicholas asked, sounding pleased. "I found that quite to my liking, if I must admit it. Where did you learn it?"

"That is a very long story . . ."

Amanda watched them walk off together and felt her heart begin to ease. They were walking together with no sharp implements of death bared. This was very good. They were of a height, quite the same in build, and somewhat the same in nature. But just the same, they were quite different and she couldn't help but believe that, for her, she had chosen the right one.

"At least Nick has stopped plotting how best to do him in," Robin remarked lazily. "You should be relieved, sister."

"I am. I will leap up and dance a jig tomorrow—when I am more myself." She wanted to lean back, but couldn't. Instead, she pulled the blanket more closely around herself and leaned toward the fire. She looked up at Robin carefully. "Where do you think Jake was all that time?"

"Haven't you asked him?"

She shook her head. "I couldn't bear to know."

"Well, he was certainly not whoring his way from here to London and back."

"Robin!" Anne exclaimed.

Robin winked at Amanda. "Forgive me. And if you'll know the truth of it, sister, he was off retrieving bags of gold and jewels to pay your purchase price. Who knows where, though."

Amanda stared into the fire for a very long time before she spoke again. "Montgomery thinks he's a fairy and that he was trapped in their land until he could convince them to let him go."

"Montgomery would be better served to think less and practice with his sword more."

Amanda smiled at Robin. "Didn't you watch him follow Jake and Nicky just now? He loves Jake well, no matter where he's been." She sighed and looked back at the fire. "I only hope all Jake's time in the lists will be sufficient, sufficient to merit his gold and jewels."

"It will be."

"There is a part of me that grieves that he should spend all he's worked for just to have me."

Robin drank deeply of his wine. "You, sister, have little idea of what he's sacrificed to remain here with you—and that includes far more than his gold."

"Does he love London so much, then?" Amanda asked wistfully.

"London is the very least of the things he's given up."

Anne laughed. "By the saints, Robin, can you be any more mysterious? Either give the poor girl the details, or cease with tormenting her."

"I'll say no more—"

"The saints be praised," Amanda muttered.

Robin frowned at her. "What you learn about him, you will learn from him. If you're curious, why don't you ask him yourself?"

"I will. I just felt it was appallingly impolite to inquire about the state of his purse," she said primly.

"Why?" Robin asked. "Every male of marriageable age in England has inquired about the state of yours."

"I hardly want to emulate any of them," she said. She looked down into the fire for a goodly while, listening to Robin and Anne talk softly about simple things and envying them their peace. Robin had his place assured and so did Anne. She watched them thoughtfully until Anne looked at her and smiled.

"What is it, Amanda?"

Amanda shook her head. She would have preferred to shrug, but that hurt too much. "I worry."

"You probably should," Robin said helpfully. "Not only will he have to impress Father, he'll have to wrench a title from the king."

"Robin," Anne chided. She looked at Amanda. "Rhys will help him, I'm sure."

"Hmmm," Amanda said, but she wasn't sure at all.

"Don't give up hope," Anne said gently.

"Listen to her," Robin advised. "You gave up hope before and look what it got you."

"Many thanks for the reminder," Amanda said, pulling at her hair.

"That won't help it grow," Robin pointed out.

Amanda glared at him. "Have you nothing useful to say? Perhaps you should repair to the lists and favor them with your sunny words."

Robin rose and stretched, then looked at Anne. "Do you mind?"

"Do I ever?"

He smiled and leaned down to kiss her. "You are a most

remarkable woman, Anne of Artane," he said quietly, "and I love you deeply."

Anne glowed. Amanda smiled at the sight. Robin could be a boor, true, but he could also be very sweet and she was happy to see that Anne could at least see that part of him that the rest of them so seldom did.

Robin ruffled her hair on his way by. "You are almost tolerable as well," he offered generously.

Amanda blew her hair out of her eyes and looked at Anne. "Can you see why he drives me mad?"

Anne laughed. "He loves you well. And he's quite fond of Jake. I wouldn't worry overmuch. He'll see that Jake is prepared."

"For what?" Amanda asked. "To have my father come home and grind him under his heel?"

"Rhys will look upon him favorably," Anne predicted cheerfully. "What choice will he have? You love Jake."

"His choice will be to choose someone for me who has a title and lands!" Amanda exclaimed.

"Jake will buy those. What cannot be bought, my dearest sister, is a man who will love and honor you all your days and that is what you have found. Your father will see that."

Amanda unclenched her hands, only then realizing how tightly she had them clasped together. "I hope you're right."

"What you need is a walk on the shore," Anne said. "Take Jake tomorrow, away from the keep, away from the lists, and enjoy the sunshine. You won't have many more days of warmth. Take Jake and tell him what is in your heart."

"I would hope he knows."

"Tell him again. They need to hear it often."

Amanda nodded. "I will. The sea air will do me good as well."

"I don't know why you thought Seakirk Abbey was a good choice," Anne said with mock horror. "So far from the sea. How would you have survived it?"

"I didn't care," Amanda said. She drew her hand across her eyes and sighed. "I didn't care and I was a fool. I should have waited."

"Love makes fools of us all," Anne said.

"Whom are you quoting?"

"I don't know, but it is the truth, isn't it?"

"Aye," Amanda said, with feeling.

But at least she would be a happy fool and for that she was enormously grateful.

Chapter 33

Jake looked at the sea and wondered how he was ever going to get his toes in the water again without baring more of himself than was proper. He weighed that sacrifice against the pleasure of holding Amanda's hand and decided it was no sacrifice. Besides, the sea was cold. He could do without it easily.

The day was beautiful. It was cool, but not unpleasant, and the sun shone. It was probably one of the last days before the fall rains began and Jake was very grateful to be on the beach for a change and not in the lists.

Not that he didn't appreciate his time in the lists. But somehow, walking with Amanda was much more enjoyable than being reduced to a quivering mass of abused muscles by one of her elder brothers. Though he generally sparred with Robin, when Robin needed to take a drink or visit the loo, Nicholas was always there, ready and willing to take up a sword and do his best to send Jake into oblivion. Jake didn't complain. The more practice he had, the better his chances of impressing Amanda's father. And given that his future depended on the latter, he was more than willing to accept instruction from either elder de Piaget brother.

Besides, he was really starting to like Nicholas. Nicholas

was more laid back than Robin, sneakier, more liable to slide a knife in between your ribs with a smile than Robin was. Jake understood that. He hoped that someday Nicholas would have forgiven him enough that they could just sit down and have a friendly conversation without worrying about that knife. Stranger things had happened.

As if there hadn't been things strange enough in his life already.

Strange and completely marvelous.

He looked at the marvelous part walking next to him. She was silent, but he supposed some of that was likely due to discomfort. She still walked with a limp, and more often than not she would gasp when her back pulled.

Busting the abbess down to scullery maid had been too kind.

Without warning, Amanda stopped and looked up at him. "Montgomery says you are a fairy," she said suddenly.

Well, apparently she was going to forgo the pleasantries and get right down to business. He supposed there was no time like the present to answer a few of her questions.

"Did Montgomery give you proof of that?" he asked.

"He said I should ask you for it."

Apparently Montgomery was very good at keeping secrets. Good for him.

"So I am asking you," Amanda continued. "Are you a fairy?"

"Do you believe in fairies, Amanda?" he asked, after a moment or two.

"I believe," she said, "in what I can touch, in what I can see, in what I can hold in these two hands. But," she admitted with a smile, "I am willing to consider other possibilities."

He looked at her, with her shorn hair blowing around her head, her clear aqua eyes, and her painfully beautiful face, and had the unsettling feeling that none of it was real.

And then she took both his hands in her own.

"So tell me," she said. "Tell me the entire tale, for I suspect there is much more to it than a simple trip to London. And if you want to tell me that you sprang up from the grass, then I will likely believe that as well."

He smiled. "I won't tell you that. But there is certainly more to it than just a trip to London."

"That eases my mind."

He supposed he would see as time went on just how much the truth eased her mind. He put his arm around her shoulders, gently, and turned to walk with her down the shore. "How much faith do you have?"

"In you?"

He nodded.

She walked with him for several moments in silence, then looked up at him. "I've watched you for a goodly part of the summer, and now part of the fall, driving yourself in the lists in a manner than makes Robin look lazy. Am I wrong in assuming you're doing that for me?"

"No," he said slowly, "you aren't wrong."

"Robin says you have given up the life you knew in return for gold and gems that you might buy a title to appease my father. Is that so?"

"That is so," he said.

"Then how can I not have faith in you?"

"You haven't heard all the facts."

"I am not a weak-kneed maid unable to bear up under strain," she said tartly. "Have you no faith in me?"

He leaned over and kissed the top of her head. "I do."

"Then cease with your kissing of every place but where it might do the most good."

He laughed, then turned her gently toward him. He slipped his hand behind her neck, then proceeded to kiss her quite thoroughly. He looked down at her with a smile. "Better?"

"You may proceed," she said, somewhat breathlessly.

He took a deep, steadying breath of his own, then nodded. "All right. But let's walk, if you can. I talk better when I'm walking."

"As you will."

He tightened his arm around her briefly, then looked down at her as they slowly paced down the sea's edge, so she would be able to judge for herself if he was lying. "Montgomery has good reason to think I'm a fairy, but not for the reason he might think. I wouldn't have believed this if it hadn't happened to me, and please do not look at me as if I've lost my mind, but there are, scattered all over England and Scotland . . ." he had to pause for a moment to see if he could manage to say it without sounding like a complete whacko, "gates through time."

She stopped. "What?"

"Gates through time."

She was every bit the poker player Robin was. She merely looked at him for a very long moment, then looked out over the sea. "Through time," she repeated thoughtfully.

"Just like the gate in and out of a castle. On one side is a certain year; on the other is another."

She chewed on that one for a minute or two. "Have you an example?"

"I do. On one side of a certain gate is the year 1227. On the other is the year 2005."

"2005," she repeated, her breath catching. She looked up at him suddenly. "Surely you jest."

He shook his head slowly. "I don't."

"And what have these gates to do with you?" she asked, but he could tell she already knew the answer.

"I used one of them."

"You used one of these gates."

"I did. From 2005."

"From the year of Our Lord's Grace 2005," she repeated with a shiver. "Even saying as much is almost beyond me." She paused. "I am not an uneducated woman, but this stretches the bounds of what I can comprehend."

"Let me finish the story, then you decide what further proof you need," he said easily.

She was silent for several minutes, then she nodded. "'Tis fair," she agreed. "Very well, how did you come to be, um, here?"

"I was traveling along, and my," he paused and decided that he would have to sit down with a sketchbook at some point and draw things for her, "cart rolled off the road. The spinning seemed to take a very long time and when I woke, I was in your father's solar."

She considered. "What language do they speak in 2005?"

"A variant of the peasant's English. The French I know is much changed from the one we speak together right now."

"And how do you defend yourselves?"

"With lawyers, generally," he said dryly. "No, in my time, we do not fight with swords, or ride horses, for the most part, except for entertainment, or live in castles. Well, there are some who do, but most don't. It costs too much."

"And merchants?"

"That is the business of a great many people," he said. "And my business, the business of gems, requires much education and skill."

"But you do live in London?"

"I did," he said.

"How old are you?" she asked, then she smiled, almost shyly. "I never asked you that."

"Thirty-two."

She shot him a look before she nodded and started to walk with him again. She looked down at her feet as they walked for so long that he wondered if she was really deciding that he'd lost it and it was better to cut her losses and run before she got in any deeper with a lunatic. Jake spared a moment for regret that he hadn't held out his hand when he first met her and given her the whole story. Then again, he hadn't known enough Norman French to have done it justice.

She stopped suddenly and looked up at him. "I am trying to take this on faith."

"Would you like proof?"

She blinked suddenly, several times, as if she were trying not to cry. "Damned sand," she said with a scowl. She dragged her sleeve across her eyes. "I do not doubt you," she insisted. "But . . ." She looked up at him, pained. "Proof would help."

He laughed, took her face in his hands, and kissed her softly. "The proof will take time to come, but I will give it to you. The baby Anne is carrying now? It will be a boy and his name will be Kendrick. Anne will have two more children, a girl and another boy. Mary and Jason."

She took a deep breath. "Anything else you feel to share?"

"I have a coin from 2005. Robin has it."

Her mouth fell open and she pulled away from him. "*Robin* knows? You trusted *Robin* with this secret and not me?"

"He watched me walk through a time gate and disappear," Jake said simply. "I had no choice but to tell him."

She folded her arms over her chest and glared at him. "I cannot believe you trusted that bumbling oaf before you trusted me."

"I thought you had enough on your mind."

"Next time," she said, her eyes flashing, "do not do my thinking for me, Jackson Alexander Kilchurn."

"IV."

"The Fourth, damn you to hell."

He laughed. "I promise, I won't."

"If you think I have forgiven you for this, you are sorely mistaken, good sir. It is simply beyond my ability to believe that you would trust my inept brother with a secret of this import before you could see your way clear to take me aside and give me the tidings first." She looked at him furiously. "I am quite angry."

"So I see. How do I apologize?"

She continued to glare at him for several minutes during which time he wondered if he should just excuse himself and go fetch that box of very expensive chocolates Kendrick had put in with his gear.

But before that became absolutely necessary, Amanda suddenly sighed. "Tell me you can do this thing," she said. "I am so afraid—"

"That I will fail?"

"That others will prevent it," she said miserably.

"Let me understand this," he said. "You can believe I am from the future, but you can't believe I can talk Henry out of a title?"

"There are many intrigues at court."

He smiled. "Here's something that might ease your mind. The night before I came to your time, I was standing in a long hallway in Seakirk castle and I watched two ghosts fighting over who was more beautiful, Anne of Artane or the lady Gwen."

Amanda took a deep breath. "Is that so?"

"That is so," he said. "The fight went on for some time. Until a third man, Robert of Conyers, said your name. The other two ghosts put up their swords and agreed in glowing terms that indeed you had been the fairest of them all. When I asked them about you, they looked at me as if I'd lost my mind. Perhaps they knew something I didn't. Perhaps they knew me from 1227. Perhaps Robert had watched me with you for years and wondered why I'd forgotten it all."

"Robert is one of my guardsmen," she said weakly.

"Apparently, eight hundred years in the future, he still thinks you are beautiful."

"Long after I'm dead," she murmured.

"Long after we're both dead," he said.

She hesitated, then put her arms around him and leaned her head on his chest. "I will trust you, though this is difficult for me to believe."

He put his arms around her very carefully. "Is it easier to believe I'm just a simple merchant setting my sights far above my station?"

She laughed briefly. "Aye, I daresay it is."

"Until you decide, trust me. And keep the things I've told you to yourself until you see the truth of them."

"Jake! Amanda!"

Jake looked back up the way to see Montgomery racing toward them, waving his arms above his head.

"Company," Jake said with a sigh.

"Kiss me," she commanded. "I'll have one last bit of peace before he hounds us for the rest of the day."

Jake obliged until Montgomery's hollering came so close that he knew he had to pay attention. He sighed and looked at Amanda's brother.

"What is it?"

"Father's home," Montgomery said breathlessly. "And he wants to see you both."

Jake thought he was far too old to have his stomach flip as it was currently doing. Amanda looked up at him seriously.

"The test is now," she said quietly. "Are you certain?"

"Do you think I'm going to walk away now? Unless there is someone else you would rather have fighting for you—"

"Well, Lord Ledenham *is* rather appealing," she said with a smile.

"Liar," he said, turning her toward the castle. "Let's go. Best to plead my case sooner than later."

She only shot him a look full of unease. Jake took her hand and walked with her down the beach and slowly back over the dunes to the castle. He kissed her hand once more under the outer bailey barbican, then let go.

"I'd better not take liberties," he said solemnly.

"You aren't taking this nearly as seriously as you should," she chided.

"Of course I am. My future is at stake and so is yours." He put his shoulders back. "I wish I had another year to perfect my swordplay."

"I do too," she said helpfully. "He'll cut you to ribbons."

"Thank you so much for your confidence in my abilities."

"Should I lie?" she asked simply. "My father grew to manhood with a sword in his hands, just as Robin did. How can you possibly hope to match that skill in a single summer?"

"I can't," Jake said easily. "I'll just do the best I can."

"I know."

He walked up the way with her to the great hall. Men were milling about the courtyard, going up and down the steps and refreshing themselves in the hall. Jake walked in with Amanda, only to have the throng part. He saw, standing near the high table, an older couple. They were dressed simply, but Jake had no trouble realizing that these were Amanda's parents.

He allowed himself to wonder for what was honestly the first time, what in the *hell* he was thinking to walk up to Amanda of Artane's father and declare his intentions of buying her for his wife. To cross swords with the man who had taught Robin of Artane everything he knew?

He was out of his mind.

He felt Amanda looking up at him. He returned her gaze with what he was certain was a slightly sick smile.

"Do not force me to carry you the rest of the way," she warned.

Jake felt some of the tension ease from him. "Thank you."

"Nay, my thanks to you. You look to be quite heavy."

And then she went and put her arms around her mother.

And Jake understood why Seakirk's ghosts had found Gwennelyn de Piaget worthy of being championed.

Jake admired her from a bit of a distance and knew he was seeing Amanda in twenty years. Gwen was breathtakingly lovely, with highlights of silver in her long, dark hair, and only a few lines of character in her face. Her eyes, though, were Amanda's and Jake found himself being assessed quickly and thoroughly.

And then he realized she was holding out her hand to him.

He wondered if falling to his knees would be overdoing it.

Instead, he stepped forward, took her hand in his, and bowed low over it. He straightened and gave her his most deferential, sincere, please-let-me-have-your-daughter kind of smile.

"I understand," she said, keeping Amanda close to her with her arm around her shoulders, "that I have you to thank for rescuing my daughter from a very poor decision."

"Let us hope she doesn't make another one in its stead," Rhys de Piaget said sternly.

Jake flashed Gwen a grateful smile, then turned to bow to Amanda's father.

"My lord," he said, straightening. He wasn't sure if now would be the proper time to lay out his scheme for Rhys or not, so he kept his mouth shut. He felt Amanda's father take his measure; he wasn't sure if he had been found wanting or not.

"I have spoken to Robin," Rhys said. "He says you are the reason my daughter stands before me."

"Your sons were there as well, my lord, in the rescue."

Rhys considered that, his arms folded over his chest, his expression anything but welcoming. Jake wondered, not for the first time in the past five minutes, if he was actually going to pull this off.

"You are a merchant, I understand," Rhys said.

Bingo. Jake nodded. "I am, my lord."

Rhys's expression didn't change. He looked suddenly at his wife. "We will settle ourselves, then I must speak with Sir Walter to see if there is aught left in the larder or in my coffers. I will give thought to this other matter later."

And with that, and no more than that, he turned and strode off.

"He had you for supper, didn't he?"

Jake looked at Robin and suppressed the urge to punch him. "Do you always sneak up on people like that?"

Robin grinned. "I've been standing next to you for several minutes. Didn't you notice?"

"Of course he didn't notice, you dolt," Amanda snapped. "'Tis a horrible habit you have and one you should rid yourself of. Jake has enough on his mind without you troubling him."

"What's to worry about?" Robin asked pleasantly. "Father

hasn't even met you on the field and already he's thrashed you."

"Are you being helpful?" Jake asked. "I'm confused."

Robin only laughed, clapped him on the shoulder, and winked at Amanda. "Poor lad. Best bring a shovel, Amanda, to scoop up what Father leaves of him."

"Begone, you vile cur," Amanda snapped. "If you cannot be useful, be somewhere else."

Robin cheerfully kissed his mother on both cheeks, then ambled off, humming pleasantly to himself.

But at least Gwen was smiling. "Master Kilchurn, is it?" she asked.

Well, at least she knew his name. That had to be a good sign.

"Jackson," he said with another deferential nod. "Jake, if you prefer."

"Hound fodder, if you want to be most accurate," Robin called back at them.

"I will kill him this time," Amanda vowed. "Watch and see if I don't."

Gwen held onto Jake's arm and drew him along with her toward the stairs.

"Robin must find you to his liking," she said easily, "else he would be snarling instead of chortling. Now, I've only heard the briefest of rumors from Montgomery, and I can see for myself what Amanda has done to her hair, but perhaps you would care to join me in my solar and describe the events of the summer whilst we take our ease?"

Jake nodded and escorted them up the stairs and down to a room he had never been in. He supposed there were many rooms he'd never been in, and wondered how that boded for his future.

"Ah, Anne, my love," Gwen said, greeting Anne with kisses on both cheeks. "How well you look."

"I am much improved," Anne agreed with a smile. "I'm sorry not to come down to greet you. Phillip was asleep here and I didn't want to leave him. Was your journey enjoyable?"

Gwen smiled. "You know I would rather be home, but we did pay visits to those we needed to. Now we return to find that you all have had a most interesting few months."

Jake procured chairs, helped Amanda sit as best she could, then stood behind her with his hands clasped behind his back.

He put on his most medieval, most how-could-you-not-want-me-as-a-son-in-law look. Amanda reached for his hand.

"Sit next to me, Jake," she said quietly. "If you will."

He found a very small stool and perched on it gamely, trying to get his sword to stop sticking him in the ribs. He finally had to get up, unbuckle it, then sit back down with a relieved sigh. He found that the women in the room were all looking at him with varying degrees of amusement and fondness.

Well, fondness from Amanda. Amusement from Anne and Gwen.

"Which of you wishes to take the first turn?" Gwen asked. "Ah, here is Isabelle. Thank you, love, for the wine. Jake, would you pour?"

Jake hadn't expected Isabelle to equal Gwen and Amanda in beauty, but when he saw her, he wondered why not. He vacated his stool, then took the tray from her. Having nowhere to put it, he set it down on the floor, poured five goblets of wine, and handed them all around. He sat himself comfortably on the floor next to Amanda's chair and wondered if he would survive the afternoon.

"You needn't remain on the floor," Gwen said with a smile.

"It's best I do," he answered frankly. "If one more beautiful woman walks in the room, I'll fall there anyway."

"Flatterer," Amanda said, stroking his hair idly.

"I never flatter. I am used to being dazzled by perfect gems. I am not used, however, to being dazzled by four of them at the same time."

Anne laughed. "By the saints, Jake, Robin's grandmother would find you much to her liking. Don't you think, Mother?"

Gwen nodded. "My mother has despaired of ever teaching my boys polite speech. They are fine warriors, but their tongues are anything but gilded. Now, Jake, if you don't mind, perhaps you would begin with why my daughter's hair is no longer than a hand's breadth and how you managed to rescue her before she cut any more of it off. We'll work our way back from there."

Jake spent the rest of the afternoon in very pleasant company, finding himself more at ease than he could ever remember feeling before. Gwen had a way about her that gave the impression that everything he said was of overwhelming interest to her. Anne came in and out of the room, depending on what her son was combining. Isabelle merely watched him with wide eyes.

But it was Amanda who left him catching his breath every time he looked at her.

It wasn't that she was beautiful, because she was, or that she didn't look hopeful, because she did. It was that she looked at peace. As if she'd found her heart's desire and was content with it.

There was still a part of him that couldn't believe that, against all odds, against lack of skill and title, against centuries of time passing, he was the one she had wanted.

Amazing.

The door to his right opened and Montgomery peeked in. "Are you finished here?"

"For the moment," Gwen said.

"Supper is ready. Then Father plans a parley in his solar." He looked at Jake. "You aren't invited."

"Montgomery," Gwen chided, "it isn't polite to single someone out thusly."

"But, I didn't, Mama," Montgomery said simply. "Father said not to invite him. I was going to keep Jake company, but Father says I must come too." He smiled at Jake. "You are welcome to come to supper, if you like. At least Father isn't starving you."

"Thank heavens for small favors." Jake rose, saw the ladies escorted out of the room, then found himself stopped at the door by a hand in the middle of his chest. Amanda reached up with a wince and pulled his head closer. She kissed him softly.

"My father's torturing you. He has done this to every man who has come to court me."

"Then this is a good thing."

"He's treating you as he treated the others. 'Tis a very good thing indeed."

"I'm relieved."

"I daresay that relief won't last long."

But she smiled deeply when she said it and he thought he might endure quite a few tormenting dinners to see that smile again.

* * *

D*inner* was an uncomfortably short affair. He had barely managed to get a few bites past the crushing hand squeezing his heart unmercifully before Rhys had risen and was leading his family off. Amanda, who had been placed at the opposite end of the table from him, spared Jake one last look.

Jake remained where he was, finished what he could of his meal, and wondered what would happen next.

He could only hope that Robin had pointed out to Rhys that those little brown bags of coins in his trunk were not a miraculous windfall Rhys should spend as quickly as possible.

The evening dragged on.

Montgomery appeared at his elbow suddenly. He did not look happy.

"Well?" Jake asked.

"They're discussing your flaws."

"Not good?"

"Nicholas is leading the charge."

"Damn him."

John popped up behind Montgomery. Jake looked at him grimly.

"More good news?"

"Robin is dissecting your swordplay."

"Not good?"

John looked somewhat baffled. "Of course it isn't good. It is Robin, after all."

Jake toyed with his trencher. He had finished examining it and was well on his way to reducing it to crumbs when Miles sauntered over with an enormous yawn.

"Well?" Jake demanded.

"They're still discussing," Miles said, casting himself down into the chair next to Jake. "Father wants to see your wares."

"Is that good?"

Miles smiled. "It is, if you want to earn more gold. It isn't if you want to wed his daughter. I would think he would be more interested in your potential as a husband."

"And what is Amanda saying?" Jake prodded. "Is she defending me?"

"She fell asleep an hour ago," Miles said pleasantly. "She's snoring quite happily with her head in Nicholas's lap."

Jake threw up his hands. "This is a catastrophe!"

"You haven't heard the worst of it," Robin said, appearing suddenly in front of him.

"Damn it, will you please *stop* that!" Jake demanded.

Robin leaned on the table and smiled pleasantly. "Tomorrow morning in the lists."

"I can do that," Jake said confidently.

"You'll start with Montgomery and work your way up. My father is saving himself for last."

Jake choked. He finally had to allow Miles to pound him on the back. "Wonderful," he gasped. He looked at Robin. "Do we go train some more, or should I just fall on my sword right now?"

Robin grinned. "Get a good night's rest. Nick said you may have his bed. I suppose he's taking pity on you."

"Nice of him."

"Either that, or he wants something left of you by the time 'tis his turn."

Jake couldn't laugh. He looked at Robin seriously. "And if I fail?"

"You lose the prize," Robin said simply.

Jake sat back and sighed. "Well—"

"Do not fail," Robin said.

"All I can do is—"

"Win," Robin said simply. "There is no other choice. There is no try. There is no 'This is my best.' You must win."

"Robin, I appreciate your faith in me, but I don't stand a snowball's chance in hell of taking on your entire family and still remaining on my feet at the end of it."

"Don't you?" Robin mused. "Perhaps not. But there is more to being a canny warrior than skill with a sword."

And with that, he turned and walked away. Jake watched him go, then looked at Montgomery. "Will you be my squire? Well, after I'm done with you, of course."

Montgomery smiled. "Happily. I'll show you Nick's bed now. You'd best have sleep while you may. And don't worry. No one bests my father. Not even Robin."

"I feel better already."

Miles laughed at him and Jake felt an unaccustomed warmth

in his heart. He looked at the three young men still left at the table with him and thought that having brothers might be a very good thing indeed.

If he survived the morning.

He had no other choice, because if the thought of having brothers was a nice one, the thought of having Amanda was nothing short of cataclysmic.

He rose and walked with Montgomery up the stairs to attempt at least a few hours of sleep.

Chapter 34

Amanda paced slowly along the inner bailey wall, finding it impossible to sit, not only because it pulled on her back but because she was nervous enough to be quite thoroughly sick.

"He is doing well."

Amanda looked at her mother, who was walking along slowly next to her. "Mother, he's fighting Miles. How poorly can he possibly be doing?"

A sword went flying. Amanda watched it as the sun glinted off it in its arc. It fell to the ground with a thud at her feet. She was vastly relieved to see that even though it was quite a plain sword, it did have a blue stone in the hilt.

Miles's, not Jake's.

"The saints be praised," Amanda said fervently. "Perhaps I should retreat to the chapel for the duration of the day."

Gwen drew Amanda's arm through her own. "My love, you would be no less unsettled there than you are here. Perhaps 'tis best you remain and watch."

Amanda stopped and looked at her mother. "How did you bear it?" she asked. "The waiting? The wondering if Father would manage it?"

Gwen smiled ruefully. "I daresay I did much as you are

doing now. I fretted and paced and spent a great deal of time on my knees."

"Mama, do you care for Jake?" Amanda asked. "Or am I making a grave mistake?"

Gwen considered for so long, Amanda began to wish she hadn't asked the question.

"This is what I think," Gwen said slowly. "He reminds me somewhat of your elder brothers, save he is not so hardened from warring. I find it difficult to believe that he is but a merchant. He is well spoken, intelligent, and quite sure of himself. Any man who has the cheek to offer for you without being your equal in station is a man who is either the greatest fool in England, or a man who loves you enough to risk everything to have you. How can I not find that sort of man to my liking? The better question is, do you care for him?"

"Aye," Amanda said glumly.

"Hence your shorn hair."

"I thought to have no other alternative."

Gwen squeezed her hand. "Love, you have always had a different choice."

"Father wanted me to wed. I thought I had lost the man I wanted. What else was I to do?"

"Oh, Amanda," Gwen said, reaching up with her other hand and touching Amanda's face, "forgive us, love. We just wanted you to be happy."

"Then pull Father aside and tell him not to kill Jake."

"I don't think 'tis your father you should worry about." Gwen nodded toward the field. "Look."

Amanda looked and wished she hadn't. Jake was facing Nicholas and Nicholas was not showing him any mercy. The only helpful thing Amanda could say was that Jake hadn't expended all that much strength besting her youngest brothers—though with Montgomery and John, he had dragged things out far longer than he'd needed to. She had looked at her father at the time to see how he felt about that, but his expression showed nothing. Her mother, however, had smiled at her and nodded her approval.

That Jake had finished Miles off in such a short time and without expending all his reserves of strength and ability boded quite well.

Then again, Miles was not Nicholas and the morning was wearing on.

The sun wended its way toward its zenith and still Jake and Nicholas continued to fight.

"This is good," Gwen said firmly.

"Good?" Amanda echoed incredulously. "How can you possibly say that?"

"Nicholas is sweating as well, my love."

"Aye, well, I wish he would sweat less and give in," Amanda said flatly. "There will be nothing left of Jake by the time Nicholas is through with him."

And then, quite suddenly, Nicholas was standing with his sword point down in the dirt and Jake's sword at his throat.

"Merciful saints above," Amanda breathed.

"Aye," Gwen agreed. "And fairly done, as well."

Nicholas called peace. Amanda watched as her brother clasped hands with Jake and walked off the field. He walked past her to where drinks were standing ready on a bench. He drank, poured the rest of the water over his head, then came to stand next to her. Amanda wrinkled her nose.

"You should bathe."

Nicholas smiled pleasantly. "I will. Once this is all over. Having come this far, I cannot miss the end."

The ring of swords had hardly begun before it was over. Amanda watched in horror as Jake's sword went flying out of his hands. Robin showed him, unsurprisingly, no more mercy than Nicholas had, pressing Jake as if he had every intention of killing him. Amanda wondered how it was that Jake held up in the face of Robin's completely unforgiving expression. She would have called peace merely not to see any more of it.

Jake leaped out of the way to miss a particularly vicious thrust. Robin scowled.

"Real knights don't flinch."

Jake smiled.

Robin was not amused.

But Robin was also, quite suddenly, without the knife in his belt. He looked at Jake, who now was in full possession of Robin's own knife, and his expression darkened.

"Jake's done it now," Nicholas said pleasantly. "Do you think he would mind if I helped myself to his gold after he's dead? My roof is proving to be quite an expensive venture."

"Be silent," Amanda whispered, too terrified to even berate him as she should have. "If you've any mercy at all, say a prayer or two for him."

"He doesn't need them," Nicholas said confidently. "Why do you think I haven't murdered him in his sleep long before now? He's quite canny. If you must wed, then wed with him."

She looked up at him, open-mouthed. "In truth?"

He smiled faintly. "We'll continue to train him. There is more to being a lord than swordskill. I know several lords who can't wield a sword to save their lives. Then again, they aren't seeking to wed with my sister, but that is another tale entirely. Now, this Kilchurn—"

Gwen's gasp interrupted him. Amanda looked to find Robin without his sword as well.

From there, it was a very brief fight and it ended with Robin face down in the dirt with Jake pinning him there.

Amanda looked about her. There wasn't a soul in the lists who didn't look on with expressions of complete astonishment.

But by the time she looked back, Jake was standing and had hauled Robin to his feet, leaving her wondering if she had imagined the entire thing. Robin was loudly pointing out to anyone who would listen that Jake had indeed not bested him with the sword.

And then a voice cut through Robin's babbling like a sword through flesh.

"Pick up your sword, if you will."

Amanda looked to her right to find her father standing there, his arms folded across his chest, his sword still sheathed.

Even Robin seemed to realize that silence was the wisest course of action because he retrieved his own sword and sauntered off the field with his normal victor's swagger. He had himself a refreshing drink, then came to stand next to his mother. He looked at Amanda.

"Damned chameleon," Robin said cheerfully. "I thought I had him there, but obviously lowering your guard to a Kilchurn is a poor idea. You'll note, however, that he did *not* best me with the sword."

Amanda snorted at him, but that was apparently not enough

to deter him. He continued to babble about his own prowess until Amanda had to fold her arms over herself to keep from reaching over and slapping him. "Mother," she said finally, in exasperation, "please shut him up or remove him from the field. He's distracting me."

"Robin, love, give your sister a bit of peace," Gwen said, "before she takes a blade to you and you find yourself bested by her as well."

Robin had quite a bit to say about that, leaving Amanda no choice but to merely do her best to ignore him. She watched her father and noticed immediately what he was doing. He started Jake out slowly, with the simplest exercises he used with his own young pages. That didn't last long. He moved on quickly to more complicated defenses and a thorough test of everything he taught first to his squires, then to his knights.

Jake held his own.

"You know," Robin whispered in her ear, "I don't think any of the other baggages you've endured ever made it this far, do you?"

"What I think is that if you creep up on me thusly one more time," she said, finding it quite easy to glare at him now that he was suddenly standing next to her, "I will plunge the dagger you so kindly chose for me into your belly and count myself well rid of you!" She elbowed him in the ribs for good measure. "Go stand by your mother where she might protect you from me."

"Well?" Robin asked. "Do you?"

She wanted to wring her hands, but that would have looked weak. Instead, she clasped them demurely in front of her and looked at the field where Jake and her father were still hard at it. "I cannot bear to think," she said. Then she looked at her brother. "He's not showing that poorly, is he?"

"He stands, still," Robin said simply. "What else is there than that? It isn't as if it is in his best interest to humiliate his future father-in-law now, is it?"

"He would never manage that," Amanda said quietly.

"Not if he's wise," Robin said cheerfully. "Though Jake certainly could hold his own if he needed to. He could relieve Father of his sword, use his hands and feet, break a bone or two—by the saints, Amanda, have you no idea whom you're giving yourself to? Not my equal, of course, but a lethal man just the same."

Amanda couldn't do anything but nod weakly. Indeed, there was much more to Jake than met the eye.

"Ah, but look you there, Amanda. See how Father begins to fight truly? It won't last long now."

Amanda watched, winced, and prayed. It lasted far longer than she suspected it would, but in the end, Jake was forced to cry peace. He resheathed his sword, then made Rhys a low bow.

"Good," Robin murmured. "Flatter him, then plead your case."

Which Jake seemed to be doing. Rhys put his hand on Jake's shoulder and they walked off together, chatting amicably. Amanda looked for somewhere to sit. Robin provided a stool and Amanda sank down upon it gratefully.

Her father and Jake walked to the far end of the lists, spoke for an impossibly long time together, then turned and came back toward where Amanda was fair to swooning off her stool. Rhys smiled at her.

"Not a bad showing," he said magnanimously. "Of course, there are a few more things I must discuss with this man before I come to a decision about him."

Amanda swallowed finally, realizing that it had been some time since she'd done so. Whilst it wasn't a final word of approval, it wasn't instructions on how to find the front gates either.

And she had heard her sire deliver those more than once.

Rhys did invite Jake in for supper and a parley after the meal. Amanda would have congratulated Jake on his efforts, but her father pulled him away. Jake shot her a look, then continued on with her sire. Amanda sighed and walked back to the house with her mother and her babbling brothers. Even Isabelle seemed to have far too much to say.

But the first test was over. Now all Jake would have to do was tell her father the truth about himself and avoid the gallows.

Supper was an unusually merry affair. Amanda found herself favored enough to sit beside Jake as he sat beside her father. Rhys and Jake were well into a very pleasant meal, discussing in a very animated manner the idea of a free Scotland, when the door to the great hall burst open and half a dozen men strode inside.

Men leaped up and would have stopped the intruders if Rhys hadn't suddenly called on them to halt. He remained seated, though, looking completely at ease.

Lord Ledenham strode to the high table, then tossed into Rhys's supper a large sack of gear and a smaller, black folded purse. His other arm, apparently a broken one, was strapped to his side. He gestured with his good hand at Jake.

"His gear. The warlock at your table."

Jake was halfway to his feet before Rhys pulled him back down calmly.

"Ledenham," Rhys said without inflection. "Gifts? How kind."

"You'll think differently when you examine those things," Ledenham said coldly. He fixed Jake with a scorching look. "I think a charge of witchcraft is not unlikely—"

Robin stood and hopped over the table before Amanda could gasp.

"By the saints," he drawled, leaning back against the table and folding his arms over his chest, "can you not do better than that, Ledenham? I know Amanda is fetching, but is she worth this? Accusing an innocent man of something so foul . . ." He shook his head sadly. "It bespeaks a man so desperate to have what he wants that he has forgotten there is a price to be paid for lying."

Even Amanda wasn't past the point of misunderstanding his meaning.

If Ledenham didn't retreat, Artane would attack.

Under the table, she put her hand on Jake's knee and squeezed. She didn't look at him and she supposed he wasn't looking at her, but his hand covered hers.

By the saints, 'twas a disaster.

Rhys picked up the little black purse from out of his stew and dried it on a cloth. He lifted the sack with equal ease and handed it and the purse behind him to Christopher.

"Take these to my solar, little one. We'll repair there momentarily." He looked back at Ledenham. "I would offer you the hospitality of my hall, but unfortunately we are just finishing supper and preparing to retire. Perhaps another time."

Lord Ledenham glared at Rhys. "I tell you he is a warlock. His gear—"

"How do you know 'tis his?" Rhys asked, with a puzzled frown.

"Because I took it off h—" Ledenham suddenly stopped, then fell silent.

Rhys looked at him quizzically. "You took it off him? Do you imply that you *stole* from this man here?" He put a possessive hand on Jake's shoulder. "This man who is a welcome guest at my table?"

Ledenham's face was a very unattractive shade of red. "I will accuse him before every soul who will listen," he spat. "I have proof."

"Show it," Rhys said easily.

Ledenham glared at Jake. "Fetch me the purse."

Jake blinked in confusion. "Purse? What purse?"

"That ruse will not suffice you," Ledenham said with a sneer. "All my men here saw it and they will swear to its supernatural contents."

"And all my men will swear they saw nothing," Rhys said. "Sir Walter," he called, "have our good men seen anything odd?"

Sir Walter was standing near the door with his arms folded across his chest in his most intimidating pose, flanked by a handful of Artane's guardsmen and faced across the way by a handful more.

"Odd?" Sir Walter asked. "We've seen nothing odd, but my lord, I must say that there is a remarkably foul smell which has wafted inside the great hall just recently."

Rhys smiled pleasantly. "Apparently, my good Ledenham, there is nothing to be seen here."

"Will your children perjure themselves for you as well?" Lord Ledenham demanded furiously.

"I believe," Robin said, giving Ledenham a shove, "that you just called my father a liar."

"You too, Rob, I'd say," Nicholas offered.

Ledenham was fool enough, unsurprisingly, to draw his sword inside Artane's hall. It was not easily done, nor was it easily wielded, given that Ledenham's right arm was the injured one. Robin chortled, then swore once he realized the weakness of his opponent.

"Oh, by the saints, return when you can fight," he said in disgust.

"I can fight," Ledenham boasted. "Raise your sword like a man and let us see if you can hold your own against me and my weak hand."

Robin shrugged, then paused. "I'll fight with my left," he said magnanimously. "To give you a sporting chance."

"I could best you with my sword held in my teeth," Ledenham boasted.

"We'll try that later," Robin promised, then, with a grin, threw himself joyously into the fray.

"I should help," Jake said, starting to rise.

Amanda stopped him with a hand on his arm. "I understand you humiliated him at the abbey. Allow Robin his little pleasures, if you can."

Jake sat back down. "I suppose."

Amanda leaned back gingerly against her chair and watched as Robin humbled the man in a matter of minutes, not bothering to rid him of his sword in any impressive manner. Robin merely stepped in at an opportune moment and grasped Ledenham's good wrist.

"Will you die," Robin asked, "or will you leave?"

"I'll kill you," Ledenham spat. "See if I don't."

Robin yawned. "As you will." Then he took his sword hilt and pressed it quite firmly against Ledenham's forehead.

The man slumped to the ground with a groan.

"Remove the refuse," Robin boomed.

Ledenham's men collected him and scurried from the great hall. Sir Walter and a large contingent of Artane lads followed them out the door. Amanda looked at her sire.

Would he think Jake was of that supernatural ilk?

Jake cleared his throat. "My lord, there are things we should discuss—"

Rhys rose. "Then come with me, if you will. Robin, Nicholas, you two will come as well. Miles, stay here and see to your mother and the girls." He smiled at Montgomery and John at the end of the table. "You lads can see to yourselves, can you not?"

"I would like to come, Father," Montgomery said, rising quickly and making Rhys a low bow. "I like Jake, you see, and I might be a voice in his favor where he has none other."

Amanda thought she just might have to make certain her youngest brother had many, many fine things from the kitchens in the future.

Rhys nodded at his youngest son. "I suppose you may come. Jake will no doubt appreciate your presence." He put his hand briefly on Amanda's head as he passed behind her. "Daughter."

"Father," she whispered. She looked at Jake as he rose. "Good fortune to you, good sir."

He smiled in a most determined fashion and left to follow her father from the great hall. If he were ill at ease, he hid it well. Amanda looked up as her mother moved to sit next to her.

"Interesting," Gwen said.

"Mother, he is no warlock."

"And why ever would I think that?" Gwen asked, blinking in surprise.

"You wouldn't," Amanda said, chewing on her lip to keep herself from blurting out things she shouldn't. She wasn't certain what Ledenham had thrown at Jake, but she suspected it was something containing items from the future.

Proof, perhaps.

She toyed with the remainder of her dinner and gave that a goodly bit of thought. Would she wish to see those things, to prove to herself that he was what he said he was, or would she take him on faith?

She thought about that for a very long time.

Her answer might make all the difference.

Chapter 35

Jake listened to the study door shut behind him with a click. His gear and his wallet sat on what served Rhys for a desk. Well, no sense in not getting it all over with at once. If Rhys de Piaget was going to have him burned for witchcraft, he might as well have a full complement of reasons for doing so.

Rhys lifted the rustic sack, then looked at Jake.

"With your permission?"

Jake nodded. What else could he do?

Rhys emptied out the sack. Jake watched as his clothing was laid out: his jeans; his shirt; his jacket.

Of course his boots were missing. A nicely broken-in pair of Doc Martens were just too good to pass up, apparently.

Rhys examined the items one by one with meticulous care. Then he carefully folded them and set them aside.

"More light, if you please."

Robin fetched two candles, lit them, then put them on the desk. Rhys sat down and took Jake's wallet in his hands. He turned it over this way and that, then opened it.

He looked at the paper money, the fifty-pound and the one-hundred-pound notes, with no noticeable change in expression. He held them up to the window to stare through them, then held them close to the candle. Not close enough to burn them but close enough to see.

A man used to using firelight for reading, apparently.

Rhys set those things aside. He then searched further in the wallet, pulling out credit cards.

And a driver's license.

Jake watched him closely, but Rhys's face gave absolutely nothing away. If he thought he was handling devilish things, he gave no indication of it.

Rhys fingered the credit cards over and over again, looking at their markings and setting them aside one by one—only after a lengthy examination.

But it was Jake's license that he lingered over the longest.

Rhys looked at the photo—a bad one, as usual—then looked up at Jake. He compared the two, holding the card up and studying it. It was a New York license. Jake made a point of returning to the States every four years to get one. He'd never been sure why he did so, but he carried a US passport and a US driver's license. Much as he loved England, he was, after all, an American first and foremost, and giving up tokens that said as much had been unacceptable.

It occurred to him finally that as calmly as Rhys was taking things, there were those in the room who were taking those same things less well. Noises of alarm, dismay, and the purposeful repeated clearing of throats finally forced Rhys to look at his sons. Jake did as well.

Robin was rocking from foot to foot, barely able to restrain himself.

Nicholas was gaping.

Montgomery was crossing himself again.

"Montgomery," Jake began in exasperation, "I am *not* a fairy!"

"He is not a fairy," Rhys agreed. "He is a man, just as you or I find ourselves to be. These are merely things of a merchantry nature which Jake has acquired in his travels. Am I right?" Rhys asked, looking at Jake with eyes as gray as a stormy, midwestern sky.

"Yes, my lord," Jake said.

"But—" Montgomery said miserably.

Rhys smiled at Montgomery. "You have done your service to Jake just by being here thus far and I will press on as if you were here to speak for him. But now I wish you to go and see how your mother fares." Rhys paused for a moment. "If you do so quickly, and without complaint, then perhaps Jake will take you on one of his travels someday and you will see the same wonders he has."

Montgomery looked at Jake rapturously, all thoughts of fairies apparently forgotten in the possibility of a good adventure. "Will you?"

"Merchantry is a dodgy business," Jake said with a nod. "It never hurts to have a fine swordsman at your side. I would welcome your company."

Montgomery threw his arms around Jake, then bolted from the room, slamming the door shut behind him. Nicholas put his hands on his hips.

"There is something very odd going on here," he said sternly, "and I for one would like to know what it is."

Jake looked at Nicholas and smiled. "I'm a fairy."

"Not amusing," Nicholas snapped.

"The truth is odder than that."

"I am not witless, nor am I possessing a faint heart."

It sounded hauntingly like Amanda. Jake took a deep breath. "All right, then, here it is. I was born eight hundred years from now. In the Year of Our Lord's Grace 2005, I heard ghosts talking about your sister, and believe me that eight hundred years from now she is still causing a stir. The next day, I was out traveling and found myself thrown through a gate from my time to yours. After I fell in love with your sister, I determined the only way to have her was to return to the future to retrieve my fortune. And now here I am, back in the past and hoping that your father will refrain from marrying your sister off to someone else until I can get a title and some land."

Nicholas looked at him in complete silence for several moments, then he looked at his father. "He's mad."

"He seems quite in possession of all his faculties to me," Rhys said blandly.

Nicholas came to stand very close to Jake. "You're mad."

Jake shook his head slowly. "I'm not."

Nicholas scowled. "And I was beginning to like you." He

turned and walked from the chamber, slamming the door behind him.

Rhys looked at Robin. "And you? Have you anything to say?"

Robin shrugged. "I saw him disappear through a time gate with my own eyes. Whilst I cannot answer for Jake, I can assure you that *I* am not daft." He clapped a hand on Jake's shoulder, then walked toward the door. "Ledenham put me off my food. I'm off to find more."

And with that, he left the chamber, shutting the door behind him.

Jake turned his attention from the door back to Rhys, who was sitting back in his chair. Jake managed a brief smile.

"And you, my lord?"

Rhys shook his head slowly. "If I was not viewing this with my own eyes, I daresay I wouldn't believe it."

"I could say the same," Jake said dryly.

Rhys indicated the chair opposite him. "Sit."

"Thank you, my lord." Jake sat. All right, so he collapsed more than sat, but he'd had a very long day so far and it didn't look to be shortening any time soon. He smiled. "Thank you."

Rhys studied him for what seemed an eternity in silence. Then he looked at Jake's driver's license again. "2005," he said, chewing on the numbers as if he'd never considered them before. "'Tis unbelievable."

"I know, my lord."

Rhys looked back at him. "And yet you are here. And these things prove it beyond all reasonable doubt." He shook his head again with a smile, then set the license aside. "You showed well today," he noted.

"Thank you, my lord."

"You have more work to do."

"I know, my lord."

"I understand 'tis only a pair of months you've been at it."

"That is true, my lord."

Rhys nodded. "Very well. You may continue to use Robin as practice, if you will, but I would like to see to your training as long as you are within my walls."

"Thank you," Jake managed. He wasn't sure if that was a good thing to have been offered or not. He wasn't one to jump to conclusions, but *as long as you are within my walls* didn't exactly sound like a rousing endorsement of Jake as husband material.

"Robin says these heavy brown bags of gold in my coffers are yours."

A knock sounded on the door before Jake could answer. Robin stuck his head in politely, then entered and dropped three more brown bags and four navy-blue velvet bags on the table in front of Jake.

"Thought those might be useful," he said, then started toward the door. "You'll note that I didn't lose any."

"Duly noted," Jake said as Robin was closing the door.

Rhys looked at the new offerings, then retrieved the rest from his trunk. He shot Jake a look. "May I?"

"Of course, my lord."

Rhys poured all the gold out, counted it very carefully, then sat back and looked at it for another protracted, excruciating amount of time. Jake was very thankful for an adulthood spent dealing with just these sorts of situations. He'd sat for hours with gem traders, playing chicken, waiting for the first move not to be his.

Only those had been just rocks at stake.

This was Amanda.

Rhys looked at the blue sacks. "And those?"

"Gems."

"May I?"

"Of course, my lord."

Rhys spilled the bags out one at a time. He was fairly impassive about it all until he opened the bag with the finished jewelry. Those he removed piece by piece, slowly and very carefully. He looked at Jake briefly after he'd examined each piece. When he finally pulled out the diamond and aquamarine ring, he spoke.

"This is for Amanda," he said.

"Yes."

"You fashioned this yourself."

"I did."

Rhys took a deep breath, blew it out as he looked heavenward, then fixed his gaze on Jake. "I have never seen anything like it. Even the king has not jewels this fine."

"His gemsmiths probably don't have the tools I had."

"Or the imagination," Rhys said, with another smile. He looked at everything spread out in front of him and shook his head. "Impressive."

"Is it enough?"

Rhys looked at him with a glint in his eye. "For me, or for Henry?"

"Either."

"It was enough this morning for me," Rhys said. "For Henry?" He shrugged. "The lad is still young and barely in control of his crown, but his regent Lord de Burgh is not an ungreedy man. Still, this will be enough."

"All of it?" Jake asked, blinking in surprise.

"Is my daughter not worth it?"

"I had hoped to keep a little back to feed her with," Jake said honestly.

Rhys very carefully wrapped up the jewelry and replaced it. He put the gems back in the bags. He divided the coins into piles, then replaced them as well. He pushed the gem bags to one side, along with two bags of coins. The others, which Jake was unsurprised to find were in the neighborhood of six, remained grouped together, as if they planned a bit of subterfuge.

"These will do," Rhys said.

"I'm relieved."

Rhys looked at him with one raised eyebrow. " 'Tis not too much?"

"I would have given all of it," Jake said honestly.

"Not the ring."

"Well," Jake said with a smile, "perhaps not the ring."

Rhys looked at the bags. "Shall I keep these safe for you until we go to Seakirk to meet with the king?"

"Do you have a reason to?"

Rhys smiled and nodded toward the door. "Go fetch your lady and we'll see what she thinks of you."

"Of course, my lord." He hesitated. "And if I obtain land and a title?"

Rhys smiled. "Then you shall have your heart's desire." He paused. "You have given up much for her."

"I would do it again a thousand times."

Rhys smiled. "Well spoken."

Jake hesitated. "You know, my lord, about Seakirk," he said slowly. "I'm not popular there."

"Neither am I, though I daresay I don't have the distinction of having terrorized hapless nuns," Rhys said with a smile, then he sobered. "Your gear here," he said, nodding toward Jake's things. "'Tis damning."

Jake nodded. "It is. How hot is your cooking fire?"

"Hot enough. We'll descend there later tonight and see to the deed together. No one will gainsay me, though Cook may rifle through the ashes after the fact to make certain I haven't assaulted her domain and left something foul behind." He nodded toward the door. "For now, go fetch Amanda."

Jake smiled. "Thank you."

"Well, you've won one battle, but the war is not over yet. And I haven't heard her say you aye," Rhys said, with a twinkle in his eye.

"True," Jake said, but he walked toward the door just the same.

Rhys cleared his throat from behind him.

"Jake?"

Jake turned with his hand on the door. "My lord?"

Rhys was silent for several moments, looking for the first time to be almost hesitant. Jake almost asked him what troubled him, but suddenly, he suspected that he might know.

After all, it wasn't every day that a medieval lord was faced with a man from the future.

Silence fell between them, as peacefully and still as snow descending in the depths of winter. Jake was quite certain that the moment would be etched upon his memory in much the same way his first sight of Amanda had been, or his first glimpse of a medieval Artane. For the rest of his life, every time he sat in Rhys de Piaget's solar, he would be able to bring to mind this precise point in time when he looked at Artane's lord and gave him answers to questions the man seemed reluctant to ask.

"My lord," Jake said gravely, "is there something I might tell you?"

Rhys nodded with an almost imperceptible sigh. "If you would." He paused. "Three things."

Jake was tempted to ask him if he might not have more

than three questions about the future, but couldn't bring himself to do so. There would be time enough, he supposed, if all went well, to tell Amanda's father all he might wish to know about the marvels that lay ahead of mankind. For now, he would satisfy the man's curiosity on a small scale in the best way he could.

"Three things," Jake began, waiting for Rhys to nod in agreement. "Very well, my lord, the first thing you should know is that the world does not end in the Year of Our Lord's Grace 1300."

Rhys raised an eyebrow. "It doesn't?"

"It doesn't."

Rhys absorbed, then nodded. "Go on."

"The world is round."

"Indeed," Rhys said, looking surprised. "Is it, indeed? They say otherwise, but I must admit, the thought of falling off its edges never sat well with me. Very interesting," he said with a nod. "Now, the last, if you please."

Jake considered what else he might say that would suffice the very proud, very astute man sitting in front of him. He took a moment or two to look around Rhys's study. There were signs of medieval affluence, certainly. It was, oddly enough, the same feeling of subdued power and influence that Jake had noticed in Gideon de Piaget's office. Auras of power and influence were the same, apparently, no matter the century. Jake spared a kind thought for Gideon and his nod to Fate's hand, and another handful of kind thoughts to Gideon's family and extended relations.

And even as he did so, Jake knew quite suddenly just what would matter the most to Rhys de Piaget.

"The third thing," Jake began slowly.

Rhys nodded, just as slowly.

"Eight hundred years from now, my lord, Artane still stands."

Rhys smiled faintly. "Does it now?"

"Yes. And your descendants still inhabit it."

Rhys's eyes were suddenly quite moist. He looked around his own study, then put his hands on his desk for a moment or two before he cleared his throat roughly. "You should go fetch your lady," he said, his voice hoarse. "Before she wears a trench in my floor that will leave my posterity stumbling centuries from now."

Jake smiled, made Rhys a low bow, and left the room to give the man some privacy. He pulled the door shut behind him, then stood there for a moment or two to gather his own thoughts. He looked up and blew out his breath.

He'd done it.

All right, so there was still the hurdle of the king to be surmounted. But now, Jake had the feeling that he might have an ally in his cause, an ally who was sitting back behind that door no doubt contemplating the state of his castle centuries in the future. And who could blame Rhys for it? Artane was a magnificent place. And, as Gideon had once said, the family was a decent bunch, all through the centuries. Jake knew he would be grateful for the rest of his life to claim them as well.

But they were, after all, just the setting for the true gem whom he didn't doubt was doing just as her father said she was, and wearing a trench in the great hall floor.

Jake smoothed his hand along the stone as he walked down the passageway, stone that would last at least eight centuries into the future.

With any luck, and enough gold in his fists, he would win the woman of his dreams and begin a family that would last just as long.

He smiled, and quickened his pace down the hallway.

Chapter 36

Amanda walked along the beach, dragging her bare feet through the sand and shivering because of it. She pulled her cloak more closely around her and wondered if she'd lost what little wits remained her. It was cold; it was rainy; it was windy. She would have been better served to be inside where she might sit by a fire and be warm.

But the thought of sitting inside when she had no idea what her future might hold was as appealing as a few fortnights in her father's dungeon. She had to pace. Best that she pace where there was room for it.

It had been almost a month since her father had returned home. She had watched Jake train with her sire during the mornings and continue with Robin in the afternoons. He spent his evenings discussing affairs of the realm with anyone who could stomach it. It was generally her sire to indulge him in such discussions, which somehow seemed to please her sire. Amanda supposed that it was because Jake was interesting to talk to, or it could have been that he was interested in what Rhys had to say about things, or it could have been just that Rhys favored him. Amanda couldn't have said. All she knew was that her father, Robin, Nicholas, and Jake had ridden to

Seakirk Abbey almost a se'nnight ago and she'd had no word from any of them since.

Louts. Had they no idea of her torment?

She rubbed her arms vigorously, wished for another cloak, then turned her face into the wind and stared out over the sea. She had spent copious amounts of time doing just that over the past fortnight—even before Jake had left for Seakirk. She'd had much on her mind.

Not the least of which had to do with the year he'd left behind.

She'd seen the coin he'd given Robin. She'd seen his Future gear. She'd had all the proof she could have wanted.

And more than she'd needed.

He'd confessed one evening as they'd stood on the roof together that he regretted not having told her sooner. At the time, the admission had soothed her pride, but now she suspected that he'd been wise beyond knowing.

2005. The very numbers still felt foreign in her mind. She had never considered that the world might last so long, or that someone from that Future might come to her keep.

And steal her heart.

But now, now that he was gone again trying to secure a future for her, she wondered how it was she had ever managed the future without him.

Nicholas had reminded her every chance he had that Jake was daft. Montgomery gave her knowing looks now and then and made a shape with his hands that looked remarkably like two fairy wings flapping. But even with those votes of no confidence in Jake's origins, Nicholas had warmed to him. Montgomery adored him.

Amanda understood.

The man was fascinating, like a gem that never ceased to please the eye or invite scrutiny as it was turned this way and that.

Amanda hugged herself, grateful for a form that didn't protest when she did so, and said a little prayer. She likely should have been on her knees in the chapel, but she was far too restless for that.

King Henry had just declared his majority and ascension to the throne. Surely he would be hungry for more support in the north. Surely Jake would look at him with that way he had that demanded ever so easily that he be taken seriously and agreed with. And surely that hefty bag or two of gold he was taking with him would speak more loudly than any of that.

The wind grew stronger. Amanda shivered. The chill had become stronger than what even she could bear. She turned to start back for the keep, then froze.

Jake was standing a hundred paces down the strand from her, simply watching her. He wasn't moving. She couldn't even tell if he was smiling.

She started toward him. And then she started to run.

He met her halfway.

And he swept her up into his arms with a jubilant laugh and spun her around until she begged him to stop.

"Well?" she demanded.

He set her on her feet, took a step or two backward, and bowed low.

"If I might present myself to my lady," he said formally. "Jackson, Lord of Raventhorpe. At your service. Night. Day. All hours in between."

Amanda gasped. "Raventhorpe?"

Jake grinned. "Brilliant, isn't it?"

"Dangerous," she corrected promptly. "On the border with those savage Scots. Perilous. Dilapidated. Unsecured."

"Mine," he said, pulling her to him and wrapping his arms around her. "It is also right on the sea, my most lovely Amanda, and I understand that on a clear day, you can see Artane in the distance. If you squint," he added.

She hugged him tightly. "Congratulations."

"Not condolences?" he murmured against her ear.

She smiled in spite of herself. "I love the unknown. Look whom I'm wedding."

He pulled back and looked at her. "Are you betrothed, then?"

She scowled at him. "You know what I meant."

"I haven't asked you yet."

"Then you'd damned well better be about your business, *my lord,* lest I change my mind."

But she smiled as she said it, so hard that her cheeks ached. He was just as merry. He went down on one knee, right there in the sand, and looked up at her.

"Amanda of Artane, love of my life and light of my heart, will you marry me?"

"Are you certain you want me?" she asked. "Now being lord of your own hall and all."

"I traveled a *very* long way to have you and you were *very* expensive," he said, his eyes twinkling. "But I see you are unconvinced of my sincerity." He reached down into his boot and pulled out something that he subsequently slipped onto her finger. "Does this improve my chances of having your heart?"

Amanda looked down at the band of stars that went all the way around her finger, shining even in the gloom of a rainy fall day. Then she found that they sparkled even more through her tears.

"Stardust," she said, unable to tear her gaze away from her trembling hand. Then she put her hands on his cheeks, then leaned over and kissed him softly. "You did it all. Just as you said."

"Is that my answer?"

She shook her head, then pulled him to his feet. "Nay, but this is: Aye, I will wed with you, Jackson, lord of that renegade-infested Raventhorpe keep, and count myself the most fortunate of women."

"And I the most fortunate of men," he said.

And then he kissed her.

Amanda closed her eyes and melted against him. It was all more than she had ever expected, and so much more than she had ever dared dream. A man she loved, desired, and couldn't imagine life without.

Stardust dreams indeed.

Jake pulled his head away from hers finally and took a ragged breath.

"We should go back inside."

"Why?"

"Because if I don't find a chaperone very quickly, we'll be in trouble."

"My guardsmen won't do?"

"Damn, I forgot about them." He smiled down at her. "Well, we should go in anyway. I imagine you've been out here all week. I don't want you repeating your vows with a stuffy nose.

People will think you're weeping because I forced you to the altar."

"No one will think that," she promised. "I will make certain of it. But I could do with a bit of a fire now that I've no more need for pacing." She took his hand and walked with him back down the shore toward the keep. "So, tell me of your time with Henry. He is quite young, is he not?"

"Twenty-five. But I think he's been seasoned in court for years, so he's definitely not easily fooled."

"What did you say to him?"

"I didn't see Henry at first," he admitted. "Your father managed an audience with Hugh de Burgh. Apparently, he didn't start out with much either, so my tale appealed to him."

"It would," she agreed. "From minor nobility to regent of England. So," she said, "you used your glib tongue to plead your case?"

"Words and gold. A potent combination."

"And with Henry?"

"Words, gold, and a contingent of Artane males standing behind me," Jake said with a grin. "A *very* potent combination. I promised the king to be on his side here in the north, handed him a gem or two and, again, bags of gold, and the deal was done."

She looked up at him, unable to stop smiling. "You did it."

"I couldn't have, without your father and brothers. Though I will admit," he said modestly, "that while I was waiting, I sketched a little portrait of His Majesty. When I handed that to him with the rest of the goods, he was pleased."

"How pleased?"

"So pleased that he's invited us to come to London as soon as we're able to travel so I can do his likeness justice."

"Jake," she breathed. "In truth?"

"Are you interested?"

"I haven't been to London in years," she admitted. "I would enjoy it very much."

"I wouldn't mind seeing it either," he said. "Besides, I don't think we're supposed to refuse. I don't know. What do you think?"

"I think you'd best discuss proper comportment before royalty with my father," she said dryly, "lest we find ourselves painting the inside of a cell in the Tower."

"Never fear, no medieval lock can hold me," he boasted. "Though I daresay it might have been a bit dodgy there for a moment or two when Ledenham arrived, frothing at the mouth."

She gasped. "Ledenham? And he said . . ."

"More of the same," Jake said with a shrug. "I had given my defense quite a bit of thought, but de Burgh made it unnecessary. When Ledenham began to spew out his accusations, de Burgh looked at him as if he'd lost his mind, wondered aloud if the bump left on Ledenham's forehead from Robin's sword hilt had damaged his wits permanently, then threw him out on his, ahem, backside."

Amanda shook her head. "Jake, it won't be the last of him. He'll never give up now."

"It will be his word against mine," Jake said. "And your father's, of course." He shrugged. "An air of mystery will cling to me and, I apologize in advance, to you."

"Which will only increase when you take up residence in Raventhorpe," she pointed out with a smile. "Congratulations again, my lord, on it all just the same. A fine coup."

He ran his hand over her sopping hair. "You were my inspiration."

"And your prize."

"Is tomorrow too soon to claim you?"

She laughed. "We are, if you can fathom this, already prepared."

"You had faith in me," he said, sounding pleased.

"I did."

He smiled at her. "Let's go home, then."

"As you wish, my lord."

She sat in her father's solar later that day, on the eve of her wedding day, and looked around at the family surrounding her. And she enjoyed, for once, not being the center of attention. It would seem that Rhys and Robin had seen several quite fetching maids at Seakirk Abbey who were surely not of the ilk to be taking their vows any time soon. Nicholas was sitting in his chair, rolling his eyes at their suggestions and vowing that he would not wed until he found someone who loved him for him and not just for his ability to liberate her from a nunnery.

Amanda smiled as she held Jake's hand, feeling quite content, for a change, in that chamber. She looked down at her ring, sparkling in the firelight, and marveled that Jake should have made such a thing. Perhaps the king would be well served to have Jake create a bauble or two for him. He certainly would if he could see the other pieces of work Jake had brought with him.

Anne was wearing one of his brooches. Gwen periodically admired the bracelet surrounding her wrist, done in the same blue stone that Amanda found sprinkled throughout her own ring. Isabelle was not so subtle. She clutched her necklace in her hand and divided her time between gaping at it and gaping at Jake.

Talk turned to the state of affairs in the north. Amanda was enormously glad to no longer be a pawn in those affairs. Now 'twas Jake who had an interest in how things might come about.

She held his hand and looked at him as he talked as an equal with her father and brothers, and she marveled at him. How he had changed, yet in truth, he had not changed at all. Even from the first, he had carried himself as a man of means and learning. 'Twas her bias that had made him seem less to her than he was. Indeed, she had learned a great deal in the past few months about a man's worth and his place in life.

She supposed she might never be the same.

So she looked at her man of worth and found it difficult to believe how much he had given up for her. The Future and all its wonders. She sincerely hoped she was worth the price.

She sighed and leaned back against her chair, then realized she was being watched. She met Robin's gaze and expected him to smirk at her or laugh at her mooning.

Instead, he was watching her with one of those expressions of genuine affection he reserved for Anne and Phillip.

"Happy?" he mouthed.

She nodded, her heart suddenly too full for speech or jest. So she let a tear or two slip down her cheeks and nodded again. Aye, she was happy. She was again in the bosom of her family, but now her heart was not only whole but full of love for the man sitting next to her who would in time hold court with their family in his own solar.

Jake raised her hand to his lips suddenly, kissed it, then held it in both his own, rubbing his thumb gently over the ring on her finger and looking down at it now and again, as if he assured himself it was still there.

She looked at Robin, who regarded them both with a satisfied smile. She nodded.

She couldn't have agreed more.

$Chapter\ 37$

$J$$ake$ stood at the front of a medieval chapel on the morning of his wedding day and paused in the midst of waiting for his bride in order to review the events of the past few months, to see where he'd gone right.

First on the list was getting mugged in Artane Enterprises, Inc.'s car park. That had sent him careening down a path through ghost-filled hallways, time gates, and past a medieval monarch, to land at the front of a relatively new chapel, where he was waiting for his bride to come give herself to him.

From mugging to marrying.

He had no complaints.

He looked around him at the souls gathered to watch the ceremony. Gwen, Anne, and Isabelle stood on the far side of the aisle. They all wore expressions of happiness, so he supposed he could safely assume they weren't dissatisfied with the prospect of him taking Amanda for his wife.

Montgomery and John stood on the near side of the aisle with Miles, looking pleased as well. Nicholas and Robin stood with Jake at the altar. Jake thought he was showing a great amount of trust by having Nicholas de Piaget standing at his back with a dagger in his belt. Stranger things had happened than a stabbing in a chapel in England. Maybe Robin would keep him safe.

Then the door opened and Amanda walked in with Rhys. Jake found that the sight of her after any sort of absence, as always, was like a fist to his gut. He was almost certain he swayed.

"Steady," Robin murmured from behind him. "Though 'tis not too late to flee."

"Shut up," Jake muttered.

"A leap or two over the benches and *voilà*, you're off."

Jake turned his head to glare at his future brother-in-law, only to find Robin grinning at him.

"I'd label you appropriately," Jake whispered, "but we're in church."

"There are always the lists later."

"I'll be busy."

"Dawn, then?"

"By the saints," Nicholas hissed, "will you two cease? We've a wedding to see accomplished."

"I'm distracting him," Robin said cheerfully. "If he catches a full view of that wench, he's liable to swoon."

"Be a man," Nicholas advised under his breath. "Bear up under the strain."

"Gladly," Jake said, smiling as Rhys deposited Amanda at the altar. Jake nodded to Rhys, then took Amanda's hand and faced the priest.

Her fingers were like ice. He looked at her in surprise, but she gave no sign of distress. In fact, she looked up at him and smiled, so brilliantly that he had to blink. He supposed he swayed; that was probably why Robin elbowed him in the ribs. Jake took both Amanda's hands in his and let yet another moment of unreality wash over him—not unlike that moment in Rhys's solar when he and Rhys had spoken of the future.

He stood in a medieval chapel, holding the hands of a medieval noblewoman, wearing a medieval title on his shoulders, and he was getting married on top of it all.

It was not, as he had decided earlier, what he had expected that morning when his dad had forced him out of bed before dawn to send him fatefully to Artane Enterprises.

"Holdings?" the priest asked.

Before Jake could wonder what he was supposed to do, Rhys stepped forward. "I will name my daughter's dowry. Scribe, are you ready?"

"Best find a chair," Robin whispered loudly.

Jake caught the glare Rhys threw his oldest son, but Robin only smiled pleasantly. Jake stood there holding onto Amanda's hand and found out for the first time just how very wealthy his bride was. He realized he was listening with an open mouth only because he eventually had to swallow and had to close his mouth to do it. He looked at Amanda.

"Wow."

She smiled. "Didn't you know?"

"Didn't know, didn't care."

"You'd best care now," Rhys said.

Jake smiled at Amanda's father. "Of course, my lord. You know I will do everything necessary to see to it properly."

Rhys nodded, apparently satisfied, though Jake knew that there had never been any question about it. He supposed it did a father good to know that the man he was giving his daughter to would take his responsibilities seriously when the time came.

"My lord Raventhorpe?" the priest inquired.

"I'll name his," Robin said. "Groomsman's duty and all that." He cleared his throat and flexed his fingers purposefully. "In holdings he brings Raventhorpe, of course. In gold and gems, he brings the equivalent of several hundred knight's fees."

"Is that all?" the priest asked.

Was that all? Jake smiled. His wealth was not Amanda's, but it was something at least.

"Nay, that is not all," Robin said archly. "I have things yet to name. Scribe, are you ready?"

"Aye, my lord."

"My lord Raventhorpe also brings to the table a fine blacksmith, furnishings for his bedchamber, great hall, and private solar." Robin smiled. "Courtesy of me."

"Thank you," Jake said, surprised and touched.

"And horseflesh for his stables and a hound or two for his kennels," Nicholas said with only the slightest bit of dourness. "From me."

"Thank you very much," Jake said, even more surprised and touched.

"Squires!" Montgomery and John chimed in.

"That would be us," Montgomery added.

"A gift of us, from us," John said with a grin.

Jake looked at Amanda's younger brothers and smiled. "I'll take you."

"And a steward," Rhys added, "from her mother and me. But a cook you can find on your own."

"Find a cook quickly," Miles advised. "She burns everything she touches."

Jake laughed and looked at Amanda, who had tears running down her cheeks. But she was smiling as well.

"What a family," he said.

She nodded, then turned to the priest. "I daresay, good father, that those things are enough. Let us be about the rest, if you will."

Jake concentrated on what was being said, on responding in all the right places with all the right words, but the back of his mind was spinning with all the revelations already that morning.

All right, so he was used to having money. His father might have been a reprehensible cad, but he had spared no expense to see Jake educated or treated properly while he'd been at Eton, and later at Cambridge. Jake himself, once his years of scrimping and saving to start his business were behind him, had certainly not lacked for the finer things of life. He'd traveled in luxury, bought whatever pleased him, surrounded himself with things of beauty.

But somehow, such abundance in medieval terms was positively overwhelming.

"Jake?"

He blinked and looked at Amanda. "What?"

"You may kiss me now."

He blinked again. "Is it over?"

Nicholas made a noise of despair and Robin laughed. Jake looked at Amanda.

"I suppose that's a 'yes'?"

She leaned up on her toes and kissed him. "Aye."

He wrapped his arms around her and kissed her back, not as thoroughly as he would have liked. He was, after all, standing right in front of her father. But he would later, when they didn't have an audience.

"Are you certain you don't want a brief foray into the lists?" Robin asked politely.

"Shut up," Jake said, just as politely.

"Then food for the man," Robin said, slapping Jake heartily on the back. "Strength for his labors."

Jake looked at Amanda, who merely laughed. There was no stopping Robin of Artane when he was on a roll, and apparently he was on one now. Jake took Amanda's hand and turned around to leave the chapel. But he couldn't leave without shaking hands with Rhys, or bowing low over Gwen's hand and thanking her again for the gift of her daughter. And on the way from the chapel, he found himself being congratulated by Miles and the twins, and shyly taken by his free arm by Isabelle who, as usual, looked up at him worshipfully.

Robin and Anne followed, with Anne making hushing noises as Robin continued his wedding monologue.

They were soon seated comfortably at the high table in the great hall. Jake supposed he was fed, but he didn't remember much of it. For the most part, he simply stared at Amanda.

He smiled to himself. No wonder the ghosts had made whacko motions when he'd asked them about Amanda. He should have taken that as a positive sign.

Robin clapped his hands together suddenly, then rubbed them. "I daresay 'tis time for the standing up, wouldn't you say?"

"Standing up?" Jake asked.

"Robin," Anne chided, "leave him be. And leave Amanda be."

Jake looked at Amanda. "Standing up?"

"Don't answer him, sister," Robin said, grinning. "We'll just show him."

"You will not," Amanda said. "My lord is not finished with his wine, and when he is, he will retire without help from you. Or any of the rest of you," she said, sweeping the males at the table with a warning glance. "I for one will not be stripped naked to stand before my sire and brothers," she huffed. "I daresay after all Jake has gone through to have me, he's not about to repudiate me."

"You can say that again," Jake said, with feeling. He looked at Miles, who sat on his other side. "You really don't do that kind of thing, do you?"

"Of course," Miles said with a smile. "How else would you have one last chance to refuse your knock-kneed, sunken chested, spindly elbowed bride?"

"I can assure you I am none of those," Amanda said sharply. "Now, leave Jake alone and let him finish his meal. For all we know, he may wish to have a small walk along the beach on the afternoon of his wedding day."

Robin spewed his wine all over the table. "Surely you jest," he gasped. "A walk along the beach? On his wedding day?"

Jake looked at Amanda. "Is it possible to have any privacy today?"

"Privacy?" she said with a snort. "Aye, at Raventhorpe."

"Too far. We'll have to settle for somewhere closer."

She pushed her chair back and stood. She leaned over and kissed her father's cheek. "My lord is weary. Of his new brothers-in-law," she said with a glare thrown Robin's way. "If you will excuse us, Father? Mother?"

"Are you asking permission of me as well?" Robin asked with a grin.

Jake rose with her and gave Robin the cuff to the back of the head he deserved as he passed.

"You'll pay for that, Kilchurn," Robin blustered. "Later, when I don't still have wine in my cup."

"Sure," Jake said. He walked to the end of the table with Amanda, then paused and excused himself. He walked around to the front of the table and stopped in front of Rhys and Gwen. He made them a very low bow.

"Thank you, my lord, my lady, for the gift of your daughter," he said simply.

Rhys nodded seriously. Gwen smiled through her tears. Jake looked at the rest of Amanda's family, made them a bow as well, then walked around the table to collect his bride. He paused at the bottom of the steps and smiled at her.

"My lady?"

"My lord?"

He laughed and took her hand to lead her up the stairs.

*H*e woke sometime during the middle of the night. He rolled from the bed, found a candle, then wrapped a blanket around himself and went out into the hallway for a light. He carried the candle back into the room and set it down on the bedside table.

He retrieved a sketch pad and a pencil, then found a stool and sat down. It took him perhaps an hour to capture her on the page as he wished, then he set aside his pencil and merely stared at her. He supposed there weren't enough hours in every day from now until he died to look at her, to drink in her spirit, to marvel that this magical, spectacular, outspoken woman was actually his to love. After all the time he'd spent combing the world for the perfect gem, here was the one of the most value.

A true one-of-a-kind.

She opened her eyes slowly, looked at him, then smiled.

"Hey," she said.

He smiled reflexively. He was going to have to be careful how he talked to her or he was going to have a medieval Valley Girl on his hands. He'd already corrupted her with chocolate earlier in the evening. Who knew what other anachronisms he would inflict upon her, given enough time?

"Hey, yourself," he said.

"What are you about, here in the middle of the night?"

He held up his sketch pad. "Drawing my favorite subject."

She caught her breath. "Ah, Jake, 'tis beautiful. Far more beautiful than I deserve."

"It is not," he said. "I'll have you know that I am a very fine artist, rendering my subjects with complete accuracy and a jaundiced eye."

"If you say so." She leaned up on one elbow. "Will you draw something else?" she asked hesitantly. "More things from the Future? Not right now, but later?"

"If you like," he said with a smile. "But what I would really like to do is paint a portrait of you. Once I can find paints and such."

"In truth?" she asked, sounding pleased.

"Yes. In that blue dress you wore today. You were very beautiful in it."

"You must paint me with long hair."

He laughed. "Why is that?"

"I do not want my posterity to see what a fool I was whilst waiting for their progenitor to return to me."

"Done," he said. "Hair to your waist, if you wish."

She smiled lazily. "I wish it. Now, put away your pencils, my lord, and come you here. I've other work for you."

How could he refuse? He put away his gear, but left the candle. After all, when you had a treasure to hand, it was best to look at it in the light.

The candle had burned low before he was finished with the work she had for him, but he didn't mind. He would burn up a thousand candles and more to please her.

He fell asleep with Amanda of Artane in his arms.

He was smiling.

Chapter 38

Several months later, Amanda stood at the end of another bed and wished she dared pace. But she feared to be a distraction, so she stayed where she was and looked at the occupant of that bed, wincing at the moans that had once been easy enough to listen to, but now were quite loud.

"Soon," Gwen said. "Soon."

"Not soon enough," Anne said, through gritted teeth.

Gwen laughed. "'Tis the same amount of work, my love. Wishing to hurry will not help."

"'Twill be over with faster," Anne gasped.

Amanda put her hand over her own belly that showed nothing as yet and wondered how it was she would manage when her turn came to be laboring to bring forth a babe.

Time passed, and Amanda wasn't sure for whom it passed more slowly. At least Anne had something to do. All Amanda could do was watch.

"Where is Robin?" Anne panted.

"Downstairs," Amanda said.

"Why?"

"I think he fears what you will do to him if he is within reach," Amanda said honestly.

"Fetch him," she said, then cried out in pain.

Amanda ran to the door and threw it open. She didn't have to go far. Her brother was standing uncharacteristically still, leaning against the far wall. In his own way, he was as pale with strain as Anne was with the pain.

"She wants you," Amanda said.

He nodded and pushed away from the wall. Amanda caught him by the arm and smiled.

"She's strong and healthy. The babe will be fine."

He looked at her sharply. "Think you?"

"I know so," she said confidently.

She wasn't about to tell him how she knew, though she supposed he guessed.

But he put his shoulders back just the same and followed her inside the chamber.

A n hour later, Amanda walked down the stairs to the great hall. Isabelle was upstairs, cooing over the babe already. No doubt her brothers, husband, and father were distracting themselves in the lists.

But on the chance she was mistaken, she tried her father's solar. She knocked, then entered to find Jake sitting across the chessboard from her father. They both looked up.

"The babe is born?" Rhys asked.

She nodded.

"Lad or lass?"

Amanda looked at Jake for a moment before she turned back to her father. "A wee lad," she said gravely.

"And the name?" Rhys asked. "And please let it be something I can pronounce."

She smiled dryly. "Phillip was not hard, Father."

"With Robin, I just never know."

Amanda looked again at Jake. He was watching her placidly, with no worry or concern in his eye, just the quiet confidence she had come to count on, even when he was feeling his way through unfamiliar situations. He merely waited, sure and steady.

"The name?" Rhys prompted.

She shivered. "Kendrick."

"Kendrick!" Rhys echoed. "what kind of name is that?"

"Something Robin heard somewhere." She swallowed. "It was something he decided the moment he found that Anne was with child again." She paused again. "He's said nothing to anyone about it, not even Anne."

"Well," Rhys said, "to each his own." He shook his head. "Kendrick, indeed. I suppose I'll grow to like it well enough."

"I'm sure he'll be a fine lad," Jake said confidently. "Indeed, I make a prediction that he will be a marvelous warrior in the tradition of his father and grandfather."

"And his uncle," Rhys said seriously.

Jake smiled. "You are too kind, my lord."

"He's screaming like a banshee already," Amanda muttered.

Rhys stood. "Do you think I might venture a visit, or is it too soon?"

Amanda shook her head. "The babe was born half an hour ago. I daresay you might go have a wee peek at your new grandson."

Rhys smoothed his hand over her hair as he walked toward the door, then paused and smiled at her. "All will be well with you, too, love, when your time comes."

"I know, Father," she said softly. She waited until he had gone, then looked at her husband.

He merely sat in his chair, watching her with half a smile. She walked across the room and sat on his lap.

"Oof," he said.

"Oaf," she replied, putting her arm around his neck. "I am not so heavy."

He kissed her gently. "I was teasing. So, Anne is safely delivered, I see."

"Are you surprised?"

He smiled. "What do you think?"

"I think you were unsurprised," she said, resting her cheek against his. She closed her eyes and sighed. "I am happy for them."

"So am I." He paused, then pulled away to look at her. "Are you convinced now?"

She smiled, knowing of what he spoke. "I was not unconvinced before."

"Is the proof reassuring?"

"Jake," she said with a laugh, "I never needed any proof."

"Did you never doubt me?" he asked. "Not once?"

"Never. Well," she said tugging on her hair, "apart from the time I didn't think you were coming back, nay, not once. Especially not once I knew for myself that you didn't have wings like a fairy."

"Thank heavens for that."

She looked at him in silence for a moment or two, then spoke carefully. "Two more?"

"Two more that live," he said quietly. "As far as any Robin and Anne might have who don't, I can't say."

"And about ours?" she asked carefully. "Do you know anything about ours?

He shook his head. "I don't."

"Couldn't you have looked?" she asked plaintively. "Whilst you were about that fetching of your gold and gems?"

He drew her close and stroked her hair. "In all honesty, Amanda, I couldn't make myself look in any of the books that would have told me just what had happened to you." He sighed. "I suppose I was afraid I would find out you'd married some hulking brute named Sven who would have sired on you a dozen lads named Sven and you would have lived out your life in Swedish bliss."

She smiled and pulled back to look at him. "And if you'd discovered that? What would you have done then?"

"Changed history," he said confidently.

"The saints be praised."

He stroked her cheek. "You know, while we were in London and you were bringing all the men at court to their knees, I nipped out and found paints and brushes. I would like to paint that portrait of you I promised, if you would allow it. In your wedding gown."

"If you like," she said, pleased. His portrait of the king had been a great success and they had invitations to do the same for many of the nobles in London. "With long hair," she reminded him.

"Of course."

She sat on his lap, and snuggled close to him for a great while in silence, so long that she wondered if he had gone to sleep. She finally lifted her head from his shoulder and looked at him. His eyes weren't closed, but they stared at nothing.

"Jake?" she asked.

He shook his head and smiled. "Yes, my love?"

"Do you regret it?" she asked.

"How can you ask?"

"Because you've drawn me the marvels you left behind. I wonder if you miss them."

He stroked his chin. "Hmmm, let me see. I traded in a life of travel, luxury, and ease without you for a life of travel, luxury, and ease *with* you. How can that possibly be a poor trade?"

"You do not have luxury and ease," she pointed out.

"Don't I?" he mused. "A fine castle—"

"With rats in your cellar and birds nesting in your bedchamber."

"True, but that can be fixed," he said. "No, it does seem very luxurious, that rat-infested castle on the sea."

She laughed and kissed him. "Very well, my lord, I agree. 'Tis marvelous fine, that hall of ours, and I look forward to living there once Nicholas and his lads repair the roof. Though why you allowed Nicholas anywhere near that keep . . ."

"He knows you'll be living there as well. He'll see it repaired properly," Jake said confidently. "It is a good life, Amanda, and one I will be forever grateful for. And you are the reason for it."

She put her arms around him and hugged him tightly. She had to agree with him. She had traded a life of ease without Jake for a life of wonder with him.

She thought about that night on the roof, when he'd promised to pull down the stars from the sky and give them to her.

If stars were happiness, he had done that and more.

She pulled back and kissed him. "Come with me and see your nephew. He's a fine, strong lad."

He smiled. "I'm quite sure he is. I can hardly wait for him to grow up so I can begin to torment him as he deserves."

"I think you have a tale for me."

"I do," he said with a grin. "And it is a most remarkable one. But no more remarkable than ours." He put her off his lap and rose. "Maybe I'll begin the torment today," he muttered as they left the solar. "He will deserve every moment of it, the little brat."

"Jake!"

He smiled at her. "I'll wait until he's older before I make his life hell." He squeezed her hand. "Let's go."

Amanda followed him, wishing she knew the future, but perhaps just as happy that she didn't. After all, her future was walking beside her, humming in that way that Robin tended to do when he was feeling particularly pleased about something. She smiled to herself, understanding that as well.

After all, they had their entire future before them and nothing but love to fill it with.

Stardust dreams, indeed.

Chapter 39

Genevieve de Piaget sat in a comfortable chair in what had served as the Lord of Artane's private study for centuries and sighed happily. It had been a wonderful two weeks that had stretched into a month. Watching Kendrick with his family had been wonderful, but what she had really enjoyed had been roaming with him over his boyhood home, listening to his memories, laughing at his antics . . . seeing him at Artane.

He was sitting next to her, laughing with Gideon over one of Gideon's childhood debacles. Genevieve looked at Megan, very pregnant and obviously ready to be not so anymore, but happy as well. The children had been in various stages of sprawl on chairs, benches, and carpets until Kendrick had taken them all upstairs and put them to bed. The baby, as always, slept peacefully in her mother's arms.

All was right with the world.

"Do you think he made it?" Megan asked suddenly.

It was the question no one had asked in the month since Jake had disappeared. Genevieve was certain the others had been wondering, but no one had apparently had the guts to just blurt it out. She supposed she couldn't blame them. It was just so strange to think of a modern man giving up his life for nothing more than a dream in the past. She'd broached the subject with Kendrick more than once, late at night, but each time he'd suddenly begun to snore. Either he didn't have the answers, or didn't want to break it to her that Jake was lost in Anglo-Saxon England where he would no doubt find himself either killed outright or taken aboard a Viking sailing ship as a galley slave.

"I called Alex yesterday," Gideon offered with a smile. "His words were, and I quote, 'No body, no problem.'"

"So like a lawyer," Megan laughed.

"Well, maybe it's time for the one in the know to cough up some information," Genevieve said pointedly. She looked at Kendrick. "That would be you, my lord. Do you think he made it? And isn't it about time you opened that box he left you?"

"He left a box?" Gideon asked, his ears perking up.

Kendrick sighed and rose. "I'll return in a moment."

Genevieve was certain that had been one of the longest moments of her life. She didn't consider herself overly curious, but she had to admit that in this, the suspense was killing her.

Kendrick came back inside the study. Genevieve shivered in spite of herself. How many times had he done that eight hundred years ago?

Probably too many to count.

Kendrick resumed his seat and held out the box for inspection. "Here it be," he intoned. "The box that may well answer all our questions."

"Just open it," Gideon said with a laugh.

Kendrick made a great production out of opening the box. He removed a small canvas. He handed it to Genevieve.

"Here, curious one. You look first."

Genevieve looked at the subject. She was dressed in a dark blue gown and sat on a stone bench near a window. A sword was propped up at her side and loose gemstones spilled over her lap and onto the bench. The woman was, Genevieve admitted readily, exceptionally beautiful, with long dark hair and arresting aqua eyes.

"Amanda?" she asked.

"Amanda," Kendrick agreed. "She was passing fair."

"No, she was stunning," Genevieve corrected him. "No wonder I hear your ghostly lads talking endlessly about her in the lists, in the garden, in the kitchen—"

"When they're not singing your praises," Kendrick reminded her.

Genevieve smiled. "It's all right. She can be beautiful and it won't bother me. I wonder, though, why Jake left you this and where he got it?"

"It was in one of the cabinets in the new wing," Gideon supplied. "Well, new is relative, I suppose. It was built in the eighteenth century."

"Positively modern," Genevieve said dryly. "I wonder how Jake got hold of it."

"He pinched it, the rogue," Kendrick said. "As for the reason why, look on the back."

Genevieve turned the small portrait over and read:

To my love Amanda, always and forever, JAK IV

Genevieve looked up at Kendrick quickly. "Then he made it."

Kendrick handed her a piece of paper. "Apparently so. I daresay he found the portrait before he wrote this."

Genevieve handed the portrait to Megan, then read the note:

Kendrick—I won't let them destroy Seakirk in 1260, though I should, you closed-mouthed bugger. No thanks necessary. JAK

She put the paper down and then smiled at Kendrick. "Well, there are a couple of clues, at least. I wonder what else happened to them?"

"We have a very large volume of family history," Gideon said. "But why use a book when you have an eyewitness?"

"Yes, Kendrick, spill the beans," Genevieve said. "You promised you would."

"And so I did." Kendrick rubbed his hands together, smiling. "Very well, what will you know first?"

"How many children did they have?" Megan asked.

"Eight," Kendrick replied. "Six that lived past infancy."

"Oh," Genevieve said with a wince. "Poor Amanda."

"Aye, well, it grieved her greatly, as you might imagine, and I daresay it changed her, but she was never one to shy away from the difficult. She was grateful for the children she had, as was right."

"Were they happy?" Genevieve asked, feeling rather wistful about it all of the sudden.

"Aye, very," he said. "Jake became quite powerful in his own right and many came from far and wide to seek his counsel." He looked at Gideon. "Perhaps that book would be interesting. I for one would like to see what it says about quite a few things."

"I'll go fetch it, if you like." Gideon disappeared into the depths of the castle, then returned quite a while later with a large book in his hands. He sat down at the table with them, then opened the book and flipped through the pages until he slowed, then stopped. He read in silence for several minutes.

"Well?" Megan prompted. "Gideon, what does it say?"

He looked at them and smiled. "They were indeed the proud parents of eight children and not a one of them was named Kendrick."

Kendrick laughed. "In truth, what does it say?"

"It is as Kendrick said in regard to the children," Gideon said with a smile. "And apparently Jake became quite a famous painter of portraits and much sought after not only for his skills with silver and gems, but also with the sword."

"Aye, I can vouch for the latter," Kendrick said, stretching in satisfaction. "After all, I taught him a goodly bit of what he knew."

"Which you probably learned from him in the first place," Gideon said. "It says here that you squired for him for a pair of years."

Kendrick shrugged with a grin. "I cannot deny it. Auntie Amanda could neither cook nor sew, but she set a famously fine table in spite of that, and looked lovely doing it. She had men lining up at her gates, vying for the chance to prepare delicacies to tempt her notoriously discriminating palate and create beautiful gowns for her pleasure. Besides, Raventhorpe was right on the border. Scads of brilliant adventures waiting there for the lad with the right set of skills."

"Troublemaker," Genevieve said fondly.

"Aye, that and more," he agreed.

"Jake said he wouldn't let your family destroy Seakirk," Genevieve said. "How did he stop it? Did he try to talk you out of going to marry Matilda of Seakirk? Did he try to warn you what her plans were for you?"

"Ah, now there is a tale indeed," Kendrick said with a nod. "Oddly enough, Jake had little to say about Matilda or my bargain with the king. That was unusual, for he was never shy about expressing his opinions. My greatest friend, Richard of Burwyck-on-the-Sea, was most adamant that I not wed with her, but Jake, nay, Jake said very little indeed. My father finally pressed him for an opinion and he unbent far enough to remark that he was certain things would work out in the end."

"Mysterious," Megan said.

"Well, I daresay my father trusted him completely. I had no idea at the time of Jake's true identity. My uncle Montgomery swore until his dying day that Jake was really a fairy, but none of us younger generation believed him. To us, Jake was a marvelous treasure who brought us back astonishing things from his travels."

"Did they travel much?" Gideon asked. "He and Amanda?"

"Aye, and with their children as well," Kendrick said. "Jake took the entire family on magnificent trips all over what of the world he could reach. He thought experience was the best teacher. Indeed, he was in Italy with Amanda when I was . . . well, murdered."

Gideon coughed and Megan had to slap him on the back several times to get him to stop.

Genevieve laughed. Maybe Gideon wasn't as accustomed to Kendrick's history as he pretended to be.

Kendrick looked at them with twinkling eyes. "My kin, as you might imagine, were desperate to find me, and then when they did not, to exact revenge. It was only later that I realized that a messenger had brought my father a missive from Jake in private. My friend Richard was beside himself that my father merely turned away and didn't raze Seakirk when they realized that I had met my end there."

"How timely that the messenger found Robin when he did," Genevieve said dryly.

"Indeed," Kendrick agreed. "In truth, I think the lad had been following my father's company and was waiting for the moment Jake had predetermined. Anyway, what I learned later from other ghostly companions was that the missive had warned my father Robin to simply walk away and Jake would give him all the details later."

"And Jake did?" Genevieve asked softly.

"Jake did," Kendrick said with a smile. "He told my father that he had known me in the future, that I had a wife, a large family, and had become Lord of Seakirk. It was cold comfort to my sire at the time, but he was grateful for the knowledge. Of course, my father did not see fit to share that knowledge with anyone but my mother, so the rest of the family grieved more than they should have, but that was his choice."

Genevieve looked at him and shook her head. "And you didn't tell Jake any of this when he was here. Why not?"

"He teased me unmercifully when I was a lad. I owed him for years of torture."

"Which he dealt out no doubt because of your treatment of him these past few weeks," Gideon pointed out.

"And so we go on," Kendrick said with a contented sigh. "Circles and circles of time and family." He took Genevieve's hand and held it gently between both his own. "I would not have traded a minute of it."

Genevieve understood. She sat with her husband in his ancestral hall and looked around her at the place in which he'd grown to manhood—yet another circle going 'round again. Megan would have her baby soon and there would begin another one with Gideon, Megan, and their child.

But now she and Kendrick would be a part of that, along with their children. Families, love, memories, all flowing in and out of a keep that had stood on the edge of the sea for eight hundred years.

She turned the portrait over again where she could look at Amanda's beautiful, smiling face. She looked content, as if she'd found all her heart desired.

Genevieve understood.

She understood very well indeed.

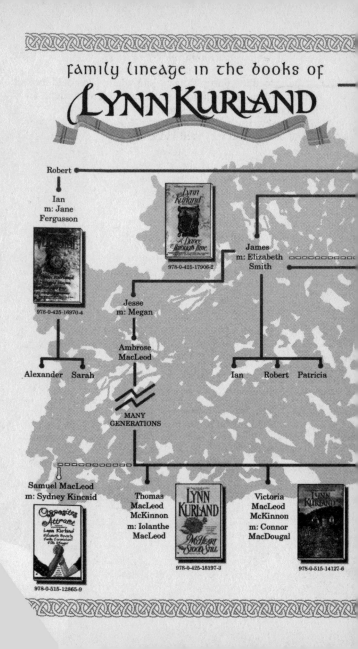

family lineage in the books of
LynnKurland

Robert

Ian
m: Jane
Fergusson

978-0-425-16970-4

978-0-425-17906-2

Jesse
m: Megan

James
m: Elizabeth
Smith

Ambrose
MacLeod

Alexander   Sarah

Ian   Robert   Patricia

MANY
GENERATIONS

Samuel MacLeod
m: Sydney Kincaid

Thomas
MacLeod
McKinnon
m: Iolanthe
MacLeod

Victoria
MacLeod
McKinnon
m: Connor
MacDougal

978-0-515-12865-9

978-0-425-18197-3

978-0-515-14127-6

MACLEOD

Douglas

Patrick
m: Madelyn Phillips

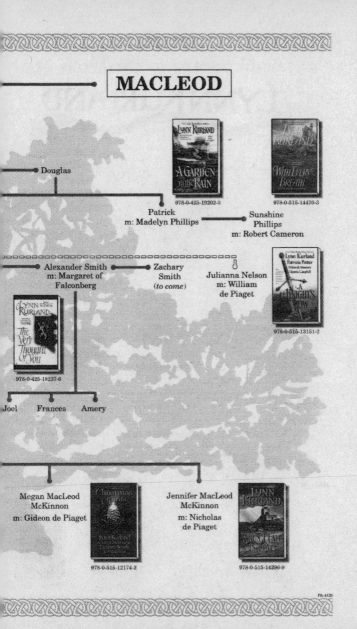

978-0-425-19202-3

978-0-515-14470-3

Sunshine
Phillips
m: Robert Cameron

Alexander Smith
m: Margaret of
Falconberg

Zachary
Smith
(to come)

Julianna Nelson
m: William
de Piaget

978-0-515-13151-2

978-0-425-18237-6

Joel   Frances   Amery

Megan MacLeod
McKinnon
m: Gideon de Piaget

978-0-515-12174-2

Jennifer MacLeod
McKinnon
m: Nicholas
de Piaget

978-0-515-14296-9

PK-4129

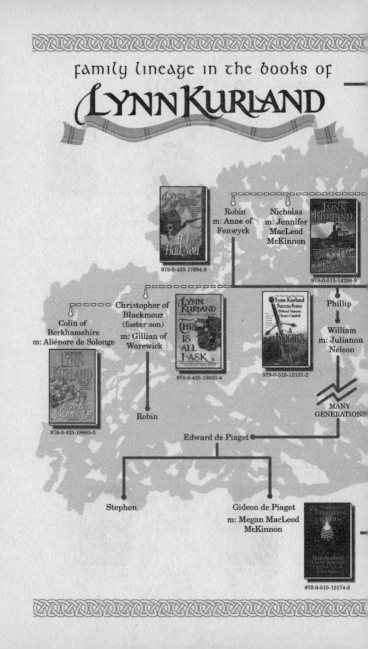

family lineage in the books of LynnKurland

Robin
m: Anne of
Fenwyck

Nicholas
m: Jennifer
MacLeod
McKinnon

978-0-425-17694-8

978-0-515-14296-9

Colin of
Berkhamshire
m: Aliénore de Solonge

Christopher of
Blackmour
(foster son)
m: Gillian of
Warewick

Phillip

William
m: Julianna
Nelson

978-0-425-18685-5

978-0-425-18033-4

978-0-515-13151-2

Robin

MANY
GENERATIONS

Edward de Piaget

Stephen

Gideon de Piaget
m: Megan MacLeod
McKinnon

978-0-515-12174-2

DE PIAGET

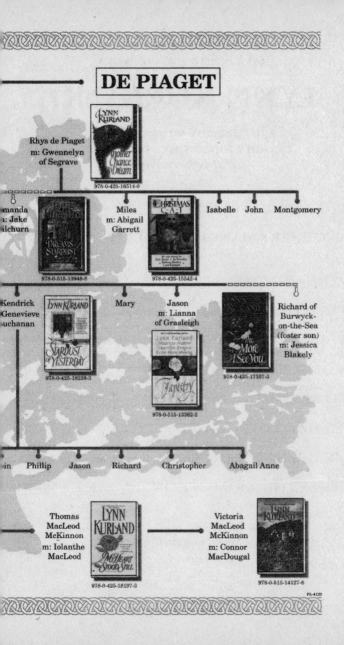

Rhys de Piaget
m: Gwennelyn
of Segrave

978-0-425-16514-0

...manda
...: Jake
...ichurn

Miles
m: Abigail
Garrett

Isabelle   John   Montgomery

978-0-515-13948-8

978-0-425-15542-4

Kendrick
Genevieve
...uchanan

Mary

Jason
m: Lianna
of Grasleigh

Richard of
Burwyck-
on-the-Sea
(foster son)
m: Jessica
Blakely

978-0-425-18238-3

978-0-515-13362-2

978-0-425-17107-3

...in   Phillip   Jason   Richard   Christopher   Abagail Anne

Thomas
MacLeod
McKinnon
m: Iolanthe
MacLeod

Victoria
MacLeod
McKinnon
m: Connor
MacDougal

978-0-425-18197-3

978-0-515-14127-6

PA-4320

To Weave a
Web of Magic

USA Today bestselling author
Claire Delacroix

USA Today bestselling author
Lynn Kurland

World Fantasy Award-winning author
Patricia McKillip

National bestselling author
Sharon Shinn

0-425-19615-1